D0779609

Culture and Social Behavior

McGraw-Hill Series in Social Psychology

CONSULTING EDITOR

Philip G. Zimbardo

Culture and Social Behavior

❖

Harry C. Triandis
University of Illinois, Urbana-Champaign

McGraw-Hill, Inc.

New York   St. Louis   San Francisco   Auckland   Bogotá   Caracas
Lisbon   London   Madrid   Mexico City   Milan   Montreal   New Delhi
San Juan   Singapore   Sydney   Tokyo   Toronto

To Pola & Louisa

Culture and Social Behavior

Copyright © 1994 by McGraw-Hill, Inc. All rights reserved. Printed in the United States of America. Except as permitted under the United States Copyright Act of 1976, no part of this publication may be reproduced or distributed in any form or by any means, or stored in a data base or retrieval system, without the prior written permission of the publisher.

This book is printed on acid-free paper.

1 2 3 4 5 6 7 8 9 0 DOC DOC 9 0 9 8 7 6 5 4 3

ISBN 0-07-065110-8

This book was set in Palatino by Better Graphics, Inc.
The editors were Christopher Rogers, Nomi Sofer, and Fred H. Burns;
the production supervisor was Friederich W. Schulte.
The cover was designed by Joan Greenfield.
R. R. Donnelley & Sons Company was printer and binder.

Library of Congress Cataloging-in-Publication Data

Triandis, Harry Charalambos, (date).
    Culture and social behavior / Harry C. Triandis.
        p.   cm.—(McGraw-Hill series in social psychology)
    Includes bibliographical references and index.
    ISBN 0-07-065110-8
    1. Social psychology.   2. Culture.   3. Cross-cultural studies.
    I. Title.   II. Series.
    HM251.T677   1994
    302—dc20
                                                    93-33418

About the Author

❖

 **HARRY C. TRIANDIS** obtained his Ph.D. in social psychology from Cornell University in 1958. He is professor of psychology at the University of Illinois. Other appointments have included the Center of Advanced Studies at the University of Illinois (1972, 1979), the Center for International Studies at Cornell University (1968–1969), and the East-West Center in Honolulu (1987, 1993). He is a fellow of the American Association for the Advancement of Science and president of the International Association of Applied Psychology (1990–1994). He is past president of the International Association of Cross-Cultural Psychology (1974–1976), the Society for Psychological Study of Social Issues (1975–1976), the Society for Personality and Social Psychology (1976–1977), the Interamerican Society of Psychology (1985–1987), and the Society for Cross-Cultural Research (1991–1992). He has received awards from the Interamerican Society of Psychology (1981), the American Psychological Association's Committee for International Affairs (1992), and an honorary doctorate from the University of Athens, Greece.

Contents

❖

Foreword

❖

*D*iversity is one of the most important new areas of research not only in psychology but in many areas of American life. At its best, the current focus on diversity represents an appreciation of the basic value of differences between people. That appreciation goes beyond mere tolerance as we realize the need to support and encourage the variations that exist between people as a function of their race, ethnicity, gender, religion, sexual orientation, and other aspects of their lifestyle. Such diversity adds rich, new coloration to the fabric of our existence.

This emphasis on cultural differences runs counter to the long dominant orientation that the United States should be the "melting pot." Immigrants from diverse cultures throughout the world have blended into that cauldron of powerful norms and been poured into The American Way Mold. With the threat of any and all differences being labelled as deviant, and the offenders thereby rejected by their new society, the quest for homogenization extended beyond culture to most aspects of individual lifestyle. Such pressures to conform made many of them voluntarily give up their native languages, customs, rituals, and even their names—to be more "American." For many, their differences from the narrow prototype was ignored by dedicated neglect, as witnessed in their absence from textbooks and the media, and thereby seemingly invisible to the educated eye.

Social psychology has helped us understand these forces of conformity, group pressures toward uniformity, the nature of deviance, prejudice, and social conflict. But it did not really advocate the appreciation of diversity until recently. However, many social psychologists who wanted to expand their focus beyond the ethnocentric myopia that afflicted their peers became cross-cultural psychologists. Some studied basic psychological processes across different cultural settings in order to determine their universality or specificity. Others investigated phenomena that were unique to certain cultures and alien to our own. They brought new methodologies and alternative perspectives to field work, originally the province of anthropologists. Yet, the work of cross-cultural psychologists has remained on the periphery of general psychology, given short shrift in introductory texts and even in many social psychology texts.

That peripheral status of cross-cultural psychology is all changing for the better. The *Zeitgeist* is finally right for the emergence of cross-cultural psychology into the mainstream of social and general psychology. And the new orientation being demonstrated by a host of cross-cultural psychologists is ripe for the fuller appreciation of their work by other psychologists. Part of this new view shows us how cultural variations in basic values shape the process by which certain basic aspects of human functioning develop. So, for example, we are learning how the central concept of "the self" is shaped by many aspects of our socio-cultural worlds that support values of either individual control and personal achievement, like ours does, or the bonds of social solidarity, as do many other cultures. Those differences, essential for adaptation to, and even survival in, a given culture, have an enormous ripple effect that impacts one's thoughts, feelings, and actions—the key triad of psychology.

Harry Triandis, one of the twentieth century's foremost contributors to research and theory in the field of cross-cultural psychology, is now showing his colleagues why and how this field of study is indispensable to a fuller understanding and enriched appreciation of the nature of human nature. In this book, he breathes new life into the body of established research on cross-cultural phenomena. He gives us a real sense of both the breadth and depth of this field of inquiry by detailing how cultural processes create psychological products. His extensive experiences across many cultures are revealed in the host of anecdotes and personal examples that he uses to make abstract concepts more vivid and immediate to readers of his story. He wants his student readers to relate actively to these new ideas, to get excited by them, and be able to incorporate them into a new way of thinking about the psychology of the person and the sociology of groups and institutions. What is the role culture plays for both of these fields? Through a unique set of self-tests at the end of each chapter, the author enables readers to relate in a special way to what they have just learned. The addition of Triandis' personal collection of photos lends a vivid visual detail to this learning experience. I know that my own teaching has been enhanced by the new lessons I have learned from reading this manuscript.

The *McGraw-Hill Series in Social Psychology* has been designed as a celebration of the fundamental contributions being made by researchers, theorists, and practitioners of social psychology to our understanding of human nature and to the potential for enriching the quality of our lives through wise applications of their knowledge. It has become a showcase for presenting new theories, original syntheses, analyses, and current methodologies by distinguished scholars and promising young writer-researchers. Our authors reveal a common commitment to sharing their vision with a broad audience starting with their colleagues, extending out to graduate students, but especially to undergraduates with an interest in social psychology. Some of our titles convey ideas that are of sufficient general interest that their message needs to be carried out into the world of practical application to those who may translate some of them into public action and public policy. Although each text in our series is created to stand alone as the best representative of its area of scholarship, taken as a whole, they represent the core of social psychology. Teachers may elect to use any of them as "in-depth" supplements to a basic, general textbook, while others may choose to organize their course entirely around a set of these monographs. Each of our authors has been guided by the objective of conveying the essential lessons and principles of his or her area of expertise in an interesting style, one that informs without resort to technical jargon, and that inspires others to utilize these ideas at conceptual or practical levels. I hope that you will enjoy the feast we have prepared for you, especially this new main course created by Harry Triandis.

Philip G. Zimbardo
Consulting Editor

Preface

———— ❖ ————

Social psychology is a product of Europe and North America. Almost all that we know systematically about social behavior was derived by studying individuals and groups from those regions of the world. However, 70 percent of the earth's population lives outside Europe and North America; in cultures that are quite different from those of the "West." In addition, as more and more non-mainstream individuals join the North American and European work place, and as global organizations and markets are being formed, no educated person can afford to be ignorant of cultural differences and the way they influence our psychological functioning, especially our social behavior.

While this textbook is designed to expand the horizon of social psychology undergraduates, it also has relevance for professional social psychologists. It is the first book with the narrow focus on culture and social behavior specifically written for American undergraduates and professionals.

Much of what I present here, in language directed to undergraduates, is available in an extensive literature scattered in professional journals and books. However, it has never been brought together in a coherent theoretical framework, such as this book provides.

I wrote this book so that it can be used either as a companion to a regular social psychology textbook, from which the instructor can assign a few chapters, or as a text for a course on cultural differences in social behavior. It aims to broaden the student's perspective. Instructors and students will find this text directly relevant in courses designed to increase the cultural pluralism of the curriculum. These courses include business administration, communication, education, international relations, sociology, social work, environmental sciences, and labor/industrial relations in which cross-cultural training is required. In addition, the book will serve well as a core text for most areas of study involving minority student or overseas affairs and professions where a culturally mixed clientele is served.

Humans all over the world have a lot in common, and social psychology courses often cover that commonality well. But people are also different, and it is those differences that I will emphasize.

During the past forty years I learned a great deal from colleagues and friends all over the world. Here I merged their work, ideas, data, and insights to form a framework for understanding the link between culture and social behavior. Many colleagues from abroad have contributed by collecting data that I was able to analyze. Several graciously entertained me when I visited their country. It would require a small volume to mention the specific ways in which each of them was helpful to me. The list that follows is to say "thanks" and mentions specific contributions in a couple of cases; it also shows how spread out around the globe these colleagues are: Michael Bond (Hong Kong); Alan Fiske (Philadelphia, Pennsylvania); C. Harry Hui (Hong Kong); Uichol Kim (Honolulu, Hawaii, who organized a conference on collectivism in Korea); Shinobu Kitayama (Kyoto, Japan); Hazel Markus (Ann Arbor, Michigan); Gerardo Marin (San Francisco, California); Shalom Schwartz (Jerusalem, Israel); George and Vasso Vassiliou (Athens, Greece, with whom I collaborated on my first cross-cultural book); and Susumu Yamaguchi (Tokyo, Japan).

Also, I profited very much from research funds I received from the Office of Naval Research, the National Science Foundation, the U.S. Public Health Service, the Guggenheim Foundation, the Fulbright Program, the Ford Foundation, the Ford-Rockefeller Population Program, the Cornell University International Studies Center, the Institute of Anthropos in Greece, the East-West Center in Hawaii, and the University of Illinois, which enabled me to visit all inhabited continents and observe and study social behavior both casually and systematically.

The inspiration for this book came from Phil Zimbardo of Stanford University and Chris Rogers of McGraw-Hill. They proved quite helpful in shaping it. Very useful comments provided by John Adamopoulos, Grand Valley University; John Berry, Queens University, Kingston, Ontario, Canada; Rich Brislin, East-West Center, Institute of Culture and Communication; and David Myers, Hope College further strengthened it. However, the most help came from Nomi Sofer of McGraw-Hill, who provided detailed comments.

Finally, my wife Pola was in some ways a true collaborator, since she read the manuscript of this book more than once and provided insightful comments.

Harry C. Triandis

1

Our Culture Influences Who We Are and How We View Social Behavior

❖

Culture: An Interplay of Sameness and Differences ◆ A Taste of Cultural Differences ◆ Culture Imposes a Set of Lenses for Seeing the World ◆ Definitions: Ecology and Culture ◆ *On the Definition of Culture* ◆ *Transmission to Others* ◆ *Emic and Etic Aspects of Culture* ◆ *Where Is Culture?* ◆ *Cultures Are "Superorganic"* ◆ *How Many Cultures Are There?* ◆ *A Definition of Culture That Follows from Our Discussion* ◆ A Theoretical Framework for Studying Ecology, Culture, and Behavior ◆ Summary

Culture is to society what memory is to individuals. In other words, culture includes traditions that tell "what has worked" in the past. It also encompasses the way people have learned to look at their environment and themselves, and their unstated assumptions about the way the world is and the way people should act.

The most inclusive definition of culture—that culture is the human-made part of the environment—was given by Herskovits in his book *Cultural Anthropology*

(1955). Since I learned my first cultural anthropology from that book, I am still partial to that definition. Granted, it is very broad, but we can break it down. By distinguishing objective aspects of culture (tools, roads, radio stations) from subjective aspects (categorizations, associations, norms, roles, values), we can examine how subjective culture influences behavior (this is taken up in Chapter 4).

When we analyze subjective culture, we learn how people perceive, categorize, believe, and value entities in their environment. In short, we discover the unique ways in which people in different cultures view their social environment.

The elements of subjective culture are organized into patterns. Although in each culture these patterns have unique configurations, we can identify some general schemas that apply to all cultures: These are *cultural syndromes*. A cultural syndrome is a pattern of beliefs, attitudes, self-definitions, norms, and values that are organized around some theme that can be identified in a society. This book deals with four such syndromes:

- *Complexity.* Some cultures are more complex than others.
- *Individualism.* Some cultures structure social experience around autonomous individuals.
- *Collectivism.* Some cultures organize their subjective cultures around one or more collectives, such as the family, the tribe, the religious group, or the country.
- *Tightness.* Some cultures impose many norms, rules, and constraints on social behavior, while others are rather loose in imposing such constraints.

Culture influences our behavior in subtle ways. In reading this book you will discover quite a lot about yourself, your culture, and other cultures. In addition, you will see that your understanding of social behavior has been shaped by Western culture, because social psychology is the product of Europe and North America. Almost all social psychologists are from that part of the world, as are almost all the data. The West is an increasingly shrinking part—approximately 27 percent—of humankind, whereas 35 percent of all humans live in China and India! This book is designed to provide a broader view of social behavior by paying attention to the impact of culture on social behavior.

Although culture shapes social behavior, it is not the single most important factor. Biology and ecology also play a crucial role. Their relative importance varies with the situation. Certainly, if we found ourselves in an environment with too little oxygen, our behavior would primarily be determined by the fact that we couldn't breathe. But as we will see, culture too is very important.

We are not aware of our own culture unless we come in contact with another one. To illustrate this point, let me tell you what happened to me the first time I went to India in 1965. I wrote to the only Western hotel in Mysore and asked the hotel to reserve a room for me for certain dates. I received a reply card that had two lines, one of which read: "We are unable to provide a room for the dates indicated." There was an X next to that statement. Assuming that the hotel had no room, I wrote to A. V. Shanmugam (my coauthor in Triandis, 1972) and asked him to find me another place. He did not bother to check with the hotel, because he knew that a large group of movie actors making a film in the nearby jungle were staying there. When I arrived in Mysore, I found the alternative accommodation unsatisfactory. In the hope that someone might have canceled a reservation, I went to the Western hotel to see if a room was available. When I gave my name, the desk clerk was astonished and said they had been expecting me! I pointed out that the card they sent had an X next to the words "We are unable . . . " and the astonished clerk replied: "Of course! We cross out the categories that do *not* apply."

Our habitual patterns of thought are so well entrenched that it never occurred to me that the way we do things in the West, placing a check (or an X) next to the category that *does* apply, is not done universally. It is important to note that the system used in that hotel is as efficient as our system of placing a mark next to the category that does apply. Our culture is not superior; it is just different.

While this anecdote is amusing and instructive, it raises an important issue: How much of the content of psychology may in fact be a distortion when applied to other cultures? When I started editing the six-volume *Handbook of Cross-Cultural Psychology*, I asked myself that question. I wrote to some forty colleagues, all over the world, and asked them to send me psychological findings from their culture that are not totally in agreement with findings published in the West. I got back very little. I was frustrated until Terry Prothro, then at the American University in Beirut, Lebanon, pointed out to me that our *training and methods* are also culture bound, and it is difficult to find new ideas without the theoretical and methodological tools that can extract them from a culture. Most of the people I had written to had gotten their doctorates in Western universities and would not have been especially good at analyzing their own cultures from a non-Western viewpoint. Examining one's own culture takes a special effort. It is only in the last thirty-five years or so that systematic attempts have been made to analyze social behavior cross-culturally.

There are barriers to such understanding. During my travels to Africa, Asia, and Latin America, I met many psychologists and was especially impressed by the fact that many of them had an inferiority complex. The West is the standard, especially in psychology. Many of these psychologists assume that if their own data do not match the Western theories, something is wrong with the data, not the theories.

I also encountered another type of problem: In most traditional cultures, modesty is a much greater virtue than in the West. Thus, most of these social psychologists consider it in bad taste to say: "Your theory is wrong"; they would rather keep quiet. Among the non-Western cultures, only the Japanese (e.g., Iwao, 1988) feel sufficiently sure of themselves to tell us: "*You* are wrong." However, they do it so politely that most Western social psychologists fail to notice!

One of the cultural differences that I have investigated more than others, because I suspect it is the most important kind of difference, is the difference between cultures that are individualistic and cultures that are collectivist. (We will describe these constructs in considerable detail in Chapter 6.) Individualists think of themselves as autonomous, independent of groups, and believe that it is okay to do what they want to do, regardless of their groups' wishes. Collectivists, on the other hand, tend to see themselves as appendages or aspects of a group, such as the family, the tribe, the corporation, the country; they feel interdependence with members of this group; and they are willing to subordinate their personal goals to the goals of the group. For example, during World War II the Japanese used kamikaze pilots, who crashed their planes into American naval vessels. Such suicide missions clearly subordinate personal goals to those of the group. Such behavior is rare in individualistic cultures.

In collective cultures people are often more concerned about acting appropriately than about doing what they would like to do. As a result, there is less consistency between attitudes and behavior than is likely to be found in individualistic cultures. This results in differences in the importance of attitudes as predictors of social behavior and places less emphasis on consistency between what is "inside" the person and that person's behavior. The Japanese often say: "You can think what is in your mind, but shouldn't say that. It's rude" (Kidder, 1992, p. 387). In other words, even expressing a thought that does not match the norms is inappropriate.

Iwao (1988) has pointed out that the Japanese are much less concerned with consistency than are Westerners. Yet much of Western social psychology deals with consistency. A thick volume of consistency theories was published by Abelson, Aronson, McGuire, Newcomb, Rosenberg, and Tannenbaum (1968) which attests to the importance of these theories. We have theories of "cognitive balance," "cognitive dissonance," "cognitive congruity," and so on that are based on Western thinking going back to the early Greeks. We in the West think that "if X is true, non-X cannot be true." But this view makes relatively little sense in cultures such as India, where philosophical monism is widely used; i. e., "Everything is one" and "The opposite of a great truth is also a great truth." For instance, Ghandhi (Ghandhi Museum in Ahmedabad, India) said: "All religions reflect the same great truth."

CULTURE: AN INTERPLAY OF SAMENESS AND DIFFERENCES

Even while we point to differences between cultures and philosophical outlooks, our discussion is complicated by the fact that humans are more similar to one another than they are different (Brown 1991). We belong to only *one* of the many species of animals. This fact is extremely striking when we consider that in one New Guinea lagoon there are more than 600 species of fish!

Universals of social behavior and experience exist and are important (Lonner, 1980; Triandis, 1978; Brown, 1991). For example, all humans think of social behaviors that are *associative* (supportive, admiring, giving resources) as similar to each other, and as different from social behaviors that are *dissociative* (avoiding, aggressive); all humans think of *superordinate* behaviors (criticize, give orders) as different from subordinating behaviors (obey, conform). Most humans understand the difference between *intimacy* (e.g., self-disclosure) and *formality* (doing what etiquette requires). In Chapter 8 we will discuss culture and social behavior by organizing the material in these categories.

The problem is that many people think that either everybody is the same or everybody is different. Neither view is correct. I think that this happens because we are all a bit lazy, and it is simpler to think that everybody is the same or everybody is different than to think that people are similar on A, B, C . . . N and different on X, Y, and Z. The tendency toward least effort is one of the universals of human behavior (Zipf, 1949).

All humans have language, food habits, art, myths, religious practices, family structures, economic systems, "truth," government, war, kinship, shelter, training systems, hygiene, and incest taboos (Brown, 1991). However, these categories are broad, and they hide many differences. Consider that all humans share food habits, but what they eat, when they eat, where they eat, whom they eat with, and how they eat are different. Similarly with the other categories mentioned above, the general category is universal, but there are numerous differences in the details. The Indian hotel clerk is very much like me. He sits at a desk, he answers the mail with a pen, and he reads and writes just like I do. But because he put the X in a different place from where I would have put it, a misunderstanding occurred. It seems clear that it is the details of cultural differences that matter for understanding social behavior.

For example, while all humans use categories, the content of these categories is often very different; e.g., some tribes place their relatives and certain animals in the same category. While all humans use personal names, in some cultures such names are used rarely and consist of nonsense syllables. (I was very honored when a former Indonesian student of mine named his son Triandis, until I discovered that many Indonesians use nonsense syllables as personal names! When they address each other, they use *teknonyms*, such as "second son of the Brown family." The meaning of words tells a lot about a culture. (In this case it tells us that the individual is not important; the family is.) We will discuss these points in greater detail in Chapter 4.

Many categories are universal and have fairly similar meanings—e.g., incest taboos, myths (as a category, not the content), human suffering (is bad everywhere), predictability and order (are generally good everywhere). Our job, then, is to sort out what is universal from what is culture specific. For example, there are some values that Americans and Chinese have in common—e.g., both cultures think that persistence is good, though the Chinese are more convinced of its importance than are Americans (Triandis, Bontempo, Leung, & Hui, 1990).

For important values both cultures have one word, or one Chinese character. However, there are also Chinese values (Bond & Pang, 1989) that can only be expressed by using many English words (e.g., "ordering relationships by status and observing this order"). When you see that many words are needed to express an idea in one language while only one word is used in another, you can bet that the idea is indigenous to the one-word culture. Usually, when members of a culture have an idea, they also have a word for it, and the more they use it, the shorter the word becomes (e.g., *television* becomes *TV*).

We can see, then, that cultural similarities and differences are two sides of the same coin. All cultures are simultaneously very similar (Lonner, 1980) and very different. Psychologists can expect similarities when they examine a behavior or a phenomenon that has largely biological bases and is also found among other animals (Klineberg, 1954), or is strongly influenced by social structure. And they can expect similarities when they compare cultures that have emerged in similar ecologies. On the other hand, when these conditions do not hold for social behaviors (Pepitone & Triandis, 1987), they should expect to encounter differences.

A metaphor may help summarize this issue. Consider the following hierarchy of concepts:

Objects
Furniture
Places to sit on
Chairs, sofas, beds, cushions, hay, tatami-mats
Texture of the materials making up these objects
Atoms, molecules
Subatomic particles

A similar hierarchy can be found with social science concepts. At the tip of the hierarchy we have broad categories like "government," "religion," or "science." At the bottom we have basic generalizations, such as "behavior is a function of its consequences" (Skinner, 1981). In the middle of the hierarchy, i.e., at intermediate levels of abstraction, we have people "constructing" their behavior out of cultural elements that are quite variable. Thus, in some sense, the cultural differences in the middle of the hierarchy are greater than those at the top and bottom. In sum, the meaning of "object" in most languages is more or less the same. But in the middle of the range of level of abstraction, we have maximum cultural differences. The way people construct their social behavior is susceptible to many cultural differences.

In any case, while some aspects of social psychology are universally valid, others apply only in the West. If we want a universal social psychology, we need to find out what is universal, what is culture specific, and how various dimensions of cultural variation change the phenomena that we are studying. This universal social psychology will include the social psychology that is in your textbook, but it will include it as "a special case" of the universal social psychology.

A TASTE OF CULTURAL DIFFERENCES

Most readers are likely to have been exposed to only one culture. As the example of what happened in the Mysore hotel suggests, even after exposure to many cultures we are most likely to use the framework of our own cultural region (e.g., the West, the East) in interpreting events. To broaden your perspective, let me describe some surprising cultural differences.

Among the Karaki of New Guinea a man is "abnormal" if he has not engaged in homosexual behavior prior to marriage; the "missionary" coital position we consider "normal" is used only in about a quarter of the societies of the world; in cultures where hunger is endemic, fat women are much more attractive than slender ones; hissing is a polite way to show deference to superiors in Japan. There are also culture-specific disorders that occur just in one culture and can be understood only if one knows the myths and legends of that culture. Kluckhohn (1954, pp. 927–940) provides an extensive set of interesting examples of such cultural differences.

If you read ethnographies about Asian and African cultures, or about nonliterate cultures, you will get a picture of ordinary life that is very different from the picture you get talking with Europeans or North Americans. For example, Phillips (1965) described the village of Bang Chan in Thailand. In this culture affability, gentleness, and good humor are typical attributes of the villager's social behaviors. Face-to-face conflict must be avoided to the point of not saying something important that happens to be unpleasant. For example, you would not say: "Your house is burning." Instead you would say: "Why don't you go see your house?" Detailed

Important Qualification Concerning Cultural Attributes

BOX 1-1

In this book there will be many occasions to say "People in culture X are like this" or "People in culture Y do that." It is very important to keep in mind the following points:

1. Cultures and societies are enormously heterogeneous. This is especially the case when large national entities are mentioned as substitutes for culture. Strictly speaking, nations and cultures are very different concepts, but it is convenient to use the nation label to describe a sample if the data have been collected in one place and there is no adequate other information about the sample.

    Within each culture there are large variations in personality that require that we qualify every statement. For example, the statement "Americans eat pizza" is reasonably accurate, but there are those who do not like it, or are on a diet, or are allergic to an ingredient in it, and so don't eat it. At best, we are really saying "Many Americans eat pizza."

2. Any description of a culture focuses on the prototypic individuals in that culture. When we use a particular word, e.g., the word "yellow," we are dealing with discriminably different stimuli as if they were identical.

Our eye can discriminate 7.5 million colors, but we very rarely use more than 40 color names, since we group a lot of different color stimuli into one category. Similarly, there are large numbers of people who may be members of the same culture.

3. "Culture" is a label that gets mixed up with language, geography, history, religion, social class, race, rural-urban residence, nationality, and many other categories. If we are to do justice to what we are talking about, we should specify all the relevant categories, but most of the time we lack the necessary information to do this. When people are about to engage in a behavior, they "sample" elements of the cultures that correspond to their occupational group, their religion, their social class, or other demographic categories, to create a "culture" of their own that may or may not correspond to their national culture. Also, people are at different levels of acculturation, have experienced different amounts of travel, have had different amounts of contact with other cultures through the mass media, and so on, all of which do change their culture. If cul-

BOX 1-1 continued

ture consists of the memories of what "has worked" in the past, national culture is only one of many influences. Nigerian and American jet-setters are overwhelmingly similar in an airplane and may be different only in the kinds of prayers they use during take-off.

4. Any data that I mention have been obtained at one point in time. An ethnography (usually a book written by an anthropologist who spent one or two years studying a culture) may be based on data collected in 1950, with no further published information about that culture. By 1995 this may be a very different culture. Cultures are constantly changing and are strongly affected by world events, such as wars. In short, *do* pay attention to the date of a reference I quoted. The longer the interval between publication and your reading about that culture, the less likely that the culture is still the same.

5. The most important point for you to learn is *not* that a particular culture has this or that characteristic. Rather, you should learn that there *may* be a culture that has this characteristic. I hope to expand your way of thinking, so that you will not be surprised when you encounter a different way of life.

6. Cultures influence each other through travel, commerce, the mass media, missionaries, and other sources of change. For example, the mass media are introducing American cultural elements to remote parts of the globe. As a result, you will find members of other cultures selecting some of those elements—say, how to greet people. Their friends in turn imitate this "neat" idea, and soon that element of American culture gets incorporated into their own culture.

Some of these influences of one culture on another have a long history. For example, a Japanese psychologist visited my home and revealed that his religion was Russian Orthodox and that his baptismal name was Alexander! The name Alexander was originally Greek (remember Alexander the Great whose army reached India?) and became a very common name in Russia; Russian missionaries went to Japan. When the Russians adopted Christianity from the Byzantines, who spoke Greek, about 1,000 years ago, they also picked up many "prestige" names from the Greeks.

interviews with women whose husbands had taken additional wives indicated that although the women were greatly disturbed, they said nothing to their husbands (p. 69). They did not want to put anyone on the spot!

In this culture, conflict is usually followed by one of the parties' leaving the scene without explanation, confrontation, or argument. As a result, many families are dissolved with little ceremony. The polite way to say "no" to a request is to giggle; that communicates the person's intentions perfectly.

Throughout the world, religion governs the life of most people. However, the extent that this is true varies enormously from culture to culture. In Japan, for instance, only about a fifth of the population takes religion seriously. In fact, some baptize their children the Shinto (traditional Japanese religion) way, marry the Christian way, and have Buddhist funerals. It is a matter of taste, similar to eating Chinese food or pizza. By contrast, about two-thirds of the population in the United States and six-sevenths of the population in India take religion very seriously (Gallup International Research Institute survey, 1977).

The ideas of the world's main religions are often mixed with traditional beliefs, and frequently scientific beliefs are mixed in as well. For example, people will recognize that lightning is caused by electricity but will explain that phenomenon by saying that it is discharged by such and such a god. Common traditional beliefs are often animistic: The event is explained by a spirit that was mad, happy, angry, disturbed, satisfied. Illness is not considered in terms of the germ theory but is viewed as a spiritual event. For example, enemies have bewitched the sick person.

There are traces of magical thinking, not only in traditional cultures but also in the United States. For example, the belief that "once in contact, always in contact" (known as the law of contagion) and the idea that the image equals the object (known as the law of similarity) were identified as the essence of magic by Frazer (1890–1959) and have been demonstrated to be active among American undergraduates (Rozin, Millman, & Nemeroff, 1986). Specifically, Rozin et al. (1986) showed that drinks that have been in contact with a sterilized dead cockroach become extremely undesirable (law of contact), even when people are certain that the sterilization made the cockroach perfectly clean. A well-laundered shirt worn by a disliked person is less desirable than one worn by a neutral person (again the law of contact). Desirable foods (e.g., fudge) are disgusting when they come in the shape of disgusting objects (dog feces), showing the operation of the law of similarity. People are less accurate in throwing darts at the faces of people they like than at those they dislike, again showing the operation of the law of similarity.

The strong association of emotions with magic indicates that some very basic, possibly universal, processes are in operation. Since we all use a bit of magical thinking, we should have no trouble understanding how

African ideas about illness occur. Following are some of these ideas. They are presented to give you a taste of a very different culture and to introduce you to a world that is different from the West.

Traditional healing is much more widely used in Africa than is modern medicine, and the obvious question is why? Vontress (1991) did fieldwork in Africa and also conducted interviews with African traditional healers and those who use their services, to answer this question. On a continent where there are only about 100 psychiatrists for 342 million people, where transportation to remote communities is difficult (80 percent of the population lives in such communities), and where there is little Western medicine (75 percent of the population is illiterate), it is not surprising that the vast majority of the population depends on traditional healing methods.

These methods are derived from animism, the belief that all things have spirits in them. Stones, leaves, trees, rivers, even the earth itself, are considered inhabited by spirits, and people believe that illness occurs when a spirit has been offended or when some of the natural relationships among the spirits have been disturbed. It thus is up to a traditional healer, who has the ability to "control" the spirits, to intervene.

Do *not* look down on these healers; they are by no means ineffective. They have studied their craft for as long as nine years. In some cases they have their own "association" that awards certificates and makes them swear that they will not harm their patients—a form of the Hippocratic oath! During their studies, traditional healers generally learn to be exceptionally good observers and to become familiar with the medicinal properties of plants. They learn how to see what is wrong with their patients, and they take extensive medical histories. They also know how to identify and use botanical substances. Botanists have classified about 350,000 known plants, but the systematic study of the effects of touching, eating, or inhaling such plants has only just begun.

In fact, modern historians of pharmacology are discovering that ancient peoples effectively used some plants for medicinal purposes. An interesting example is a plant called silphion that is now extinct but used to grow on the Cyrene coast of North Africa. Greek and Roman women used it for birth control. It was "the pill" of the ancient world (Riddle & Estes, 1992). While this plant was harvested to extinction, plants that are genetically related to it still exist and do have contraceptive effects when used on laboratory animals.

African healers learn about plant attributes and uses from their teachers, who in turn learned from traditions developed over millennia of trial and error. They are quite skilled in their use of plants for healing, though they do make occasional mistakes with dosage. Through careful observation and through a broad knowledge of the patient's environment, healers are in a better position to detect psychosomatic disturbances and to use shock treatments (such as immersing their patients in cold water, or

Read about Other Cultures

BOX 1-2

Novels and plays are a quick way to get a taste of a very different culture in a highly entertaining and effective way.

To sample another culture, read the work of one of the following:

- Nigerian-born Chinua Achebe, who lives in Nsakka, provides a vivid account of African life in her book *Arrow of God* (1967), including the struggle between tradition and modernity, colonialism and anticolonialism, and the old and the new religions.
- In her novel *Return to Laughter* (1954/1964), American anthropologist Laura Bohannan, who used the pseudonym Eleanor Smith Bowen, depicts African rural life (e.g., the aged father in a polygamous family asks one of his older sons to have intercourse with one of his wives, so he will not lose face by not having an offspring).
- Ruth Hill sets her novel *Hanta Ho* (1979) in the second half of the eighteenth century. Hill, who lived with a Native American tribe, uses the way members of a

Native American tribe from the Dakota region think and speak to tell her story. For example, in this tribe they identify a year by referring to the notable events of that period, such as the "deep-snow winter" or "when the arrow hit the leader's neck." A swallow is a "bird that carries mud in mouth." There are monoleximic (one-word) terms for complicated ideas, such as *blotahunka* for "advisers to a large war party." *Ptepazo* is "something that points in the direction of the herd," a *teya* is "a relationship between the two wives of one husband," *wasicun* is "messenger delivers a message to an individual" but also means "white man," and *witanhantahipi* means "they come from the place of sunrise." These examples point to an important observation we already noted above: Cultures develop efficient (one-word) ways of talking about things that matter a lot to their members. This is why when we learn a language, we also learn much about a culture.

scaring them with masked invaders who threaten to kill them) than are modern psychiatrists (Torrey, 1986) who typically can take little time to work with patients who have no money. Traditional healers can ask countless questions and talk to the patients and their relatives to obtain clues that can lead to useful cures. They can impress their patients with colorful costumes and a variety of objects (e.g., roots, insects, monkey skulls, shells) and deal effectively with a wide range of problems (e.g., from impotence to depression). They are a combination of physician, priest, and psychologist. Torrey (1986), an iconoclastic American psychiatrist, doubts that the cure rates of such healers for psychological problems are different from the cure rates of modern psychiatrists.

Of course, the total picture is not entirely positive. We find that 75 percent of Africans believe in sorcerers (evil people, who can make you impotent or even kill you) and see almost everything that is bad as due to some form of sorcery. You might want to read a play by Ousmane (1976), called *Xala* (impotence), which dramatically illustrates how beliefs about sorcerers shape social behavior in Africa. It is the story of a very successful businessman, with two wives and several children with each of them, who is persuaded by a young girl's relatives to take her as his third wife. As soon as the third marriage is announced, much conflict develops between the man and his other two families. As a result he becomes impotent. However, in "good" traditional thinking, the man's impotence is attributed to sorcery. Efforts are made to get rid of the curse, but they are all ineffective. By the end of the play the man's business is ruined and he is abandoned by all his wives and children. Like a Greek tragedy, once the fatal decision to take a third wife has been taken, fate inescapably and inevitably leads to total ruin. (See Box 1-2 for other reading suggestions.)

CULTURE IMPOSES A SET OF LENSES FOR SEEING THE WORLD

In observing other cultures it is useful to keep in mind that we see the world less "as it is" and more "as we are." Depending on the experiences *we* have had, the habits that *we* have acquired, we see events differently.

For example, even the perception of visual illusions, such as the Müller-Lyer illusion show in Figure 1-1, depends on prior experience. Africans who have been socialized in environments that do not have many right angles are not as susceptible to this illusion as those people socialized in "carpentered" environments (Segall, Campbell, & Herskovits, 1963). Look around you. How many right angles are in your environment? In the West, people are inundated by right angles and learn to see Figure 1-1 as the edges of boxes—the line that looks smaller is assumed to be the back of the box and the line that looks larger is assumed to be the front.

An anthropologist from a culture that does not use our way of toothbrushing is likely to describe our procedure as follows: "It is reported to me that the ritual consists of inserting a small bundle of hog hairs into the mouth, along with certain magical powders, and then moving the bundle in a highly formalized series of gestures" (Miner, 1958). This passage is from a spoof written by an anthropologist about the way the "Nacirema" ("American" spelled backwards) engage in various rituals to improve

FIGURE 1-1
The Müller-Lyer illusion. Two equal lines seem unequal
when the context suggests that they represent the edges
of a box.

their bodies. In a very amusing way, it points to how ordinary behaviors can be seen very differently from diverse cultural perspectives.

Our experience with past events influences the way we judge present experiences. This is a very important idea for understanding cultural differences. When we judge any phenomenon, we use a neutral point that shifts around with experience. It is called the *level of adaptation* (Helson, 1964). For example, those who lift light weights (e.g., watchmakers) judge most objects in the world as "heavy," while those who are used to lifting heavy weights (e.g., professional weight lifters) judge most things to be "light." The same idea applies to many other kinds of judgments, such as whether something is good or bad, strong or weak, active or passive. Even when we judge attitude objects (e.g., the President of the United States), we do so differently, depending on our past experiences. For example, a person who has lived for years in a very corrupt society will see the current President as more honest than will a person who has not had that experience. The reason is that the level of adaptation is a kind of summary of past experiences (strictly speaking, psychophysicists have found that it is the geometric mean of the reactions to the stimuli that a person has been exposed to). So what looks good to one person can look bad to another, depending on the experiences that they have had.

In summary, in this book we will try to broaden social psychology by examining what must be modified if it is to be valid for the majority of humans. This can be done only in a preliminary way since there are not enough social psychologists in the non-Western world and so our data are very limited.

The next section of this chapter presents some definitions of key constructs, like culture. The final section provides a theoretical framework for examining relationships between culture and social behavior.

*D*EFINITIONS: ECOLOGY AND CULTURE

Humans live in enormously varied physical environments. *Ecology* refers to where people live. Ecology consists of the objects, the resources, and the geography of the environment, and the ways one can make a living and survive. For example, if there are fish, people may become fishermen.

The ecology shapes the cultures that emerge in it, and in turn culture shapes particular kinds of behaviors (Berry, 1979). In short, a simplified way of thinking about culture is to place it between ecology and social behavior, as follows:

Ecology → culture → social behavior

Humans like to feel in control of their environment. In fact, people who do not have a sense of control often become demoralized and even depressed. Among the very old this condition can hasten death (Langer, 1983). Cultures increase the sense of control over the environment. They provide humans with customs, myths, norms, etc., that allow them to feel good about themselves.

I said earlier that culture is to society what memory is to individuals. I stole this definition from Kluckhohn (1954, p. 967). Culture provides traditions that tell people what has worked in the past and makes it easy for humans to pick behaviors that may work again in the present. Customs make the social environment more predictable. For example, if you go to a social event and you know the customs, you know how to behave. Usually if you do what is customary, few eyebrows will be raised.

Myths explain what has happened in the past and why. Magic gives a sense of control over the present and the future. Even if a particular piece of magic does not work, it feels good to believe in it, and usually an explanation can be found of why it did not work that reinforces the belief. Norms (ideas about what should be done in a social situation) tell us what behaviors have worked well in the past and assure us that they will work again in the future. Values direct humans to aspects of the environment to which they should pay attention and to goals they should reach. They provide standards people can use to evaluate their own behavior and that of others.

Culture influences the way humans select, interpret, process, and use information. In many cases, customs can be substitutes for thought (Kluckhohn, 1954) and can save time. Imagine how difficult it would be if you had to decide on which side of the road to drive each time you got into your car!

The cultural elements that we might use when we think about culture include the following: patterns of dress, specific technological innovations (e.g., tools), methods of getting food (e.g., hunting, agriculture), economic activities (e.g., trading), patterns of social interaction (e.g., does one talk to one's mother-in-law? In some cultures that is not allowed), patterns of child rearing, ways to educate the young, ways to make decisions, ways to resolve conflict (e.g., politics), beliefs and behaviors regulating the relationship of humans to the universe (religion), aesthetic preferences, behaviors that increase understanding of the way the world is (philosophy), patterns of communication (language, gestures), and so on. In short, culture is multifaceted.

On the Definition of Culture

There is a wide range of definitions of culture. One of my favorite definitions (as noted before) is that culture is the "human-made part of the environment" (Herskovits, 1955). That allows me to talk about objective culture (chairs, tools, jet planes) and subjective culture (categories, norms, roles, and values).

Other abstract definitions, such as "culture is a set of schedules of reinforcement" (Skinner, 1981), or "Culture is like a computer program that controls behavior" (Hofstede, 1980), or "Culture is the software of the mind" (Holfstede, 1991), also make a contribution.

One useful way to think about culture is to think of *unstated assumptions,* standard operating procedures, ways of doing things that have been internalized to such an extent that people do not argue about them. For example, the American Constitution is a part of American culture. You will not find many people who say, "Let's get rid of it." We have long discussions about whether or not something is constitutional, but not about the merits of the Constitution itself. On the other hand, in places where constitutions are just being written, they have not yet become part of the culture and are debated at great length (e.g., Russia). One way to think about culture is that it includes ideas and behavior patterns that are "obviously valid" for members of the culture and that need not be debated.

There are many definitions of culture (Kroeber & Kluckhohn, 1952), but there are certain aspects that almost all researchers see as characteristics of culture. First, culture emerges in adaptive interactions. Second, culture consists of shared elements. Third, culture is transmitted across time periods and generations. We will consider each of these aspects of culture in turn.

Adaptive Interactions

As humans talk to each other, they reach agreements and develop language, writing, new tools, new skills, and definitions of concepts. They create ways of organizing information. They develop symbols; evaluations; patterns of behavior; intellectual, moral, and aesthetic standards; knowledge, religion; and social patterns (e.g., marriage, kinship, inheritance, social control, sports). They construct systems of government and of making war, and they formulate expectations and ideas about correct behavior that are more or less effective (functional).

One way to think of cultural evolution is to think of Darwinian mechanisms (Campbell, 1975). People tried this and that, selected what worked, and passed what worked on to their children and friends. Elements of culture that have been effective, e.g., resulted in solutions to everyday problems of existence that were satisfying, became shared and were transmitted to others (e.g., the next generation of humans).

Note also that circumstances keep changing and that what was functional in one period (e.g., having six children when infant mortality was very high) can become dysfunctional in another.

Some anthropologists take the view that cultures should be studied, but the scientist should not change them. I don't agree with this viewpoint. If elements in a culture are dysfunctional, it seems reasonable to change them. When a corporation brings a new activity into an area, it changes the culture. Usually, such a change is not evaluated from an ethical point of view. Why, then, is it unethical for a scientist to try to change a culture (e.g., teach its members agriculture when they know only how to hunt)? Of course, this is a little like "playing God," and each point of view is defensible.

In Figure 1-2 you will find another example of what I consider to be "cultural lag" (where the environment has changed but the culture keeps traditions that may be dysfunctional).

There are many cultural elements, such as national symbols, flags, and insignia, that make social interaction smoother. *Common ways of dealing with social problems* are elements of culture and can be helpful. For instance, in the United States, if several people disagree, one way of deciding what to do is to vote. That is an adaptive way of resolving conflict. In Japan the custom is to talk until there is agreement by consensus. In other cultures people who disagree leave the group. In still others, people who do not agree are killed.

We should keep in mind that humanlike creatures hunted and gathered food on the face of the earth for about 2 million years, but only in the last 15,000 or so years did humans cultivate the land and live in fixed communities. Today, when we study some of the remaining hunting-gathering people, such as the tribes of the Kalahari Desert (DeVore & Konner, 1974; Draper, 1973; Eibl-Ebersfeldt, 1974; Truswell, Kennelly, Hansen & Lee, 1972), we are studying what humans have been like for 99 percent of their existence. Viewed in this time frame, modern cultures are evolving very rapidly. Many "inventions," such as voting, occurred only "yesterday" (2500 years ago).

Still another way to think about culture is to consider the "rules of the game." If you know a culture, you know how the game is played. Of course, knowing the rules does not mean you can predict the outcome, but you can understand the games you see. If you went to a game of cricket, you would probably have a hard time figuring out what the players are doing. But as you learn about that element of British culture, you would be able to follow what was happening very well.

Shared Elements
Since interaction normally requires a shared language and the opportunity to interact (e.g., interaction usually occurs when people live next to each other), one can conveniently use (1) shared language, (2) time, and

FIGURE 1–2

A lingam yoni. This is a symbol of fertility found in many temples in India, usually bedecked with fresh flowers. Lingam means penis and yoni means vagina, and the symbol represents the gods of creation. We must remember the anxiety of most cultures about the survival of their group. It was important to stimulate fertility in an environment where infant mortality was high and life expectancy short. Now India has a population of more than 800 million, expected to grow to 1.6 billion by the year 2020. Its environment cannot sustain that size population and yet the culture and other symbols that evolved to stimulate fertility still exist and people still pray to them. That is cultural lag.

(3) place as hypotheses to identify those who are likely to belong to the same culture. However, one must agree that interaction can take place among individuals who do not share a language (e.g., via interpreters), or time (e.g., reading a book written centuries earlier), or place (e.g., via satellite). When this is the case, some elements of culture diffuse from one culture to another. In fact, diffusion and acculturation (people move to other cultures and pick up the local culture) are two important ways in which cultures influence each other.

Common fate and other factors resulting in easy, positive interaction among individuals can also form cultures or subcultures. Thus nations, occupational groups, social classes, genders, races, religions, tribes, corporations, clubs, and social movements may become the bases of specific subcultures.

This way of thinking about culture suggests that there are hundreds of thousands of cultures. In India when people were asked what language they spoke, the researchers got over 600 answers! Shared elements of culture can be found when people can interact, and so a common language is an important clue that there is a distinct culture.

There are certain geographical regions that have rather similar cultures. They are called "culture regions" because there is much similarity within the region and considerable differences across regions (see Chapter 2 for details).

When you think of culture, try to avoid thinking of nationality, religion, race, or occupation as the only criterion that defines culture. The use of a single criterion is likely to lead to confusion, as would happen if you put all people who eat pizza frequently in one cultural category! Culture is a complex whole, and it is best to use many criteria to discriminate one culture from another. Most modern states consist of many cultures; most corporations have unique cultures; most occupations have some aspects of distinct cultures (special vocabulary, unstated assumptions).

An important thing to keep in mind is that cultures are in constant flux, but the change tends to be slow (one or two generations are required before you can see a major transformation). Cultures change because of wars (think of Japan in 1940 and in 1990); commerce (think of the globalization of U.S. corporations); contact through tourism, missionaries, migration (a menu in Frankfurt, Germany, included the item "Gyros mit Tsatsiki und Sauerkraut!" combining two Greek specialties with the German favorite); and other factors.

Transmission to Others

Cultural elements are transmitted to a variety of other people, such as the next generation, coworkers, colleagues, family members, and a wide range of publics. Modern communication results in cultural diffusion via films and television. Tourism, commerce, war, and other factors also play a role in cultural transmission.

Emic and Etic Aspects of Culture

Humans have largely overlapping biologies and live in fairly similar social structures and physical environments, which create major similarities in the way they form cultures. But within the framework of similarities there are differences.

The same happens with language. Phonetics deal with sounds that occur in all languages. Phonemics are sounds that occur in only one language. The linguist Pike (1967) took the last two syllables of these terms and coined the words "etics" for universal cultural elements and "emics" for the culture-specific, unique elements.

Although some students of culture assume that every culture is unique and in some sense every person in the world is unique, science deals with generalizations. The glory of science is seen in such achievements as showing that the laws that govern the movements of planets and falling apples are the same. Thus the issue is whether or not the emic elements of culture are of interest. When the emic elements are local adaptations of etic elements, they are of great interest. For example, all humans experience social distance from out-groups (an etic factor). That is, they feel closer to their family and kin and to those whom they see as similar to them than to those whom they see as different. But the basis of social distance is often an emic attribute: In some cultures, it is based only on tribe or race; in others it is based on combinations of religion, social class, and nationality; in India, caste and ideas about ritual pollution are important. In sum, social distance is etic; ritual pollution as a basis of social distance is emic.

Scholars have divided the work of describing differences among humans. The unique attributes of individuals are described by literary scholars; the unique aspects of cultures are examined by some cultural anthropologists. The etic aspects of culture and the way etic variables are manifested as emic variables in each culture are of interest to both cultural anthropologists and cross-cultural psychologists. All these activities are valuable, and complementary, to one another.

To summarize about emics and etics, when we study cultures for their own sake, we may well focus on emic elements, and when we compare cultures, we have to work with the etic cultural elements.

Where Is Culture?

One of the controversies in anthropology is between the *realists*, who think of culture as "out there" or "in the heads of the members of the culture," and the *nominalists*, who emphasize that culture is in "the head of the investigator" (Rohner, 1984). Can we obtain a satisfactory definition of culture by using only one or the other perspective? An empirical investigation by Triandis et al. (1984) suggested that the answer is "no." While the individual models of social behavior of monolingual people from different cultures were quite distinct, the information about cultural differences, by itself, did not make enough sense. It needed to be "interpreted" by an outsider who knew something about the ecology and history of the groups under study. In other words, both sides of this dispute have a point. Culture is in the heads of its members, but we cannot fully understand it without knowing a great deal more, which is likely to require the study of how the ecology and history shaped the culture.

Cultures Are "Superorganic"

Culture is "superorganic" (Kroeber, 1917),which means that it does not depend on who (you or I) is in it. Members come and go; the cultures remain more or less stable. For example, when I was a teenager in Corfu, Greece, I used to observe people walking up and down particular streets at specified hours. The function of this activity, locally called *sergyani* and found in all the countries of the Mediterranean (e.g., *corso* in Italy and *paseo* in Spain), was to give young people a chance to determine who was attractive and worth courting. A specified set of behaviors during this activity often resulted in a "secret rendezvous," which sometimes resulted in formal engagement. Fifty years later, I observed the grandchildren of those teenagers do almost exactly what was done fifty years earlier! Same walk, same time, same place. The people were different; the culture had changed very little.

How Many Cultures Are There?

This is a difficult question to answer. If we use distinct languages as the criterion, where the speakers of one language do not understand the speakers of the other, there are several thousand cultures. If we pay more attention to details, the number grows enormously. For example, Roberts (1951) studied three Navajo households in the Southwest in the United States. He identified 578 cultural elements and examined how many of these elements were shared. He found that only 154 of these elements were held in common. There were 58 held in common by groups A and B, 50 held in common by only B and C, and 33 held in common by only A and C. (Only 13 elements were held by A, B, and C, and the remaining elements were unique.) That means that there were many unique elements, elements held by only one of these groups. In short, to the superficial observer, the Navajo have one culture. After all, they do understand each other. But once you start looking at other cultural elements (e.g., the way they skin a sheep), you can find behaviors that are shared by very few people. Similarly, in a modern hospital there may be several subcultures, such as doctors, nurses, patients, families, accountants, lawyers, government inspectors. From this point of view, the number of cultures is enormous. Interestingly, even cultures that are geographically distant will share some cultural elements.

A Definition of Culture That Follows from Our Discussion

Since, as we have seen, it is difficult to provide an adequate definition of culture (e.g., see Shweder & LeVine, 1984), I would recommend using this approach: There are many definitions of the concept, and they are all valid. However, depending on what a particular investigator wishes to study, it may be optimal to adopt one or another of the more limited definitions. For example, if the investigator is a behaviorist, Skinner's definition (culture is a set of schedules of reinforcement) may be quite satisfactory; if the investigator is a cognitive psychologist, a definition that emphasizes information processing may be optimal.

In summary,

Culture is a set of human-made objective and subjective elements that in the past have increased the probability of survival and resulted in satisfactions for the participants in an ecological niche, and thus became shared among those who could communicate with each other because they had a common language and they lived in the same time and place.

Culture can be studied by examining its emics, its etics, or both of these aspects; it is necessary both to study the members of the culture and to consider historical and ecological factors that explain why the particular elements of culture have become important.

A THEORETICAL FRAMEWORK FOR STUDYING ECOLOGY, CULTURE, AND BEHAVIOR

A simple way of thinking about culture and behavior is to consider the following framework:

Ecology → culture → socialization → personality → behavior

Let us begin by considering ecology (physical environment, geography, climate, fauna and flora), which contains some *resources* (e.g., fertile land, animals for hunting, oil, metals). These resources make it possible for certain behaviors (e.g., fishing) to lead to rewards (schedules of reinforcement); behaviors that are rewarded become automatic and become the customs of the culture.

These factors create a particular way of looking at the social environment, and (as noted before) are factors that make up subjective culture. Subjective culture includes how events are categorized and named (language), associations among the categories, norms, roles, particular kinds of self-concepts, and values. When attitudes and norms are shared, they are part of culture. When they are held by an individual, they may or may not be shared; then, they are part of personality. Habits, self-definitions, norms, attitudes, and beliefs are linked to behavior (Triandis, 1972, 1980) in ways we will describe later.

Consider this example. Ecologies where survival depends on hunting and fishing are different from ecologies where survival depends on successful farming. An analysis of what people do to survive in these two kinds of ecologies is useful. In hunting and fishing societies, people must be able to move around, to follow their prey. These cultures then acquire elements that encourage physical mobility. People who are resourceful, self-reliant, and independent do well in such environments. Thus, child-rearing practices emphasize these qualities. As a result, parents socialize their children by giving them much freedom and by encouraging independence.

In agricultural cultures, cooperation is often required. For example, many farmers work together digging irrigation canals or constructing storage facilities. A person who is not dependable or does not conform would not be a good coworker. As a result, socialization in such cultures emphasizes dependability, responsibility, and conformity.

The realities of the environment create conditions for the development of particular cultural, socialization, and behavioral patterns. For example, in particular parts of Africa, it used to be the case that living in an environment infested by tsetse flies (ecology) had far-reaching consequences (Whiting, 1964). Because the flies decimate the herds, it is difficult to keep cattle. With no herds it is difficult for babies to obtain milk. As a result, mothers feed their infants their own milk. Since women do not lactate if they become pregnant, this results in a long postpartum sex taboo—women are not supposed to have sex with their husbands for three years after giving birth. But, then, what will the men do? That makes polygyny functional! In turn, polygyny results in children's sleeping in the same bed with their mothers until they are quite old. Male children thus become very attached to their mothers and so do not learn the male roles very well. To overcome this, the cultures develop severe initiation ceremonies that clearly separate the "child" from the "adult" male.

In other words, from the presence of an ecological condition (tsetse flies) we can trace the development of several cultural features—a long postpartum sex taboo, polygyny, sleeping arrangements, close mother-son relations in early life, initiation ceremonies, and more distant relationships in later life.

Some researchers (e.g., Berry, 1979) have speculated that even shifts in the gene pool may be associated with such ecological variables. It is possible that very independent, socially unresponsive individuals in farming communities are removed from the breeding population either through ostracism or death. In hunting bands, also, highly dependent individuals may be a nuisance and similarly be removed from the gene pool. In both cases we can speculate that there is a change in the gene pool that makes the genes consistent with the ecology, thus increasing the chances of adaptation to that particular ecology.

Boyd and Richerson (1985) have provided a sophisticated account of how biological and cultural evolution have taken place. The basic idea is that random variations occur in both the genes and the cultural patterns, and natural selection results in different gene patterns, while selective retention of cultural patterns results in new cultures.

Ecology is not the only factor that shapes culture; history is just as important. Think of what happens when a war changes the way people view themselves. For example, the Japanese changed the way they thought about themselves after World War II. Although one might argue that they have not changed radically, they certainly have changed from military aggressors to economic competitors. So, historical events can shape cultures as much as ecologies. In short, ecology and history shape culture, and that includes the way people raise their children.

Different cultures have different ways of raising their children. Socialization differences can lead to personality differences. For example, Rohner (1986) has shown that parents who are warm, supportive, and cuddling toward their children have children who are optimistic (positive world view) and well adjusted. Parents who are cold, indifferent (unavailable), and rejecting (use frequent physical punishment, much verbal abuse) toward their children have children who are pessimistic (negative world view); do not like themselves; are emotionally unresponsive, hostile, aggressive, emotionally unstable, and poorly adjusted (disturbed friendships and peer relations); have physical health problems (e.g., allergies, asthma, hypertension); and show intellectual performance problems.

A major correlate of parental acceptance, worldwide, is the voluntary physical presence of the father in the household. Second in importance is the presence of the "stem" family (grandparents, parents, and children). Rohner theorizes that women raising children alone feel overwhelmed and unable to provide sufficient acceptance. This is also supported by the observation that children with more than four siblings report less acceptance than children with fewer than three siblings. It appears that the presence of a large number of care-givers in the household improves the chances of acceptance. Such caregivers can be, in addition to parents and grandparents, older siblings or even well-trained staff. The point is that there must be enough caregivers, who have enough time to give, to provide the kind of emotional support needed.

Since Rohner published his studies, several researchers confirmed his findings in other cultures (e.g., Erkman, 1992, in Turkey). The findings are sufficiently consistent and clear to be useful for social policy. One implication is that it is undesirable to bring up children when one is a single parent, unless other adults (such as friends or kin) can help.

In sum, socialization depends on many factors, such as what resources are available to the parents, how much help the parents can get from others, and what kind of family structure there is. We can now go back to the larger question of how the ecology shapes the culture.

In some cases, features of the culture itself require particular socialization practices. In the Andaman Islands (Gupta, 1976; Sen, 1962), located between India and Malaysia, women in one of the local tribes customarily carry their babies on their backs at all times, including while working in the field. However, this tribe does not have diapers for their babies. Of course, mothers are highly motivated to toilet-train their babies. Not surprisingly, this culture has the world's record on early toilet training— they train their babies completely by age six months! This is one case where Freud's (1909/1976) theory about socialization and personality was supported. Freud thought that an emphasis on cleanliness during early childhood will make people obsessively and compulsively neat. Such people would want "everything in its own place" and things to be done "just so." That is exactly what was observed in the tribe just described. They are very clean and compulsive. (However, they also suffer from many cases of "autointoxication"—something that happens when a person does not expel bodily fluids and excrements as needed.) In any case, in this example we see how a particular norm (carrying the baby on the mother's back) results in a socialization pattern (severe toilet training), which results in a personality pattern (compulsiveness), which results in certain behaviors (being superclean, superneat).

Now that you have seen the way socialization links with personality and the way some behaviors are associated with that personality, consider how personality is linked with behavior. While generally the situation is a more powerful predictor of behavior than is personality (see Ross & Nisbett, 1991), there is a tendency for people with certain personalities to select situations that fit their personality. Aggressive people are more likely to join the military than a monastery. Contemplative people are more likely to do the opposite.

In another sphere of culturally linked behaviors, cultures with severe socialization practices have gods that are severe (Lambert, Triandis, & Wolf, 1959). That is, we find in the same cultures either very lenient, non-punishing parents *and* gods or very severe, punishing parents *and* gods.

When we predict individual behavior, we need to consider the entire range of influences—from ecology, social organization, community, family, and personality (Georgas, 1989). In addition we need to consider the behavior setting (Barker, 1968). People behave in specific ways in each setting, e.g., praying in a church, dancing at a party, depositing money at a bank, reading in a library. The setting is one of the most powerful predictors of behavior. But cultures shape their settings differently, depending on the ecology, social organization, community, and family structure. For example, in individualistic cultures, such as the United States, people are likely to deal with conflict via legal means, and there are many more lawyers, courts (a behavior setting), law offices (a behavior setting), and records of legal precedents than in collectivist cultures, such as those found in the Far East, where conflict is resolved informally, by using intermediaries, mediators, and other specialists.

To get a sense of the meaning of settings, examine Figure 1-3 from a study by Adamopoulos, Smith, Shilling, and Stogiannidou (submitted). They found that behavior settings are perceived rather similarly in the United States and Greece. Four dimensions were needed to show the judged similarities and differences of these situations. I will not burden you with the details of all these dimensions, but will mention only the first two, the most important.

Dimension I contrasts settings where great variability in behavior is not appropriate (e.g., doctor's office, library) with settings where one can do many different things (party, cocktail lounge). In the settings on the left side of Figure 1-3 people saw more interactions and more cooperation as appropriate than in the settings on the right side of the figure.

Dimension II contrasts settings where there is a lot of chatting (beauty parlor) with those where there is less (gymnasium).

S UMMARY

Culture as the precipitate of history reflects many of the things that previous generations have learned work well in their particular ecologies. Of course, ecologies do change, and then cultures become obsolete. But, on the whole, most of the links between ecology, culture, and behavior can be understood from a functional point of view. Since most of the phenomena of social psychology have been discovered in specific ecologies and cultures, the chances are that as we examine the same phenomena in other cultural settings, we will observe some differences. Much of the time these differences are small, but some of the time the phenomenon is completely reversed. When this happens we must incorporate cultural variables into our theory of the phenomenon. Essentially our theory changes. Instead of "the more of X, the more of Y," it might become "in cultures high on Z, the more of X, the *more* of Y"; "in cultures low on Z, the more of X, the *less* of Y."

This kind of theorizing is clearly more complicated than the kind that has been used in psychology so far, and it is legitimate to ask: Do we need to bother with culture to develop a good social psychology? The next chapter will tell you that we do need to bother, and why.

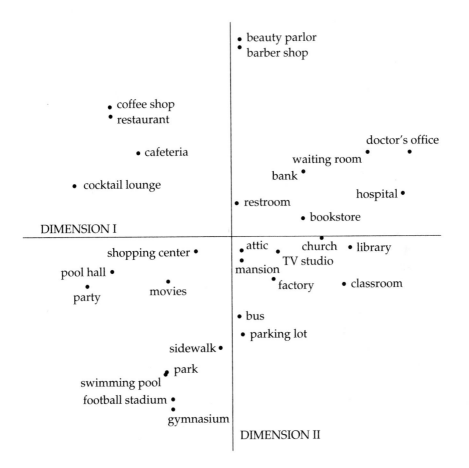

FIGURE 1–3

The location of different behavior settings on the two most important dimensions that people use to discriminate such settings. Behavior settings that are perceived to be familiar are close to each other; "hospital" or "cocktail lounge" are very different from each other. (Adamopoulos et al., submitted. Reprinted by permission.)

QUESTIONS AND EXERCISES

1. Find students from another culture and interview them. Ask them to tell you what they found different here compared with their own culture.

2. Read one of the books (such as the play *Xala*) recommended in the text and list some of the major cultural differences you encountered while reading.

3. Use a ruler to measure the central lines of Figure 1-1, to satisfy yourself that they are equal. Do they look equal? What is the explanation of the difference between how things are and what they seem to be? *Hint:* Use previous experience, the level of adaptation.

4.   Review the discussion about adaptive and dysfunctional cultural elements. Do you think it is ethically permissible for scientists to change the cultures they study?

5.   Consider the discussion about child rearing, personality, and behavior. What kind of advice would you give to parents in your culture so that the frequency of delinquency would become lower?

Hint: While delinquency depends on many factors, does Rohner's research suggest that children who are rejected are more likely to become delinquent than children who are accepted? If that is the case, what are the implications for the debate about abortion, for changes in the economy, and for reforms of the rules for aid to dependent children?

2

Why Bother to Study Culture-Social Behavior Relationships?

On January 9, 1991, the foreign minister of Iraq, Tariq Aziz, and the secretary of state of the United States, James Baker, met in Geneva to attempt a last-minute compromise that would avoid a war. Seated next to Aziz was the half-brother of Iraq's president, Saddam Hussein. The half-brother kept calling Baghdad to provide Hussein with his evaluation of what was going on. Baker used the verbal channel of communication almost exclusively, and said *very* clearly that the United States would attack if Iraq did not move out of Kuwait. The Iraqis, however, paid less attention to *what* Baker said and most attention to *how* he said it. Hussein's half-brother reported to Baghdad that "the Americans will not attack. They are weak. They are calm. They are not angry. They are only talking." Six days later the United States unleashed Operation Desert Storm.

We know what happened to the Iraqis after they made this cross-cultural communication mistake. The best estimate is that they lost about 175,000 of their citizens, they sustained $200 billion in property damage, and some of their population were reduced to refugees.

While this incident describes a *major* cross-cultural mistake, Western businesspeople, diplomats, academics, and others make myriads of *minor* mistakes of this kind each year. Most of the time they do not know they are making them. People tend to be polite in intercultural encounters. People in collectivist cultures, such as Africa, Asia, and Latin America, are sometimes more polite than people in Europe and North America, especially when they are dealing with a person who has power and resources. So they will not criticize, and they will not point out mistakes. Unfortunately, without feedback it is impossible to learn. Thus billions of foreign contracts, advantageous common projects, and the opportunity to form better human relationships are lost because of ignorance of the way culture influences social behavior.

We know that all people express themselves not only linguistically but also paralinguistically (e.g., gestures, tone of voice, looking or not looking in the eye, firm or loose handshake, orientation of the body, level of voice). In some parts of the world, such as the Middle East or the Far East, people pay more attention to paralinguistics than do people in such parts of the world as Northern Europe, or even America. In Chapter 7 we will discuss findings (e.g., those of Gudykunst & Ting-Toomy, 1988) that suggest that in collectivist cultures people use context more than content.

Another cultural difference is how extreme the linguistic statement has to be to be believed. Some cultures, e.g., the Japanese, use very mild, moderate expressions, and consider it very bad manners to use an extreme statement. Other cultures, such as the Arabs, believe that a truly sincere person will not equivocate with a moderate statement but rather will express ideas forcefully and with some exaggeration: "If you attack, you will face the mother of all battles." Had Baker wanted to use the Iraqi communication pattern, he would have used extreme language (e.g., "We are going to make hamburgers out of you!"), banged the table, and looked ferocious and angry; and if he had really wanted to make an impression, he would have thrown a large telephone book at Aziz!

Most Westernized Arabs would deny that this was necessary, but they also do things the Western way and may be embarrassed by the traditional Arab behaviors. Hussein and his half-brother, unlike many Arabs who have studied in the West, know relatively little about that part of the world and thus may well misunderstand a message produced there. Similarly, Baker may not have understood the extent to which his message did not get through. Thus, an opportunity for peace apparently was lost because neither side knew enough about cross-cultural social psychology.

An important point about this example is that we must not stereotype and that we must differentiate when we are meeting members of other cultures. There are many kinds of Arabs, some highly Westernized, and others not. Baker probably has learned about Arabs mostly from interactions with Arab diplomats, who tend to be Westernized, and did not take into account the relative importance of Hussein's half-brother as a member of the Iraqi delegation. Diplomacy in a multi-cultural world is not easy.

In a world that can become extinct in a nuclear holocaust, can we afford to neglect a better understanding of the relationship of culture and social behavior?

In the previous chapter you learned that social psychology is mostly a Western-cultural product and that we are still quite unsure about the extent to which the important findings of social psychology apply to the majority of humans. This chapter expands on this point and discusses some other advantages of cross-cultural studies.

ADVANTAGES OF CROSS-CULTURAL STUDIES

Checking the Generality of Social Psychological Findings

Most of what we know about social psychology comes from studies that were done with respondents from Europe or North America. A reasonable guess is that more than 90 percent of social psychology has been generated in North America (including Mexico), which represents less than 7 percent of humankind. To get a sense of that proportion, let us say that if the earth had 100 people, 55 would be Asians, 21 Europeans, 9 Africans, 8 South Americans, and 7 North Americans.

But even that poor sampling does not take into account that most of the information comes from college sophomores, and they are not especially representative of the population at large (Sears, 1986). If science aspires to be universal, we need cross-cultural research to check the generality of what has been found.

Another deficiency of sampling is that, at least in the pre-1970 social psychology literature, the majority of the empirical data were based on males. Women were "invisible," and in many cases the tasks were more appropriate for men than for women (Nielsen, 1990).

It is acknowledged that working outside the university setting poses special difficulties for academic psychologists. It is increasingly difficult to study institutional populations (schools, prisons), because their administrators feel that their wards have been overstudied, they worry about bad publicity, and they would rather not be bothered. But even if we did study noncollege samples, they would hardly be representative of humankind. While there are special methodological difficulties in doing cross-cultural work (Triandis & Berry, 1980), if we don't engage in this type of research, it is impossible to differentiate between those studies that report phenomena of local interest and those that report universal phenomena.

The importance of checking our findings with other populations is illustrated by the work of Amir and Sharon (1987). They began by considering all articles published in the top social psychological journals between 1973 and 1975. They divided these articles into seven topical categories and randomly selected five articles from each category. Next they examined these thirty-five articles to see if the studies could be replicated. This judgmental review indicated that six studies had a good chance of being replicated, because they did not deal with a unique American issue or require complex equipment. Their paper reports their attempt to replicate these studies with samples of Israeli college and high school students.

Thirty-four of the sixty-four results (more than half) did not replicate. Some pessimistic social psychologists have argued that many of these results would not have replicated even in the United States. That may be true. We need a similar study done in some very American environment (Decatur, Illinois?) to answer this point. In any case, the authors add: "The low replicability is even more striking if one keeps in mind the fact that when studies were selected for replication, the method of selection biased the results towards the 'etics,' excluding very specific probably non-reproducible experiments" (p. 468).

In short, we should be cautious in assuming that the studies published in our best journals generalize to humankind, particularly if the phenomenon is complicated. We must be even more cautious if we take into account the fact that literate people tend to be more similar to each other than to illiterates, and schools have the effect of closing the cultural gap (Rogoff, 1981). Moreover, the cultural distance between the United States and Israel is not as large as the cultural distances between the cultures where most social psychological findings have been obtained and the cultures where the majority of humans live.

Anthropologists consider six or seven "cultural regions" (there is much current research on this issue based on similarities in social structure, language, and religion; see Burton, Moore, Whiting, & Romney, 1992) as most distinct from each other:

1. Europe and regions where the people heavily influenced by Europe live, such as North America. This region also includes the people who live in the area around the Mediterranean, such as North Africa and Israel. (Remember the monotheistic religions—Judaism, Christianity, Islam—have a lot in common.)
2. Africa south of the Sahara.
3. East Asia (Japan, China) and South Asia (e.g., India).
4. Pacific Islands, including the Australian aboriginals.
5. North American Indians.
6. South American Indians.

More recently, a group of anthropologists has argued that there are seven regions (Burton et al., 1992), but that is a detail of little importance to us. The important point is that Israel is largely in the same cultural region as North America, and so we expect American studies to replicate better in Israel than in, say, India or China, and much better than they would replicate if a tribe on the Amazon River had provided the respondents.

In measuring cultural distance we must think of at least five facets: language, family structure, religion, level of affluence, and values.

1. We know that languages have "families." Comparative linguists have discovered these families by examining similarities in words and patterns of language. For example, the Indo-European languages range from India to Iceland, with a few pockets of non-Indo-European languages (the Hungarians, the Finns, the Basques) in between. That is a different language family from, say, Japanese or Zulu.

2. Family structures range from polygynous (husband has many wives) and polyandrous (wife has many husbands) to monogamous (one spouse) and from extended (e.g., all resources are shared by all the brothers and their families) to nuclear (father, mother, children). Todd (1983) identified eight types of family structures.

3. Religions come in many varieties within the Christian, Jewish, Muslim, Hindu, Buddhist, Shinto, and animist categories.

4. To measure wealth, gross national product per capita (GNP/cap) is frequently used. The range between countries is enormous, e.g., $150 for Bangladesh to $23,000 for Sweden (of course, these numbers change as the value of the dollar changes).

5. Values (Schwartz, 1992) differ in important ways. For example, there are cultures where "tradition" and "honoring parents and elders" are much more important values than "pleasure" or an "exciting life."

Minimal cultural distance will exist when the same language, family structure, religion, GNP/cap, and values can be identified. The largest distance will occur when all five facets are different. In the case of the United States and Israel, the language belongs to different families (but most Israelis learn English); family structure is quite similar; religion is somewhat different, but monotheism results in common traditions; the GNP/cap is different, but not very different; values are different, but compared with the world relatively similar. All in all, in worldwide perspective, the two cultures are a lot more similar than different.

Some readers may conclude from these results that we should not trust any of the findings reported in our journals. However, before we get carried away with the idea of cultural specificity, it is important to point out that humans do have a lot in common, so that some hypotheses that reflect human commonalities are likely to be replicated. Klineberg (1954) used the idea of a "dependable motive" for certain behaviors (e.g., seeking food, sleeping) which makes them universal (1) when they have a physiological basis and (2) when they can be found among other animals as well as humans. There are also linguistic universals and other kinds of universals (Brown, 1991).

Lonner (1980) reviewed evidence that in all cultures we find athletic games, courtship, dancing, feasting, funeral rites, games of chance, gift giving, greetings, hospitality, joking, kinship nomenclature, and visiting. But the form of the behavior can be very different. For example, around the world, greetings can involve rubbing noses, lying prostrate on the floor, crying, and other behaviors that almost never occur in Western greetings.

It is also a universal that for nonneurotic development to occur, babies must be close to some adult during early socialization (Harlow & Harlow, 1962). As well, if there is insufficient social involvement, there is social disorganization (e.g., divorce, crime, child abuse; see Naroll, 1983).

In sum, there are many cases of universality, even though many of our findings do not replicate in other cultures, as Amir and Sharon have suggested. We need a more balanced view about what is or is not likely to be culturally general. Pepitone and Triandis (1987) point out that some phenomena are strongly connected with biology, or features of the ecology or social structure that are common to humankind. Thus, theories that deal with such phenomena are likely to be universal. But for these theories to be universal it is also important that the *meaning* of the stimulus conditions be universal, i.e., the same across cultures. Our problem is that since culture is the ultimate source of meaning, we cannot take meaning constancy for granted. Thus, we must check each finding cross-culturally before we assume its generality.

One conclusion that is easy to derive from a reading of the six-volume *Handbook of Cross-Cultural Psychology* is that almost every important phenomenon in psychology has both a universal and a culture-specific aspect. Some examples will clarify this point. Take learning in Japan and the United States: Does the way the Japanese learn vary from the way Americans learn? To find out, we can use a graph. We can plot the number of trials required to learn on the x axis and the number of correct responses on the y axis. When we do this for Japan, we get a line that shows that the more trials there are, the fewer errors are made. Since we get the same general line shape for the United States, the more trials–fewer errors relationship is a cultural universal. Another variable that we might consider is, Who gets rewarded for learning when the learner makes the correct response: the learner or the experimenter? Haruki,

Shigehisa, Nedate, Wajima, and Ogawa (1984) explored this question by sometimes rewarding the learners with candy and sometimes rewarding the experimenters. They discovered that in America, people learned under both conditions, but they learned *more* when the learner was rewarded than when the experimenter was rewarded. In Japan, people also learned under both conditions, but they learned *as much* when the experimenter was rewarded as when the learner was rewarded. The researchers explain these findings by pointing out that Japanese mothers usually reward their children by saying "I am happy" when they act correctly and "I am sad" when they behave inappropriately. The Japanese thus learn to pay attention to how others feel and to change their behavior so that others will feel good. Thus, the Japanese learn as much when an important other person gets rewarded as when they themselves get rewarded. That is cultural specificity, and it reflects the "individualism" of the United States and the "collectivism" of the Japanese. In sum, the main phenomenon, learning when one gets rewarded, is culture general, but the details are culture specific.

Similarly, Ekman and Friesen (1971) have shown that emotions have the same connections with different types of situations in different parts of the world. However, the "rules" for displaying emotions are culture specific. For example, in Japan, when a subordinate suffers a misfortune and must report this misfortune to a supervisor, the subordinate is supposed to smile when he recounts what happened. The misfortune would normally result in a frown, a sad expression, or tears, but one is not supposed to upset a high-status person, and by smiling the stress of the other person is reduced. In Japan, people are expected to control normal emotions.

We can also see this in an experiment in which Americans and Japanese were shown a movie of someone's hand being cut. The subjects of the experiment were shown the movie under two conditions: alone and in the presence of others. The Americans and Japanese expressed the same emotions in the "alone" condition, but the Japanese expressed less emotion in the "presence of others" condition (Ekman, 1992; Ekman & Friesen, 1971; Lazarus & Averill, 1972). Thus, while the emotional experience appears to be universal, the rules for expressing the experiences are culture specific.

In summary, an important benefit from cross-cultural studies is that it is possible to differentiate the universal and the culture-specific aspects of each psychological phenomenon.

Cultures Provide Natural Experiments

Strodtbeck (1964) has pointed out the advantages of using the natural experiments that culture creates for us in order to learn about social behavior. Some of these allow variables to have much more range than they have in our culture. For example, Whiting (1968) has pointed out that in the West there is a linear relationship between the age of weaning and the extent a child is assessed to be anxious at a later time. The older the age of weaning, the more anxious the child tends to be.

But this conclusion is based on the fact we wean most of our children by the age of six months. If we look at other cultures, we see that the age-of-weaning-versus-anxiety curve rises linearly only up to age eighteen months and then reverses and so the relationship is curvilinear: the older the age of weaning, the higher the anxiety up to age eighteen months and the lower the anxiety after age eighteen months: thus, children weaned at thirty-six months are no more anxious than children weaned during the first weeks of life.

Remember the example in Chapter 1, that in some African cultures where there are many tsetse flies, weaning occurs at thirty-six months? Well, weaning-derived anxiety is one problem these cultures do not have! If a missionary/pediatrician working in Africa were aware of only the American data, she would probably strongly advise against weaning at thirty-six months, but this would be the *wrong* advice. Often a behavior that is functional in a particular ecology may be abandoned because of the ignorance of the adviser. Unfortunately, much cross-cultural advice is equally flawed.

A problem with research in the United States is that we are not allowed to vary the range of variables beyond what is natural in our culture. Institutional review boards that approve our studies before we collect data want to ensure that we do not expose our subjects to unnecessary risks. Except for unusually important scientific studies, we can get our studies approved only if we expose our subjects to no risks or at most to "risks of ordinary life." Our professional ethics (American Psychological Association, 1973; Tapp, Kelman, Triandis, Wrightsman, & Coehlo, 1974) also require that we avoid stressing our subjects.

But cultures vary so much that what is considered an unethical manipulation here may occur naturally in some other place. For example, an experiment that deprives children of the chance to go to school would be unethical, but unfortunately in many cultures children are unable to attend school, and in that setting it is ethically acceptable for us to test the effects of this deprivation.

Unconfounding Variables

In science we need to find out precisely what causes what. Unfortunately, this is difficult to do outside the laboratory, because many variables are confounded—that is, they are strongly associated with other variables. For example, we might have a situation in which a child who went to a school with pupils mostly from other cultures did poorly on a test. Was the fact that the child went to that school the cause of this poor showing? Would that particular child have done poorly in any school? Was the test valid for that child? Would testing at another time have given a different result? There are a dozen possibilities, and our job is to find the one factor or combination of factors that caused the event. To do so we must "unconfound" the variables that we study.

Many variables of interest are confounded in our culture, but cultures can allow us to unconfound them. For example, it is difficult to find totally illiterate fifteen-year-olds in the United States, but there is no difficulty finding such a sample in parts of Africa. Thus, if we want to separate the effects of age from the effects of schooling, we can study African children aged four, eight, twelve, and sixteen with schooling and without schooling.

Studying Culture Change

Cultures change in many ways (Berry, 1980b). They influence each other; war, commerce, tourism, missionaries, and other factors change them.

It is often difficult to study some kinds of change in our own culture, since it has already occurred, but we can study the same kind of change in other cultures. For example, what is the effect of the introduction of television on the behavior of children (Lonner, 1985)? We can study social life in communities that do not now have television, before and after its introduction, and see how social behaviors change.

In many of these studies, television has had the effect of reducing the frequency of social behavior. By comparing what people did before with what they do after the introduction of television, researchers have found that people spend more time watching television and talk less to each other, play fewer games, and tell fewer tales. It is probable that such changes have also occurred in American culture as a result of the introduction of television, but we can no longer study them. We can guess that it is undesirable for children to watch television forty hours per week, but we cannot document it until we have solid data. Such data can be obtained in cultures where television is only now being introduced.

Even more important changes can be identified in American culture during the last half century. I am old enough to remember when a faculty member was fired by a small college (1960) because he was getting a divorce. Today most colleges would not dream of taking steps against professors who choose to get a divorce—or to live with a partner out of wedlock. That is change!

In 1958 my university fired a professor who wrote an article in the student newspaper suggesting that perhaps it was desirable for young people to "test" their relationships with others before marriage. Now such tests, in the form of living together, are fairly frequent, so much so that another of my colleagues has found enough cases to study and has concluded that the fired professor was wrong. Actually, the data indicate that people who pretest their relationships have a higher probability of getting a divorce than people who do not. That may be explained by the argument that the more "conservative" are less likely to enter into such pretest arrangements and also less likely to divorce. The only point I want to make is that sexual freedom is greater in American culture now than thirty-five years ago.

Another phenomenon of cultural change is acculturation. We will discuss this phenomenon in more detail in Chapter 9. Here we will discuss only the acculturation of recent Hispanic migrants (from Mexico in particular) to the United States to provide a concrete example.

We might think that this change is linear, but in fact it is more complex. Triandis, Kashima, Shimada, and Villareal (1986) have shown that there are three patterns of acculturation, and they occur for different cultural traits. First, it is common for Hispanics to acquire some of the attributes of non-Hispanics—that is called *accommodation*. Second, there are cases of *overshooting*; that is, some Hispanics become even more extreme on some trait than are non-Hispanics. Finally, there is *ethnic affirmation*; that is, Hispanics who have been in this country for some years become more like their culture of origin (Mexico, Puerto Rico) on some attributes than Hispanics who have just arrived. In the Triandis et al. study most of the data showed accommodation or overshooting.

Patterns of acculturation also depend on which generation is studied. The children of new immigrants are eager to merge and be like the local children. But the grandchildren of the immigrants tend to be quite comfortable with their ethnicity and often show ethnic affirmation (Waters, 1990) to distinguish themselves from the masses.

Newcomers may want to become absorbed by the host culture (assimilation), or they may prefer to stay separated from the host culture. If they want to assimilate, a major factor that determines if people will show accommodation, overshooting, or ethnic affirmation is whether there is prejudice and discrimination toward the newcomers. The more the newcomers can "pass," the more likely they are to accommodate or overshoot; the more the newcomers are rejected, the more likely they are to show ethnic affirmation, especially in those domains where their ethnic affirmation cannot be observed by the mainstream of the society, so there are no punishments for being different.

Reducing Ethnocentrism

In a world of satellites and jet travel, which has the capability of total annihilation through nuclear war, we have to shift from our "natural state" of ethnocentrism (using our own culture as the standard for judging how good other cultures are) to an understanding of other cultures and the development of skills for successful social behavior with members of other cultures. We have to develop new ways of thinking. For example, when we make a comparative judgment that our culture is in some ways better than another, we need to learn to follow this judgment with two questions: Is that really true? What is the objective evidence? If we find ourselves judging a culture that is not our own as better than our own, the chances are that the judgment has some basis. But when we judge our culture as better than another, it is likely that this is an illusion. For example, I feel secure in judging French and Chinese food or Japanese gardens as better than American or Greek food or gardens, because I was not brought up eating such food or viewing such gardens. I have acquired the taste. I note also the painstaking work that goes into such activities—several years of study to become a master chef in France and as much as three years of study to place the boulders in the garden of the Katsura villa in Kyoto, Japan. When members of a culture spend so much time and effort on an activity, the chances are that they do it well.

To reduce ethnocentrism we must learn to appreciate the best that humans have produced, no matter where it was developed. We must learn to analyze cultures (some of the methods and information presented in Chapters 3 to 5 will be helpful); also, we need culture training (some of the information in Chapters 8 to 10 can be useful) to understand the mechanisms of social behavior across cultures and to learn skills that will increase successful social behavior across cultures.

In the next several sections we will review some important social issues, examining them in the light of what we can learn by paying attention to cultures. And we will see that we can learn a lot—which is one more reason for undertaking cross-cultural studies.

*C*ULTURE AND SOCIAL ISSUES

Culture and Health

There is considerable evidence that culture is related to the health status of individuals. For example, there are large cultural differences in life expectancy. In most traditional cultures life expectancy is somewhere between forty and fifty years. In most developed cultures it is somewhere between seventy and eighty-six years depending on other factors, such as ecology, the accuracy of the statistics, diet, customary exercise levels, and so on.

Diet is largely an ecologically (what is available in the environment) and culturally (traditionally, what do we eat?) determined factor. Here we see the opposite trend from the one just mentioned, because the developed countries have diets that are rich in fat and fat intake is strongly correlated with age-adjusted death rates (Cohen, 1987). Many poor countries have better diets than rich countries, since affluence increases meat consumption and heart attacks! For example, Greece has increased meat consumption sixfold in twenty-five years, and heart attack rates have also increased. That is, for any age group, the more fat in the diet, the more likely people are to die. In the developed, rich countries people eat more meat and hence absorb more fat; in the less developed, poor countries people have to limit themselves to vegetables and often eat fewer calories. These contradictory trends imply that the improved life expectancy in the rich countries is more closely linked to sound public health measures and good medicine than to diet.

If we use life expectancy as the standard, the rich countries of the world have the highest expectancies, but even among those countries there are large differences. For example, life expectancy is higher in Sweden, Norway, and the Netherlands than in the United States. This probably reflects the fact that many Americans do not have health insurance, which could help them to take preventive measure to increase their life expectancy. Consider also that the *custom* of an annual checkup is an element of culture!

As well as there are differences among countries, there are differences within countries. Black Americans have distinctly lower life expectancies than do white Americans. This is due to many factors, such as greater poverty, less concern for diet, higher probabilities of death from homicide, and, for some, greater demoralization (why live when you are unhappy?).

There are also differences in the amount of stress experienced by people in different cultures. Fast-changing cultures and those cultures where individuals have to fend for themselves without the help of an extended network of family and friends are characterized by higher levels of stress than stable cultures and cultures in which people receive social support from many people.

Henry and Stephens (1977) reviewed studies of the systolic blood pressure of a wide range of people which showed that mean blood pressure is lower in traditional societies than in modernizing populations. Statistical controls for diet and other factors do not change the results. Rapid social change and isolation from a stable network of social support appear to be the main causes of increased mean population levels of blood pressure.

It has been shown that a tense occupation does not necessarily mean high blood pressure. Test pilots, for example, do not have unusually high blood pressure, suggesting that it is possible to adapt to tense conditions. High blood pressure is more closely linked to frustration, such as not being able to control one's environment, than to job type.

Another quantifiable aspect of health is mental health. Mental hospital admissions per year per 10,000 people range from 121.1 in Panama, 99.5 in Finland, and 93.7 in Sweden to 31.4 in the United States, 1.5 in Burma, and 1.4 in Tanzania. Here, again, several cultural factors are likely to be involved, such as definitions of the kind of behavior that requires hospitalization, the degree of environmental stress that is likely to precipitate a mental breakdown, the probability that a person will receive social support when in distress, the availability of alternative ways to deal with the undesired behavior (e.g., indigenous healers), and other factors.

These differences in frequencies may also reflect additional cultural factors, such as the extent to which a person feels in control of life's situations. Some mental disorders, such as depression, are caused by situations in which individuals experience a loss of control and feel helpless. There are many ways to improve the sense of control. For example, prayers coupled with a deep emotional attachment to religious beliefs result in the person's feeling more in control. From a scientific viewpoint this is probably a case of self-deception, but that is irrelevant when it works for the individual. Similarly, in many traditional cultures people believe strongly that the spirits of the ancestors are active in a person's life and that traditional healers can "call" them to cure the sick. Some psychiatrists, such as Fuller Torrey (1986), have argued that psychiatrists have about the same success rates with mental diseases as traditional healers. If that statement is correct, then it is not surprising that people who believe in the efficacy of traditional healers will not visit mental health facilities, and that will influence the mental health statistics.

Another serious health problem in many industrial countries is alcoholism. A relevant statistic is the amount of alcohol consumed per person per year. The top consumers, Portugal and France, consume seven times as much as the bottom consumer (Israel). In the middle of the range are the United States and the former U.S.S.R.

The greater the culture's pressure on children for personal achievement, the lower the nurturance of children. The lower this nurturance and the emotional dependence of adults upon other adults, the greater the frequency of drunkenness (Naroll, 1983, p. 190).

In addition, in cultures (e.g., France) where people drink low-alcohol-content drinks, such as wine, the *volume* is higher than in cultures (e.g., Russia) where people drink high-alcohol-content drinks, such as vodka, gin, or whiskey. Studies also show that cultures that encourage people to depend on others for their emotional and nonemotional needs have lower rates of alcohol consumption than cultures where people try to face their problems alone.

Figure 2.1 presents a theory of the antecedents of disease that is consistent with a variety of evidence but that has not been tested as a

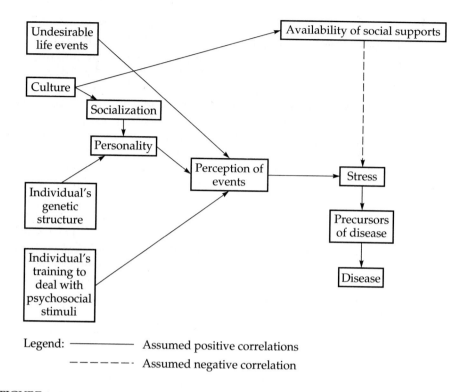

FIGURE 2-1
Cultural antecedents of disease. (Triandis, Bontempo, Villareal, Asai, & Lucca, 1988.)

single entity. "Undesirable life events" are one important factor in poor health. Such events can include the loss of a job, the death of a loved one, or a divorce. Rahe (1972) developed a scale of such events by assigning 50 points as the amount of "life change" associated with getting married. He asked adults in Seattle, Washington, to rate numerically the amount of life change associated with various life events using the 50-point life change as a point of reference. Death of a spouse was rated 100, divorce 73, in-law trouble 29, and so on. There is evidence that different cultures rank life events more or less similarly (Rahe, 1969).

Figure 2.1 also suggests that some socialization patterns create more stress than others. Stress is more likely to develop during socialization when the signals of correct social behavior sent by adults are confusing.

Social cohesion (e.g., availability of social supports) is a factor that can reduce the impact of undesirable life events. Cultures differ in the extent to which people face their problems alone (typical of individualistic cultures like the United States; it is also more often true for men than for women) or face their problems jointly with others (typical of collectivist cultures, such as one finds in many traditional societies, where both men and women face problems jointly with others).

In collectivist cultures, consultation is used very widely, decisions are often taken by consensus, and responsibility for these decisions is shared. Thus, in individualistic cultures failure is usually the source of more stress than in collectivist cultures where failure is shared (Kashima & Triandis, 1986).

In Figure 2.1 undesirable life events are perceived as more or less stressful depending on the way culture and socialization predispose the person to look at them. For example, unemployment is much more stressful when people know that it is a consequence of their own actions than if it is a consequence of universal economic changes, and it is likely to be perceived as more of a threat if people feel alone and have to make a living entirely on the basis of their own abilities than if they feel interconnected with many relatives and friends who can help during a crisis. In many traditional cultures earnings go into a common pool, from which the expenses of the extended family are paid. If one of the contributing members is fired, the resources of the group are reduced, but it is not quite as terrible an event as when the person fired is the sole support of a family.

Moreover, personality is a moderator of the effects of unpleasant life events on the perception of a stressful event. Some people manage to see undesirable events with much optimism and others, with much pessimism. Both genetic factors (Plomin, 1990) and modes of socialization seem to be relevant. Across cultures socialization that is associated with much warmth and acceptance tends to result in optimism; socialization associated with rejection tends to result in pessimism (Rohner, 1986).

Furthermore, the individual's training in dealing with undesirable events, such as getting fired or experiencing the symptoms of a disease, can make the perception of the stimuli more or less threatening. For example, some people get used to low levels of pain while others are severely threatened by the same levels of pain. The perception of the events as threatening results in further stress. But stress can be reduced if the person receives a lot of social support. Thus, socially cohesive cultures, in which individuals are more likely to receive social support, are likely to have many members who experience relatively little stress.

There is considerable evidence that stress is a precursor of disease, because it decreases the effectiveness of the immune system (Ader, 1981) and thus is related to the frequency of peptic ulcers, cardiovascular disease, cancer, complications of pregnancy, and many other health problems (Henry & Stephens, 1977).

There is a good deal of evidence is support of Figure 2.1, some of which is presented in Henry and Stephens (1977). As mentioned above, blood pressure levels increase with age in populations where there is rapid social change and where Westernization is common. But in traditional societies blood pressure is not related to age (except after age sixty). High blood pressure, of course, increases the probability of cardiovascular disease. While diet (e.g., salt) plays a role in blood pressure levels, culture seems to play an even greater role.

Around the industrialized world, levels of cardiovascular disease differ very sharply, as is shown in Figure 2-2.

The lowest probability of cardiovascular disease was observed among Trappist monks. Trappists had rates of just over 1 heart attack per 1000 people. These monks have pledged not to speak for the rest of their lives and communicate only by writing, which is usually less emotional than Benedictine monks (who do speak but make few decisions outside the monastery), who had rates of 3.5 per 1000; Benedictine priests (who make

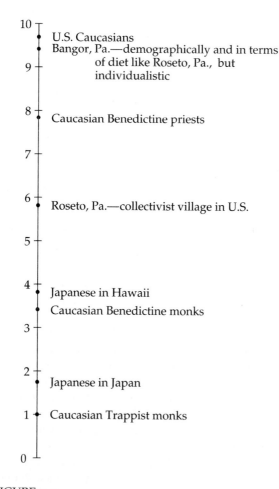

FIGURE 2-2

Heart attack rates per 1000 inhabitants in selected samples. (Triandis, Bontempo, Villareal, Asai, & Lucca, 1988. Copyright 1988 by the American Psychological Association. Reprinted by permission of the publisher.)

many decisions, because they run schools and hospitals) had rates of 7.8 per 1000. The difference is statistically reliable ($p < .0001$). In short, the more involved the sample is with decisions, the higher the cardiovascular disease rates.

In a sample of more than 3000 Japanese Americans, Marmot and Syme (1976) observed that the more Americanized the individual, the higher the rate of coronary heart disease (in this study Japanese in Japan, 1.8; Japanese in Hawaii, 3.2; U.S. Caucasians, 9.8). The more a Japanese American used English and American norms, rather than traditional Japanese behavior patterns, the higher the coronary rate. Those Japanese Americans who cannot be distinguished from mainstream Americans in culture also have the U.S. Caucasian level of heart attacks. Even after factors such as diet, cholesterol level, exercise, smoking, and weight are controlled, the relationship between acculturation to the U.S. norms and heart attack rates can be observed. One possible explanation is that the strong emphasis on politeness (no loss of face by anyone), the predictability of social behavior in Japanese culture, and the emphasis on in-group harmony and consensus create a social environment that is less stressful than the American confrontational style, which demands being "different" and "distinguished," and the American concern for individual as opposed to group-based achievement.

One may wonder if the fast pace of life in the United States is responsible for the differences just described. But Levine and Bartlett (1984) showed that the pace of life is actually faster in Japan. Table 2-1 presents one of the three measures used by these researchers to determine the pace of life. It shows that Japanese and American men living in large cities require on the average 19 and 21 seconds, respectively, to walk 100 feet; women require 21 and 25 seconds, respectively. This difference in pace of life is substantial. The table contrasts the pace in large and small cities and in industrial and less developed countries. Two other measures (time to complete a post office transaction and incorrect time on the public clocks) showed the same pattern of results (Japan fastest, most accurate). The three pace-of-life measures were correlated with each other. The important point is that the pace of life in Japan is not slow, so that this factor cannot account for the low heart attack rates among the Japanese.

Epidemiological data from Los Angeles county (Frederichs, Chapman, Nourjah, & Maes, 1984) are consistent with the above data. They show that mortality rates that are age- and sex-adjusted for European and African Americans are more than twice the rates for Asian Americans, and the difference is even larger when deaths from cardiovascular disease are examined. Some of the differences, of course, are due to diet, but it is important to keep in mind that diet is also part of culture!

Similar data emerged from the comparison of the village of Roseto, Pennsylvania, with a similar "control" community, Bangor, Pennsylvania. The only difference is that Roseto is socially well integrated because

TABLE 2-1 WALKING SPEEDS IN SIX COUNTRIES*

City size	Country											
	United States		Japan		Taiwan		Indonesia		Italy		England	
	M	SD	M	SD	M	SD	M	SD	M	SD	M	SD
Large												
Men	20.84 (n = 75)	2.89	19.10 (n = 62)	2.20	23.10 (n = 60)	3.84	24.19 (n = 84)	3.29	22.49 (n = 51)	2.59	20.07 (n = 60)	1.89
Women	24.65 (n = 75)	3.08	20.87 (n = 60)	2.78	25.72 (n = 60)	3.30	27.21 (n = 72)	3.74	24.65 (n = 60)	3.06	22.23 (n = 60)	2.39
Small												
Men	21.33 (n = 64)	2.34	20.42 (n = 62)	3.08	25.55 (n = 65)	3.99	27.82 (n = 65)	4.49	22.22 (n = 60)	2.64	20.95 (n = 60)	2.76
Women	22.99 (n = 70)	3.02	22.23 (n = 65)	3.57	27.22 (n = 65)	5.20	30.28 (n = 65)	3.92	24.08 (n = 60)	3.30	23.10 (n = 60)	2.85

* Times indicate the number of seconds taken to walk 100 feet. Thus, higher numbers indicate slower speeds.
SOURCE: Levine & Bartlett, 1984. Reprinted by permission of Sage Publications, Inc.

the residents immigrated from the same Italian village in the province of Foggia. The researchers checked if there were differences between the two communities in age, sex, weight, cholesterol level, exercise levels, diet, or smoking. They did not find statistically significant differences on these variables (Henry & Stephens, 1977). The socially well-integrated village had essentially no heart attacks before age sixty-five; the control village had some. After age sixty-five the Roseto rate was half the rate of the control village.

In addition to data of cardiovascular disease, the results of many other studies, on diseases such as cancer, on complications at the time of pregnancy, and so on, fit the general framework of Figure 2.1.

Culture and Sex-Role Inequality

The question of why there is so much difference in gender-role inequality across cultures is an interesting one. The general pattern around the world is that men have more status and power than women, but this difference is not the same across cultures (Rosaldo & Lamphere, 1974).

The level of unfairness reflected by this inequality is best summarized by some numbers: "Women constitute half the world's population, perform nearly two-thirds of the work hours, receive one-tenth of the world's income and own less than one-hundredth of the world's property" (Frankenhaeuser, Lundberg, & Chesney, 1991, p. 257).

Where do these differences come from? There are many theories (see Gailey, 1987, for a review), but the evidence in support of these theories is contradictory, and some of the theories are more inspired by Marxist ideology than by facts. Probably, each theory contains a grain of truth, but the reality is that no completely convincing, sound theory is yet available. Nevertheless, the explanation presented below appears to be the most plausible way of answering this question. We will discuss this issue in more detail in Chapter 5. It is just mentioned briefly here to stimulate your interest.

Cultures differ in the degree of inequality. Even in cultures where an ideal of sexual equality is stated explicitly (e.g., in Mao's China) the practice is inconsistent with the ideal. Men and women tend to be more equal in simple hunting-and-gathering-band societies than in complex stratified ones (Etienne & Leacock, 1980; Lebra, 1984). In band societies there is often male-female reciprocity and complementarity rather than hierarchy. In stratified societies women tend to be "put in their place."

Socioeconomic and sex inequalities are often correlated, and sexual exploitation is often consistent with economic exploitation.

In Africa, for example, in the non-Muslim areas, the status of women was fairly equal to the status of men until the colonial powers took over

(Etienne & Leacock, 1980). Under colonization there was economic exploitation, and gender inequality increased. In addition, religious authorities often provide further justification for inequality through rigid dogma (Iglitzin & Ross, 1976) and hierarchies in which male priests are dominant. The Muslim and Catholic religions have been especially supportive of gender inequality (Iglitzin & Ross, 1976).

Where are men and women more equal? One index of gender inequality is the percentage of illiterates who are women. In general, it is desirable to have an equal number of men and women who are literate, as is the case in Scandinavia and Switzerland. In many of the developing countries, however, far more women than men are illiterate. Even in the United States, women did not match the male levels of education until the late 1970s!

Another index of equality is the percentage of women in managerial positions. Worldwide it is far less than 50 percent, with 48 percent in Switzerland and 28 percent in Austria. The remaining major countries have even lower rates. The United States figure is only 17 percent. Very low rates can be seen in the Muslim countries, in South Korea (2 percent), and in Ghana (3 percent).

The sex-earnings ratio indicates how much women earn as a percentage of what men earn. Treiman and Roos (1983) provide thirty-five pages of statistics from industrial countries. Briefly, in this data set, the best ratios occur in Germany (where women earn 74 percent of what men earn) and the Scandinavian countries (Sweden 69 percent, Finland 68 percent, Norway 63 percent, but Denmark only 57 percent); in most Western European countries women earn about two-thirds of what men earn; the data for the United States, in this report, show 51 percent. Note that this is an average and that the picture is different by occupation, region of the country, ethnic group, age group, and so on. Nevertheless, on the whole, women earn less than men.

Around the world, men are more likely to be killed than women. In Northern Ireland this is a 9 to 1 ratio. In the United States it is 3.3 to 1, but in Denmark it's only 1.1 to 1. Men are also more likely to die in automobile accidents. In Chile the ratio is 4.8 to 1; in the United States, 2.7 to 1. Iceland is an exception, with a ratio of 1.0 to 1.0. Again, these numbers reflect averages—and the tendency for men to do more dangerous jobs than women.

In other words, a major factor in such differences may be that there are traditional male and female activities (e.g., occupations). Some theorists have argued that the domestic domain of women is less prestigious than the public domain of men. But why should this be the case? Starting with the reality of different biologies, hormonal levels, and physical anatomies, members of cultures exaggerate the importance of some attributes and reduce the importance of other attributes, and thus conclude that some activities are strictly for males and others strictly for females.

Gender is *constructed* out of the realities of physiology and the cultural assumptions (beliefs, attitudes, values) that emerged in different ecologies.

Men are more likely than women to engage in dangerous activities where there is a choice (e.g., to fish in the open sea or the lagoon?) and to take chances. When humans were foragers (hunters, gatherers), pregnancies made dangerous activities inappropriate for women, and so the societies glorified some activities (e.g., fishing in treacherous waters) and attached little prestige to other activities (e.g., cooking). One can take a functional viewpoint here: If the dangerous activities were not glorified, few would have done them. Thus, traditions glorifying the activities of men (e.g., war) developed through such mechanisms and remain, to some extent, in all contemporary societies.

Boys and girls are socialized differently (Barry, Bacon, & Child, 1957). Boys are raised to be independent, self-reliant, aggressive, and achieving to a greater extent than girls are; girls are socialized to be high in nurturance, responsibility, and obedience to a greater extent than boys are. A more recent study (Low 1989) found that girls were inculcated with sexual restraint and industriousness in about forty cultures, while boys received such training in less than five cultures; boys were inculcated with self-reliance, competition, aggression, and fortitude in ten of thirty-five cultures, while girls received such training in two cultures. Statistical analyses indicated that these effects were quite reliable—unlikely to be due to chance.

There is considerable agreement among both men and women in thirty countries concerning the stereotypes of males and females (Williams & Best, 1982). Males are seen as adventurous, aggressive, autocratic, daring, dominant, enterprising, forceful, independent, progressive, robust, stern, and wise in the overwhelming majority of the samples. Females are seen as affectionate, dreamy, sensitive, sentimental, submissive, and superstitious in the overwhelming majority of the countries. Thus the socialization patterns and the stereotypes converge to some extent.

In studies of fourteen countries, Williams and Best (1990) examined how individuals believe themselves to be, i.e., the actual self; how they would like to be, i.e., the ideal self; and how males and females should be, i.e., the ideology of gender. They found small cultural variations in the actual or ideal self, but large cultural variations in the ideology of gender. Specifically, in countries with high socioeconomic development and a high proportion of Protestant Christians, there were highly educated women, and large percentages of women were employed outside the home. In those countries the gender ideology was egalitarian. In more traditional cultures, especially those with large proportions of Muslims, such as India, Pakistan, and Nigeria, the gender ideology emphasized the desirability of differences between men and women.

There is considerable evidence (Campbell, 1967) that stereotypes reflect what people do: When members of a group engage in commerce, they are more likely to be perceived as "shrewd"; when members of a group live in an arid area, where they can cultivate only one crop, they are more likely to be perceived as "lazy"; and when they live in a rainy area, where they can grow two crops, they are more likely to be seen as "diligent." If the theory suggested above is valid, it leads to optimistic conclusions about the closing of the gap: In information societies, i.e., societies in which the activities of the men and women become indistinguishable, the sex-earnings ratio will move toward equality.

Of special interest is Japan, because it is a modern country with a gender ideology that is still relatively traditional. But as Iwao (1993) clearly shows, the gender ideology is very different among those born during the 1930–1946, the 1946–1955, and the 1955–1970 periods. The older Japanese are quite traditional; the youngest group is almost equal but uses a conception of equality that is uniquely Japanese.

Kidder and Kosuge (in press) provide some sense of the changing gender ideology scene in Japan. Two hundred years ago Japanese women had very little responsibility for raising their children. Most decisions were made by the family hierarchy in which the older males were the major players. Today, child rearing is the major job of Japanese women, who are educated so they can further educate their children. The "education mama" (*kyoiku mama*) is noted "for her single-minded concern with tutoring and preparing [her children] for entrance examinations, from kindergarten through university" (p. 6). These authors ask, however, whether this is *progress*.

Role differentiation is so great that Japanese women do a great deal more than Japanese men in raising children. In a study of seventy married men and women, aged twenty-two to fifty-five, with one or more children, Kidder and Kosuge found that women indicated that raising children was their chief activity. They were significantly more likely than the men to prepare all the meals, do laundry, shop, wash dishes, turn on the bath, lock up at night, take out trash, answer the phone, pay bills, meet teachers, remember birthdays, discipline children, select schools, help others relax, control the family's money, and make decisions about family savings. Men were only more likely to earn money, deal with politics, make major investment decisions, and drive the car. Even employed women showed that profile. There was little use of baby-sitters.

In a survey of boys responding to questions about spending time or playing with their fathers, the Japanese gave the "I spend *no* time" response three times more frequently (16.1 percent) than the American (5.1 percent) or German (5.7 percent) samples. Kidder and Kosuge argue that this pattern is bad for the men, who become overdependent on their mothers (e.g., mother calls forty-year-old son every morning to ensure he wakes up). Men are then caricatured as tyrants or babies.

The women in the Kidder-Kosuge sample were not attracted by work, in part because the workplace was seen as the realm of men, where women could play only supportive roles. In addition, death from over-work (*karooshi*) is occurring in Japan. About 10,000 people per year die from the stress of overwork (Kidder & Kosuge, in press, p. 21). A 1991 survey conducted by a pharmaceutical company among men and women working for major companies in Tokyo found that 30 percent of the men and 23 percent of the women feared death from overwork. Under such circumstances it is not surprising that women prefer to be education mamas. On the other hand, university graduates would love to have a job, if a good one were available. Lebra (1984, p. 309) reports a survey in which 83 percent of Japanese women university graduates indicated they would have liked to have a job. The Kidder-Kosuge paper does not agree entirely with the analysis provided by Iwao (1993), who sees a greater change toward equality of a unique Japanese type than do those authors. We will return to Iwao in subsequent chapters.

Culture and Morality

In collectivist cultures morality is much more a function of what is good for the collective than in individualistic cultures, where personal rights are emphasized. Among collectivists moral behavior is virtuous behavior, which means doing one's duty as it is defined by the in-group, carrying out one's role in the in-group in the best possible way, and doing what is best in the particular situation. In collectivist cultures, also, conflict between the individual and the group is resolved by the moral individual submitting to the will of the collective. The same conflict in individualistic cultures is evaluated with abstract ideas such as "the greatest good for the greatest number."

In individualistic cultures people are more likely to have an idea of what is "the truth," and they are more likely to use abstractions. At the same time they can do their own thing without being rejected, while in collectivist cultures those who do their own thing are often rejected.

In the study by Shweder, Mahapatra, and Miller (1990), when Indians from the province of Orissa were asked whether a widow could eat fish, they responded that she should not and would greatly suffer if she did. The Illinois samples thought that she had the right to eat fish. Careful examination of the beliefs that underlie these responses makes clear the collectivism-individualism contrast. The Indian view is that the widow is linked to her husband for eternity, and eating fish, which they believe can cause sexual excitement, may result in her having sexual relations with another man, thus breaking the link with the husband. The Illinois sample, on the other hand, sees the widow as an autonomous individual who has the right to decide for herself what to eat. In short, the Indian view is that individuals are interdependent; the Illinois view is that they are independent.

A similar point is made by Miller, Bersoff, and Harwood (1990), who show that Indians regard the failure to aid another in moral terms under all conditions, while Americans view such failure in moral terms only in life-threatening situations or in cases of parents' responding to the moderately serious needs of their children. In short, again, Indians see the self as being more interdependent and hence people must help others, while Westerners see the self as more independent and obliged to help only under certain circumstances.

A very influential theory of moral development was proposed by Kohlberg (1969, 1981). Briefly, the theory postulates the existence of six stages. In stage 1 morality, people avoid breaking rules, obey, and do not damage property simply to avoid punishment. In stage 2 morality, they follow rules when they see that this behavior is in their best interest. In stage 3 morality, they are "good" because they want to do what is expected of them by those to whom they are close; they conform because being good is important to them. People in stage 4 do their duty, act lawfully, and contribute to society or their group or institution because it is right to maintain the social system. Stage 5 people are aware that a variety of values and opinions exist but feel that the values and rules of their own group must be adhered to because there is a "social contract"; they also believe that some nonrelative values and rights, such as life and liberty, must be upheld in any society regardless of majority opinion. People in stage 6 follow universal ethical principles that are self-chosen; when laws violate these principles, one can disobey the laws; universal principles of justice, such as equality of human rights and respect for the dignity of human beings as individual persons, guide their actions; people should act out of a sense of personal commitment to the universal principles.

Supporters of this theory have used a set of scenarios describing moral dilemmas to ask people to make judgments about them. For example, one of the scenarios describes a man whose wife is very sick and will die without proper medicine. The druggist charges a very high price for the drug; the man does not have that much money, and so he steals the needed medicine. The interviewee is asked to evaluate this action. The issue is whether the man should do everything possible to save his wife's life.

The responses obtained are classified into the six stages by using a scoring manual. Snarey (1985) has reviewed forty-five studies of moral development carried out in twenty-eight countries and reports that the Kohlberg invariant sequence proposition was well supported, because stage skipping and stage regressions were rare. Nevertheless, he did identify two biases: Complex urban societies and middle-class populations reached the higher stages quite dependably, while folk societies did not. Stages 3 and 4 were present in virtually every society, and stage 5 was rare in most populations.

One interpretation of the findings is that stages 5 and 6 are culture-bound and ethnocentric. However, Snarey rejects this interpretation, arguing that members of a culture may use a particular stage most frequently although all cultures may be fully equal in moral development. In other words, the frequencies of the stages can reflect differences in age, socioeconomic level, or social-technical complexity. If a society consists mostly of children and young adults, as is common in folk societies, which have a short life expectancy, one can expect that the most frequent score will correspond to a lower stage than in a society that consists mostly of older people. The fact that the most frequent score corresponds to a low stage in moral development does not make that culture low in moral development, as long as some members of the culture are capable of higher-stage reasoning. Snarey concludes that every culture is capable of supporting higher-stage reasoning, and thus cultures are equal in moral development.

Snarey concedes that the Kohlberg scoring manual needs revision because the higher-stage moral reasoning reflects Western philosophy and neglects non-Western thought. For example, it is not that life is not valued in Hindu philosophy, but that it is valued situationally in very culturally specific ways. Values found in some societies, such as communal sharing (see Chapter 6), collective happiness, nonviolence, purity, chastity, filial piety, and community responsibility are missing from the scoring manual.

Broader criticisms of Kohlberg (e.g., Shweder et al., 1990) included the argument that his theory reflects individualism and liberalism and is androcentric (male-centered). The methodology is hypothetical and uses dilemmas that do not include enough context and with which people are unlikely to feel especially involved.

The theory is individualistic because it assumes that people are autonomous and morality is purely individual, and the values chosen, such as individual property, human life, and individual conscience, refer to individuals. It reflects Western liberalism, because it is quite likely that Marx or Buddha would have gotten a low score in moral reasoning. It is androcentric because Kohlberg's morality emphasizes values that are most often held by men, such as autonomy and rationality, and de-emphasizes values that are most often held by women, such as mercy, care (Brabeck, 1989), love, attachment, belonging, and emotional security (Gilligan, 1982).

Lykes (1985) has shown that men have more individualistic and women more collectivist notions of the self. Specifically, in a multimethod study of conceptions of the self, she found that women, especially at the lower end of the occupational ladder, perceive the self as person-in-relationships. The various measures of social individuality, such as collectivist ideology, social responsibility, and attention to social cues, were correlated with each other for women but not for men.

More recent evidence (Josephs, Markus, & Tafarodi, 1992) indicates that men and women form their self-esteem differently. Self-esteem is high when a person reaches goals that are culturally mandated. For American men that means separation from in-groups and independence; for American women that means connection with in-groups and interdependence. In this study, based on U.S. data, men's self-esteem depended on distinguishing achievements and women's on establishing successful connections and attachments. Those who had a high self-esteem and did not perform well on gender-appropriate tasks reacted in a defensive manner.

Furthermore, it is imperative to test theories cross-culturally with multimethod measurements. The use, in the Kohlberg tradition, of only one method weakens quite considerably our confidence in the results. We may wonder also about the validity of the method for collectivist cultures. Consider this response, obtained in New Guinea, to the scenario "The man steals to get medicine to save his wife's life." The respondent replied: "If nobody helped him, I would say that *we* had caused the crime."

What would be a collectivist theory of moral judgment? Ma (1988) has provided such a theory starting with Kohlberg and noting that stages 5 and 6 are not universal. Instead he provides Western and Chinese perspectives for these stages.

It seems to me that there is agreement that the more abstract principles reflect higher moral reasoning. However, each culture is likely to have a different set of supreme, abstract values, and people who reach the higher stages of moral reasoning are the ones who are guided by these values. All values are acceptable as long as they do not infringe on those who have different values. Given that all the great religions emphasize the relationships among humans, and given that the most influential view of the world, in terms of billions of people who have been influenced by it, is the view developed by Confucius, which emphasizes concern for one's family, kin, the state, and so on, I wonder if a true collectivist morality might not be the one that emphasizes concern for the well-being and care of each individual, as well as for larger and larger groups, and in the end humankind. That is quite abstract!

SUMMARY

It is important to study and understand the relationship of culture to social behavior in order to avoid significant errors in social interaction. Perhaps the mistake of the Iraqis in judging that the Americans would not attack in 1991 has the world's record as a cross-cultural blunder. But there must be myriads of potential errors that can be avoided if one knows how culture influences social behavior.

Furthermore, to develop a better social psychology we must study the way culture influences social behavior. We need to understand, for instance, that the emphasis on attitudes and consistency in social psychology reflects Western individualism, where the individual is at the center of the stage. A more collectivist culture would have developed a social psychology that put more emphasis on the study of norms, customs, group behavior, and the influence of culture on social behavior.

It is important also to study the generality of what we have learned in the West, and to take advantage of the natural experiments that cultures provide, in order to study key variables and also to unconfound variables that cannot be studied or are confounded in our own cultures.

It is clear that cultures differ very much on health, ideas about morality, and other important attributes. The reported differences provide an invitation for us to study cultures in order to understand some of the factors that cause these differences.

We have made the case, I hope, that it is worth studying the relationship between culture and social behavior. We must now face the fact that such a study is much more difficult than studying social behavior in a single culture. The next chapter will examine these difficulties and suggest ways to overcome them.

QUESTIONS AND EXERCISES

1.   There are differences between modern, rich, industrial countries and traditional, poor, agricultural countries. In your opinion, is economic development always a blessing?

2.   Many social psychological studies cannot be replicated in other cultures. What does that mean about the future of social psychology?

3.   Make a list of some of the most important findings of social psychology. Do you think they would be supported in other cultures? To what extent would this happen?

4.   Pick one of the cultural differences in a health index. To what extent is culture the important factor? Can we use some other factors to explain the difference? If your answer is "yes," are these other factors entirely distinct from culture?

3

How to Study Cultures

------------------------- ❖ -------------------------

Problems and Difficulties ◆ *Rival Hypotheses* ◆ *Some Solutions to These Problems* ◆ *Some General Comments* ◆ *Good Theory Can Eliminate Some Rival Hypotheses* ◆ *Acculturation Indexes Can Help Establish Cultural Differences* ◆ *Statistical Methods May Help* ◆ A Broad Perspective on Cross-Cultural Research ◆ Emics and Etics in Cross-Cultural Research ◆ How to Use Emic Measurements of Etic Constructs ◆ General Recommendations ◆ The Available Range of Multimethod Measurements ◆ *Ethnographic Work* ◆ *Establishing Shared Cognitions* ◆ *Interviews and Surveys* ◆ *Tests* ◆ *Experiments* ◆ *Content Analyses* ◆ *Human Relations Area Files* ◆ *In Sum* ◆ Translations ◆ Ethics of Cross-Cultural Studies ◆ The Ethnocentric and Androcentric Bias of Researchers ◆ Criteria of Good Cross-Cultural Research ◆ Summary

T he previous chapter showed why it is desirable to study the relationship of culture to social behavior. However, such studies present many difficulties. This chapter examines some of the methodological problems associated with this research.

PROBLEMS AND DIFFICULTIES

The general intent of this chapter is not to teach cross-cultural research methods, but to provide ways to tell the difference between a good and a bad study.* Many bad studies have been published. Once you learn to identify them, you need not pay much attention to them.

Good cross-cultural research is like ordinary social research, only it is more difficult because of the complexity of the issues of translation, equivalence of measurement, and the like. Those who want to do such research should become familiar with the writings of Campbell (1988) as well as the publications mentioned in the footnote.

In the previous chapter we discussed the importance of checking the generality of social psychological findings in other cultures. If the findings obtained in one culture can be replicated in another culture, the methodological problems are no more difficult than ordinary social research done in one culture.

However, if the findings cannot be replicated, we have a problem. We must then ask: Do we have a real cultural difference, or do we have an "apparent" difference due to an artifact or a "rival hypothesis"? For example, it may be that people in one culture respond to a particular *method* of data collection differently from the way people in another culture respond to it. In such a case we do not have a substantive finding but rather a finding that is best explained by the way people react to the method of data collection.

To establish a "real" cultural difference we need to eliminate all plausible rival hypotheses (Malpass & Poortinga, 1986) that may account for the observed difference.

Consider the following specific case: We tested two sample populations, representing two separate cultures, and found a difference in their intelligence (IQ). What are some of the plausible rival hypotheses?

Rival Hypotheses

1. **The two cultures may have a different definition of "intelligence."** In some cultures intelligence is defined as "slow, sure, makes no mistakes"; in others, as "does what the elders say"; and in still others, as "knows our traditions." If the two cultures define the concept differently, can we really claim that the difference we obtained with a method

---

* Those wishing to do cross-cultural studies can consult a more advanced text. The most complete one, though rather long, is by Triandis and Berry (1980). A shorter volume is by Lonner and Berry (1986). Special issues concerning the equivalence of cross-cultural measurement, as well as the unstated assumptions that are made by people who collect cross-cultural data, are discussed in Hui and Triandis (1985).

that measures intelligence well in *our* culture means the same thing in the other culture? Can we compare the two cultures? How can we claim that we found a difference between the two cultures?

A specific example, reported by Berry and Bennett (1992), illustrates how different cultures define intelligence differently. Social scientists sometimes use a statistical technique called multidimensional scaling to determine what ideas go together. This technique requires subjects to judge the similarity among different ideas (*stimuli*). It results in a map that shows the location of the stimuli in relation to each other, as they have been judged by the average respondent.

In this case the judgments were made by the Cree, a Native American tribe found in Canada. The results show that "lives like a white" is close to "stupid" and "crazy," but also "cunning"; "wise" goes with "thinks carefully" and "is respectful." The kinds of ideas we in the West would consider as going together, like "smart" and "mentally tough," are not very close to each other in the view of the Cree.

The ideas that psychologists in the West have about the intelligent way to answer a question are determined, in part, by their own culture and conventions. For example, when people are presented with a set of familiar objects and are asked to classify or sort them as well as they can, it is assumed that it is "more intelligent" to do so by taxonomic category (tools, food) than by color (white, blue) or association (hammer and nail, bread and butter). Clearly, psychologists argue, color is a superficial attribute; it is not a "mature, sophisticated way" to sort objects.

Glick (1968) asked some Kpelle farmers in Liberia to do this task; these farmers used color or association as the basis of sorting. But since they seemed to be quite intelligent (for instance, they were very good at bargaining in the market), Glick did not believe that he had actually measured their intelligence. So he asked them to do the task in a number of other ways. At no point did they use, as the basis of sorting, the attribute that Western psychologists consider intelligent. Exasperated, Glick asked them to sort the objects "the stupid way." With that instruction they sorted the objects using the criterion that Western psychologists considered to be intelligent! Thus, what psychologists, working within their cultural framework, consider an intelligent answer may be defined in another culture as stupid.

To eliminate this rival hypothesis we need to study the meaning of constructs, in the relevant cultures, *independently* of their measurement.

Even more important, when we measure something in another culture, we are most likely to get an answer to the question, Do they do *our* tricks as well as we do our tricks? rather than, Do they do *their* tricks well? The development of abilities, attitudes, and specific personality attributes depends on the extent to which these attributes get rewarded. Different ecologies reward different tricks. Now, that does not mean that it is useless to ask, Do they do our tricks as well as we do our tricks? If they are to compete with us in a particular environment, that information is relevant. The point is that we should be clear that we are not measuring their *native* abilities but rather their abilities to adjust to *our* environment.

More generally, when we compare two cultures, we are comparing entities that differ in a myriad of ways. The conclusion that the difference reflects a particular variable (e.g., intelligence) requires that we control all the interactions of intelligence with other variables.

Furthermore, we need to sort which aspect of culture is the relevant one. For example, in a comparison of black Americans and white Americans, we need to distinguish a difference due to race/color per se from differences due to nutrition, social class, neighborhood, historical influences, etc. If all the observed differences are due to social class, it is scientifically irresponsible to report them as due to race. If both social class and race are relevant, we must report that fact also.

It becomes apparent from this argument that a two-culture comparison will have almost no scientific value, since in science we want to find relationships among well-defined, clear, reliably measured variables. Suppose we want to check the relationship of nutrition to intelligence. Ideally (assuming we have the funds) we should try to include a large sample of cultures in our study. The cultures that we select should differ in all sorts of ways, except that they should be ranked on *one* clear variable, nutrition. Then the countless other variables will not be systematically associated with nutrition, and we will be able to say something reliable about the relationship of nutrition to intelligence (Leung, 1989).

Campbell (1988) makes a valid point: The comparison of any two cultures is essentially useless (except for preliminary, hypotheses-generating work). This point requires us to study *many* cultures (a minimum of two "high" and two "low" on the variable of interest). The more cultures we can include in our analyses, the better.

In addition, we must replicate the study with *many* different methods, since each method has its own meaning in each culture, but it is unlikely that an unsound hypothesis will be supported with very different methods. It is especially important to replicate the study with both non-reactive methods, such as participant observations, and more reliable (but usually reactive) methods, such as testing or questionnaires. Multimethod measurement is discussed in greater detail later in this chapter.

2. **The instructions may not be understood the same way.** This is especially likely if the members of one culture have much less experience with a method or task than the members of the other. Related to this variable is the extent to which the two populations are familiar with the measurement method. For example, multiple-choice tests are widely used in the United States, and a measure that uses such a test can give U.S. subjects an advantage over a population from a country where such tests are not used.

A special test that measures how well people understand the instructions should be used routinely to eliminate this rival hypothesis. Familiarity with this measurement format and content has to be equated. This can be done by using formats that are equally familiar (and contents that have been pretested to be equally familiar) in the two cultures.

3. **The level of motivation of the two samples may be different.** Americans are likely to be motivated if an experimenter tells them that their intelligence will be measured by how fast they will do something. But in other cultures, where intelligence is not linked to speed, people may respond with "What is the hurry? Why should I work that hard to answer these questions?" Independent measurements of the levels of motivation should be used to control for the difference statistically in order to eliminate this rival hypothesis.

4. **The reactions to the experimenter may be different.** For example, in some cultures it is against the norms to cooperate with "outsiders." In some cultures it is *mandatory* to lie to outsiders or trick them. One should use several experimenters, some "insiders" and some "outsiders," to obtain some estimate of the importance of this factor.

5. **The meaning of the test situation is not always the same.** For example, in some studies (Bond & Cheung, 1984; Bond & Yang, 1982; Yang & Bond, 1980) the language of the instructions influenced the results. When instructions were given to Hong Kong subjects in Mandarin, Cantonese, or English, the results differed. Apparently, the language of the instructions suggested to the subjects who was interested in the results of the study—the Beijing authorities, the Hong Kong authorities, or the British colonial authorities.

In testing black ghetto children, white psychologists sometimes get poor responses using certain psychological tests, such as the Stanford-Binet. But if the researchers first play games with the children, sit on the floor with them, speak their dialect, and so on, the children do score well. The difficulty is making sure that the meaning of the test situation is equivalent. Even when the psychologist judges the situation to be equivalent, it may not be. One needs some independent measurements of the equivalence of the meaning of the situation.

6. **Some people panic in IQ test situations and thus do very badly.** Others find testing a challenge and do very well. The difference may be due to the difference in the levels of anxiety that the test situation produces. While this is a problem in within-culture testing, requiring that the subject be tested several times with parallel forms under relaxed and "normal" (everyday-life) conditions, it can be a really significant problem

in cross-cultural testing. Mean anxiety levels are sometimes quite different across cultures.

7. **Response sets differ across cultures.** In some cultures people only answer the questions they are absolutely sure of; in others they answer all the questions.

In some cultures people use extreme responses; in others moderate responses (Hui & Triandis, 1989; Triandis, 1972). For example, Marin, Gamba, and Marin (1992) found that Hispanics in the United States, relative to non-Hispanics, are more likely to use extreme responses (e.g., I *strongly* agree) and to show acquiescence (agree with every question). However, the more acculturated they are to the United States (have spent a lot of time in the United States, are comfortable when using English), the less they do that. In some cultures people are *expected* to agree when asked questions; in others they are expected to disagree when asked questions by outsiders. Statistical controls of response sets may be used to eliminate this rival hypothesis.

8. **The two samples, in the two cultures, may not have been strictly equivalent.** For example, there might have been differences in social class, age, sex, religion, or some other demographic attribute that is the real cause of the difference; yet the difference is attributed to language or culture. The solution is to analyze the data separately for each demographic category. Furthermore, the two populations under study may not be stable over time (e.g., sampling in 1960 and assuming that the results apply in 1993 may well be an error). When a population is heterogeneous, sampling in one area and hoping that the results are valid in another area (e.g., sampling in New York and assuming that the results apply to the whole of the United States) may be misleading. For that reason, ideally the experimenter should obtain samples in different parts of a country, and from different occupational, sex, and age groups, and check the consistency of the findings across these samples.

9. **The ethical acceptability of the method may not have been the same.** For example, in some cultures some samples (e.g., women) are not supposed to have an opinion, let alone an opinion that is different from their husband's. If the experimenter asks about that opinion, people can be embarrassed or become angry because the experimenter "dared" to ask such a question. Pretests are needed, after which subjects are asked, "What did you think about this method?" It is useful to use a set of scales (such as good versus bad, active versus passive, strong versus weak) for the subjects to rate the test situation itself (Was the test situation pleasant or unpleasant?). One of these scales could be moral versus immoral. If the study appears moral in one culture and immoral in the other, it would be necessary to investigate the matter further before collecting much data.

It's clear from the above that there are many ways in which a difference may appear. It's easy to obtain a difference across cultures. The question is, Is the difference a substantive finding, or is the apparent difference due to something that is indirectly associated with the measurement? We can never be sure that we controlled all rival hypotheses, and so any conclusions about cultural differences must remain tentative.

Some Solutions to These Problems

The discussion presented above does not mean that we must reject all forms of testing. There are situations in which testing is useful. To repeat a point made earlier: If a psychologist is trying to predict grades in a white middle-class school, white middle-class tests can do a good job. But note the difference in the interpretation between "This child is not going to do well in *this* school" versus "This child is stupid."

We can control statistically those variables that are correlated with the dependent variable of interest. For example, if there is a response set, one way to control it is to "standardize" the data statistically.

Some General Comments

Clearly, there are many pitfalls to testing, and we need to be very careful. One of the best ways to proceed is to study the phenomenon with the help of local social scientists who understand their culture. In addition, it is necessary to *use more than one method of obtaining data,* because each method has a different meaning in each culture. If the results of several different methods converge, it is unlikely that the same bias accounts for all the results.

The researcher must also do separate *construct validations* within *each* culture. In a construct validation the researcher has a theory and tests that theory. If the data hang together the way the theory predicts, then both the theory and the measurements of the constructs must be valid.

For example, suppose we have a theory that predicts that there are certain "antecedents" of intelligence (e.g., age, stimulating social environment) and certain "consequences" of intelligence (e.g., good grades, successful problem solving). If we measure IQ with different methods in each culture and we find that the correlations between our measures of IQ and the several antecedents and consequences specified by our theory are approximately the same in *both* cultures, then we have validated our measures in those cultures. If the patterns of correlations are similar, and if certain statistical tests (discussed by Irvine & Carroll, 1980) indicate that the two measures are equivalent, then we can compare the results across the cultures.

Good Theory Can Eliminate Some Rival Hypotheses

If we have a well-developed theory that makes several predictions, and the theory is supported by the data, some of the rival hypotheses become less plausible (Malpass, 1977). Supppose our theory predicts that in a collectivist culture people will favor the goals of their family more than their personal goals, while in an individualistic culture they will favor their personal goals more than the goals of their family. Suppose we collected data in rural China and rural America and we found what we predicted. In that case many of the rival hypotheses—different definitions of the constructs, different levels of motivation, different response sets—become less plausible.

This does not mean we should not worry about rival hypotheses when we have good theory. Clearly, if the theory and a rival hypothesis make the same predictions, we cannot use the theory to eliminate that rival hypothesis. But in many cases the theory and the rival hypotheses will make different predictions, and if the data support the theory, that is reassuring.

The main point to remember from this discussion is that cultural comparisons that indicate a cultural difference are not easy. They require a lot more work, checking, elimination of rival hypotheses, multimethod measurements, and the like, before the cultural difference becomes plausible. As a sophisticated consumer of cross-cultural research, you should be looking for evidence that this extra work, checking, and elimination of rival hypotheses were actually undertaken by the researcher.

Acculturation Indexes Can Help Establish Cultural Differences

Acculturation is an important phenomenon in modern societies (Berry, 1990). As cultures mix, people acquire the cultural attributes of cultures other than their own. Some of that activity is stressful when the cultural traits of the two cultures are contradictory. However, we can take advantage of the fact that there are samples at different levels of acculturation to establish the presence of real cultural differences.

Triandis, Kashima, Shimada, and Villareal (1986) presented a method that, under some conditions, can establish real cultural differences without having to worry about some of the rival hypotheses. The logic is best explained with an example. Suppose we want to study cultural differences between Hispanics and non-Hispanics in California. We can obtain several samples of Hispanics and non-Hispanics and see if they are similar or different on the attributes of interest. Now, suppose we find that Hispanics, relative to non-Hispanics, expect social behavior to be more positive and less negative in a wide range of situations (Triandis et al., 1984).

If the difference is real, comparison of Hispanics at different levels of acculturation (e.g., as soon as they arrive, after one year, after five years, after ten years) with non-Hispanics on this tendency should show convergence toward the position of the non-Hispanics. For example, if we ask whether a son is likely to fight with his father, the answer of

FIGURE 3–1
Acculturation in buildings: McDonald's in Amsterdam. (Triandis.)

those who have just arrived would be "definitely no." The longer their stay in the United States, the more likely they would be to answer like the non-Hispanics; i.e., that this does happen some of the time.

While on the whole this expectation was confirmed in the Triandis et al. (1986) study, it was not confirmed on *all* attributes, because on some attributes Hispanics showed the opposite of the hypothesized convergence. Careful analysis suggested that on *visible* attributes (e.g., behavior) convergence was high; on invisible attributes, such as autostereotypes or stereotypes of the mainstream, *ethnic affirmation* occurred—i.e., the Hispanics became progressively *more* rather than less different from the non-Hispanics.

Theoretically, such differential effects of acculturation can be expected. On visible attributes one is likely to be rewarded for merging with the mainstream. But on beliefs, attitudes, and values the rewards may be greater for affirming membership in one's ethnic group than for moving toward the mainstream.

In any case, the value of cultural elements is not equal. In many cultures people do not care as much about what they wear, or what jobs they have, as they do about their family life and religion (Naidoo & Davis, 1988). Thus, in many studies, we see that as cultures change, they first change on superficial traits, which are usually material, and subsequently on more basic traits, such as child-rearing patterns or religion.

The advantages of the method just outlined is that it is not susceptible to rival hypotheses. If we see a convergence of the Hispanic and non-Hispanic samples, it is unlikely that it can be explained by differences in motivation, response sets, and the like. It may still be possible to explain it on the basis of "understanding of instructions," but independent tests can be constructed that measure such understanding. In fact, such tests should be used routinely (see Triandis 1976b for an example of how to do it).

We can also "triangulate" by using more than one group's acculturation. If both groups are shifting in the same way, it is likely that a real cultural difference exists between these groups and the host culture. For example, Anglos are more individualistic than either Hispanics or Asian Americans. When we see acculturating Hispanics *and* Asian Americans shifting toward individualism, we know we have identified a real cultural difference.

A visual example of acculturation is shown in Figure 3-1.

Statistical Methods May Help

Several strategies have been used to establish cross-cultural equivalence.

1. *Factor analysis* is a statistical procedure that indicates what variables go together in each sample. If the same variables go togeth-

er in each culture, that is one indication that the variables have the same meaning in the two cultures.

2. *Item response theory* (Hulin, Drasgow, & Parsons, 1983) provides a statistical procedure that indicates if a particular item has the same meaning in the two cultures. The procedure is based on the similarity in the way people respond to that item and to all the other items.

3. *Psychophysical methods* allow some physical variable (e.g., distance between physical objects) to be linked to a psychological variable ("How do you feel about social entities?"). (For an example see Triandis, McCusker, & Hui, 1990.)

A BROAD PERSPECTIVE ON CROSS-CULTURAL RESEARCH

Here are some general points to keep in mind when evaluating cross-cultural studies.

1. It is necessary to establish many similarities between cultures before it is possible to establish a difference. In short, differences must be *embedded* into a framework of similarities. The large number of similarities guarantees that many of the rival hypotheses (e.g., response sets) are not relevant.

2. Researchers must generate methods, test items, and other measurement procedures in all the cultures that are to be compared (Marin & Marin, 1991). It is generally poor research strategy to develop the method in, say, Japan and take a chance that it will work in the United States. For example, when measuring collectivism, Yamaguchi in Japan used ten questions that used "my group" and had reliabilities (internal consistencies) of .85 (that is very good). I used these items in Illinois and got reliabilities of .50 (not good enough). When I switched the wording from "my group" to "my parents" I got reliabilities of .70 (not bad). You can see that in Illinois "my group" is vague, but in Japan it has a more clear meaning.

  Focus groups (small groups that do some brainstorming) and colleagues from each culture should be used to generate the measurement procedures. If test items, for instance, are generated from only one culture, they are likely to favor that culture, placing other cultures at a disadvantage. Ideally, researchers should generate items from both men and women (Harding, 1987; Nielsen, 1990; Reinharz, 1992) as well as from all important groups that make the culture heterogeneous (e.g., social class, religion, language, age, family structure).

In addition, researchers must counterbalance the presentation of the stimuli; that is, half the people in culture A should get the items generated in culture A first, and the other half should get the items generated in culture B first. In short, the administration of the items should be done using two orders: AB and BA. This is necessary, because if the items from the "other" culture are more difficult or appear "strange," this could influence the way people will respond.

3. Cultural difference must be demonstrated with more than one method (Fiske, 1986; Fiske & Shweder, 1986). Especially important is to *diversify* the methods and use some "operant" (minimum stimulus is presented to subjects who operate on it, i.e., give many responses, as in projective tests or sentence completions) and some "respondent" (McClelland, 1980) methods (a complex stimulus is presented and the subjects make a simple response, such as agree or disagree).

Use these three criteria to evaluate the quality of cross-cultural studies. Those studies that use all three are likely to be more dependable than those that do not use these strategies.

EMICS AND ETICS IN CROSS-CULTURAL RESEARCH

Chapter 1 introduced the idea of *etic* (universal) and *emic* (cultural-specific) cultural elements. If we read cross-cultural studies, we are likely to meet these constructs.

Emics, roughly speaking, are ideas, behaviors, items, and concepts that are culture specific. Etics, roughly speaking, are ideas, behaviors, items, and concepts that are culture general—i.e., universal.

Emic concepts are especially useful in communicating within a culture, where one word can sometimes be used to convey a very complex idea. For example, a geographer who has studied the inhabitants of Tierra del Fuego, at the southern tip of South America, told me that they have a word *mamihlapinatapei*, which means "looking at each other hoping that either one will offer to do something that both desire but are unwilling to be the first to do." One can almost see the scenario when boy meets girl and they *mamihlapinatapei*! We learn quite a bit about that culture by knowing the definition of this word. Thus, by learning particular words, we get to know more about a culture.

Emic concepts are essential for understanding a culture. However, since they are unique to the particular culture, they are not useful for cross-cultural comparisons.

Let us consider an analogy, the comparison of apples and oranges. Apples and oranges have some common attributes, such as size, weight, price, and availability. They also have some unique attributes, such as flavor and aroma. Clearly, if we are going to understand what an orange is, we need to know about orange flavor. But we cannot compare apples and oranges on orange flavor, except to say that apples do not have it. On the other hand, if we want to talk about price, we can compare apples and oranges. If we want to compare price to size or weight, we can certainly do that, too. So, we can have a theory of size-weight-price relationships and see if it holds as well for apples as it does for oranges, and we can even extend it to other fruits. Emics are like apple or orange flavor; etics are like size, weight, and price. So, for certain purposes, such as comparisons, we must use etic concepts; for other purposes, such as getting a real "taste" of the culture, we must use emic concepts.

More formally, emics are studied *within* the system in one culture, and their structure is discovered within the system. Etics are studied *outside* the system in more than one culture, and their structure is theoretical. To develop "scientific" generalizations about relationships among variables, we must use etics. However, if we are going to understand a culture, we must use emics.

Many anthropologists work with emics and think that etics are silly. They would be of the opinion that you do not know about apples by just knowing about their price, weight, and size. Psychologists want to make generalizations about people, and so they do not want to get into the details of a single culture. Cross-cultural psychologists try both to understand and to compare cultures. They work with both emics and etics.

The important point is to find *convergence* between different methods of understanding reality. Some "deconstruction" humanists, or even some who pretend to be scientists, argue that nature is constructed, not discovered—that truth is made, not found (e.g., Haraway, 1991). This is an extreme position. On the other hand, subjective responses to reality are often constructed. For example, I am a realist, and so I do not believe that women do not make as good chief executive officers (CEOs) as men do just because that is the male-dominated "construction" and conventional wisdom of current CEOs. But I would agree with this view if someone showed me a convincing study, with hard criteria, that indicated that this view is correct.

Constructionism can easily result in an image of reality that is found in only one person's mind. It might be good literature, but it is terrible science. The essence of science is a conversation between the scientists and nature. It requires probing with multiple methods to replicate important findings and establishing convergence between observations and measurements. If such convergence is broad, i.e., includes humanistic "findings" as well as findings obtained through scientific methods, we can be much more certain that we have identified an important phenomenon than if we have one person's argument or a single set of findings obtained in one place with only one method. An important distinction between the humanistic and the scientific method is the contrast between the subjective and the objective. If the humanistic insight is to be taken seriously, it has to converge at some point with other evidence; it cannot remain entirely subjective.

If we take a construct generated in our culture and use it in another culture, we may have a *pseudoetic* (false etic) construct. We must get empirical evidence that the construct operates the same way in the other culture, i.e., is a true etic, before we use it to compare the cultures. Remember the discussion about construct validation above? That is what needs to be done to establish a true etic. Then we have to make sure that the etic construct is measured in ways that are culturally sensitive. That often requires the use of local terms and ideas. In short, we must use both etic constructs and emic ways to measure them. That is why cross-cultural psychologists advocate the use of *both* emics and etics (Berry, Poortinga, Segall, & Dasen, 1992; Triandis, 1972, 1992).

One advantage of such a strategy is that we can obtain more sensitive information about the relevant cultures, which implies that we can obtain more cultural differences if we use both emics and etics in the design of cross-cultural studies. In one study (Triandis & Marin, 1983) samples of Hispanics and non-Hispanics responded to either a questionnaire based on ideas generated in previous studies with American samples (pseudo-etic) or a questionnaire that used ideas obtained from focus groups (informal discussion groups that generated items to be used in the questionnaire) of Hispanics and non-Hispanics. The latter questionnaire included both emic items that were spontaneously generated only by the Hispanic focus groups and etic items that were generated by both the Hispanic and non-Hispanic focus groups. Since the questionnaires in that study had 600 questions, it was possible to get 6 cultural differences by chance (at the .01 level of significance). The number obtained by the pseudoetic questionnaire was 14, and the number obtained by the emic plus etic questionnaire was 50. In other words, we can miss a lot of subtle information about the way cultures differ if we do not use emics. (See Figures 3-2 to 3-5.)

The importance of emics cannot be overestimated. There are emic concepts that are extremely difficult to understand by people who use an etic framework.

Consider this example: What is a geisha? Most Westerners are likely to free-associate "prostitute" with that concept, and as a result they will be quite wrong. A 500+ page ethnography of geishas (Dalby, 1983) shows that the closest association to "geisha" should be "jester." Just as the jester in a king's court had the function of diverting the king and his guests, so a geisha has as her chief function entertaining the clients of an establishment. Most geishas spend their time reciting poetry, singing, dancing, and serving their clients while they eat and drink.

Furthermore, there are many kinds of geishas, and only a minority are actual prostitutes (*yujo*). Most do other things, including greeting people at the door or playing musical instruments. The most highly

FIGURE 3–2
Consider the concept of "city transportation" and compare this picture (from Nanking, China) with what you see where you live. There are some etic elements (people move from one part of the city to another) and some emic elements (separate paths for pedestrians, bicycles, and cars). (Roy S. Malpass.)

FIGURE 3–3
Another emic view of city transportation, this time from Kathmandu, Nepal. (Roy S. Malpass.)

FIGURE 3–4
Compare this market, from Bogotá, Colombia, with a market near you. What are some of the etics and some of the emics? (H. Triandis)

FIGURE 3–5
Another emic view of markets, from Ibadan, Nigeria. (H. Triandis.)

sought geishas are older and more experienced and thus able to act more appropriately. President Ford, the first U.S. President to visit postwar Japan, had dinner with several geishas as part of his touring experience. The most beautiful were placed next to him, but the ones who did most of the entertaining were the older, more experienced ones. Of course, without knowledge of Japanese, President Ford may not have been able to appreciate the entertainment.

The contrast between "geisha" and "wife," in terms of the free associations of these words among Japanese males, is also instructive. The former is seen as sexy, artistic, witty, and economically self-sufficient; the latter as sober, humdrum, serious, and economically dependent. The former is likely to be well read and know the latest poems and songs; the latter is likely to talk about the problems of the children.

Now that you have gotten a glimpse of the meaning of geisha, do you see that it is a culturally specific role, one that corresponds to an emic Japanese term, and that the Western view that a geisha is a prostitute is a pseudoetic and becomes a true etic only when it uses the idea of "jester"? In any case, the Western view does her an extreme injustice.

HOW TO USE EMIC MEASUREMENTS OF ETIC CONSTRUCTS

Any theoretical construct of some generality in social psychology is likely to have both etic and emic aspects. For example, the concept of social distance makes sense in every culture and even among animals where territoriality is a well-established phenomenon. We allow some people to come close, while we keep others away from us. The original concept, developed by Bogardus (1925), was operationalized by asking people if they would like to "marry," "live in the same neighborhood as," "exclude from the country," etc., certain groups of people. It was found that Americans in the 1920s showed little social distance toward Western Europeans, especially those who came from the United Kingdom, and much social distance toward "Negroes," "Turks," and "Jews."

While the social distance concept is etic, the way it is operationalized can vary with culture. In India, the idea of "ritual pollution" results in social distance, and while a person may not mind living in the same neighborhood with a member of the lower castes, especially if the lower-caste individual is a servant, that person can mind very much if a member of the lower castes "touches my earthenware." Thus, in India, social distance is indexed differently. Touching earthenware is an Indian emic; social distance is a theoretical concept, an etic.

In sum, clearly, there are behaviors we can use to measure social distance in one culture that do not make sense in other cultures. If we ask an American if he would mind having a Turk touch his earthenware, we would probably not get as good a measure of social distance as by asking one of the original Bogardus questions.

For a specific example of how emic items can be used to measure etic constructs, look at Table 3-1 (from Triandis & Triandis, 1962, p. 208). The items were obtained by using separate focus groups, in Greece and in Illinois. Some of the items were translation equivalent, so they were used

TABLE 3–1 SCALE VALUES OF SOME SOCIAL DISTANCE STATEMENTS IN TWO CULTURES

Statement	American scale value	Greek scale value
I would marry this person.	0.0	0.0
I would accept this person as an intimate friend (in Greek: "best friend")	11.1	13.5
I would accept this person as a close kin by marriage.	21.5	28.5
I would accept this person as a roommate.	29.5	—
I would accept this person as a member of my social group (in Greek: parea).	—	31.1
I would accept this person as a personal chum in my club	31.1	—
I would accept this person as my family's friend.	40.9	24.0
I would accept this person as a neighbor.	38.7	—
I am going to invite this person to dinner.	—	33.3
I would live in the same apartment house with this person.	49.4	—
I would rent a room from this person.	57.5	42.8
I would accept this person as a speaking acquaintance.	52.4	45.6
I would accept this person as a step-father.[a]	—	46.1
I would exclude this person from my country.	95.0	82.6
I would be willing to participate in the lynching of this person.	97.2	—
As soon as I have a chance I am going to kill him.	—	100.0

[a] For brevity, not all of the statements used in the study are included in the table.
SOURCE: Triandis & Triandis, 1962.

in both countries, while others were different. All the items were subjected to a procedure developed by Thurstone (well described in Edwards, 1957) that uses judges.

These judges examined each item and placed it on an 11-point scale, according to how much social distance was implied when a person agreed with that item. These judgments were treated statistically, and scale values for each item, standardized so they were on an equal-interval scale, were generated in each culture.

In this case the top and bottom of the scale were called 100 and zero, for easy comprehension. As you can see, the scale values of translation-equivalent items were quite similar (e.g., 11.1 versus 13.5) in some cases, but not in others. For example, "I would accept this person as my family's friend" corresponds to more social distance for the Americans than for the Greeks. Since Greece was at that time (1960) traditional and collectivist, accepting a person as a family friend implied very little distance. In other words, Greeks at that time felt closer to persons who were friends of their family than did Americans.

When the actual people are studied, the items of the social distance scale are presented to them in a scrambled way. They are asked to pick three statements that best represent how they would act toward a particular stimulus person, for example, a "fifty-year-old unskilled Chinese laborer." The respondent's social distance is the average social distance value of the three items (statements). Interested readers can read the details of this method in Triandis (1992).

We can generate stimuli systematically, by varying, for instance, the age, nationality, and occupation (or whatever we are interested in studying) of the stimulus person and then obtain the social distance each respondent feels toward that stimulus. This allows for complex statistical analyses (such as analyses or variance) that show the relative importance of the attributes, such as age, nationality, and occupation, as determinants of the social distance judgments. Note that the data come from the scale values of the statements that have been generated and standardized in *each culture separately*. Thus the fact that the statements have different scale values in different cultures does not produce a problem. They are emic values, but the construct is etic.

The same strategy can be used with most concepts. They may have a universal meaning, one that most researchers understand the same way; yet these concepts must be operationalized and measured differently in each culture, because behavior has different meanings in each culture (Triandis, Vassiliou, & Nassiakou, 1968).

*G*ENERAL RECOMMENDATIONS

For good cross-cultural work we must start with the theoretical construct and discuss it with local informants to see how it is best operationalized. It is then useful to use focus groups and come up with around 100 ideas about how to measure the construct. While these ideas will probably be different in each culture, chances are that some of them will be generated in both.

Next, we should take each of these 100 ideas and scale them *separately* in each culture. This means local standardization of the items. One of the techniques that is very useful was developed by Thurstone (1931) and is explained very clearly by Edwards (1957, chap. 5). With this method a small set of fifteen or so items, which have been locally standardized but link to the etic continuum under study, can be identified in each culture.

This method provides excellent locally standardized and *equivalent* equal-interval scales in the two cultures (that means that the difference between, say, 2 and 3 in one culture means the same thing as the difference between 2 and 3 in the other culture). Then the fifteen items are scrambled and presented to the subjects under study in each culture with the instructions: "Pick three of the following fifteen items that describe your most likely behaviors toward (the social category of interest)."

*T*HE AVAILABLE RANGE OF MULTIMETHOD MEASUREMENTS

We have already emphasized the desirability of using multimethod measurements in cross-cultural studies. A range of methods is available.

Ethnographic Work

Ethnographic work (see Goodenough, 1980, for details) is based on observations, with some questioning of informants and occasionally an experiment or survey. In such work an anthropologist spends one or two years among a group of people as a participant observer. After learning the local language, the scientist becomes a member of the culture and often assumes one of the existing roles within the culture (e.g., the chief's son). After that, observations can be done informally or formally (see Longabough, 1980, for details) using videotapes or films that are later coded by several coders to establish interrater reliability.

Establishing Shared Cognitions

This approach involves measuring a psychological construct with several methods in each culture and checking if the measurements converge. However, it is important to be able to distinguish a psychological from a demographic or cultural construct. The definition of culture in Chapter 1 specified that culture has shared elements. When we measure a psychological construct, we do not know if it is shared, and so it may or may not be part of culture.

Triandis, Bontempo, Leung, and Hui (1990) have developed a method that allows a researcher to sort the personal, demographic, and cultural constructs. The basic idea is to have triads (groups of three respondents) hear a question and answer it while the time it takes for them to agree on the answer is measured. Cultural elements do not require debate. For example, if you ask three Americans whether fairness is important or unimportant in everyday life, they are likely to supply a "yes" in less than two seconds, and over 85 percent of the triads that are tested will agree. But if you ask if fame is important or unimportant, they engage in a debate. Being famous is not a widely shared element of American culture; some want to be famous and others do not. For those who want to be famous, this is a *personal* construct.

Using these two criteria (length of time to respond, percentage of the triads that agree), the researchers can pick those elements of culture that are widely shared.

The study by Triandis, Bontempo, Leung, and Hui was done in Hong Kong and Illinois as a demonstration of what can be done to measure cultural elements. The same could be done with demographic elements (men versus women, old versus young, rich versus poor) by assembling appropriate triads and measuring how much time it takes for them to agree on how to answer a question and what percentages of the triads do agree. Also, this study was limited to values, but it could be done with other elements of subjective culture.

Unfortunately, this method requires that many people be involved in the study. For example, to have 50 triads, which is not an especially large number for a somewhat heterogeneous culture, 150 people are needed in each culture.

The examples that follow illustrate this method. Table 3-2 presents the most important values in Hong Kong and Illinois. Some ideas were valuable in both cultures. For example, "to be well-adjusted, in harmony with my environment, in good relationships with others" was agreed upon by 100 percent of the triads in both cultures, with an average time of 2.8 seconds in Illinois and 3.4 seconds in Hong Kong. In order for a value to be considered part of the culture, at least 85 percent of the triads of that culture had to agree that it was in a short time. Some were only Hong Kong values because they did not reach an 85 percent consensus in Illinois. For example, "persistence" (100 percent agreement in 2.1 seconds), "courtesy" (100 percent in 2.7), and "filial piety" (obedience to parents, respect for parents, honoring ancestors, filial support of parents) resulted in 92 percent agreement in 13.4 seconds in Hong Kong.

Some were only Illinois values, because they did not meet the 85 percent criterion in Hong Kong. For example, "to be content, happy, feel enjoyment, joy" was agreed on by 100 percent of the Americans in 4.1

TABLE 3–2 HONG KONG CHINESE VALUES RANKED ACCORDING TO PERCENTAGE AGREEMENT AND SHORT REACTION TIMES

Value	Percent	Time (sec)	U.S. Value Rank
1. Persistence (perseverance)	100	2.1	
2. Courtesy	100	2.7	
3. To be well-adjusted, in harmony with my environment, in good relationship with others	100	3.4	1
4. To have a close, intimate friend	100	4.1	
5. Prudence	100	5.0	
6. Adaptability	97	3.3	
7. Patience	97	7.7	
8. To be able to take advantage of opportunities, to not miss opportunities	95	4.1	3
9. Kindness (forgiveness, compassion)	95	7.2	
10. To be able to properly balance action, enjoyment, reflection, behavior, feeling, and thought	92	5.1	5
11. Tolerance of others	92	5.7	
12. To be self reliant, independent, not depend on others, stand on my own two feet	92	7.1	6
13. Filial piety (obedience to parents, respect for parents, honoring ancestors, filial support of parents)	92	13.4	
14. Ordering relationships by status and observing this order	92	13.9	
15. Personal steadiness and stability	90	7.5	
16. Sense of righteousness	87	6.3	
17. Harmony with others	85	3.7	
18. Thrift	85	9.4	
19. To be content, happy, feel enjoyment, joy, feel I have good fortune	77	15.2	2
20. To have intimacy, be close to others, know a lot about others who know a lot about me.	67	5.5	4
21. To have nice children who are just like I want children to be, children who are good	59	14.3	24
22. Patriotism	56	17.8	
23. Moderation, following the middle way	56	15.6	
24. To have a high income that allows me to live just as I want to live	54	16.6	26

SOURCE: Triandis, Bontempo, Leung, & Hui (1990). Reprinted by permission of Sage Publications, Inc.

seconds; in Hong Kong, only 77 percent agreed, and the time was long (15.2 seconds). Finally, some values did not reach sufficient consensus in either place. For example, "to have a high income that allows me to live just the way I want to live" was agreed on by 52 percent (Illinois) and 54 percent (Hong Kong) of the triads in 16.6 seconds (in both samples). While the percentages were similar and the times were identical, the 85 percent agreement criterion was not reached, and so this cannot be considered an element of either culture.

It is possible to compare the data of this method with the results obtained by questioning one person at a time using other methods. If the results are similar, we have evidence about the convergent validity of both methods. The Hong Kong–Illinois study did that, and convergent validity was obtained.

Interviews and Surveys

These methods are often used (Pareek & Rao, 1980). Some of them are informal and allow for questions to be asked as the interview proceeds, while others follow a rigid schedule. Interviews can be based on limited or representative samples of the culture.

Tests

One might also use tests (Irvine & Carroll, 1980), attitude scales, personality scales, projective tests (Holtzman, 1980), and psychophysical tests.

Experiments

Experiments can be done in more than one culture, but they present special difficulties (see Brown & Secrest, 1980; Ciborowski, 1980). For example, it is extremely difficult to ensure that the same degree of manipulation of the independent variables has been used in each culture.

However, some interesting results can be obtained when the same experimental procedure is used in each culture. Strodtbeck (1951) provides an interesting example. He examined whether culture is related to the probability that the wife or the husband will win an argument. He tested ten husband-wife pairs in each of three cultures: Navajos (where the custom is for the husband to live with his wife's relatives, and hence one might expect husbands to have less power), Texans, and Mormons (where traditional male supremacy is used).

The study began by asking each spouse a number of questions separately. The researcher noted on which questions the spouses disagreed. He then put them together and tape-recorded their interactions while they discussed their answer to a question and attempted to reconcile their differences. If the couple finally agreed with the husband's original position, that indicated husband dominance; if the couple finally agreed with the wife's original position, it indicated wife dominance. The results were as follows:

| | Number of decisions won by | |
	Husband	Wife
Navajos	34	46
Texans	39	33
Mormons	42	29

SOURCE: Strodtbeck (1951).

The hypothesis was supported. Culture predicts who wins, with the Navajos more likely to agree with the wife and the Mormons with the husband.

Content Analyses

Content analyses (see Brislin, 1980) of children's stories, newspaper stories, myths, formal and informal communications, speeches, or movies produced in several cultures are used to measure attitudes, motives, opinions, values, and other attributes.

Human Relations Area Files

These files contain (Barry, 1980) a very useful data set. They consist of photocopies of much of the world's ethnographic records classified alphabetically according to the content of each paragraph. Thus, for instance, a researcher who is interested in checking if the age of weaning of a child is related to the level of anxiety in adult personalities would look in the files under "age of weaning" and would find the ages in several cultures. Similarly, this researcher would find some categories that might index the extent to which adults in the culture are high or low in anxiety. Then the researcher would either plot the data or compute statistics to check the relationship of age to anxiety.

Of course, ethnographies do not include every type of information, and so it may be that there is no information relevant to anxiety in a particular culture. The result is "missing data."

After the information on the two variables has been extracted from the files, certain statistical analyses, such as the computation of a correlation or a chi-square test, can indicate whether or not the two variables are related. In these analyses the number of cultures is the number of observations on the basis of which the correlation is computed, or N cultures are classified as "high" or "low" on each of the variables to compute the chi-square test. In other words, we can establish an association between two variables, based on holocultural data (all cultures on which there is information; see Naroll, Michik, & Naroll, 1980, for details).

In Sum

It is ideal to test a hypothesis with as many of these methods as feasible. Some of these methods are "operant" in the sense that the researcher provides a minimal stimulus and the subjects provide many responses (*operate* on the stimulus as they see fit when responding). For example, sentence completion or projective techniques, ethnographies and the Human Relations Area Files, observations, unobtrusive measures (see Bochner, 1980, for details), and content analyses are operant techniques. In most cases the researcher does nothing to stimulate the production of the data. In some cases a minimal stimulus, such as "Please write twenty statements that begin with the words *I am*," is provided.

By contrast, experiments, surveys, and interviews are "respondent" methods; the subject is *responding* to stimuli presented by the researcher.

Respondent methods are more obtrusive, and they are more likely to be distorted by reactivity. The respondents are more likely to distort their answers, so that they will appear to be socially desirable people to the researcher, their peers, or the authorities in their culture, or from the point of view of their culture's ideal. In short, respondent methods are more likely to result in cultural differences due to the *method*. However, it is easier to control artifacts when using respondent methods, because the study can be replicated under a variety of conditions.

Operant methods are generally less reliable. Many observations or responses are obtained, and it is not clear which ones are the most important. Operant methods also have a high "dross rate" (irrelevant information is a high proportion of the total information obtained). Furthermore, the observer may be biased and see or hear only what is consistent with the hypothesis.

Both kinds of methods are appropriate at different points in the research sequence. At the initial stages of the research, when we know little about the culture, lack good hypotheses, and are dealing with respondents who are not familiar with social science methodologies, it is best to use operant methods. Such methods are especially good when investigating complex relationships. These relationships can be kept in mind while making additional observations. However, since these methods are not sufficiently reliable and are difficult to check for reliability and validity, we should not reach definitive conclusions with them. Rather, it is best to refine existing hypotheses, develop new ones, and keep an open mind about the culture while using them.

At a later stage in the research process when more is known about the culture, the hypotheses are more likely to be supported, and then it might be possible to design experiments, questionnaires, and interview schedules that are appropriate for the problem. It helps also if the subjects are familiar with the researcher's methods, since they may then be more likely to give the same meaning as the researcher to the testing situation.

In other words, no method is perfect; each method has both advantages and disadvantages. The sophisticated consumer of cross-cultural research will give more weight to findings that have been supported by more than one method, particularly if the methods were very different.

Separate tests of hypotheses within cultures and between cultures, and with more than one method, increase the confidence in our findings.

However, we must not assume that a test at the between-cultures level will *necessarily* give the same results as a test at the within-cultures level. For example, consider the variable "degree of industrialization" and correlate it with the variable "probability that a worker will vote for the Communist party." In both India and the United States, there is a greater probability of a Communist vote in a highly industrialized voting district than in a less industrial one. In other words, within the countries there is a *positive* relationship between the variables of interest. However, when we compare the two countries, we see a *negative* relationship between these two variables. In the United States, there is a higher level of industrialization but a *low* probability that anyone will vote for the Communist party; in India, there is less industrialization but a relatively *high* probability that a worker will vote for the Communists. In short, there is a reversal of the sign of the relationship between the two variables when we study the phenomenon across versus within cultures.

This means that while we should do our analyses at both the between-culture and within-culture levels, we need not become discouraged when these results are inconsistent. Of course, consistency boosts our confidence that the relationship is robust. There are examples (e.g., Rohner, 1986; Schwartz, submitted) in which a hypothesis has been tested at both levels and was supported consistently.

T*RANSLATIONS*

It is ideal to gather the data in each culture by using the same procedures, but without translating specific items. This view is supported by the realization that translation is at best approximate.

See Box 3.1 for some hilarious examples of poor translation that suggest how difficult it is to translate.

BOX 3-1 *Examples of Translations*

Outside a Hong Kong tailor shop: "Ladies may have a fit upstairs."

In a Thailand dry cleaner's store: "Drop your trousers here for best results."

Outside a French dress shop: "Dresses for street walking."

In a Greek tailor shop: "Order your suits here; because of a big rush we will execute customers in strict rotation."

A Hong Kong advertisement: "Teeth extracted by the latest Methodists."

An Italian laundry: "Ladies, leave your clothes here and spend the afternoon having a good time."

A Czechoslovak tourist agency: "Take one of our horse-driven city tours— we guarantee no miscarriages."

Advertisement for donkey rides: "Would you like to ride on your own ass?"

In a Romanian hotel lobby: "The lift is being fixed for the next day; during this time we regret that you will be unbearable."

In a French hotel: "Please leave your values at the front desk."

In a Greek hotel: "Visitors are expected to complain at the office between the hours of 9 and 11 a.m. daily."

In a Yugoslav hotel: "The flattening of underwear with pleasure is the job of the chambermaid."

In a Japanese hotel: "You are invited to take advantage of the chambermaid."

On the menu of a Swiss mountain inn restaurant: "Our wines leave you nothing to hope for" and "Special today—No ice cream."

In the window of a Swedish furrier: "Fur coats made for ladies from their own skin."

A Danish airline: "We take your bags and send them in all directions."

A Norwegian cocktail lounge: "Ladies are requested not to have children in the bar."

At the office of an Italian physician: "Specialist in women and other diseases."

A Mexican hotel: "The manager has personally passed all the water served here."

A Japanese hotel air conditioner: "Cools and Heats: If you want just condition of warm in your room, please control yourself."

Detour sign in Japan: "Stop! Drive sideways."

(Source: Lederer, 1987; miscellaneous newspapers.)

In short, one can make the case that translation should be avoided. But that is not always practical, and so a word about translation is necessary.

Translation of single words is unwise, because it is extremely difficult to establish exact equivalence in meaning for single words. Only if the study focuses on the meaning of single words, and uses several methods to tap that meaning, is translation of single words acceptable.

The greater the context of a text, idea, or concept, the more likely it is that it can be translated properly. If an idea is expressed in more than one way, translation has a chance of reaching linguistic equivalence. Thus, it is helpful to introduce redundancy, synonyms, and context.

Brislin (1980) provides many useful suggestions on how to maximize linguistic equivalence. A good approximation to the ideal translation uses the Werner and Campbell (1970) method of double translation with decentering. This method is based on the realization that there are many ways to say the same thing, and careful adjustments to the original language of the research project may not produce any difficulties for the research but may facilitate the translation.

For example, the researcher starts with an English text (E) and asks a bilingual person to translate it into Japanese (J). Then, he or she asks *another* bilingual person to translate it back into English to obtain E'. Now E and E' can be compared for discrepancies. If the discrepancies are significant, the researcher can "decenter" the text by producing a new text (E") that is satisfactory for the purpose of the research but is closer to E' than to E. Such a text is likely to translate into Japanese more easily, since E' was an English version of a Japanese text. Then, a new bilingual person is asked to translate, and this provides J'. Still another bilingual person translates J' into English, which results in E'''. The researcher now compares E" with E''', and the chances are that these two texts are identical. But if they are not, the researcher continues the process by producing an E"" version that is closer to E''' than to E". The process continues until a back translation is just like the "acceptable text" in the original language.

Although back translation is a good way to obtain linguistic equivalence, it has its problems. First, many words in languages from the same language family (e.g., Indo-European languages cover a wide area from India to Europe to the Americas) have the same roots but different meanings. For example, in the Latin-based languages, the term "sympatique" (French) or "simpatico" (Spanish) means "pleasant or agreeable." In English "sympathetic" means "feeling like the other person does." Clearly, the meanings are not the same. Yet people who are bilingual are apt to translate, say, "sympathetic" as "simpatico" and back-translate it into the original language when in fact the translation is not correct.

Second, skilled bilinguals are good at imagining what the original text might have looked like. So suppose a Japanese text is being translated; the interpreter may be able to guess what the original E or E' was and produce an E" that is just like it. The researcher would be reassured, but the translation is imperfect. In short, while back translation is desirable, it does not guarantee linguistic equivalence.

One technique that is useful, continuing with our example of English and Japanese, is the administration of both the English and Japanese version of a questionnaire to a sample of Japanese bilinguals. In such a case one can compare the responses of the *same* person when answering in the two languages. This can provide a check on the translation, since the same answer would indicate good translation. However, even this technique is problematic, because people who are bilingual have a tendency to present themselves in a more socially desirable way to "outsiders" than to "insiders" (Marin, Triandis, Betancourt, & Kashima, 1983). Thus, it is likely that a Japanese bilingual will present a more favorable set of answers when answering in English than when answering in Japanese.

In sum, it is safest not to translate. Basically, the same data-gathering operations can be carried out in each culture, and the only text that needs to be translated is the instructions, which usually have a good deal of context. Then, standardization is done separately in each culture. Various statistical tests and comparison of distributions (e.g., item response theory checks; highly correlated factor structures in the two languages) can be used to establish equivalence before any comparisons are made. If we find a large number of cultural similarities, and if the differences are embedded in the similarities, then we may be more confident that there is a cultural difference rather than an artifact.

ETHICS OF CROSS-CULTURAL STUDIES

Unfortunately, not all researchers carry out their work ethically. Some study what is easy to study, and as a result we know a lot more about the disadvantaged than the advantaged segments of most cultures. When two groups are in conflict and a researcher offers to study the conflict, the weak are more likely than the strong to accept the study. The powerful do not submit to research very easily; that means our picture may be distorted.

Ethical research requires that subjects be informed about the study before they give their consent to participate (*informed consent*). That way they can avoid participation in studies they consider unethical or disadvantageous to them. But in many nonliterate societies the concept of research is nonexistent, and it is impossible for the prospective participants to provide meaningful informed consent.

With most operant methods the chances are that people will not be exposed to stress or risks. But with respondent methods some risks can be significant. If risks beyond those of ordinary life are involved in a research method, it is essential that the risks be explained to the subjects, and the subjects should have the opportunity to decline participation. This, of course, produces other problems, such as distorted samples consisting mostly of volunteers. Nevertheless, if risk is involved, the subjects must be informed.

Since risk is perceived differently in each culture, it is important to bring research collaborators into the decision-making process at the earliest points of a project. If a method that appears risk-free in one culture is not risk-free in another, the method may have to be changed. There are many ways to collect data, and so it does not follow that because we change the method, we cannot test an important theory.

There are special problems of research collaboration across cultures that are discussed in detail in an article by Tapp et al. (1974). Before doing cross-cultural research, consult that article or the chapter by Warwick (1980). For example, a research collaborator may be harmed by collaborating with someone from a culture that is politically taboo in his or her country. In addition, it is generally believed that the researcher must leave something of value in the culture, such as information, procedures, material goods, payments. Exactly who is to be paid, how much, and other details are beyond the scope of this book but are covered in Tapp et al. (1974).

THE ETHNOCENTRIC AND ANDROCENTRIC BIAS OF RESEARCHERS

Most cross-cultural researchers, including myself, are Western men; we all have difficulties in escaping our ethnocentric (my culture is the standard of comparison) and androcentric (my gender offers the only valid perspective on an issue) biases. We can try to control such biases, but the choices of problems, theories, and methods are likely to reflect such biases. For example, we cannot be sure that we have controlled such biases when we evaluate whether or not gender inequalities are similar or different across cultures. Thus, when evaluating cross-cultural research, it is wise to ask ourselves whether such biases may have colored the reported findings, interpretations, and conclusions.

CRITERIA OF GOOD CROSS-CULTURAL RESEARCH

- The study included many similarities across the cultures, and the differences were embedded inside the similarities.
- Multimethod procedures were used, and they converged.
- Tests within and between cultures were consistent, or when inconsistent were expected from theory.
- Rival hypotheses were checked and eliminated.
- Etic constructs were measured emically, with emic items generated in each culture to tap the etic constructs.

- The study was conducted ethically.
- The researchers made an effort to control ethnocentric and andro-centric biases.

Summary

Cross-cultural research faces many difficulties: It is necessary to (1) eliminate or control rival hypotheses, (2) establish many cultural similarities so as to provide a framework within which to examine possible cultural differences, (3) use multimethod measurements that converge, (4) attend to emics and etics, and (5) use a theory about the attributes of the relevant cultures to overcome some of the difficulties of cross-cultural research.

There is much cross-cultural work that simply collects data in different cultures and claims to have established some point. Most of this work is uninterpretable and hence of doubtful utility.

Fortunately, there are a number of methods for cross-cultural research. When several of these methods converge, we can be confident that some phenomenon has been identified. It is best to avoid translations; this can be done by working with focus groups in each of the cultures using parallel methods and by developing locally standardized and culture-equivalent (emic measures of etic constructs) measures.

In the next chapter we will discuss the concepts that should be studied when we analyze cultures and try to understand them.

QUESTIONS AND EXERCISES

1. How do you feel about research that does not conform to the points made in the summary? Will you pay attention to the results? Under what conditions?

2. How do you feel about research that was not done ethically? Will you pay attention to the results? Under what conditions?

3. What is your position concerning the testing of minorities in U.S. schools? When should it be done? Under what conditions are the results useful?

4. Suppose you went to another culture to study it. What would you do first, second, and so on? Outline for yourself the full course of your studies.

4

Analyzing Subjective Culture

❖

Categorization ◆ Associations ◆ Beliefs ◆ Evaluations ◆ Connotative
Meaning ◆ Expectations ◆ Norms ◆ Roles ◆ Rules ◆ Self-
Definitions ◆ Stereotypes ◆ Ideals and Values ◆ The Meaning of In-groups
◆ The Meaning of Social Behavior ◆ Subjective Culture and Social Behavior
◆ Summary

P eople in each culture have characteristic ways of viewing the human-made
part of their environment. We call this their *subjective culture*. The ideas, the
theories, the political, religious, scientific, aesthetic, economic, and social
standards for judging events in the environment are human-made and shape the
way people view their environment.

In this chapter we examine ways to analyze subjective culture. To do that, we
need to study the way people categorize experience, their ideas about correct
behavior, the way they view other people and groups of people, and the way they
value entities in their environment. We will see that many of the elements of
subjective culture, such as categorizations, associations, and beliefs, to name just a
few of the ones we will touch on, form coherent structures that have their own
internal logic.

87

CATEGORIZATION

All known cultures use categories (Kluckhohn, 1954). But what they include in the categories and what they choose to categorize are to some extent arbitrary decisions. For example, our eye is capable of discriminating about 7.5 million colors, but we find it quite unnecessary to pay attention to that many distinctions. The English language is very rich in color names (it has about 4000), but most of us get along with the names of no more than 40 colors. While some artists and interior decorators may distinguish many more colors, no one uses all the colors that humans are able to discriminate.

That means that we categorize colors. Categorization is defined as "making the same response to discriminably different stimuli." Color is a good domain to study because we can use objective stimuli. Munsell color chips vary in hue (color), lightness (also called "strength" or "chroma" in some textbooks), and saturation (also called "density" or "value"). The scientist, armed with a color chart that consists of thousands of such chips, can go to different cultures (e.g., as did Landar, Ervin, & Horowitz, 1960) and ask people what names they use to call each region of the color chart. When this is done, we find that different cultures give somewhat different responses. So, for example, if we were to show a chart with color chips to people in one culture and ask them to draw a line that will enclose all the color chips that they call with their name for "yellow," and then show the chart to people in another culture and ask them to do the same, we would get much consistency within cultures, but not across cultures. While the chips located in the middle of the yellow patch are pretty much the same (they are known as *focal colors*), the periphery of the color patches show cultural differences. A hypothetical diagram appears in Figure 4-1.

It is also interesting that people who are bilingual tend to have color categories that are averages of the categories of their two languages (see Triandis, 1964, for a review of studies showing this). In other words, our language determines to some extent whether we will use one or another color name for particular chips.

Languages differ in the number of color names that they have. In all languages people have names for something equivalent to black and white or dark and colored. But there are languages that have no other color names. If a language has a third color name, then it will be the name for red. If a language has four color names, the additional name, after black, white, and red, will be either yellow or green. In more complex languages there is a name for blue. In still more complex color vocabularies there is a name for brown. Finally, the most developed color vocabularies include names for purple, pink, orange, and gray (Berlin & Kay, 1969). Figure 4-2 shows the sequence. This sequence of color names

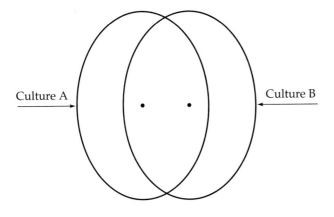

FIGURE 4-1

Even concepts that translate easily across languages do not
have identical meanings. This can be seen when we study
two cultural groups, identify translation-equivalent color
names, and ask monolingual people of each culture to draw
lines around the color chips they call by a specific color
name. The lines drawn by people from different cultures
are not identical. They may look like the two diagrams
shown above. The "pure colors" (shown as dots) of a particular color name are usually in the common space, and that
is why the two color names appear to be translation-
equivalent. People who are bilingual draw lines that are
compromises between the lines drawn by monolinguals.

found in languages is also found developmentally. Children first name
black and white and later learn the other eleven basic color names; they
learn purple, pink, orange, and gray last.

You might ask what this has to do with social behavior. The answer is
that children develop their ideas about social behavior in a sequence, from
simple to complex, that is parallel to the simple-to-complex sequence for
learning colors. Specifically, when children first categorize social behavior, they use the difference between positive and negative behaviors (e.g., I
love you; I hate you). Then they learn what it means to give or deny a
resource (Foa, 1961). For example, they learn the differences among to *give*
love, to *get* love, and to *deny* love. As they grow older, they develop more
complex categories of social behaviors and family roles (Foa, Triandis, &
Katz, 1966). They also learn to exchange six kinds of resources, which are
organized as indicated in Figure 4-3.

The reason these resources are organized in this way is that resources
such as love, status, and information are abstract and resources such as
services, goods, and money are concrete. Resources such as love, status,
and services are *particularistic*, in the sense that we pay attention to the

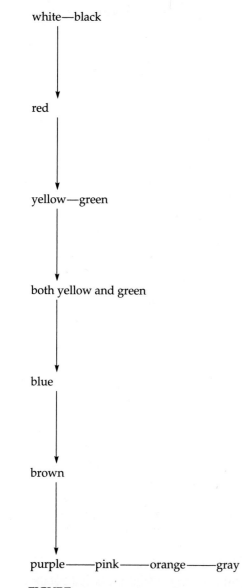

FIGURE 4–2

Berlin and Kay (1969) discovered that if a
language has only two color names, it will
have names for black and white; if it has
three color names, it will have a name for
red. If it has four names, it will also have a
name for yellow or green, and so on. If a
language has more than seven color names,
it will have names for pink, purple, orange,
and gray. Children learn color names in this
sequence also, suggesting that there is something fundamental about the structure of
color names shown here.

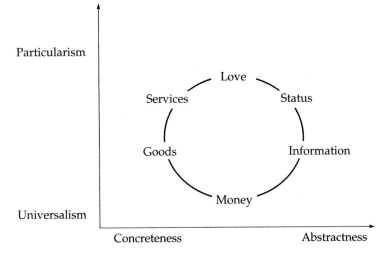

FIGURE 4-3

Foa and Foa's theory of interpersonal exchanges. (Foa & Foa, 1974.)

particular individual who gives or takes them away (e.g., if you are a woman, it makes a big difference to you if you love Joe or George). Resources like money, information, and goods are *universalistic*, because we can give money to anyone (e.g., as occurs in the stock exchange), or information to anyone (e.g., by way of TV), or goods to anyone (e.g., sell to anyone who pays). We generally do not care who gets these resources as long as we get from them what we consider a fair exchange, such as the right amount of money.

Adamopoulos (1984) has analyzed social behavior by paying attention to the ideas of Uriel and Edna Foa (1974). He has suggested that association-dissociation (e.g., love-hate) is the first discrimination we learn to make, and it corresponds to giving or denying a resource. Then we learn to pay attention to the interpersonal orientation—are we dealing with a particular other person or just any person? Then we pay attention to whether the resource exchanged is concrete or abstract. On that basis we develop a typology (that is, a set of related categories) of social behavior (Figure 4-4) that corresponds to the typology found empirically across cultures (e.g., Triandis, 1978). This means that in all cultures, people distinguish between associative and dissociative behaviors, between subordinate (e.g., obey) and superordinate (e.g., give orders) behaviors, and between intimate (e.g., reveal inner thoughts) and formal (e.g., send a written invitation to) behaviors. Adamopoulos added a category he calls "trading," which is also found in all cultures.

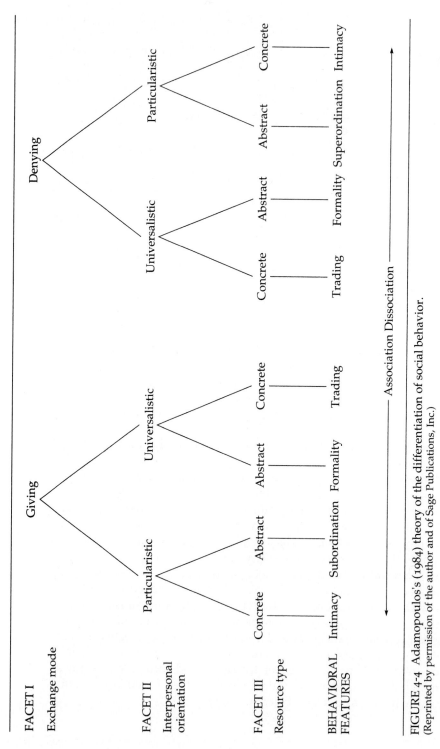

FIGURE 4-4 Adamopoulos's (1984) theory of the differentiation of social behavior.
(Reprinted by permission of the author and of Sage Publications, Inc.)

Adamopoulos and Bontempo (1986) found that social behavior develops as suggested above. By analyzing the content of written texts (e.g., Homer's *Iliad*) they showed that in early human writing there is much talk of associative-dissociative behaviors (e.g., Achilles loved Patroclos and hated Hector), some mention of subordination-super-ordination behaviors (e.g., Agamemnon was too bossy; Achilles refused to fight), some trading (e.g., a horse in exchange for a slave), but little evidence of intimacy-formality (e.g., no revelations of inner life to others; no statements that there was a certain protocol for getting something done).

Categorization is functional because it simplifies the environment for us. Imagine how difficult it would be if we really paid attention to 7.5 million colors! But, at the same time, there is a large loss of information. We ignore more than we attend to. In addition, it is common for misinformation to link with the category. So, for example, when we categorize people as European or African American, we lose information and we also add invalid information to the categories (usually so as to maximize our self-esteem and support our values).

When we assign attributes to a category, we stereotype: We might say: "All professors are absentminded" or "All Americans eat ice cream." You know these are not accurate statements, but they simplify the processing of information. Stereotyping occurs because we cannot handle all the information that is available. Of course, stereotypes are inaccurate, and we lose a lot of good information when we use them. Also, we often attach misinformation to the category that maximizes our self-esteem. Avigdor (1953) found that when two groups are in competition, they are likely to have negative stereotypes of each other; when two groups are cooperating, they are likely to have positive stereotypes of each other. In these experiments, objectively the groups were the same. The only difference was that in one condition they competed and in the other they cooperated. Thus, it is not the reality that is different but the construction of the reality. Such constructions serve our prejudices.

Most categories are defined in relation to other categories with which they are related (Trier, 1931). For example, the definition of "hot" depends on the definitions of "cold" and "warm." You cannot fully understand "night" unless you understand "day."

In culturally important language domains there is rich differentiation of categories within these domains. For example, the Arabs are said to have about 6000 words that have something to do with camels, and 50 or so of these words refer to stages of camel pregnancy (Klineberg, 1954). Americans have a very rich vocabulary concerning cars (Ford, Chevy, sedan, convertible, etc.).

To take another example, Kitayama (see Markus & Kitayama, 1991) found that the Japanese language has many more interpersonal emotional terms than English. English has a rich vocabulary for self-focused emotions (e.g., anger), while Japanese has a large vocabulary for other-focused emotions (e.g., sympathy). This kind of analysis gives us a clue about the two cultures. In other words, we can learn quite a lot about cultures by studying their categorizations.

The content of categories can vary widely. For example, among the Nootka of British Columbia, Canada, it is necessary to mention a physical feature when you refer to a particular person. You might say the equivalent of "the fat Mr. Jones," or "The astigmatic Mr. Jones," or "Mr. Jones with the large appetite," or "The bald-headed Mr. Jones." Some languages have two "we" terms: one that is "you and I" and the other "I and other people, excluding you."

In Japanese the status of the people in the social relationship is reflected in the language they use. This is one reason Japanese often exchange cards when they meet. They literally do not know how to talk to each other until they know something about where they belong in a status hierarchy.

We can learn a lot by studying such content. For example, the Pawnee, of Oklahoma, use the same word for "mother's brother's wife," "ego's wife," and "sisters of ego's wife." Study reveals that a Pawnee man is allowed to have sexual relations with all three of these women.

Cognitive anthropologists have developed methods for obtaining indigenous taxonomies of various domains, e.g., diseases, botanical terms, and animals. They try to determine the features of objects or events that define a category. They attempt to develop these taxonomies only from data from the local culture, and only after the taxonomy is developed do they compare it with Western "scientific" taxonomies. For example, in rice-eating cultures people use cues that we do not use at all to talk about rice, such as "sticky brown rice" or "fluffy white rice" (these are monoleximic terms, i.e., one word is used for what requires three words in our language).

The attributes used to define categories may be very different from the attributes we use. For example, a male Ojibwa (the Ojibwa tribe is scattered throughout the U.S. Midwest and Canada) looks at a woman by first noticing whether she is a totemic sister, which makes her sexually taboo. The Balinese, in Indonesia, use the directions of the compass much more than we do. For example, a musician may say: "Hit the key to the east of the one you are hitting." The Papago, of southern Arizona and northern Sonora, Mexico, have a grammatical category that includes "mass nouns" such as water, coffee, wine, salt, sand, clouds, and rain.

A useful way to study categories is to ask: "What do you call this?" Once the informant has given a name, say a *zib*, taking objects that are like that object one asks: "Is this also a *zib*?" This way you can gradually learn the limits of the term.

Another good research strategy is to focus on communication. Can a person describe an object quickly and accurately using a particular language? It turns out that it depends on the precision of the vocabulary. There are categories of "high codability" (Brown & Lenneberg, 1954) where people (1) use a single word to name the object, (2) communicate about it very quickly, and (3) agree among themselves concerning what to call it. By contrast other categories are of "low codability"; i.e., people cannot communicate either quickly or accurately about the subject. This again tells us much about the importance of the subject in the particular culture. The reason we have so many different words for cars is that it is functional for us. Being able to tell quickly and unambiguously that it was the "blue Cadillac" that hit the pedestrian is much better than saying a "blue car."

In sum, we can learn a fair amount about a culture by examining the kinds of categorizations, words, word sizes, and number of words used in each domain.

A SSOCIATIONS

Categories become associated to each other by frequent co-occurrence. Szalay (1970), for instance, noted that the category "democracy" was associated with the category "socialism" in those cultures where there was a Democratic Socialist party. By studying the kinds of associations that people use with important words we can learn a good deal about a culture. For instance, we can ask people to talk into a tape recorder and mention any idea that comes to mind when they hear a particular word. When two people make similar associations, there will be more successful communication than when the associations are dissimilar. For example, a person who associates "socialism" with "democracy" will have trouble communicating with a person who associates "socialism" with "communism."

One can even develop a "dictionary" (Szalay, 1970) that contains such associations and tells quite a lot about the particular cultures. For example, Szalay (1985) found that the word "I" produces more associations from Anglo-Americans then from Hispanics, but the word "friend" produces more associations from Hispanic Americans than from Anglo-Americans. In one study (see Triandis, 1964, p. 11) "mother" was associated with "food" in 16 percent of the American sample, 51 percent of the Lebanese, but only 7 percent of the Sudanese.

B ELIEFS

Links between categories, e.g., "African Americans are handsome," are beliefs. Chains of associations, such as "African-Americans moving to a white neighborhood improve the chances of friendly relationships between the races," can be studied as beliefs. This sentence can be modified in many ways, and people can be asked to agree or disagree with each modification of the sentence. For example, instead of "African Americans" we can use "Hispanics," "Native Americans," "Asians," etc. For a "white" neighborhood we can substitute other ethnic groups. Instead of "improve," other verbs can be used, and other characterizations of the relationships can replace the description "friendly."

Thus, from a sentence like this one, a researcher can generate a large number of other sentences that can be used to obtain information about many aspects of subjective culture by having people agree or disagree with them.

One category of beliefs is especially important. Beliefs that refer to the cause of behavior, or attributions, are very important because the way we understand (interpret) a behavior depends on the attributions we use. For example, if a person hits another person, it makes all the difference if the attribution made was "It was an accident" versus "He intended to hurt the other person."

Cultures differ in the attributions they make. For example, Miller (1984) found that Americans are much more likely to use internal dispositions as attributions of behavior (e.g., "He did it because he is dishonest" or "because he has a negative attitude") than external, context factors (e.g., "He did it because it was a hot day" or "because the room was crowded). Conversely, Indians tended to use context factors more often than dispositions.

These kinds of differences are also quite important in making social or political judgments. For example, we can ask: "Why are these people poor?" The answer could be dispositional (e.g., "because they are lazy") or contextual (e.g., "because there are no jobs"). Individualistic cultures, such as the United States, often make more dispositional judgments, and collectivist cultures (e.g., China, India) make more contextual judgments.

E VALUATIONS

Beliefs have an evaluative component; i.e., they make people feel good or bad. Also, categories can become closely associated with positive or negative emotions. For example, Razran (1940) asked students to evaluate a set of slogans, such as "Workers of the world unite," to express their personal approval and to judge the social effectiveness and literary value of the slogans. He then presented one set of slogans while the students were enjoying a free lunch and another set while they were required to inhale unpleasant odors. After five to eight "conditioning trials" the slogans were reevaluated by the students. Razran found that the slogans that were associated with the lunch increased in rated personal approval and literary value, but the slogans that were previously associated with unpleasant odors showed a decrease in these qualities. Razran included a number of control slogans, not associated with anything, and also checked if the students were able to identify which slogans had been presented with the lunch, with the odors, or in the control conditions. The students were *not* able to identify which slogans went with what condition. There is a large literature that makes similar points about the way rewards are associated with the way we process information and look at the world.

CONNOTATIVE MEANING

One of the more important ways to study cultures is to analyze what people mean by the words they use. A major cross-cultural study provided such data (Osgood, May, & Miron, 1975).

First, 32 samples of male high school students, located in 23 countries, were presented with 100 culture-fair nouns. Culture-fair nouns like "mother," "fire," and "god" usually translate easily into other languages and can be back-translated into English without difficulty. The high school students were asked to complete sentences like the ones below in their own languages:

The _____ mother. The mother is _____.

Since 100 students completed 100 such sentences in each language, there were 10,000 "qualifiers" available in each language. Of course, many of these were the same adjectives. Osgood and his collaborators selected 50 of these qualifiers, according to the criteria that they (1) were very frequently given and (2) were elicited by different nouns.

Second, they presented these 50 qualifiers and their antonyms, e.g., "good-bad," "passive-active"—as well as the original 100 culture-fair nouns—to a new sample of high school students. In this step the students were asked to rate each noun on 50 scales, according to the extent to which the noun implied, was associated with, or meant what the scale measures. This method is called the *semantic differential*. For example:

FIRE

good___'___'___'___'___'___'___bad

The students were asked to indicate whether fire was good or bad by placing an X on the scale at the extreme left for good or at the extreme right for bad. If they though it was slightly bad, they placed an X somewhat to the right, like this:

good___'___'___'___' X '___'___bad

In each culture the students made 5000 such judgments. The judgments were randomly divided among 10 groups of students. Thus, each student sample in each culture made only 500 judgments, a task that takes about an hour. Then the judgments concerning a particular noun and a particular scale obtained in each culture were summed so that 5000 numbers (100 nouns on 50 scales) were retrieved.

Third, the 50 by 50 matrix of correlations of each scale with every other scale was computed based on 100 observations per scale. This matrix was reduced to a simpler pattern by a statistical technique called *factor analysis*. The point of this step is to find out what scales go together in the sense that when something is rated high on one scale it is also rated high on other scales.

From this step it was found that in every one of the thirty-two samples, evaluative qualifiers went together. That is, "good," "kind," "beautiful," and so on were used by the students more or less the same way in making their judgments. This was called the *evaluative* factor (E). In addition, qualifiers like "large," "heavy," and "male" formed another factor called potency (P), and qualifiers like "active," "alive," and "fast" formed a third factor called *activity* (A). So, E, P, and A were found everywhere. However, while E, P, and A were etic, i.e., the same across cultures, the position of the 100 nouns on these common yardsticks was not. Some very emic information was obtained. For example, "Wednesday" was "good" in those cultures where high school students only have to attend school for a half day on Wednesday and was neutral in meaning in those cultures where students have to go to school all day!

Osgood found that some scales are linked to the E factor in almost all cultures. For example, "nice-awful," "sweet-sour," "heavenly-hellish," and "good-bad" seem to measure E everywhere. "Big-little," "powerful-powerless," "deep-shallow," and "high-low" measure P almost everywhere. "Fast-slow," "noisy-quiet," "young-old," and "dead-alive" measure A almost everywhere. This means that if you want to find out the meaning of some words in a new culture, but cannot take the time to do the elaborate Osgood pretests, you can use these scales to get a fairly good measure of E, P, and A that will be more or less equivalent to the measures of E, P, and A obtained in other cultures.

Next, Osgood and his associates developed an "atlas" of 620 words rated in each culture on E, P, and A. The atlas provided a lot of information, such as the average location of each noun on E, P, and A and how much agreement there was in the culture among those who rated that noun.

From this information it was possible to find out if cultures are similar or different. It turns out that in certain domains some cultures are extremely similar, and in others they are not. For example, on food nouns ("rice," "bread," etc.) Greece, former Yugoslavia, and Lebanon were extremely similar, which is not surprising if you eat in Greek and

Lebanese restaurants or know some history. The Ottoman Empire dominated that part of the world from about the middle of the fifteenth to the nineteenth century, and the food of these countries was strongly influenced by Turkish food. On other topics these three cultures were different.

When Osgood studied the cultures of North America, Western and Northern Europe, Latin America, the Mediterranean countries, West Africa, India, and East Asia, a pattern emerged. The world was divided into Western cultures that are very individualistic (Chapter 6 describes this pattern in detail) and traditional cultures that are characterized by different forms of collectivism. Greece and Yugoslavia were marginal on this division, because on some topics they were Western and on others traditional.

Here are some more examples of the kinds of things found in Osgood's studies: The words "discipline" and "duty" produce a lot of conflict (disagreement among the respondents of the same country) in the Western cultures. People are not sure whether they are good or bad, strong or weak, or active or passive. But in Greece and Japan there is no doubt: they are good, strong, and active.

We can interpret this finding as an aspect of the individualism of the West. Individualism is reflected in people's placing their personal goals above the goals of their groups (e.g., family, coworkers). "Discipline" and "duty" are not compatible with "doing your own thing," "pleasure," and the other values of individualists. In the East, and in most traditional cultures, people are socialized to place the goals of their groups ahead of their personal goals. So, "discipline" and "duty" are just fine.

In addition to studying the meaning of words with the semantic differential, as was done by Osgood and his collaborators, there are other methods for the study of word meanings. One of the methods is called the *antecedent-consequent method* (Triandis, 1972, pp. 181–262). Again, students complete sentences as the first step. The antecedents use sentences of the form "If you have_____, then you have *progress*," and the consequents sentences are of the form "If you have *progress*, then you have_____."

In the second step of this method, people are shown both the sentence and a list of antecedents obtained in different cultures during the first step. For example,

If you have _____, then you have *progress*.
Ambition _____
Drive _____
Hard work _____   (Please select one)
Research _____
Unity _____
Or they are shown both the sentence and a list of consequents:
If you have *progress*, then you have _____.
Civilization _____
Expansion _____

A good name _____   (Please select one)
Satisfaction _____
Well-being _____

In each culture, the frequencies of endorsement of each specific antecedent-consequent reflect, in part, the meaning of "progress."

EXPECTATIONS

Our expectations reflect our previous experiences. Since in different cultures there are major differences in experience, we can anticipate that cultures differ in what they expect. Obviously, when the gross national product per capita is high, people expect to be paid better than when it is low; when everybody else pays high taxes, a person expects to pay high taxes too. If we examine economic indexes, we find major cultural differences, such as in income and tax rates.

We can get data that reflect such differences by asking questions like this: "What is the average vacation length in your country?" In some countries there is no such thing as a vacation; in the United States two weeks is common; in Western Europe a month is more common than in the United States. Customs of this type are quite influential in shaping lifestyles. While it may be obvious that we should have this kind of information in order to understand a culture, we might forget to look for it exactly because it is so obvious.

NORMS

Norms are ideas about what is correct behavior for members of a particular group. For example, suppose two friends, Bill and Joe, worked for an employer who gave them $50 as pay for their work. How should they divide the money? In the United States the *equity* norm is very strong, so that the answer is very clear: They should divide the money according to the contributions of each friend to the total job. But in other cultures other norms are much more likely to be used. In most collectivist cultures *equality* and *need* are more likely norms.

For example, the herders of Sardinia use the equality norm. They can be paraphrased as saying: "God wants everyone to have the same; when someone has more, we take it away (i.e., steal) to do God's work." The norm of stealing is of course inconsistent with Italian law. However, the herders have had this norm for centuries, certainly long before Italy became a state.

A similar situation can be found in many cultural groups where the laws of the state are viewed as unrealistic or inconsistent with traditions. Nader (1975) provides several examples, not only from Sardinia where cattle theft is not viewed as a crime (p. 155), but also from other cultures. In such situations there are *two* normative structures: One set consists of traditional norms, and the other set reflects the laws of the state. The Basques versus Spain and the Provisional Irish Republicans versus Britain are but two of many examples. In such cases the populations are not culturally integrated in the country (i.e., they do not accept the idea that they are ultimately responsible for obeying the laws of the country), and are in a relationship of a "working misunderstanding" (Nader, 1975, p. 157) with their governments. If we keep in mind that people may be dealing with two or more normative systems, we may be able to under-stand somewhat better the behaviors that occur during race riots by minority groups in the United States.

I personally feel sympathetic to these subgroups, because during the Second World War, I lived under German occupation in Greece. We Greeks had norms about how to behave (e.g., listening to the British Broadcasting Corporation's news); the laws that the Germans imposed on us (listening to the BBC became a crime) were in conflict with our norms. Of course, we behaved according to *our* norms.

Now let us go back to our friends, Bill and Joe, who have to divide $50. They may use the norm of equality because Bill and Joe are friends, so why not split the money equally?

Or they may choose the norm of need: Bill's parents are rich and he does not need much, while Joe's parents are poor so he needs more money.

Still other principles might be used. In some cultures people pay a lot of attention to "who the other is." So, for example, the son of famous parents "naturally" should receive a larger share of the $50. In other cultures people pay attention to previous accomplishments, to level of ability, to effort. Thus, they might agree that the higher-ability friend should receive a larger share; or they might decide that the one who worked obviously harder, even if his output was not high because he was inefficient, should receive more. The supply and demand of the market might be considered in other cultures, and the friend who did the part of the job that required skills in short supply would get the larger share. In still others, the major consideration is the common good. If the common good requires an unequal distribution of the $50, then that is just fine. In most cultures reciprocity is very important, and if Bill has done Joe a favor, that will affect the way they decide to divide the $50. Finally, the norm may say that no one should get less than a certain percentage, regardless of the contributions or other factors, because to get less is clearly unfair (see Deutsch, 1975). In short, what is equity in one culture may not be so in another.

Norms differ sharply. Perhaps the best examples contrast the United States and India. Table 4-1 shows some of the thirty-nine cases used in research that contrasted these two cultures. They are presented ranked in order of perceived "seriousness of breach" as judged by eight- to ten-year-old Hindu Brahmans (Shweder et al., 1990, p. 165). It is notable that the more serious cases, such as cases 1 and 2, are not even considered to be wrong actions in the United States. In the United States only the ninth (bigamy) is a serious breach. To study how people react to these cases, Shweder et al. (1990) used the questions shown in Table 4-2.

Many of the stories that indicate a serious breach in India are not a breach in the United States and vice versa. For example, American adults and five-year-old children ranked the seriousness of the breach in the thirty-nine stories consistently (rank-order correlation of .85), but the American adults and Indian adults (untouchables) ranked them differently from each other (correlation of $-.29$). A wide range of Indian samples ranked them consistently, e.g., Brahman adults and untouchable adults had a rank-order correlation of .70. In other words, each culture has its own point of view in judging these thirty-nine events.

Special kinds of norms are discussed in some of the social science literature. First, there are *folkways*, such as particular ways of doing things found in a small subculture, e.g., having a farmer's market on Sunday in

TABLE 4–1 TEN CASES IN ORDER OF PERCEIVED "SERIOUSNESS OF BREACH" AS JUDGED BY HINDU BRAHMAN EIGHT- TO TEN-YEAR-OLDS

1. The day after his father's death, the eldest son had a haircut and ate chicken.
2. One of your family members eats beef regularly.
3. One of your family members eats a dog regularly for dinner.
4. A widow in your community eats fish two or three times a week.
5. Six months after the death of her husband the widow wore jewelry and bright-colored clothes. (the widow)
6. A woman cooked rice and wanted to eat with her husband and his elder brother. Then she ate with them. (the woman)
7. A woman cooks food for her family members and sleeps in the same bed with her husband during her menstrual period. (the woman)
8. After defecation (making a bowel movement) a woman did not change her clothes before cooking.
9. A man had a wife who was sterile. He wanted to have two wives. He asked his first wife and she said she did not mind. So he married a second woman and the three of them lived happily in the same house. (the man)
10. Once a doctor's daughter met a garbage man, fell in love with him and decided to marry him. The father of the girl opposed the marriage and tried to stop it because the boy was a garbage man. In spite of the opposition from the father, the girl married the garbage man. (the daughter)

SOURCE: Kagan and Lamb, *The Emergence of Morality in Young Children.* Reprinted by permission of the publisher, The University of Chicago Press.

TABLE 4–2 THE STANDARD QUESTIONS

1. Is (*the behavior under consideration*) wrong?
2. How serious is the violation?
    (*a*) not a violation
    (*b*) a minor offense
    (*c*) a somewhat serious offense
    (*d*) a very serious violation
3. Is it a sin?
4. What if no one knew this had been done. It was done in private or secretly. Would it be wrong then?
5. Would it be best if everyone in the world followed (*the rule endorsed by the informant*)?
6. In (*name of a relevant society*) people do (*the opposite of the practice endorsed by the informant*) all the time. Would (*name of relevant society*) be a better place if they stopped doing that?
7. What if most people in (*name of informant's society*) wanted to (*change the practice*). Would it be okay to change it?
8. Do you think a person who does (*the practice under consideration*) should be stopped from doing that or punished in some way?

SOURCE: Kagan and Lamb, *The Emergence of Morality in Young Children*. Reprinted by permission of the publisher, The University of Chicago Press.

Main Square. Second, there are *mores*, e.g., the accepted ways of doing things in a society, e.g., asking for a woman's hand in marriage. Third, there are *taboos*, specifying what should not be done, e.g., not eating pork. Finally, there are *laws*, which are enacted by an elected body or a government authority.

Norms are needed in order to control the behavior of people, and they function very much the way roads function for transportation. If there were no roads, we would drive chaotically anywhere a car could go. Roads ensure that we drive in a more orderly, safe, and rapid fashion.

ROLES

There is a special kind of norm that consists of ideas about how a person in a certain position in a social system (e.g., father in the family) should behave. For example, how *do* fathers behave?

We can study this with the role differential. Here is an example of a role differential item:

father-daughter

would ——————————————————————— would not

ask for money from

Studies of this kind have shown that, for example, the husband-wife role is more intimate in individualistic than in collectivist cultures, but the parent-child role is more intimate in collectivist than in individualistic cultures.

An interesting observation (seen on the Public Broadcasting System television network): A twenty-one-year old Vietnamese American, son of an American soldier and a Vietnamese mother, was given permission by the U.S. government to emigrate to the United States. The permission allowed him to take with him either his mother or his wife and child. He chose his mother, in keeping with the cultural parents–children bond of collectivist cultures. Later he managed to convince the U.S. government to allow his wife and child to come to the United States as well. Note that he played his cards correctly. The U.S. government, given American culture, was more sympathetic to the request to bring his wife and child here than it would have been to a request to bring his mother.

Hsu (1971) has identified cultures where the most important role is the mother-son (India), father-son (China), or spouse-spouse (the West) role. In father-son cultures, for instance, other roles are likely to have much of the character of the father-son role. Thus, for instance, the supervisor-subordinate, teacher-student, and official-citizen roles have a lot in common with the father-son role. Similarly, the spouse-spouse role tells much about equality, and this influences other roles, so that in Western cultures supervisors feel the need to deal with subordinates as if they are equal.

In a study that compared roles in Indonesia and the Unites States (Setiadi, 1984), the most important elements of roles in Indonesia reflected *subordination* to authorities; the most important elements in the United States were related to *having fun*. Again, that fits the collectivism-individualism contrast: Indonesia is collectivist, and respect for in-group authorities is an important element of role perceptions; the United States is individualistic, and "having fun" is an important value that can be used in thinking about many role relationships.

One of the studies of role perceptions (Triandis, Vassiliou, & Nassiakou, 1968) sampled 100 roles and examined 120 behaviors that may occur in such roles in Greece and Illinois. The behaviors were extracted from a content analysis of Greek and American novels to represent the kinds of social behaviors commonly found in each culture. Ratings of the roles on the behavior scales and factor analyses followed procedures similar to those already described for the semantic differential. The role differentials were developed independently in the two cultures. Here are a few of the findings:

How much love would a son show toward his mother? On a 9-point scale where 1 is the maximum love and 9 the minimum, the Greek mean was 1.8 and the American 2.4. Americans value independence, and that distances people from each other.

What about a daughter loving her father? In Greece 2.9 and in the United States 1.6. In the United States it is acceptable for a daughter to be close to her father, but in traditional Greece there is the notion that fathers are disciplinarians, highly concerned that their daughters remain virgins. There is therefore less closeness in that relationship.

And, lastly, how do athletes feel toward their opponents in athletic games? Greece 5,0. United States 4.4. Americans feel fairly positive, and Greeks are neutral.

RULES

Cultures differ in the kinds of relationship rules they endorse. Argyle, Henderson, Bond, Iizuka, and Contarello (1986) studied thirty-three rules (see Table 4-3) that British, Japanese, Hong Kong, and Italian samples use when they think of twenty-two social relationships. A cluster analysis of twenty-two social relationships was carried out in each culture. The relationships had different meanings in the West and in the East.

The authors discuss these differences by pointing out that in the "East there are more rules [than in the West] about obedience, avoiding loss of face, maintaining harmonious relationships in groups, and restraining emotional expression" (p. 312). They also point out that the "strongest cross-cultural differences emerged on rules dealing with intimacy" (p. 313). We will discuss the theoretical understanding of these differences in Chapter 6.

TABLE 4–3 THIRTY-THREE COMMON RULES USED
ACROSS RELATIONSHIPS

1. *First name*: Should address the other person by their first name.
2. *Self-disclosure*: Should not disclose to the other person one's feelings and personal problems.
3. *Paying for others*: Should offer to pay for the other person when going out together.
4. *Acknowledging birthdays*: Should give birthday cards and presents.
5. *Social visits*: Should not visit the other person socially, unannounced.
6. *Swearing*: Should not use swearwords in the company of the other person.
7. *Discussing religion*: Should not talk to the other person about religion and politics.
8. *Discussing sex*: Should not talk to the other person about sex and death.
9. *Showing anger*: Should not show anger in front of the other person.
10. *Showing anxiety*: Should not show distress or anxiety in front of the other person.

TABLE 4–3 continued

11. *Obedience*: Should obey the instructions of the other person.
12. *Public affection*: Should not show affection for one another in public.
13. *Handshake*: Should shake hands with one another on meeting.
14. *Touching*: Should not intentionally touch the other person.
15. *Material help*: Should not ask the other person for material help.
16. *Personal advice*: Should not ask the other person for personal advice.
17. *Public criticism*: Should not criticise the other person publicly.
18. *Stand up for*: Should stand up for the other person in their absence.
19. *Discussing confidences*: Should not discuss that which is said in confidence with the other person.
20. *Sexual activity*: Should not indulge in sexual activity with the other person.
21. *Family invitations*: Should invite the other person as a guest to dine at a family celebration.
22. *Repayment*: Should seek to repay debts, favours or compliments no matter how small.
23. *Joking*: Should not engage in joking or teasing with the other person.
24. *Appearance*: Should appear neatly or smartly dressed when with the other person.
25. *Self-presentation*: Should strive to present oneself to the other person in the best possible light.
26. *Time taking*: Should feel free to take up as much of the other's time as one desires.
27. *Discussing finances*: Should not discuss personal financial matters with the other person.
28. *Positive regard*: Should show unconditional positive regard to the other person.
29. *Informing of schedule*: Should inform the other person about one's personal schedule.
30. *Sharing news*: Should share news of success with the other person.
31. *Privacy*: Should respect the other's privacy.
32. *Eye contact*: Should look the other person in the eye during conversation.
33. *Emotional support*: Should be emotionally supportive.

SOURCE: Argyle, Henderson, Bond, Iizuka, & Contarello (1986).

S ELF-DEFINITIONS

The self consists of all the statements that a person makes that include the words "I," "me," "mine," and "myself" (Cooley, 1902). A good way to study the self is to ask people to write twenty sentences that begin with the words "I am." The responses reveal a lot about a culture. Triandis (1989) examined three aspects of the self: the private self (e.g., "I am kind"), the public self (e.g., "Most people think I am kind"), and the collective self (e.g., "My family thinks I am kind"). He argued that these three kinds of self are sampled with different probabilities in different cultures. In individualistic cultures people sample mostly the private self; in collectivist cultures they use mostly the collective self. The more complex the culture (e.g., many levels of political authority, many different groups and occupations, a large urban population), the more people will sample the private and public self rather than the collective one. Collectivism, external threat, competition with out-groups, and common fate increase the sampling of the collective self.

Aspects of the environment, such as the need to cooperate in order to survive, result in more use of the collective self. Collectivist cultures raise their children by emphasizing obedience, reliability, duty, cleanliness, and order. Individualistic cultures raise their children by emphasizing creativity, self-reliance, independence, and the freedom to do your own thing. These qualities are associated with the use of the private self.

When the collective self is sampled, people are more likely to behave according to norms, roles, and customs. When the private self is sampled, people are more likely to behave according to their attitudes, feelings, and beliefs, or their personal philosophy.

S TEREOTYPES

Stereotypes are ideas about the characteristics of groups of people. It is important to distinguish *autostereotypes* (e.g., what Americans think about Americans) from *heterostereotypes* (e.g., what Americans think about the Japanese, or what the Japanese think about Americans). Some stereotypes are accurate, in which case we call them *sociotypes*. For example, the stereotype that African-Americans in the northern United States vote for the Democratic party is a sociotype because there is empirical evidence that about 90 percent of them do so.

Stereotypes vary in *complexity* (e.g., how many independent ideas are included in them), *clarity* (e.g., how much agreement is there that the particular attribute is characteristic of the specific group), *specificity* (e.g., "good at arguing a case in a court" versus more abstract, such as "intelligent"), *validity* (e.g., how much agreement is there between the stereotype and objective social science evidence), and *value* (e.g., includes mostly good or bad attributes).

The clarity of the relevant stereotypes often increases when two groups are in contact. When one cultural group has many resources that are admired by another group, the richer group is seen more favorably, and so the value of the heterostereotype is positive. The greater the similarity between two cultural groups, the more positive the value of the corresponding heterostereotypes.

Examples of autostereotypes and heterostereotypes are provided in a study by Triandis, Lisansky, Setiadi, Chang, Marin, and Betancourt (1982). They identified all Hispanic-name Navy recruits arriving at three Navy recruiting stations (in Florida, California, and Illinois) during a specific time period, and asked them if they thought of themselves as "Hispanics." They randomly selected an equal number of non-Hispanics from the same cohort. Next they selected fifteen attributes by asking samples of Hispanics and non-Hispanics to indicate the attributes that were most important in describing their own group and the other ethnic group.

Then they asked the recruits to rate the extent they believed different ethnic groups to have a particular attribute. For example, "Chicanos tend to be uneducated" was rated on a 1=never to 10=always scale. Table 4-4 shows the way Anglos and Hispanics rated the attributes for Chicanos as well as for Mexican Americans.

To understand this table you need to know a bit more about the way the judgments were analyzed. First, the fifteen attributes were intercorrelated, and a factor analysis was done. This method shows what attributes people perceive as going together. Second, the percentages of each sample that selected those attributes in describing a particular group were recorded. So, for example, the first column of Table 4-4 tells us that Anglos perceived Chicanos as cooperative, ambitious, and hardworking, a factor that was given the name of "well socialized" by the researchers. (These factor names are matters of opinion, and as you read the tables, you may want to use other names for them.) The numbers of the first column also tell us that the correlations between the particular attributes and the factor were about .70. The numbers in parentheses tell what proportion of the Anglo sample used that particular attribute to describe Chicanos. So, for example, 59 percent of the Anglos used the attribute "cooperative" when rating Chicanos. You can read the rest of the table and study subtle differences in the heterostereotypes (Anglos judging Chicanos, Mexican Americans) and autostereotypes (Hispanics judging those stimuli). Note that some of the factors ("well socialized") are similar, but the endorsement levels are a bit different (around 60 percent endorsement of "well socialized" by Hispanics and only about 50 percent endorsement by Anglos).

Table 4-5 shows the same kind of data for the stimuli black and white Americans. Here the autostereotypes on the "well socialized" factor is endorsed at around the 85 percent level. As you study these tables, you will see a number of interesting similarities and differences.

TABLE 4-4 HOW ARE CHICANOS AND MEXICAN AMERICANS PERCEIVED BY ANGLOS?

Scales	Chicanos – As seen by Anglos — 1 L (%)	2 L (%)	3 L (%)	Chicanos – As seen by Hispanics — 1 L (%)	2 L (%)	3 L (%)	Mexican Americans – As seen by Anglos — 1 L (%)	2 L (%)	3 L (%)	Mexican Americans – As seen by Hispanics — 1 L (%)	2 L (%)	3 L (%)
Factor Name	Well socialized	Not anti-social	Good citizens	Well socialized	Not backward	Good citizens	Well socialized	Not anti-social	Underprivildged	Well socialized	Not backward	Not under-socialized
Uneducated		.61 (45)			.70 (31)				.49 (44)		.64 (20)	
Educated				.66 (56)			.74 (49)			.71 (64)		
Family Oriented			.40 (71)			.60 (72)	.46 (79)			.70 (79)		
Friendly				.79 (62)						.85 (74)		
Unfriendly		.57 (34)						.64 (35)				.58 (13)
Competitive						.56 (62)	.63 (58)			.61 (67)		
Cooperative	.72 (59)		.53 (42)				.77 (59)			.60 (69)		.61 (38)
Dependent												
Independent					.69 (30)						.47 (47)	
Unambitious		.67 (37)				.52 (58)						
Ambitious	.74 (48)									.75 (73)		.52 (17)
Lazy		.52 (39)			.71 (20)			.63 (32)			.58 (17)	
Hardworking	.72 (44)			.68 (64)			.65 (53)			.75 (68)		
Ethical			.62 (51)			.68 (61)			.58 (51)			
Unethical		.67 (30)			.67 (23)			.70 (24)			.46 (14)	

SOURCE: Triandis et al., 1982. Reprinted by permission of Sage Publications, Inc.

TABLE 4-5 HOW ARE BLACK AMERICANS AND WHITE AMERICANS PERCEIVED BY ANGLOS AND HISPANICS?

Scales	Stimulus: Black Americans						Stimulus: White Americans					
	As seen by Anglos			As seen by Hispanics			As seen by Anglos			As seen by Hispanics		
Factors	1 L (%)	2 L (%)	3 L (%)	1 L (%)	2 L (%)	3 L (%)	1 L (%)	2 L (%)	3 L (%)	1 L (%)	2 L (%)	3 L (%)
Uneducated	-.55 (36)									-.58 (18)		
Educated				.71 (69)			.57 (92)	.58 (92)		.61 (88)		
Family Oriented							.67 (82)					
Friendly		.57 (60)		.59 (67)		-.51 (67)	.54 (81)					
Unfriendly			.50 (24)			.74 (18)						
Competitive									.51 (12)		.64 (79)	
Cooperative		.56 (50)		.54 (56)				.49 (75)	.44 (88)			
Dependent											.71 (77)	
Independent												
Unambitious					.68 (33)					.51 (61)		.63 (61)
Ambitious								.60 (23)				
Lazy	-.59 (38)				.62 (30)							
Hardworking				.60 (54)								
Ethical	.53 (51)									.60 (51)		.73 (65)
Unethical			.58 (32)		.47 (28)				-.44 (73)			
Factor Name	Good citizens	Well socialized	Not antisocial	Well Socialized	Not backward	Not unfriendly	Well socialized	Go-getting	Not calculating	Enlightened	Subject to situational ethics	Protestant ethic

SOURCE: Triandis et al., 1982. Reprinted by permission of Sage Publications, Inc.

*I*DEALS AND VALUES

Ideals are ideas about the most desirable possible state of the world. *Values* are principles that guide our lives. *Value orientations* are conceptions of the desirable.

Kluckhohn and Strodtbeck (1961) argued that cultures differ on five value orientations:

1. Innate human nature—can be evil, neutral, or good; can be mutable or immutable.

2. Human-nature relationships—can reflect subjugation to, harmony with, or mastery over nature.

3. Time focus—can be focused on the past, present, or future.

4. Modality of human activities—can emphasize doing, being (the experience), or becoming (growing, changing).

5. Modality of social relationships—can be lineal (do what authorities say), collateral (do what peers say), or individualistic (do what you think is right).

Let us consider these in more detail. When members of a culture think that humans are evil, they are likely to favor arrangements that will control free human activity, such as police action; if they think that people are basically good, they are likely to favor freedom and self-determination. If members of the culture believe that humans are mutable, they will favor education and other methods of changing them, but if they think humans are immutable, they will not want to waste resources in such activities.

Subjugation goes with reverence for nature, changing oneself to fit in with nature; conversely, mastery means changing nature to make it fit with humans.

A focus on the past leads to paying a lot of attention to ancestors; a focus on the future results in little interest in tradition.

A doing orientation implies counting actions and valuing action for its own sake; a being orientation implies valuing experience; a becoming orientation implies valuing change and growth.

Diaz-Guerrero (1977) reports that his samples of Mexicans valued "being" (the experience), while Americans valued "doing" (the action). Furthermore, they valued different ways of dealing with the environment. When there is an inconsistency between what is demanded by the environment and what the person is doing, most Mexicans are likely to change themselves (passive coping), while most Americans are likely to change the environment (active coping).

Other literature as well suggests that people in collectivist cultures are more likely to change themselves to adjust to the environment and people in individualistic cultures are more likely to try to change the

environment. Thus Americans are more likely to show active self-assertion, while many Mexicans show affiliative obedience to powerful others.
Americans are more likely to try to cope on their own, and Mexicans are
more likely to ask for help from others. In my observations, in both kinds
of cultures, men are more likely than women to try to cope on their own,
e.g., refuse to ask for directions when they are driving. I am especially bad
in this respect! I feel a loss of self-esteem if I have to ask for directions. I
realize that I am wasting time, but it is a matter of pride to be able to get
anywhere with a map.

A lineal orientation implies paying attention to authorities; a collateral
one implies paying attention to those of the same status; and an individualistic orientation implies paying attention to one's own needs, goals,
and views.

This set of values has been researched to some extent. However, the
methods for study proved to be too abstract for most respondents, and for
that reason more specific value methods have been developed. Specifically, extending the Rokeach (1973) method, Schwartz (1992) has worked
with a focused definition of values and developed a more manageable
method that we will review below.

Schwartz defines values as (1) concepts or beliefs (2) that pertain to
desirable end states or behaviors, (3) that transcend specific situations, (4)
that guide selection or evaluation of behavior and events, and (5) that are
ordered by relative importance (Schwartz, 1992, p. 2).

He asks people to rate the importance of a value to them "as a guiding
principle in *my* life." People are presented with fifty-six values; they are
asked to rate them from −1 (I reject this) to 7 (of supreme importance). For
example:

Equality (equal opportunity for all): 5

The instructions specify that the respondent should not use a 7 more than
twice when rating the fifty-six values.

A statistical treatment of the ratings, called *smallest-space analysis*, is
used to see how the values go together. There are ten sets of values that
appear repeatedly in a wide range of cultures (Schwartz, 1992). They are

1. Self-direction (e.g., creativity, freedom, choosing own goals,
   curious, independent)
2. Stimulation (e.g., a varied life, an exciting life, daring)
3. Hedonism (e.g., pleasure, enjoying life)
4. Achievement (e.g., ambitious, successful, capable, influential)
5. Power (e.g., authority, wealth, social power, preserving my public image, social recognition)
6. Security (e.g., social order, family security, national security,
   reciprocation of favors, clean, sense of belonging, healthy)

7. Conformity (e.g., obedient, self-disciplined, politeness, honoring parents and elders)

8. Tradition (e.g., respect for tradition, humble, devout, accepting my position in life, moderate)

9. Benevolence (e.g., helpful, loyal, forgiving, honest, responsible, true friendship, mature love)

10. Universalism (e.g., broadminded, social justice, equality, world of peace, world of beauty, unity with nature, wisdom, protecting the environment)

These value patterns have emerged in data collected in more than 30 countries from samples of about 200 teachers and about 200 others. "Others" were generally university students, but in some countries they were workers or a national sample representative of the society. The results from the teacher and student samples generally were fairly similar. However, the teachers in almost all cultures were higher in collectivism than the students. Schwartz (1992) gives the details of this method. The project is still in progress, and new data arrive daily.

*T*HE MEANING OF IN-GROUPS

People are ready to cooperate with and even sacrifice themselves for some groups, their in-groups, and are ready to fight with, oppose, or be indifferent to other groups, their out-groups. When people feel that they have a "common fate" with a set of other people, they often feel that these other people belong to their in-groups. The definition of an in-group differs across cultures.

In some cultures the in-group is very narrow (e.g., the family, southern Italy in the 1950s), and no other collectives are important; in others there are several important collectives, and some are very broad (e.g., in Japan the whole country is one of the collectives).

In addition, the strength of the link between the individual and each collective can vary. In some cultures the strongest link is with the nuclear family; in others with the tribe, the extended family, the work group, the country. In some cultures (e.g., the rural United States) the neighbors are a very important collective; in others (most cities) most people don't even know their neighbors.

Triandis, McCusker, and Hui (1990) presented to students in Illinois and the People's Republic of China the task of judging the distance between themselves and twenty social stimuli. Table 4-6 presents the stimuli and the scale values obtained by using a psychophysical method called the *method of direct estimation* (Stevens, 1966). The subjects were

TABLE 4–6 SCALE VALUES OF SOCIAL DISTANCE ITEMS USED IN CHINA AND THE UNITED STATES

		Illinois	
Stimulus	PRC sample (n = 27)	Allocentrics (n = 71)	Idiocentrics (n = 71)
Spouse	.18***	.39	.31
Mother	.24***	.41	.35
Father	.34*	.57	.50
Closest friend	.44	.43	.37
Roommate	1.19***	.67	.78
(All) friends	.81*	.61	.66
Neighbors	.93**	1.23	1.35
Extended family	1.06	1.05	.90
Coworkers	1.08	1.24	1.09
People whose politics you like most	1.08***	1.87**	1.36
Acquaintances	1.27	1.14	1.22
People of your own occupation	1.39	1.35	1.17
People from country you like most	1.23**	1.98	1.63
People of your own race	1.63	1.99	1.49
People of your own religion	1.70	1.78	1.55
A stranger you see first time	2.19	2.55	2.29
People whose politics you like least	2.36	3.19	2.35
People whose race you like least	1.71	1.80	1.74
People whose religion you like least	2.65	3.18	1.36

NOTE: Sixty percent of the stimuli have similar scale values when the PRC and U.S. allocentrics are compared, and 95% have the same values when the two U.S. samples are compared.
a Subsets of subjects, who completed all instruments.
* $p<.05$. ** $p<.01$. *** $p<.001$.
SOURCE: Triandis, McCusker, & Hui (1990). Copyright 1990 by the American Psychological Association. Reprinted by permission of the publisher.

asked to consider "the person with whom you feel closest" and use one unit of "distance" from that person. For instance, if a student said "father" was the closest person in the world, one would ask what the distance is to "mother," *expressed in the same units.* This psychophysical method provided the scale values of the stimuli seen in Table 4-6.

The Chinese felt closer to their mother, father, and spouse than did the Americans. But they felt more distance from their roommate than the Americans. That is understandable, because in China roommates are assigned by the authorities, while in America roommates choose each other. The Chinese also felt more distance to the stimulus "friends" than did the Americans, probably because friends are often family friends rather than personal ones. However, they felt closer to their neighbors than the Americans. They also felt closer to those whose politics they liked (the data were collected one year before the Tiananmen Square events of June 1989) than did the Americans. Finally, they felt closer to other Chinese than Americans felt to other Americans. Probably the somewhat greater cultural homogeneity of China is a factor reflected in this result, but also collectivist cultures tend to be more patriotic (Schmitz, 1992).

Note that the remaining scale values are not significantly different from each other. That is very desirable, because as shown in Chapter 3, it is important to have a lot of similarities among the cultures under study in order to be confident that some of the obtained differences are real. Note also that the two samples of Americans, identified by their answers to a questionnaire that measured how allocentric (values like those found in collectivist cultures) or idiocentric (values like those found in individualistic cultures) they were, did not provide many differences in scale values. In other words, the American samples gave similar scale values for these stimuli.

An important cultural difference is that in some collectivist cultures, such as Japan, classmates, neighbors, and fellow countrymen constitute important in-groups to a greater extent than in more individualistic cultures, such as Australia. A suggestion of this difference is provided by Mann, Radford, and Kanagawa (1985), who asked children in Japan and Australia to divide chocolates between their own and another group formed by their own classmates. The Japanese divided the chocolates *equally* between the two groups, while the Australians gave more to their *own* group. This suggests that the Japanese saw all their classmates as an in-group, while the Australians did not. Similarly, the Japanese are ready to cooperate with their neighbors or other Japanese to a greater extent than are people from the United States.

Cultures differ on which collectives are considered the most important in-groups. For example, in Africa the tribe is a very important in-group, and in some tribes facial scarification is practiced so that members of the tribe can be identified immediately. National and ethnic groups are important ingroups in Europe. especially in the Balkans and the former Soviet Union. In many countries tribes are more important in-groups than the state (e.g., the Kurds who live in Iran, Iraq, and Turkey), since the national borders were established by colonial powers, who did not pay much attention to the desires (or relationships) of the people.

In-groups are based on similarity and common fate. However, the situation or setting itself is also crucial. Two Muslims in Saudi Arabia may not be part of the same in-group, but in a remote part of North America they may well be in-group members. The criterion that will be used to form in-groups depends on the importance of that attribute in the particular situation and culture. Muslims pay more attention to gender than do Europeans. In fact, in the Middle East it is rather difficult to interact across sex lines if there is no kinship relationship that allows such interaction.

Age is often the key attribute for the formation of in-groups. In some cultures age-mates form a definite in-group based on both similarity of age and common fate (people are treated by others the same way).

Social class is another very important attribute for in-group formation. In Marxist thought, "class struggle" was a key idea. It has been more relevant in Europe and Latin America than in the United States or Canada. During the French (1789), Russian (1917), and Mexican (1910) Revolutions, for instance, many people were killed simply because they were rich. Again, there is more than similarity that is relevant; common fate is often also important.

THE MEANING OF SOCIAL BEHAVIOR

Social behavior does not mean *exactly* the same thing across cultures. Triandis, Vassiliou, and Nassiakou (1968) studied the meaning of specific behaviors in Greece and the United States by asking samples from these two cultures to rate each behavior on different dimensions. For instance, one dimension (association versus dissociation) was defined by the behaviors "to love," "to admire," "to help" versus "to hate," to despise," "to be prejudiced against." Another dimension (subordination versus superordination) was defined by the behaviors "obey," "be commanded by," "accept the criticism of" versus "treat as subordinate," "command," "give advice." A third dimension (intimacy versus formality) was defined by "have sexual intercourse with," "marry," "pet" versus "appoint to important position," "send letter inviting to dinner," "invite to join own club." A fourth dimension, hostility ("throw rocks at," "insult," "exclude from the neighborhood"), was also used. In each culture, each behavior was rated on scales anchored by such sets of behaviors. For example, is "inviting to dinner" more like "obey" or "command"? Numerous cultural differences in the meaning of behaviors were identified.

In the U.S.-Greek study, the Greeks saw more "giving of status" implied by the behavior "compete with," and less "giving of status" for the behavior "accept as close kin by marriage." The specific findings need not concern us here. Just remember: (1) There are subtle differences in the meaning of social behavior across cultures, and (2) there are methods for identifying and measuring them so that we can train people to take these differences into account.

We have already discussed the shifts in the level of adaptation. Think of the frequencies of different behaviors in a culture as the determinants of that level. In a culture where people invite others to dinner very frequently, the level of adaptation would be on the side of getting invited, and a person who did not get invited would feel offended. You can extend this logic to any social behavior. The frequency of the behavior in the culture is a major determinant of the meaning of the behavior.

By knowing about differences in the meaning of social behavior we can train people who have to interact with members from other cultures (see Chapter 10) to understand how members of these cultures view social behavior. For example, the fact that Greeks see less intimacy than do Americans in the behavior "to invite to dinner" is a useful piece of information. It means that Americans should not expect a dinner invitation in Greece to mean they have been accepted as close friends. Each culture has its own standards for social behaviors. For example, it is more intimate to be invited to dinner in France than in the United States, and so one would not expect such an invitation in most work relationships in France. Getting to know such subtle differences in the meaning of social behavior can facilitate social interaction and avoid misunderstandings.

S UBJECTIVE CULTURE AND SOCIAL BEHAVIOR

When we know how people categorize events, what associations among categories they stress, what norms, roles, and values they have, we can predict some behaviors. For example, Heise (1979) used the evaluation, potency, and activity (from Osgood et al. (1975); see above) aspects of the meaning of roles and behaviors obtained from samples in a given culture as the basic information from which to predict what a person will do in

FIGURE 4–5
Subjective culture and social behavior.

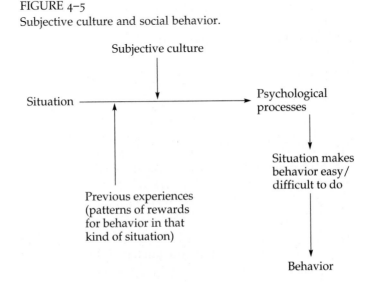

response to the behavior of another. His predictions were reasonably successful.

The other elements of subjective culture also predict behavior. The model (Triandis, 1972, 1977, 1980) in Chapter 8 shows how we can integrate these predictions. Here is just a brief introduction to the model. Note in Figure 4-5 that the *situation* and *previous experiences* are *interpreted* in the light of the individual's subjective culture. These processes activate various *psychological processes* that make the person ready to carry out a behavior. The behavior will occur if the *situation* makes it easy to do it. Chapter 8 will give you details about the psychological processes that get activated.

SUMMARY

In this chapter we examined some of the concepts we need to use for the analysis of culture. These concepts are not the only ones available, but they do provide an introduction to the topic. Pay attention to categorizations, associations, beliefs, evaluations, norms, roles, goals, values, and other elements that may be revealed in interaction with people from another culture. Try to learn some of the language, because that will tell you much about categorization and you will be able to observe some of the other constructs. Ask people about their beliefs, evaluations, norms, roles, goals, and values. Do not assume automatically that their subjective culture is like the subjective culture of your own ethnic group. Keep your mind open for possible differences. But also look for similarities. If you find only differences, you may not be able to organize the information into a meaningful pattern, and you may even be using the wrong methods for the study, as discussed in Chapter 3.

In the next chapter we will explore further cultural differences in some of the elements of subjective culture.

QUESTIONS AND EXERCISES

1. In a company consisting of men and women, use some of the methods suggested in this chapter to determine the meaning of interesting categories. For instance: What events are included in the category "to flirt"? What are the associations? What is the connotative meaning of the category (use a semantic differential)? What is the denotative meaning (use the antecedent-consequent method)?

2. Repeat what you did in exercise 1 for the category "sexual harassment."

3. What personal values do you have? (Look at the Schwartz values mentioned in the chapter.)

4.   Use the rules of Table 4.3 to study whether you and your friends use these rules the same way for the following relationships: a heterosexual couple living together, a same-sex couple living together, a dating couple, close friends, siblings, teacher–student, work superior–subordinate, work subordinate–superior.

5

Some Interesting Differences in the Elements of Subjective Culture

❖

The Sapir-Whorf Hypothesis ◆ Gender Inequalities across the World ◆
Foragers ◆ *Horticultural Societies* ◆ *Pastoral Societies* ◆ *Agrarian Societies* ◆
Industrial Societies ◆ *Socialist Societies* ◆ *The Third World* ◆ *Information
Societies* ◆ What Is Functional Is Good ◆ Cultural Differences in
Attributions ◆ Cultures and Dealing with Time ◆ Culture and Marriage ◆
Culture and Social Distance ◆ Culture and Stereotypes ◆
Sex Stereotypes ◆ Summary

T he previous chapter discussed ways to analyze subjective culture. This chapter begins by examining the theory that language influences and perhaps even determines how people view the world. The chapter then presents some examples of specific, broad cultural differences.

THE SAPIR-WHORF HYPOTHESIS

In the late 1920s the linguist Edward Sapir (1951) suggested that language influences the way we think. His student, Benjamin Whorf (1956), proposed that the "world view" of members of a culture depends on the structure of the language they speak. The so-called Whorfian hypothesis resulted in much research, debate, and argument. The conclusion that is widely accepted today is that language has an effect on some aspects of our experience of the world, but the effect is relatively minor, and it certainly is an exaggeration to say that language affects the world view of members of a culture.

Let us examine this debate a bit more closely. When you speak English you *have* to pay attention to some aspects of the environment, such as the sex of the person you are talking about, so you will use the words "his" and "her" correctly, and the number of cases involved, so you can use the singular or plural form. While Indo-European languages pay attention to sex and number, other languages pay attention to other attributes. For example, in Japanese you must know the relative status of the speakers in more detail than in most European languages.

The importance of language structure is indicated in research reported by Guiora (1985), which includes the finding that children who spoke languages with greater gender loadings (e.g., Hebrew) developed a gender identity sooner than those who spoke languages with little gender loading (e.g., English) or none (Finnish). To the extent that "I am a man" or "I am a woman" constitutes a different world view, Whorf was correct. But it can also be argued that a world view is something more than gender identity. In sum, it is largely a question of definition: What do we mean by a "world view"?

In many European languages there is a polite, respectful form (*vous* in French, *usted* in Spanish, *Sie* in German, *esis* in Greek, and corresponding plural grammatical forms) and a familiar form (*tu, du, esi*, and corresponding singular grammatical forms). But in Japanese there are more gradations on the respect dimension. We can conclude from this observation that the Japanese must pay more attention to status differences, and indeed we can observe that when Japanese businessmen or professionals meet, they immediately exchange cards so they can determine relative rank. They are literally unable to speak until they know the other person's rank, since much of the selection of words depends on that.

In many countries if you use the wrong term, you are committing a faux pas that is equivalent to using a swear word in the presence of a high-status, prim and proper person. In the French upper class the use of the *vous* form reflects *savoir vivre* (knowing how to live) and proper etiquette, and it is used even between spouses and parents and children.

The Luganda language, in Uganda, compels its speakers to note whether an event occurred within or before the twenty-four-hour period immediately prior to the time at which the event is described. That observation would suggest that the Luganda consider today versus the past an important way of thinking about events.

There are thousands of such examples, especially in comparisons of the language of the Hopi Indians of New Mexico and English, the two languages that Whorf studied in detail. Whorf reasoned that those attributes that people *have* to pay attention to in order to speak correctly will influence them when they think, and so their world view is going to be influenced by the structure of their language.

That position proved too vague. We can break it down by examining four levels: (1) differences in linguistic codability (see Chapter 4), (2) the influence of codability on behavior, (3) differences in language structure (i.e., what distinctions are mandatory in order to speak correctly?), and (4) the effects of differences in structure on behavior. (See Triandis, 1964, pp. 37–38, for more details.)

A difference in codability means that people can say certain things in one language more quickly and more accurately than in another. If codability influences behavior, it will be mostly in the domain of communication. Since I can say: "Go to the parking lot and find the gray 1986 Ford Lynx," I can communicate more effectively than a person who has to say "... gray automobile." But that is hardly a difference of world view.

The differences in language structure mean that people pay more attention to one clue than to another. We do code in our language the present versus the past, but we are not as precise as the Luganda on what we mean by the "present." If I say, "I am on my way to San Francisco," as opposed to, "I went to San Francisco," the coding is present versus past, but the past does not have to be within a twenty-four-hour period. I could be on my way to San Francisco for several days. The Luganda would have made a finer discrimination. But such differences hardly mean that English and Luganda speakers have entirely different world views.

When differences in structure show up in behavior, it is fair to conclude that more weight is given to one kind of information in one language than in another. Thus when two American executives meet and they ask each other what positions they have in their respective corporations, that says something about relative status, but it is not likely to result in significant differences in respectful behavior. However, when two Japanese executives meet and they exchange cards, this may lead to major differences in respectful behavior, such as in the depth of bowing. But, again, are these cultural differences in world view?

Research has uncovered evidence of "Whorfian effects" (e.g., Kay & Kempton, 1984; Witkowski & Brown, 1982). The issue is not whether such effects occur, but what their practical significance is. Consider the study by Kay and Kempton who used blue- and green-color chips. They presented them in triads to respondents in California and northern Mexico (the Tarahumara Indians of Mexico, whose language does not have separate names for blue and green). The respondents were required to "pick the one of the three chips that is most different from the other two." The responses to this task can be analyzed by a statistical technique called *multidimensional scaling*, which results in a multidimensional map on which the chips are located. The map would show mostly blue chips in one part and green chips in another. The maps obtained from the two cultures indicated that the distances between blue chips and green chips were greater in the English sample than in the Tarahumara. That is a Whorfian effect, but is it of great significance?

In sum, Whorf made a contribution in alerting us to the fact that language influences in subtle ways how we think and behave. When we translate poetry or philosophical discussions from one language into another, we see that we have greater difficulties than in translating information about everyday affairs. If the difficulties we have in translating poetry or philosophical discussions are due to the fact that language structures are different, we must give Whorf some credit for identifying this phenomenon.

We now turn to a number of interesting topics about cultural differences. The first one concerns gender inequalities.

GENDER INEQUALITIES ACROSS THE WORLD

In Chapter 2 we examined sex-role inequalities in the context of the argument that we can understand such phenomena better when we examine them from a cross-cultural perspective. In this chapter we look at gender inequalities in more detail.

Note that I used both the words "sex" and "gender." Exactly what do these mean? Schlegel (1989) argues convincingly that we should use the word "sex" to refer to the biological features that distinguish men and women and the word "gender" to distinguish the behaviors that are considered appropriate for men and women. Gender is largely "constructed" (Hare-Mustin & Marecek, 1990), in the sense that people around the world start with something real (sex) and project their own attitudes, beliefs, norms, stereotypes, and values to create gender (Moore, 1988; Ortner & Whitehead, 1981).

Biology-based differences are generally exaggerated, and people tend to see larger differences between men and women than can be identified by rigorous psychological testing (Lott, 1990). For example, a study by Lummis and Stevenson (1990), which tested thousands of elementary school children in Taiwan, Japan, and the United States, found very small gender differences. Girls were slightly better in reading and boys were slightly better in mathematics in all three cultures. But mothers in all three cultures believed that the differences were quite large. Furthermore, gender differences often appear "natural" and "biology-based" much more than is justified by the facts.

In short, reliable differences tend to be small, unstable, and situation specific, and yet people project their culturally based needs (e.g., ideas that often justify gender exploitation) to exaggerate them.

The previous chapter pointed out that the way we perceive the world is in part due to objective reality and in part due to the elements of subjective culture we have acquired during our socialization and life in a specific culture, such as our shared attitudes, beliefs, and values. In other words, sex is *real* and *etic*, and gender is *constructed* and *emic*. It is constructed in unique ways in each culture. The ideas of "maleness" and "femaleness" are even more emic.

The elements of subjective culture that are linked with sex differ across the world, because they depend on the nature of the activities in which men and women engage in order to survive in particular ecologies. Starting with the reality that women are the ones who bear children and should therefore not be put at risk during pregnancy and childrearing, societies that must engage in dangerous activities, such as fishing in open seas or hunting wild animals, develop subjective cultures to glorify these tasks. This is a way to make sure that these jobs get done. A pattern of status differentiation of activities is thus established, which in turn creates status differentiation of genders.

Of course, in information societies, such as the United States, dangerous activities are less necessary for survival. As a result, we do see evidence that the more "modern" a society, the less of a difference there is in the stereotypes that people have of men and women (Williams & Best, 1982, 1990).

The link between ecology and the status of women can be seen in the interesting case of polyandry. Fraternal polyandry (several brothers married to the same woman) is practiced by the people who live in the northwest corner of Nepal, near Tibet. There the land is barren, and it is difficult to support much population. In that part of the world families must work the fields, herd cattle, and do some trading in order to be economically independent. One man can rarely do all those jobs, and thus fraternal polyandry is widely practiced (Goldstein, 1987). The normal pattern is that the woman comes to live on the land of her husbands. Since a woman can produce only a few children, the difference between monogamy and polyandry in terms of population control is striking. Members of this culture have the option of monogamy or polyandry, but often prefer polyandry so that the land will not be divided.

Those brothers who opt for monogamous arrangements, but do not divide the land, find that the conflicts among their wives are quite significant, and thus polyandrous marriage becomes more attractive.

In short, starting from the realities of poor soil and the undesirability of the division of the land, this segment of Nepalese society has devised a marital arrangement that controls population, keeps the land intact, and provides security for many of the women and children.

What about the status of the women? Nominally, the oldest husband is the boss of the family, and all the children call him "father"; the other husbands are called either "father" or "father's brother" (varies with the region). But unlike women in monogamous marriages, a woman in that marital arrangement has ways to play one husband against another, and thus can control many situations to her advantage. It's hard to generalize about status differences in this case since some women will be more successful than others in controlling the household.

This is a concrete example of a methodological difficulty in the area of gender-status comparisons across cultures: Gender status is an emic. How can we compare emics? In Chapter 3 we argued that only etics can be compared. If we compare men and women as *biological* entities, there are no known cultural differences. It is only when we compare them as culturally *constructed* entities that we see some differences. But suppose the indicators of the differences themselves are emic. Then it is impossible to make a comparison.

As we will see below, in doing comparisons we tend to use particular ideas, such as "who makes the major decisions," to come to the conclusion that men have more power than women. But what is a "major" decision? If a major decision is one that influences the whole community (e.g., "Should we go to war?"), then indeed there is a basis for arguing that men have more power than women. But if a major decision is one that affects the household, such as "Should we have one more child?" then it is not that clear that men have more power than women in all societies. There are no studies that have "scaled" decisions on impor- tance on a worldwide basis, and so we must make our comparisons very cautiously.

An interesting case of the "emics of equality" is provided by the generation of Japanese women born between 1946 and 1955 and described in detail by Iwao (1993). Iwao argues that those Japanese women born before the Second World War are clearly traditional, and their status is inferior to that of the men, but the 1946–1955 generation is clearly differ- ent. In this generation, the wife controls the purse strings (husband brings salary intact, and wife gives him spending money) and may decide to work, thus having an average "free access" to $650 a month, while her husband has $406 (p. 87). If she works, she puts the money in her savings account, to use as she sees fit. She is free to decide whether to work, go to graduate school, participate in international organizations, run for politi- cal office, or write novels or poetry. If she decides to work, she can decide what job to do. By contrast, her husband is the "slave of the corporation." She can travel overseas, she can go to concerts and the theater, and she has appliances and fine clothing. Her husband works all his waking hours and cannot spend as much time with his family as he would like to. The Japanese say: "Men are superior; women are dominant." Japanese women see the American women's view of equality as "Since men get killed, we must get killed." They prefer to write their own agenda.

Furthermore, in a culture such as Japan, where the continuation of the family is a most important goal for both men and women, the men work to support the family and women to prepare the children for the fierce competition of the outside world. The result is that "neither men nor women in Japan think that giving birth or raising children is the source of inferior status" (Iwao, 1993, p. 129).

Americans are often impressed by the fact that Japanese wives generally do not participate in the social activities of their husbands, which the Americans consider a clear sign of inferiority. But Japanese wives see it differently: "I have to be on my best behavior in front of my husband's colleagues, and make a good impression on his superiors which is very humiliating for a woman of pride who feels that having to be ingratiating with other people she does not instinctively like is degrading and can be left to professionals like bar hostesses or geisha. . . " (Iwao, 1993, p. 91).

The women born between 1946 and 1955 make most of the important decisions, such as where to live, where the children should go to school, or what appliances to buy, especially because one-third of Japanese marriages are "commuting marriages" (the husband is away and returns once a month, for the week-end). Some decisions include going into business for oneself, so that almost 5 percent of presidents of Japanese corporations are women. In short, Japanese women see the quality of life as the criterion to be used for the measurement of equality, and they see that men have an inferior quality of life. Iwao argues that the postwar Japanese rush toward wealth and power has kept men from achieving it.

Another difficulty in comparing the status of men and women is that cultures do not have the same "models of the relationships" between men and women. In precolonial Ghana, and some other parts of Africa, for instance, men and women had a "separate but equal" relationship. The women minded their financial affairs independently of their husbands and in many cases were more successful. Men and women came together for sex and procreation, but otherwise they lived separate lives (Giele & Smock, 1977). It is unclear how we would compare statuses in this case.

In any case, there are major cultural differences in the meaning and extent of gender inequality. These differences reflect divergent subjective cultures with respect to the meaning of "men" and "women" as well as the concept of a "good life." Subjective cultures often reflect major differences in the ecologies within which the societies are surviving.

O'Kelly and Carney (1986) wrote a whole book on this subject. They examined the relationships between men and women in societies that are typed as "forager" (hunting, fishing, gathering wild plants), "horticultural" (slash-and-burn method of raising crops), "pastoral" (herding of livestock, such as cattle, camels, sheep, goats), "agrarian" (plowing, fertilizing, and irrigating), and "industrial" (producing commodities that are exchanged for other resources, such as money, information, goods, and services).

Some social scientists believe that cultural evolution has gone through these stages. For 99 percent of the time that humanlike creatures lived on this planet the cultural pattern was foraging. Other patterns evolved subsequently, but some remnants of these later patterns are still found in most societies.

There are still foraging cultures in remote regions of the world such as the Kalahari Desert and the Arctic. Horticultural cultures can be found in areas that are opening up, such as the Amazon forests in Brazil. Pastoral cultures are quite widespread and can be found in Europe (on some of the large islands of the Mediterranean and in the interior of the Balkans) and especially in Africa (e.g., Kenya) and Asia.

Agrarian cultures are the most common. Even in the United States, where only 3 percent of the population engages in farming, and where farmers tend to be "high-tech" managers, some minor elements of agrarian culture can still be found in the traditions and conceptions about women. Of course, other countries are much more agricultural. For example, 80 percent of China's 1.1 billion people are engaged in farming.

While most industrial societies are found in Europe and North America, Japan, Hong Kong, South Korea, Taiwan, and Singapore are outstanding examples in Asia. Many of the socialist countries have developed a good deal of industry as well. Sensitive to the complexities of industrial societies, O'Kelly and Carney (1986) devoted separate chapters to the United States, Sweden and Japan, the Third World, and the socialist societies.

Foragers

In foraging cultures there is little gender inequality or social stratification (rulers, bosses). There is much respect for human life; e.g., the Eskimos look down on Westerners because they "hunt each other like animals." Kinship is most important, and bilateral descent systems (equal importance of kin from mother's and father's sides) are common. Foragers tend to be serially monogamous (have one spouse at a time) and live in nuclear families of mother, father, and children. Since there is no surplus, men cannot be viewed as wealthy and, hence, powerful.

At least two factors create inequality: (1) the relative danger of the activities of men and women and (2) dependence on meat. Since most of the dangerous hunting and fishing is done by men and most of the less dangerous food gathering, home building, cooking, and child care by women, some inequality is generated by this division of labor. In addition, in foraging societies that eat much meat, there is some gender inequality when only the men supply the meat. Nevertheless, the relationship between the genders is much more egalitarian in foraging than in other societies because each gender depends on the other for specific activities. In general, the more harsh the conditions of extracting food from the environment, the more inequality there is, even among foragers. But on the whole this cultural pattern is characterized by cooperation, egalitarianism, flexibility in human relationships, and recognition of human integrity and freedom irrespective of age, gender, or personal achievement. The social order depends on neither the fact nor the theory of male dominance.

Horticultural Societies

In parts of the world that have uncleared land available to anyone who wants to work it, extended families work the land as a group. Crops are planted in the newly cleared land. These societies often have some surplus food, and those who have additional resources are in a position to impose their will on others. In advanced horticultural societies productivity is especially high because of the availability of metal tools.

The average size of the community is 40 persons among foraging, 95 among simple horticulturalists, and 280 among advanced horticulturalists (O'Kelly & Carney, 1986, p. 37).

Simple horticultural societies tend to be egalitarian, but in comparison with foragers there is more concern for prestige, boasting, and overt competition. The ability to organize kin to produce food surpluses results in "big men's" dominating the kin group. Advanced horticultural societies have even more inequality, with slavery and hereditary leadership positions found in such groups.

Usually, the task of clearing the land is assigned to the men, and women help with the cultivation of plants. In advanced horticultural societies, such as in West Africa, females do most of the trading, exchanging the surplus food for industrial goods or money. Since the women have profits, they also have much status.

Unlike the foragers, who, as mentioned above, are most likely to use bilateral descent, horticulturalists use unilineal descent. If the descent excludes the female line, it is patrilineal, and if it excludes the male line, it is matrilineal. Patrilinearity is more common, but there is a good deal of matrilinearity among horticulturalists.

Matrilinearity gives women considerable power, influence, and personal autonomy. It occurs in about 10 percent of the foraging, 27 percent of the horticultural, and 4 percent of the agrarian societies, but it is virtually unknown in the industrial societies (O'Kelly & Carney, 1986, p. 41).

When a society engages in male long-distance trading, work, or external warfare, the men tend to be away, allowing the women to have more power. In many cultures where men have to be away from the family for long periods of time, women make most of the important family decisions.

Warfare, however, is associated with gender inequality, since it is a more dangerous activity, and one of the ways to convince people to take such risks is to make the activity more prestigious.

One of the most male-dominated societies is the Yanamano Indians, who live on the border between Brazil and Venezuela. They have a "warfare complex" (Chagnon, 1968), they are patrilinear and patrilocal (bride must live with husband's relatives), and males control most resources. This society produces enough vegetables but is short on protein, which requires hunting scarce game. Conflict with neighbors over hunting territory is common. Consciously or unconsciously, there are mechanisms that keep the population under control, so that game is not hunted to extinction. Many men die during warfare, and female infanticide is also practiced. As a result of infanticide, polygyny, and strict sexual mores for women, women are in short supply and are fought over by men. The warfare complex makes women a "commodity" and degrades them. The males devote most of their energy to fighting and to maintaining an image of fierce aggressive bravery. The women are among the most brutalized in the world, because it helps a man's image to beat or stab his wife in public. Wives are obtained through raiding. The captured women are gang-raped by the warriors and then distributed to the fiercest fighters. Polygyny is extremely prestigious for the men. Thus, gender inequality in this horticultural society is among the highest on record.

In short, competitiveness, scarcity of resources, aggression, and inequality are characteristic of many of the horticultural societies. The movement from simple to complex or advanced horticulturalism is associated with increasing levels of male dominance and gender inequality.

Pastoral Societies

Here the primary source of food comes from herding livestock. Life is organized around the needs of the herds; e.g., in the summer people live at the higher elevations and in the winter in the valleys. Thus, these societies are in part nomadic.

Exchanges are through kinship ties, and there is little marketing of the animals to outsiders. Some foraging and gardening are done. Expanding the herd is an important goal, and so raiding out-groups to obtain meat or expand the herd is common. Male economic control and female economic dependence are commonplace. Males fight the other herders, and females take care of the domestic chores. Women willingly accept domination in exchange for protection and food. The concept of family honor is very important; honor can be lost if a kinsperson is killed or a woman of the in-group has sexual intercourse with outsiders. In such cases, killing a member of the out-group is mandatory. Women who dishonor the in-group are also killed.

Feuding among males is endemic because in-groups constantly look for ways to acquire the animals of the out-groups. Socialization is directed toward making the males quick-tempered, aggressive, and courageous warriors. Islam is widely accepted among herders in Asia and Africa and supports the separation of males and females and the subordination and seclusion of females. The males of the in-group cooperate to control the females.

Pastoral societies can be conceived of as being in a stage between horticultural and agrarian societies. Some pastoral societies have gender relations similar to those of the horticulturalists, and others have relations that are similar to those of the agrarian societies.

Agrarian Societies

The plow, fertilizers, and irrigation methods are some of the elements that define these societies. Work is more demanding than it is in horticultural societies. Agrarian societies first developed about 5000 years ago in Mesopotamia and Egypt and are characterized by the accumulation of considerable surpluses. Surplus food and goods lead to the development of a class structure, make large cities possible, and provide time for construction of major monuments.

Gender inequality is extreme. Agricultural labor often requires muscular strength and long hours. Since it can also be dangerous, it is done mostly by men. However, women are equally busy with child rearing and household chores. There is more of a public-domestic split in behavior in those societies than in the foraging or horticultural ones. Men engage mostly in public and women in domestic activities. The concept of a "woman's place" simultaneously combines the subordination and idealization of women. An extensive discussion of the public-domestic dichotomy can be found in Eisenstein (1983, pp. 15–26).

The genders are interdependent, because the men are often unable to cook and the women are unable to fight. Fighting for territory is common. A strong sexual double standard exists, with women frequently being seen as "property," and male honor depends on controlling the sexuality of women.

A good description of how women's seclusion and men's honor are interrelated is provided by Mandelbaum (1988), who focuses on northern India, Bangladesh, and Pakistan. Shyness of demeanor, avoidance of eye contact with men, avoidance of loud speech and laughter, and little contact with males outside the family are aspects of the code of "good conduct" for women. For example, women must veil themselves when older men pass by a courtyard where they are sitting. In many rural parts of Asia, men and women live in separate sections of the household. The husband shares his wife's bed briefly, in the still of the night. A young wife must appear completely uninterested in her husband when they are in the presence of others. On the other hand, a woman has a joking, informal relationship with her husband's younger brothers. If a woman has an illicit sex encounter, she is ruined for life. An unmarried pregnant woman is likely to be killed by her own father or brothers. The misbehavior of a married woman affects her husband and brings dishonor to his family. However, after a woman has become the mother of males, her status improves, and when she is old and the head of a household with several daughters-in-law, she reaches the pinnacle of female prestige.

Modern societies continue to be influenced by attitudes generated during the agrarian period of culture evolution.

Industrial Societies

The production of commodities that are exchanged for other commodities or for money is the key characteristic of these societies. Dependence on a money economy allows both genders to offer their services to employers. Large surpluses allow even larger cities, public works, and military expenditures than were possible in agrarian societies. Social stratification is strong, not only among economic classes, but also between feminine and masculine jobs. The domestic-public split is still important, but the women participate in both, while the men still act mostly in the public domain.

Consumerism is associated with women's escaping the dreary aspects of domestic life to go shopping. This helps business sell its excess production. Some social scientists emphasize that the exploitation of the males in the workplace is softened by the subservience of their wives. Wives are expected to tend to the physical, emotional, and sexual needs of their husbands. They relieve males of household and child-care chores and allow them to be more efficient at work.

However, as women participate in economic activities on an equal basis, they demand greater equality, and in many of the advanced industrial societies they are increasingly getting it. In the United States by the late 1970s women were as educated as men, and while they still face a "glass ceiling" (do not get to the top of the economic structures), they are increasingly closing the earnings gap between men and women. In some societies (e.g., Switzerland) the gap is now rather small.

Greater sexual freedom and the availability of alternative lifestyles have reduced the power of the sexual double standard. However, the degree of change in gender inequality varies greatly among different industrial societies.

Sweden now has one of the world's highest standards of living and ranks ahead of the United States on per capita income, health care, infant mortality, life expectancy, and measures of well-being. Every adult has the right to a job. Children are viewed as valuable contributions to society, which should shoulder the burden associated with having and rearing children. A generous parental-leave policy allows most Swedish mothers to be away from work for one year after they give birth. The rate of cohabitation (couples living together without marriage) is very high. Such a pattern inevitably means more equality, and since the burdens of child rearing are widely shared by the state, many women feel free to enter and leave relationships that do not work well for them. Divorce rates are very high. Most child care, however, is still done by the mothers. In spite of the emphasis on gender equality in the schools, females do most of the routine, secretarial, and child-care jobs, and there are more men than women in top-management positions. Women participate in the country's political life, but the top government jobs are held by men.

Socialist Societies

The ideology of socialism has been strongly associated with gender equality, but the reality remains that in most of the socialist societies women are not found in leading positions. In fact, in some ways the egalitarian ideology has resulted in women's doing more dangerous work than in societies where there is gender inequality. For instance, men and women are equally exposed to industrial chemicals, and both do heavy work, such as road building.

The Third World

Most women today live in nonindustrial societies characterized by mixed social structures. Most of these are agricultural, but pockets of industrial structures can be found in many parts of these societies, especially the cities. In many ways the position of women in those societies is less satisfactory than in foraging societies. However, it is difficult to evaluate such developments, because we are contrasting apples and oranges, e.g., comparing food shortages with the degradation of working for low wages in industrial plants. A major attribute of these societies is the diversity of gender roles that depend on social class. The upper classes in such societies, e.g., in the Philippines, often develop gender roles that copy the roles in the advanced industrial societies, while the lower classes remain very close to the models of the agrarian societies.

Information Societies

As we move more and more toward an information society, where muscular strength will no longer be required and dangerous occupations will be less common, we can expect to see greater gender equality. But as pointed out before, we perceive the world not only on the basis of realities but also according to subjective cultures that are traditional. It will take a very long time even in these societies for full equality to be reached.

There is evidence that as societies increase in "complexity" from foraging, through agricultural, to information societies, the difference in the status of men and women first increases and then decreases. Thus the relationship forms an inverted U (Giele & Smock, 1977).

A good annotated bibliography, with discussions of the status of women in India, China, Oceania, sub-Saharan Africa, Latin America, and the Middle East plus North Africa, can be found in Duley and Edwards (1986). It is recommended for further reading on this subject.

WHAT IS FUNCTIONAL IS GOOD

Societal tolerance for homosexuality has been empirically found to be greater in societies where there are population pressures, where there are food shortages, and where abortion and infanticide are common (Ember & Levinson, 1991, p. 96). One possible explanation of these findings is that in societies with tremendous population pressures any activity that reduces the population is functional, is reinforcing, and becomes associated with what is "normal and desirable." Anyone who has visited the more densely populated parts of India and China is likely to approve of activities that will relieve the population pressure. The director of a psychology institute in China told me that he called in his staff and told them how many children they were allowed to have—one. If they did not obey, they would have no job! Such an intrusion by a boss would be intolerable in the United States. But having been to that part of the world several times, I fully understand the director's actions.

CULTURAL DIFFERENCES IN ATTRIBUTIONS

If you fail an exam, your parents are apt to ask you why. In responding, you are most likely to use one of four types of explanations (Weiner et al., 1972) based on ability, task difficulty, effort, or luck. For example, you might tell your parents that you are not intelligent enough to pass, that the exam was terribly difficult, that you did not study hard enough, or that you were unlucky because the professor asked just those questions that you had not studied.

Cultures tend to use different explanations for success and failure. For example, the Japanese usually explain success by pointing to the help they receive from others (Kashima & Triandis, 1986), and failure by pointing to lack of effort (Holloway, Kashiwagi, Hess, & Azuma, 1986). In contrast, Americans are most likely to attribute success to their ability and to attribute failure to the difficulty of the task. Note that ability and effort are *internal* to the person, and task difficulty and luck are *external* to the person.

Psychologists have studied attributions extensively, and one widely held conclusion is that attributing failure to lack of effort is better than attributing it to lack of ability or to the difficulty of the task. The reason is that the person can do something about effort but may not be able to do much about ability or task difficulty. So, some psychologists train children to make effort attributions, as the Japanese are most likely to do. Children who learn to make effort attributions do better in school than children who make other kinds of attributions.

CULTURES AND DEALING WITH TIME

Doob (1971) hypothesized that the duration of an interval of time will have greater significance under the following conditions: (1) when goals are achieved more easily through coordination of the activities of more than one person, (2) when people are seeking similar goals and must coordinate their actions to achieve them, (3) when an activity involves the power relation between groups and individuals, (4) when planning and receiving communication has significance to the communicator and the audience, (5) when it is anticipated that continuation or termination of the activity will bring the relevant goal closer or will reduce frustration, and (6) when gratification is frequently deferred. These hypotheses suggest that the more industrialized the society, the greater the emphasis on time.

A study by Levine and Bartlett (1984), mentioned in Chapter 2, showed that the Japanese are more concerned with time than are Americans, who in turn are more concerned than people in less developed countries. Also, people in large cities are more time-conscious than people in small towns. One of the ways to get an idea of how people deal with time is to ask: "If you set a meeting with one of your friends for 12 noon, how long will you wait before you decide that your friend will not come?" Most people in Europe and North America give intervals of about fifteen minutes. Some, of course, use shorter and others longer periods. However, in some parts of the less developed world, it is not uncommon to obtain answers such as a day. Remember these are environments without telephones and with underemployed populations. Usually, there are few ways for people to entertain themselves. If they sit in a coffeehouse and their friend does not come today, they check again the next day. Perhaps the friend got confused about the date.

Diaz-Guerrero (1979) asked Mexicans and Americans to estimate when "a minute" had elapsed. He found that Mexicans on the average reported it had elapsed after 1.5 minutes and Americans after 0.8 minutes! This result suggests that Americans are much more active in dealing with time and that Mexicans are more relaxed.

CULTURE AND MARRIAGE

Cultures differ in the marital arrangements that are most common. In addition to the monogamous pattern that we are familiar with, there are numerous other patterns, such as polygyny, polyandry, and mandatory marriage to specific relatives (e.g., daughter of father's brother). Todd (1983) has argued that family structures have important political consequences. For example, democratic institutions are found in cultures where the nuclear family and monogamous marriages prevail.

Who is a good spouse? We see in a study by Buss (1990) that people look for rather different attributes. For example, in individualistic countries they look for an "exciting personality," while in collectivist countries they look for a "good homemaker/provider" and "virginity." Modern Japanese women look for "high income" (more than $35,000 per year), "graduation from a prestigious university," and "physical height" (at least 175 centimeters, or 5 feet 10 inches, according to Iwao (1993, pp. 67–68).

The marriage concept itself is seen very differently in those two kinds of cultures. In the collectivist cultures the whole extended family "marries" the other extended family. In the individualistic cultures it is the individuals who marry.

Arranged marriages are much more widely used in collectivist than in individualistic cultures. Even in modern Japan many marriages are arranged (24 percent according to Iwao, 1993). "How can you let emotional youths decide something that affects so many people?" asked the Indian informants in Shweder et al. (1990).

In mate selection, individualists ask: "What does my heart say?" Collectivists ask: "What will other people say?" In general, the divorce rate among those who marry according to the wishes of parents, or some other collective, is much lower than the divorce rate among those who marry for love. Whether that is desirable or undesirable can be debated at length. One can make the case that marriage, when seen as a fifty-year relationship, is more likely to be a good one if people enter into it after a careful, rational analysis, which is more likely to be provided by older adults than by sexually aroused young people. On the other hand, there is evidence that some arranged marriages involve rather formal relationships (e.g., among kings and queens), where spouses talk to each other the way they talk to acquaintances and where intercourse is a duty to produce legitimate offspring, while most love life goes on with mistresses and lovers.

To evaluate the two patterns we have to consider the evidence about the effects of divorce much more carefully. Divorce seems to be detrimental to the welfare of women, who often lose much of their economic well-being, and children, who often feel confused and hostile toward one or both parents. It is difficult to evaluate the social consequences, because dysfunctional marriages may be just as poor in their influence on children as divorces.

One point should be useful: We should not consider that what we do is universally the best! It may well be the case that what is done in other cultures (e.g., India) is as good or better. We should have an open mind. For example, a close friend of mine from India talked to me very frankly about his marriage. He was nineteen and she was fifteen; it was arranged. In the beginning she spent much time with her parents, and their relationship was somewhat strained. But over time a great fondness developed. They had two children and now have several grandchildren, though they are only in their late forties. Looking back at the whole experience, they both feel that their parents selected well for them. I could observe myself the concern that each has for the other. It was not great passion, but it was really a good relationship. The wife was very supportive of her husband's professional work and thus made it possible for him to become one of India's leading psychologists. It makes you wonder if the great passions, which result in great disappointments (more than half the marriages among teenagers in the United States end in divorce), are really preferable.

I can bolster this point with an empirical study reported by Gupta and Singh (1982), who identified fifty couples in Jaipur, India, some of whom had married for love, while the others had married by arrangement. The researchers administered a scale that measured the couple's intensity of being "in love." They found that the couples who married for love were more "in love" *only* during the first five years; they were significantly *less* in love than the couples who had married by arrangement after the fifth year, and the difference was quite large after ten years.

Psychological theory and data have repeatedly found a phenomenon called *regression toward the mean*. If you measure a psychological trait on two occasions and the first value is extreme, the second time you measure the value of the trait it is likely to be closer to the mean of the distribution. In short, it is not surprising that the in-love couples were less in love after several years. However, what is interesting is that the by-arrangement couples surpassed them in the intensity of their feelings after several years.

Don't get me wrong: I don't claim that these data can be replicated in an individualistic culture. The conditions are too different. However, it may be that our marriage arrangements are not necessarily the best. Perhaps we should introduce procedures where the two families get much more involved in marital arrangements than is the case for most American couples at this time.

CULTURE AND SOCIAL DISTANCE

Marriage implies minimal "social distance" (Bogardus, 1925). To study social distance more extensively, we can ask people in different cultures whether they would or would not do something with another person who is described by several attributes. For example, "Would you attend a dinner party given by an unskilled black worker?" Studies done in the 1960s in several countries (e.g., Triandis, Davis, & Takezawa, 1965; Triandis & Triandis, 1960) showed substantial cultural differences.

Specifically, Americans were, at that time, very sensitive to the race of the stimulus. For example, they gave very different responses to the above question when the stimulus was white versus black.

In those early studies, about 60 percent of the variability of the social distance judgments of male students was controlled by race in the United States; the corresponding figure was 6 percent in Germany and 38 percent in Japan. Occupation was most important in Germany; it accounted for 70 percent of the variability; in Japan it was 50 percent and in the United States 22 percent. Religion (e.g., Christian versus Jewish) was more powerful in Germany (12 percent) than in the United States (around 6 percent) and had zero importance in Japan. Nationality was less important for the students in the United States than for the students in Germany (2 percent) and Japan (3+ percent).

Using the same methodology in Canada twenty years later, Dion (1985) found occupation (42 percent), race (9 percent), and nationality (4 percent) effects. The difference between Canada and the United States may be due to the time period when the data were collected, but it may also reflect cultural differences, with Canada accepting the social-class ideology that comes from Britain to a greater extent.

CULTURE AND STEREOTYPES

We have seen in the previous chapters that people think of other groups of people in ways that are shared by members of their culture. We know that the greater the real differences between groups on any particular custom, detail of physical appearance, or item of material culture, the more likely it is that that feature will appear in the stereotyped image each group has of the other (Campbell, 1967, p. 821).

It is important to place this tendency in perspective. Suppose you have a group of people in culture A who wash their hands on average 100 times a day, while people in culture B wash on average 70 times a day. Figure 5-1 shows the frequency distributions. It shows that some people in culture A wash only 80 times a day and some in culture B wash more than 80 times a day. But the central tendencies are clear: 100 versus 70. The important point in this example is that on a worldwide perspective both cultures are extremely clean. But most A's will see B's as "dirty."

In other words, stereotypes are comparative judgments that people *experience* as absolute. Triandis (1972) reported studies of stereotypes that support these conclusions.

An important distinction is between a *normative* stereotype and a *personal* stereotype. In many cases we have no direct knowledge of particular groups of people. For example, did you ever meet an Eskimo? Probably not. Nevertheless, the chances are that you have a stereotype. This is a normative stereotype, i.e., a norm about how to think about Eskimos that exists in your country, influenced by teachers, writers, and others who supposedly know about Eskimos.

Some aspects of a stereotype may be accurate. As we have seen, a stereotype that is accurate is called a *sociotype*. For example, if social research has established that 90 percent of some group have a trait, if we think that a member of that group has that trait, we will be correct 90 percent of the time. In that case we would do better using the sociotype than saying "I know nothing about this person."

Figure 5-2 (taken from Triandis, 1972, p. 113) shows how sociotypes and normative and personal stereotypes are related to each other and are

FIGURE 5–1

Stereotypes are comparative judgments. People in culture A, who wash between 80 and 120 times a day, with an average of 100, are likely to call the superclean people in culture B, who wash "only" 70 times per day, "dirty"! The curves show the frequency distributions in the two hypothetical cultures.

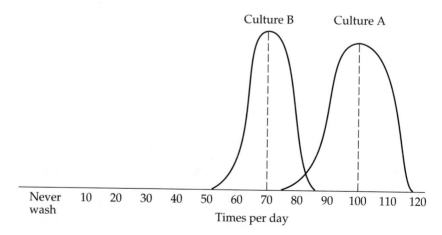

Objectively Clean Cultures

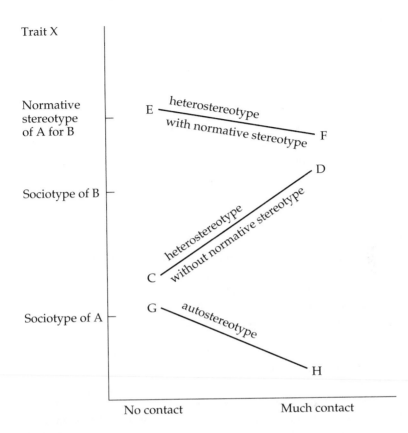

FIGURE 5-2
Theoretical changes in different kinds of stereotypes, as a result of contact.
(Triandis, 1972, p. 113.)

affected by contact. It indicates that if the sociotypes of groups A and B are different, group A is likely to have a normative stereotype that exagge-rates the difference. However, the more contact there is with group B, the more this group will be seen realistically. In short, a heterostereotype with a normative component will change and become like the sociotype.

If there is a friendly relationship between two cultures and the culture of group A does not offer a normative stereotype, then group A is most likely to think that group B is like group A. This assumed similarity between the two groups is usually an error. With more contact, that stereotype also will shift toward the sociotype.

Personal stereotypes are formed from our own experience with the other group. That experience is also likely to be faulty, but as we have more and more contact with that group, it is likely to become a bit more accurate.

Countries differ in their stereotypes as a function of the extent to which their international relations with other countries are positive or negative and the extent to which the other country is seen as dynamic (powerful and active), volatile (excitable), unique, or familiar (Tanaka, 1972).

Finally there is some evidence that the autostereotype is affected by contact. The more contact, the more "contrast" there is with the other group (Triandis & Vassiliou, 1967)—in short, the greater the tendency to see one's own group as different from the other group. This might be expected if we remember that the stereotype is a comparative judgment. The more opportunity we have to notice a difference, the more likely we are to see ourselves as different from the other group.

Sex Stereotypes

In a study of 30 widely situated countries, Williams and Best (1982) measured the sex stereotypes of these samples. They asked their subjects to indicate the typical characteristics of men and women by indicating which of 300 most often used attributes described men and women.

The sex stereotypes were quite similar around the world. The female stereotype was that women are emotional, appreciative, weak, etc.; the male, that men are aggressive, adventurous, independent, etc. Table 5-1 shows the results in more detail.

The attributes of the stereotypes had three aspects: favorability, activity, and strength. These dimensions are the same as the dimensions identified by Osgood et al. (1975) that we discussed in Chapter 4. Table 5-2 indicates whether male or female stereotypes in 25 countries were more or less favorable, active, and strong. It shows that in Japan men are seen more favorably than women. The same is true in Nigeria and South Africa. On the other hand, women are seen more favorably than the men in Australia, Italy, and Peru.

Men are seen as more active and stronger than women in all countries. However, the degree of difference varies from country to country, with Bolivia, Peru, New Zealand, and Scotland showing the greatest differences in activity and with Nigeria, Japan, and South Africa showing the largest differences in strength.

One conclusion from this study: In general, the more developed the country, the less of a difference is found in the stereotypes of men and women.

National and Gender Stereotypes

The stereotypes that people have of particular nationalities are more like the stereotypes of the men of those nationalities than the stereotypes of the women of those nationalities (Eagly & Kite, 1987). This can be explained by the fact that men and women in most cultures have different roles, with the male roles higher in self-assertion and mastery of the

TABLE 5–1 ATTRIBUTES ASSOCIATED WITH "FEMALE" AND WITH "MALE" IN DATA FROM TWENTY-FIVE COUNTRIES

No.	Defining adjective(s)	$\overline{X}F\%$	No.	Defining adjective(s)	$\overline{X}M\%$
1	emotional	.84	2	aggressive, assertive, tough, forceful	.87
4	appreciative	.74	3	adventurous, daring, courageous	.88
5	weak	.83	6	independent	.84
8	talkative	.78	7	disorderly	.76
9	rattlebrained, fickle	.69	10	ambitious, enterprising	.82
12	gentle	.79	11	jolly	.59
13	frivolous	.72	14	cruel	.79
16	fussy, nagging	.68	15	steady, stable, unemotional, unexcitable	.73
17	meek, mild	.76	18	boastful	.77
20	whiny, complaining	.78	19	coarse	.91
21	flirtatious, charming, attractive	.77	22	severe, stern	.83
24	excitable, high-strung	.67	23	loud	.76
25	affectionate	.89	26	dominant, autocratic	.87
28	soft-hearted, sentimental, sensitive	.85	27	confident, self-confident	.78
29	submissive, dependent	.82	30	logical, rational, realistic	.77
32	sophisticated, affected, prudish	.76	31	strong, robust	.89
	Grand $\overline{X}$ = 77.6			Grand $\overline{X}$ = 80.4	

SOURCE: Williams & Best, 1982. Reprinted by permission of Sage Publications, Inc.

TABLE 5–2 MEAN AFFECTIVE MEANING OF THE MALE (M) AND FEMALE (F) STEREOTYPES IN TWENTY-FIVE COUNTRIES

City size	Favorability			Activity			Strength		
	M	F	M-F	M	F	M-F	M	F	M-F
Australia (AUS)	481	509	−28	547	466	81	526	472	54
Bolivia (BOL)	491	505	−14	557	443	114	539	452	87
Brazil (BRA)	484	504	−20	540	450	90	525	458	67
Canada(CAN)	508	497	11	551	461	90	554	459	95
England (ENG)	497	508	−11	547	466	81	539	468	71
Finland (FIN)	495	496	−1	538	470	68	535	461	74
France (FRA)	494	504	−10	518	470	48	512	468	44
Germany (GER)	498	510	−12	536	463	73	532	473	59
India (IND)	492	512	−20	526	462	64	519	464	55
Ireland (IRE)	504	493	11	553	472	81	552	458	94
Israel (ISR)	514	487	27	532	453	79	542	447	95
Italy (ITA)	489	524	−35	537	466	71	516	483	33
Japan (JAP)	551	472	79	540	474	66	577	448	129
Malaysia (MAL)	528	477	51	549	457	92	561	443	118
Netherlands (NET)	511	491	20	539	465	74	544	455	89
New Zealand (NZ)	512	496	16	568	463	105	567	453	114
Nigeria (NIG)	546	469	77	556	451	105	581	439	142
Norway (NOR)	499	488	11	537	462	75	534	453	81
Pakistan (PAK)	505	480	25	547	451	96	539	445	94
Peru (PER)	489	523	−34	544	434	110	524	468	56
Scotland (SCO)	494	516	−22	581	467	114	564	469	95
South Africa (SAF)	542	464	78	549	462	87	572	434	138
Trinidad (TRI)	503	502	1	542	469	73	542	471	71
United States (USA)	495	511	−16	545	474	71	511	475	36
Venezuela (VEN)	496	508	−12	542	471	71	508	463	45

SOURCE: Williams & Best, 1982. Reprinted by permission of Sage Publications, Inc.

environment and the female roles higher in selfless concern for the welfare of others (Eagly & Kite, 1987, p. 451). As a result of this role differentiation, the mass media carry more international information about the activities of men than of women. For instance, those who carry out a domestic role are unlikely to be mentioned by the mass media.

SUMMARY

There are countless cultural differences, many of which are important in understanding social behavior. In this chapter, we touched on only a few.

We examined several examples of variations in subjective culture. Of course, these examples in no way provide a complete picture. But they do give some indication of the way people around the world feel, think, and behave. In the next chapter we will examine some important "building blocks" for constructing social behavior. These building blocks are used more in some cultures than in others, and so they result in additional cultural differences in social behavior.

QUESTIONS AND EXERCISES

1. Find a translation of a paragraph from another language into English or vice versa, and work with someone who is bilingual to evaluate its adequacy. Look for discrepancies from a perfect translation that may reflect some Whorfian phenomena.

2. Interview people who have lived for an extended time in cultures very different from your own. Ask them to give you some examples of cultural differences in attitudes.

3. Follow the directions for exercise 2, but ask for examples of cultural differences in norms.

4. Follow the directions for exercise 2, this time asking for examples of cultural differences in values.

6

Cultural Differences in Patterns of Social Behavior

❖

Exercise ◆ Elementary Forms of Social Behavior ◆ Elementary Forms and Cultural Syndromes ◆ Some Interesting Features of These Four Forms of Social Relations ◆ Elementary Forms and Values ◆ Cultural Syndromes ◆ *Cultural Complexity* ◆ *Tight versus Loose Cultures* ◆ *Individualism-Collectivism* ◆ *Relationships among the Cultural Syndromes* ◆ Summary

W e will start this chapter with an exercise, so you can see how different kinds of elements of subjective culture go together to form the cultural syndromes of individualism and collectivism.

Exercise

Method 1: Self-Concept
In the spaces below please complete the twenty sentences. Answer the question: Who am I? as if giving the answers to yourself, not to someone else. Write your answers in the order in which they occur to you. Do not worry about importance or logic. Go fairly fast.

1. I am _____

2. I am _____

3. I am _____

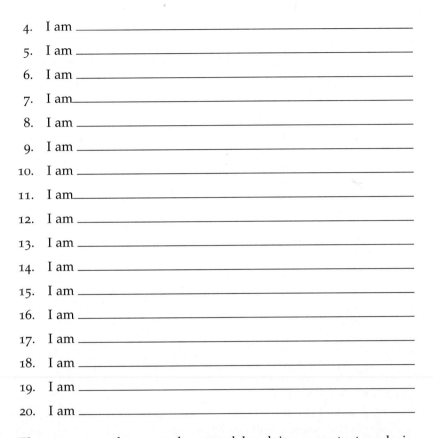

4. I am ⸺
5. I am ⸺
6. I am ⸺
7. I am ⸺
8. I am ⸺
9. I am ⸺
10. I am ⸺
11. I am ⸺
12. I am ⸺
13. I am ⸺
14. I am ⸺
15. I am ⸺
16. I am ⸺
17. I am ⸺
18. I am ⸺
19. I am ⸺
20. I am ⸺

The responses above can be scored by doing a content analysis. Examine each answer, and if it implies a social (S) response (e.g., I am a son = family; I am Catholic = religious group; I am a member of the XYZ Athletic Club = club), score it as S. In analyzing each response, check to see if you share a common fate with others who are members of a social unit. Clearly there is a common fate in those examples. Families, for instance, have a common economic fate. Also, "I am a resident of X" implies common fate (same weather, etc.). On the other hand "I am kind" or "I am happy" is not an S response, because kind people or happy people are not a group, and it is not easy to think of a common fate in those cases. Compute the percent S by noting what percentage of the 20 responses were S responses. Train a friend to code your responses. You and your friend should agree on 90 percent or more of the judgments. If you do not, you have not trained your friend adequately. Take the average S you got from your friend and yourself and use that as the final score for this method. Collectivists have scores in the 20 percent to 50 percent range, while individualists have scores in the zero to 15 percent range. The most common score (mode) of Illinois undergraduates is zero.

Method 2: Attitudes

Please use a scale from 1 = disagree (false) to 9 = agree (true) to indicate your agreement or disagreement with the following statements.

1. I would help within my means if a relative told me that he or she is in financial difficulties.
   False 1 2 3 4 5 6 7 8 9 True

2. When faced with a difficult personal problem, it is better to decide what to do yourself, rather than follow the advice of others.
   False 1 2 3 4 5 6 7 8 9 True

3. I like to live close to my good friends.
   False 1 2 3 4 5 6 7 8 9 True

4. It does not matter to me how my country is viewed in the eyes of other nations.
   False 1 2 3 4 5 6 7 8 9 True

5. One of the pleasures of life is to be related interdependently with others.
   False 1 2 3 4 5 6 7 8 9 True

6. What happens to me is my own doing.
   False 1 2 3 4 5 6 7 8 9 True

7. What I look for in a job is a friendly group of coworkers.
   False 1 2 3 4 5 6 7 8 9 True

8. I would rather struggle though a personal problem by myself than discuss it with my friends.
   False 1 2 3 4 5 6 7 8 9 True

9. Aging parents should live at home with their children.
   False 1 2 3 4 5 6 7 8 9 True

10. The most important thing in my life is to make myself happy.
    False 1 2 3 4 5 6 9 8 9 True

11. When faced with a difficult personal problem, one should consult one's friends and relatives widely.
    False 1 2 3 4 5 6 7 8 9 True

12. One should live one's life independently of others as much as possible.
    False 1 2 3 4 5 6 7 8 9 True

13. One of the pleasurers of life is to feel being part of a large group of people.
    False 1 2 3 4 5 6 7 8 9 True

14. I tend to do my own things, and most people in my family do the same.
    False 1 2 3 4 5 6 7 8 9 True

It is obvious that the odd-numbered items are collectivist and the even-numbered items are individualistic. To get a collectivist score, add your answers to the odd-numbered items together and then average them. Add and average your even-numbered answers to get an individualistic score.

Method 3: Values
In the questionnaire below, you are to ask yourself: "What values are important to *me* as guiding principles in *my* life, and what values are less important to me?" Rate the values on a scale from −1 to 7, where −1 means you reject the value, zero (0) indicates a value that is not at all important, and 7 means that the value is of supreme importance. You can use a rating of 7 only once.

Begin by reading all the values.* Decide (a) if you want to reject one or two of them and (b) to which value you are going to give a 7. Then, in the blanks below, fill in your low and your high scores (1, 2, and 5, 6, 7) and finally your 3, 4 responses.

1. _____ National security (protection of my nation from enemies)

2. _____ Freedom (my own freedom of action and thought)

3. _____ Family security (safety for loved ones)

4. _____ An exciting life (stimulating experiences)

5. _____ Honoring parents and elders (showing respect)

6. _____ A varied life (enjoyment of variety)

7. _____ Obedient (dutiful, meeting obligations)

8. _____ Choosing own goals (self-direction)

9. _____ Self-disciplined (self-restraint, resistance to temptation)

10. _____ Independent (doing my own thing)

It is obvious that the odd-numbered items are collectivist and the even-numbered are individualistic. Add the corresponding responses to get two separate scores.

The findings from these three methods tend to converge. That is, people who are collectivists have high percent S, interdependent attitudes, and interdependent values. The next step is to put the information from the three methods together. Here is how you can do that.

---

* These values are taken from a questionnaire consisting of fifty-six values developed by Schwartz, 1992.

Method 1

We have studied people in many countries, and we have some idea of how people respond to the first method. If your percent S is less than 10 percent, you are likely to be an individualist; if it is more than 30 percent, you are probably a collectivist. Let us convert your percent S score to a simpler score that reflects how collectivist you are.

Your % S is	Your score is	What the score means
Zero to 10	1	It is almost certain that you are an individualist.
11to17	2	You are probably an individualist.
18 to 22	3	This measure does not tell us what you are.
23 to 30	4	You are probably a collectivist.
More than 30	5	It is almost certain that you are a collectivist.

Methods 2 and 3

Consider your collectivism score and your individualism score on each scale. If one is high and the other is low, that means you are probably average in both attributes. Remember that every person has both tendencies, but many individuals are high in both, others are low in both, and only some individuals are clearly individualistic or collectivist. Look for consistency among the three methods to get a clue about who you are.

More importantly, ask yourself whether you "cheated" when you answered the questions above. If you cheated in the individualistic direction, your culture is pushing you in that direction; if you cheated in the collectivist direction, your culture is pushing you in that direction. This last insight is the most important one from this exercise.

I n the previous two chapters we examined the influence of culture on different elements of subjective culture, such as categorization, stereotypes, and values, and suggested how behaviors are related to subjective culture. This chapter describes how cultures differ by combining several aspects of subjective culture to form unique configurations.

Subjective culture includes *some* of the basic elements that cause social behavior. Many of these elements go together forming patterns of beliefs, attitudes, norms, values, and social behaviors that have been called "elementary forms of social behavior" (Fiske, 1990, 1992). These elementary forms of social behavior, in turn, combine to form cultural syndromes, such as individualism. Cultural syndromes are clustered into very broad attributes of culture, such as traditionalism or modernity (Inkeles & Smith, 1974).

E LEMENTARY FORMS OF SOCIAL BEHAVIOR

In every culture people have unique ways of sampling the elements of their subjective culture to *construct* their social behavior. Let us take one example. A person receives a gift. How will she respond? She is likely to consider who the giver is, what norms are operating (e.g., reciprocity), and what the situation is and then use the elementary forms of social behavior to guide her decision. If the giver is a long-time friend, there will be pressure to reciprocate, even if she has little money; she has to *share* what she has. If the giver is very rich compared with her, she might say, "Thank you very much. I appreciate your generosity," and not reciprocate; *hierarchy* allows nonsymmetric behavior on her part in some cultures. But in other cultures *equality* is important, and she would feel pressure to return a gift of about equal value; in still other cultures the recipient calculates a *proportion* as a guide for behavior. These four basic ideas, *sharing, hierarchy, equality,* and *proportion,* define the four elementary forms of social behavior identified by Fiske (1990, 1992). Exactly which form is to be used in reaction to a gift depends on the culture and the situation.

Fiske (1990, 1992) used these names for the elementary forms: communal sharing, authority ranking, equality matching, and market pricing. Let us review them in more detail.

1. *Communal sharing (CS).* This is the sort of social behavior that goes on in families in most cultures. Usually, when resources are available in a family, people *share* them according to their need. There are many cultures where land is owned "by everyone" and used "as needed." In our own culture, parks are for everyone's use. The essence of this social behavior pattern is *sharing by all those who belong to the group according to need.* (See Figure 6-1.)

2. *Authority ranking (AR).* In this elementary form, people pay attention to status and divide according to *rank.* For example, in the traditional Chinese family, the grandfather gets the food he wants first; then the other males of the family choose, in descending order of age; and finally the females of the family in descending order of age get what is left.

   In this cultural pattern the youngest females eat only if there is enough food. The essence of this behavior pattern is rank and hierarchy. The higher your rank in the group, the more you get. We see such patterns in our culture as well. For example, if the resource is "attention," the President of the United States gets a lot more than you or I. In fact, he gets more than he wants.

3. *Equality matching (EM).* In this situation reciprocity—tit for tat—is emphasized. People do not share according to what they need, or according to status, but they share *equally.* When this pattern is

FIGURE 6–1

Two girls in front of the image of a god, in Nepal. The custom is for the worshipers to offer quite a lot of food to the god, but take most of it home to eat. A small amount is left at the feet of the god, and it is understood that any member of the community may eat it. Thus, nothing is wasted and everyone is blessed. The two girls eagerly anticipate that someone will bring a good offering so that they can eat. In many community-sharing cultures, food is left in sacred places for anyone to eat it. (Roy Malpass.)

used, it is bad form for one person to get even a spoonful more than the others. One way to be sure that things are correctly divided is for one person to do the dividing and for the others to choose their share first. The essence of this behavior pattern is *equality* and equal sharing. When land was divided in the western United States, each parcel of land had to be equal. We also use this idea when we talk about equality of opportunity or equality of outcomes.

4. *Market pricing (MP).* In this social behavior pattern you receive something you want in exchange for something you give. In addition to money, you can give other resources, such as love, status, information, goods, services, labor, or time. The key feature of this form is that the *more you give*, or contribute, *the more you get.* For example, the more you invest, the more interest you receive from the investment. The essence of this social pattern is *proportionality.*

In any culture, all four social orientations can be used in the same situation, but in each culture they are likely to be given different emphases. Let us consider what happens at a party in the West. Usually, guests are allowed to eat or drink as much as they like (CS). Some resources, however, such as the party-goers' attention, may depend on rank. For example, at a company party, when the chief executive officer (CEO) comes in, chances are that most of the participants will give the floor (AR) to the CEO, who makes some remarks, cracks some jokes, and leaves. Now think of what happens at the party when some very rare wine is opened. Then, unless there are some teetotalers at the gathering, each guest asks for an equal share (EM). Finally, suppose one of the guests is selling shares in a gold mine. He tells the other guests about the great opportunity to become rich by investing in this mine. Each guest buys a few shares; the more money the guests give, the more shares they get (MP).

Thus you can observe all four behavioral patterns at a party. In no-money cultures there is very little market pricing; in industrialized cultures there is much market pricing. The environment, or situation, determines which behavioral pattern will be emphasized. Specifically, at Western family and social events there tends to be much communal sharing of food and drink, little authority ranking, quite a lot of equality matching (the cake is cut more or less equally), and very little market pricing (it is the ultimate faux pas to tip the hostess!).

But if the party is a benefit auction, the emphasis on market pricing will increase dramatically. In such a case, for instance, there is likely to be a "cash bar" (MP), those who have the most money receive special treatment (more AR), and there is less equality matching.

In each culture each institution has its own profile of emphases on the four orientations. For example, consider the institution of marriage. It is customary in some cultures to marry a person for love (CS), in others to marry a person who has status (AR), in others to marry a person who is equal in every respect (EM), and in still others to marry a person who offers the highest bride price or dowry (MP).

Fiske argues that people *construct* their social behavior by combining these four models in various ways depending on the social situation. Each culture has unique ways of using each of the four patterns. Thus, the patterns are etic; the content of the patterns is emic. For example, in one culture market pricing is done with money, in another with cows, and in still another with medals (objects that give honor but have no special value).

E LEMENTARY FORMS AND CULTURAL SYNDROMES

When we analyze cultures, we see that in collectivist cultures people use communal sharing and authority ranking more frequently than equality matching or market pricing, while in individualistic cultures the opposite pattern prevails. However, the four forms of social relations are independent of each other, because there are a few cultures that use communal sharing and equality matching most of the time and in most situations, and there are others that use market pricing and authority ranking most of the time and in most situations.

Fiske assumes that in *any* situation one can use any one of the four forms. Note, for instance, that although the United States is an individualistic culture and uses market pricing in more situations than other cultures do, the cultural ideal for marriage is communal sharing. Marrying for money is frowned upon. Paradoxically, collectivist cultures use communal sharing in many more situations than do individualistic cultures, but when it comes to marriage, they often use market pricing.

SOME INTERESTING FEATURES OF THESE FOUR FORMS OF SOCIAL RELATIONS

People organize information about other people by placing them in categories that correspond to the four social relationships just described. In other words, we think of people with whom we share, whom we obey, with whom we are equal, or with whom we have contractual, formal arrangements. This was demonstrated in a study by Fiske, Haslam, and Fiske (1991), who showed that the social errors that people make, like calling someone by the wrong name, can be explained, in part, by the fact that they use cognitive structures (schemas) that reflect these relationships.

In homes, CS is the most important behavior pattern, but that does not mean that some of the other patterns will not be used, such as a father's paying his son to mow the lawn (MP) and children's accepting the decisions of the parents (AR). It rather means that in family life CS "feels right" and MP does not.

The important thing about culture is that it creates unstated assumptions about the *desirability* of one or another of these forms of human relationships in different types of situations. For example, in collectivist cultures CS and AR are valued more than EM and MP. Thus, there is a tendency to shift the definition of relationships in the CS and AR direction, even if the behavior might best be carried out in EM or MP terms.

Traditional Japan is collectivist, and thus many modern Japanese find it offensive to jump into a bargaining session without knowing a great deal about their customers or buyers. Of course, in time-conscious modern Japan, more and more transactions follow the MP pattern, but for really important transactions it is necessary first to do a lot of CS and AR and only later to do MP. Note that this is sometimes true in the United States as well, and so the cultural difference is a matter of degree.

Kitayama (personal communication) makes the point that in Japan the most comfortable form of social interaction is CS, so that even interactions that are not appropriate for this form of social relationship are *transformed* in that direction.

Interactions that are normally CS become MP in individualistic cultures. For example, parents may pay their children to do a job for them; or before getting married, a couple might sign a contract specifying how to divide their property in the event of a divorce. In collectivist cultures that behavior would be truly unthinkable.

Thus, what we see is that in individualistic cultures more and more interactions are varieties of MP, while in collectivist cultures most interactions are shaped into a CS form.

E LEMENTARY FORMS AND VALUES

The four Fiske basic orientations have some relationships with the value structures identified in Hofstede's (1980) monumental study. Hofstede analyzed the responses that IBM employees gave to a values questionnaire developed by that corporation. The survey was conducted twice, in 1968 and 1972, producing a total of 116,000 questionnaires. The respondents were diverse in nationality, occupation within IBM, age, and sex. Four dimensions were extracted by analyzing statistically (using factor analysis) the way the respondents answered the value questions.

1. *Power distance*—reflects the tendency to see a large distance between those in the upper part of a social structure and those in the lower part of that structure. It corresponds very closely to Fiske's authority ranking.

2. *Uncertainty avoidance*—reflects the avoidance of situations where the outcome is uncertain. Cultures high in communal sharing often have very clear norms for proper behavior in social situations and avoid new situations with no clear norms. However, the relationship of this factor to Fiske's system is not very close.

3. *Individualism*—is very closely linked to Fiske's market pricing.

4. *Masculinity*—does not seem to have a relationship with Fiske's orientations. It refers to the tendency of members of the culture to value activities that are more common among men than women.

Figure 6-2 shows the location of Hofstede's national samples on the individualism and power distance factors. It is clear from the way the countries are located in this figure that the two dimensions are correlated. In fact, the correlation was almost .7, indicating that in that sample of countries collectivism is associated with large power distance. The most collectivist high-power-distance countries were Venezuela, several other Latin American countries, the Philippines, and Yugoslavia. The opposite pattern, individualism and low power distance, was found in the English-

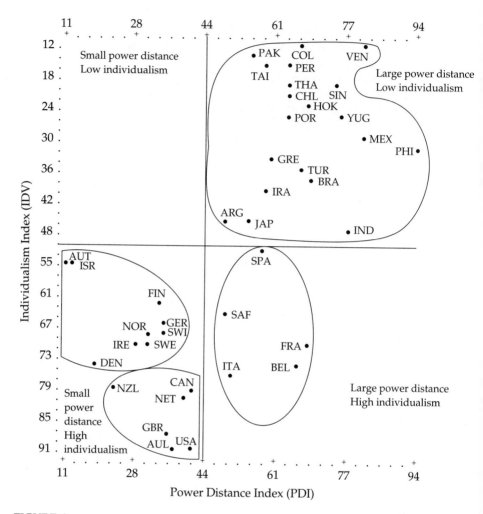

FIGURE 6–2

The location of countries on "individualism" and "power distance," as reported by Hofstede (1980, p. 223). Venezuela, Mexico, the Philippines, and Yugoslavia were high on both variables; the Scandinavian countries, Austria, and Israel were very low on power distance and moderately high on individualism. The English-speaking countries were very high on individualism and moderately low on power distance. The European Latin-based-language countries were moderately high on power distance and individualism. (Hofstede, 1980. Reprinted by permission of Sage Publications, Inc.)

speaking countries and in Scandinavia, Austria, and Israel. Countries high in power distance, but individualistic, were Spain, France, South Africa, Italy, and Belgium—for the most part, industrial Roman Catholic countries.

Figure 6-3 shows the other two Hofstede dimensions. Here the Scandinavian countries were low in uncertainty avoidance and masculinity. The Chinese were low in uncertainty avoidance and moderate on masculinity. The English-speaking countries tended toward masculinity and low uncertainty avoidance; the majority of the Asian countries, except Japan, were not high on either attribute. Japan was high on both dimensions. The countries of the Mediterranean and their culture descendants in Latin America were high in uncertainty avoidance.

In short, the Hofstede study found relationships between geography and value patterns. This is consistent with the notion that there are culture areas, as we discussed in Chapter 2. Hofstede also identified at

FIGURE 6–3
The location of the countries on "uncertainty avoidance" and "masculinity," as reported by Hofstede (1980, p. 324). The Scandinavian countries were feminine and low in uncertainty avoidance; Japan and Greece were masculine and high in uncertainty avoidance. The English-speaking countries were high in masculinity and low in uncertainty avoidance; Yugoslavia, Portugal, and Chile were high in uncertainty avoidance and low in masculinity. (Hofstede, 1980. Reprinted by permission of Sage Publications, Inc.)

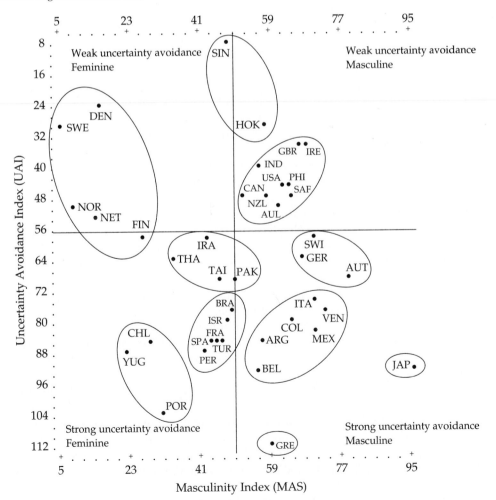

least two dimensions that have much in common with Fiske's orientations.

As noted above, the elementary forms are related to the cultural syndromes. Next we are going to take a closer look at the content of the cultural syndromes and see what kinds of cultural elements they contain.

CULTURAL SYNDROMES

Cultural Complexity

Human and cultural evolution have gone in the direction of increased complexity. For 99 percent of the time that members of the genus *Homo* have lived on this planet, the typical methods of survival were based on hunting and food gathering. Some of the nonliterate tribes that still survive in remote corners of the earth, as well as today's nomadic peoples, represent this most important period of human evolution. These groups are relatively simple in their social organization. Archaeological evidence suggests that such bands usually consisted of fewer than forty adults, and the number of relationships among forty individuals is small.

The next major stage was the development of agriculture, which allowed humans to settle permanently in particular locations. This change represented a major increase in cultural complexity. Villages of several hundred and towns and cities of several thousand characterized this phase of evolution. Of course, the number of potential relationships among thousands of people is already very large. Ancient Rome, with about a million people, was enormously complex.

Next, with the industrial revolution, population density increased, and very large cities emerged. Today, Mexico City with about 22 million people, represents enormous complexity.

Students of complexity (e.g., Carneiro, 1970; Lomax & Berkowitz, 1972; Murdock & Provost, 1973) have used several indexes. They have been able to obtain reliable rank orders of cultures by considering such variables as the development of writing and the existence of records, fixity of residence, agriculture, urban settlements, technical specializations, land transportation other than walking, money, high population densities, many levels of political integration, and many levels of social stratification. Cultures that have all these attributes, such as ancient Rome, fifth-century B.C. China, and modern industrial age societies, were on the top of the complexity scale.

In complex cultures, people make large numbers of distinctions among objects and events in their environment. For example, the number of distinct occupations reflects complexity. There are over a quarter of a million occupations in modern industrial cultures (see *The Dictionary of Occupational Titles*), while nonliterate cultures may have barely twenty. With that many potential jobs, an individual needs vocational counselors and "headhunter" consulting firms to find an optimal job. Complexity in religious functions is another clue. For instance, there are about 6000 priests in one temple in Orissa, India, each of whom has a different responsibility.

Even more complexity is observed when we examine the so-called information societies. We note that enormous masses of information are stored in computers. Analysts have access to huge data banks linking them to all parts of the world. These cultures use extremely complex systems of information (e.g., 5000 parts that make a car) and scientific/theoretical constructs (e.g., modern physics) that integrate large amounts of information.

We can learn a lot about ourselves by examining life in some of the simpler cultures. Lee and DeVore (1976) describe one of them: the !Kung (the ! stands for a click sound; put your tongue on the roof of your mouth and say quickly "ung"). Among the !Kung children are encouraged to share things with others (CS), even when they are very young. At the same time equality (EM) is encouraged, and strict obedience to parental authority is considered neither necessary nor desirable (low AR). The relationship between the sexes is not equal; men have more status, which they impose because they have more strength, but it is not as unequal as in some of the Muslim countries.

Among the !Kung, storytelling is a great art, and most old men are very good at it. An important topic of discussions is hunting techniques. The !Kung have advanced abilities to observe and assemble facts about animal behavior and to discriminate facts from hearsay. They are able to develop hypotheses about why animals behave the way they do and to improve their thinking about hunting as they go along. However, they do not teach each other very much. People have to learn for themselves.

When the !Kung are in conflict, they tend to talk it out instead of resorting to force. They dread fighting, and when fighting occurs, it is an event to be discussed and remembered for a long time. Talking keeps communication going, allows the expression of emotions, and is the basis of social discipline.

Talk is about every detail of daily life: the comings and goings of relatives, places to find food, past and future hunts, and those women who are especially quick and able food gatherers.

There is much borrowing and lending, but no stealing. Individuals never live alone. They are always in the company of others. Resources belong to the band and are distributed by it. Thus, an individual cannot exist outside the group. There is much touching and sitting close together. Yet kindness, sympathy, and genuine generosity are not common, though they do occur. Remember, these are subsistence cultures; people who can barely manage to get enough to eat to survive do not have the resources to be very altruistic.

Gift giving is very important and is followed by lengthy discussions of who gave what to whom and how soon it was reciprocated. Bursts of laughter accompany these conversations when the group concludes that the exchange was inappropriate or the reciprocation was poorly timed.

Men and women do not discuss sexual matters openly, nor do they speak the names of gods aloud, fearing that they might attract their displeasure.

When meeting strangers, good manners require laying down weapons and approaching unarmed. Visitors are received courteously and are invited to sit by the fire. Guests refrain from eating too much at one time. Both hands are used in receiving food or a gift; using just one hand suggests "grabbing." You do not say "no" directly, but indirectly. Emotional expression is not considered polite, and people manage to control their emotions to a considerable degree. Most of these behaviors remind us of the behaviors in collectivist cultures.

Meat sharing is a way to keep stress and hostility at low levels. The practical value of sharing is obvious to all. Reciprocity is widely practiced. Animals too small to share belong to the person who killed them. Large animals belong to the first person whose arrow penetrated the animal. That person is responsible for arranging the sharing. Everyone who receives meat shares it in turn with relatives, so that eventually the whole band benefits from the hunt, and there are few reasons for jealousy. Note the functional basis of CS in this setting: Everyone eats.

Gift giving consists of giving ordinary objects, and there is no trading, which the !Kung consider undignified. Asking for a gift is within the rules of propriety, as is asking that a return gift be made. If a person wants an object he or she may ask for it. That can be a problem for the visitor. I found that in this type of culture people often ask for my pen, because it sticks out from my breast pocket. Unless I have a large supply of pens, I can find myself without the means of keeping notes!

Thus we see in this description that the !Kung exhibit both individualistic elements, such as equality and self-reliance, and many collectivist elements, such as interdependence, sharing, and gift giving. On the whole, the collectivist elements are more numerous than the individualistic.

The ecology and history of a society determine its complexity. Societies that subsist on hunting, fishing, and food gathering tend to be simple; agricultural societies tend to be somewhat complex; industrial societies tend to be more complex; information societies are the most complex.

Family structures tend to be related to complexity by an inverted U-shaped function (Blumberg & Winch, 1972). Simple cultures emphasize nuclear families; complex cultures are characterized by extended families; very complex and extremely complex cultures use nuclear families again. The phenomenon of many households with only one parent and several children has become common in North America but is rare in hunting, food-gathering, or agricultural societies.

In nuclear families there is less regimentation and less emphasis on obedience, while exploration and creativity are encouraged. Extended families insist on obedience and are more organized around rules than are nuclear families.

In a review of the relevant hologeistic studies (that use the culture as the unit of analysis), Ember and Levinson (1991) conclude that the contrast between simpler and more complex cultures is the most important factor of cultural variations in social behavior. Associated with higher complexity are settlement size, level of political integration, population density, and more complex social stratification. Among preliterate people high complexity implies "more compliance and physical punishment in childhood, more restriction on premarital sexual behaviors, relatively lower status of women, warfare for political control, and more military sophistication. Furthermore, much of the expressive realm of culture (art, music, dance, games, religion) is strongly related to societal complexity" (p. 110).

Tight versus Loose Cultures

When I was in Japan in the summer of 1990, I read an account in the English language *Japan Times* about a startling event. A teacher slammed a heavy door on the head of a student who was two minutes late for class, killing her.

The discussion in the press was clearly ambivalent. While editorial writers were horrified by the event, they also showed some "understanding" of the teacher, who was trying to teach his students to be on time—a very important value in Japan. Note that the schoolgirl's "crime" was being two minutes late. In the United States few people would be punished for this, though they might be punished for exceptional tardiness.

Japan is a tight culture. People are expected to behave according to norms, and deviation from norms is likely to be punished. Some Japanese with whom I discussed the schoolgirl's death said that the teacher was "deranged." However, we must remember that psychopathology is an exaggeration of what is normal in a culture (Draguns, 1990). The culture has to provide the "theme" for the deranged person to act upon.

In the United States the culture is loose, and deviation from norms is tolerated much more than in Japan. Some would say we are too tolerant of deviation. The extraordinarily high homicide rate in the United States can partly be interpreted as the consequence of a loose culture. The culture provides the "theme" of killing in a myriad of TV images. Themes of uncontrolled, unpunished behaviors play themselves out across the movie screen (car chases, physical violence, destruction of property). One of the better theories of criminal behavior (Gottfredson & Hirschi, 1990) uses as its key concept *self-control*. It is very likely that self-control and impulse control are learned better in a tight than in a loose culture.

Tight cultures (Pelto, 1968) have clear norms that are reliably imposed. Little deviation from normative behavior is tolerated, and severe sanctions are administered to those who deviate. Loose cultures either have unclear norms or tolerate deviance from norms. Theocracies are prototypic tight cultures, but some contemporary homogeneous, relatively self-contained cultures (e.g., traditional Greeks, the Japanese) also tend to be high in tightness (Hofstede, 1980).

When I was ten years old, I spent a month in a Greek convent, at the invitation of a nun who had worked in my grandmother's house. Everyone got up, ate, prayed, and went to sleep at the same time. Deviation from the schedule was unthinkable. That is a tight culture.

In heterogeneous, pluralistic cultures, such as the United States, it is more difficult for people to agree on specific norms, and even more difficult to impose severe sanctions. Geographic mobility allows people to leave the offended community; urban environments are more loose than rural ones.

Prototypic loose cultures are the Lapps of northern Sweden and the Thais. Loose cultures are often found at the intersections of major distinct cultures that are rather different from each other (e.g., Thailand is between the massive cultures of India and China), are surrounded by a very different culture, are pluralistic, as is the United States, or are very low in population density (deserts, the arctic). Looseness is based on conflicting norms or is traceable to norms that are not especially functional. If the next human band is 50 miles away, there is no point developing elaborate norms for interacting with it.

In short, certain factors appear to lead to tightness. Cultural homogeneity (similarity among people) leads to agreement about what is correct behavior. Isolation from other cultural influences increases the importance of this variable. Population density makes clear that norms are highly functional and keep people from bumping into each other. They are like the rules of the road. If you are the only driver, you can drive on either the right or left side; if there is a lot of traffic, you had better stick to the normative side. Finally, in cultures where there is much need for coordinated action, such as in agricultural ones, norms are likely to be imposed more strictly.

Conversely, cultural heterogeneity, strong influences from other cultures, and much space between people (for example, the Lapps) can lead to looseness. If individuals are exposed to different cultures, they may decide that no norm is necessarily "correct" and become loose in following norms. In addition, if occupations permit much solitary action, such as hunting and gathering or writing a book, norms may be weak and loosely imposed.

There is also some relationship with climate: very warm climates appear to favor looseness, while cultures in cold climates are tight (Robbins, deWalt, and Pelto, 1972). One interpretation of this relationship is that *Homo sapiens* evolved in warm climates and adjusted more naturally to these conditions. Adjustment to cold climates required more "control" of self and others, and tighter regulations ensured that food resources were used optimally. Greater control of self may result in the higher suicide rates found in tight societies, but in loose societies we find more homicides (Robbins, deWalt, & Pelto, 1972, p. 338).

In very tight cultures, according to Pelto (1968), one finds corporate control of property, corporate ownership of stored food and production power, strong religious leaders, hereditary recruitment into the priesthood, and high levels of taxation. Such relationships suggest that tightness is correlated with collectivism (corporate control).

Tightness is especially high in Japan, where the Confucian teachings, the island geography, and cultural homogeneity favor it. Many of the Confucian teachings emphasize "correct action." There are rules, norms, customs to be observed. People cannot be allowed to do their own thing, whether that is jaywalking (see Figures 6-4 and 6-5) or arriving late to class.

In Japan conformity to age-appropriate norms is very high. It is seen as "the safest protection from criticism and eliminates the need to make personal judgments and errors which can bring quite devasting social

FIGURE 6–4

There is no jaywalking in Japan. One can see a tight culture. (Triandis, in M. E. Meyer, Ed., 1979. Reprinted by permission of Oxford University Press.)

FIGURE 6–5
There is jaywalking in India. On that attribute India is loose. (Triandis.)

consequences (Iwao, 1993, p. 23). In general, in a tight culture if you do what everyone else is doing, you will be protected from criticism.

Tightness is more likely when the norms are clear. This requires a relatively homogeneous culture. The existence of dissimilar norms for a particular situation leads people to take the initiative in deciding whether and which norms are to be observed. Such dissimilar norms are most likely when the culture is heterogeneous or is at the intersection of two or more important cultural traditions.

We must also note that tightness has some desirable consequences. Tokyo is one of the safest cities in the world. Women can walk at night without fear. Its size is comparable to that of New York, but the homicide rate is a fraction of that in New York.

Also, maintaining high quality in manufacturing can be seen as "natural" in a tight culture. The other side of the argument is that in tight cultures people are criticized for minor deviations from proper behavior. A Japanese child is likely to be criticized for bringing Western food for lunch; a high school student might be criticized for getting a permanent; hair length and color and speech patterns must conform to the norms (Kidder, 1992). "It was really hard," said a returning Japanese student, "because I looked different and I talked different. My hair was kind of light colored from all the sun, and my skin had a tan. And so when people looked at me they didn't think I was a real Japanese" (p. 385).

There is much tightness in Japan about crossing against red lights and jaywalking. My friend John Adamopoulos was chased for two blocks by an angry Japanese who saw him cross against a red light on a deserted street. But although the culture is tight in most situations, there are several exceptions. For example, people are permitted much deviation from norms if they are drunk or mentally ill or are foreigners (do not know better).

In loose cultures, sanctions are generally not as severe when the norm applies only to some people (e.g., unmarried adults living together) or is informal. Conversely, in tight cultures even informal norms that apply only to some people are generally followed, and sanctions are applied when they are broken.

The United States is a relatively loose culture, but it is not as loose as traditional Thailand. As reported by Phillips (1965), who lived in Thailand for a time, relationship of an employer and an employee may be broken off over matters that have nothing to do with either contract obligations or job satisfaction. An employee may become bored, have a sudden desire to take a trip, or, if he is from another village, just be homesick (p. 77). He may quit without saying a word to the employer. His absence is sufficient to indicate the termination of the relationship.

The longer Phillips lived in Thailand, the more obvious it was to him that social behavior there is characterized by lack of regularity, discipline, neatness, or regimentation. There was no administrative regularity and no sense that one had "work hours."

Psychologically the Thais were ready, at that time, to separate themselves from others. In face-to-face situations there were expressions of responsiveness, cooperation, and compliance, but once the situation changed, they did exactly what they enjoyed most.

Phillips reported that Thai villagers basically do not believe that people are predictable. Those who do not believe in predictability will not find it. They see life as a series of accidents.

In that setting, social behavior is made highly unpredictable by the very assumptions used about it. Nevertheless, most people live together as a family, "for more or less sustained periods of time, fathers do save for years in order to give their sons respectable ordinations into the monkshood, relatives and friends who have not seen each other since childhood do assemble for cremation of a late kinsman or mutual friend, and mature adults do continue to feel a profound sense of respect and obligation to individuals who were their teachers when they were youngsters" (Phillips, 1965, p. 91). The fact that the ethnographer mentions as remarkable such points of predictability reflects the unpredictability of the culture.

Typical is the view that these villagers are "free and autonomous individuals, who in a relatively opportunistic way make use of the available channels of social participation and the rewards that are attached to them" (Phillips, 1965, p. 204) to maximize their self-interest by disregarding many norms.

Phillips says that after living in Thailand for several months, "I began to wonder not about the Thai capacity to maintain loosely structured relations but about the considerably more mystifying American capacity to conform to the expectations of others" (Phillips, 1965, p. 204).

One of the major advantages of tightness is that people know what they are supposed to do and how they are supposed to behave in every important situation. For example, an Indian wedding is a very elaborate event that takes several days, and each "player" has a precise script to follow. As well, rules specify which members of the extended family are expected to contribute to the dowry. For example, the woman's maternal uncle is expected to contribute a substantial gift (usually jewelry). While there are rules in loose cultures as well, they tend to be vague. Giving jewelry commensurate with your wealth and status in the community is at a different level from consulting the bridal registry for gift ideas.

Individualism-Collectivism

Recent research has suggested that there are two kinds of collectivism: One emphasizes interdependence and oneness and might be called *horizontal*; the other emphasizes serving the group and might be called *vertical*. The two aspects of collectivism are correlated (in the .3 to .4 range in most studies). The first is very similar to Fiske's communal sharing; the second to his authority ranking.

People in individualistic cultures often give priority to their personal goals, even when they conflict with the goals of important in-groups, such as the family, tribe, work group, or fellow countrymen. Conversely, people in collectivist cultures give priority to in-group goals, and this is especially important among vertical collectivists.

In-groups become salient in situations where common fate is clearly seen by in-group members. In-groups are also determined by similarities in important attributes, proximity, and common threat by outsiders. Certain situations, e.g., emergencies, increase the salience of common fate and hence the importance of in-groups as regulators of behavior.

In collectivist cultures the self is defined in terms of membership in in-groups which influence a wide range of social behaviors.

Collectivists often, but not always (Billings, 1989), are organized hierarchically, and tend to (1) be concerned about the results of their actions on members of their in-group, (2) share resources with in-group members, (3) feel interdependent with in-group members, and (4) feel involved in the lives of in-group members (Hui & Triandis, 1986). They feel strongly about the integrity of their in-groups (Triandis, Bontempo, et al., 1986). Individualists are emotionally detached from their in-groups and emphasize self-reliance, independence, pleasure, and the pursuit of happiness.

Distribution of Syndromes
Individualism is very high in the United States and generally high in the English-speaking countries (Hofstede, 1980). It has been studied with both historical (Inkeles, 1983) and empirical (Bellah, Madsen, Sullivan, Swidler, & Tipton, 1985) methods. Collectivism can be found in parts of Europe (e.g., southern Italy, rural Greece) and much of Africa, Asia, and Latin America. A detailed comparison of Canada and the United States by Lipset (1990) shows that Canada is somewhat less individualistic and somewhat more collectivist than the United States, in spite of the extreme similarity of the two cultures.

Antecedents of Individualism
A major antecedent of individualism is affluence. Financial independence leads to social independence. However, extreme economic deprivation is also associated with individualism (Scheper-Hughes, 1985). The upper social classes and the more educated segments of a society tend to be more individualistic (Daab, 1991). In addition, migrations, social mobility, and urban residence increase individualism. The more complex the culture, the more individualistic it is, because in complex cultures a person has the choice of becoming a member of various groups.

Attributes of Individualists and Collectivists
The behavior of individualists tends to be friendly but nonintimate toward a wide range of people outside the family. However, there is a fair amount of competition (Sullivan, Peterson, Kameda, & Shimada, 1981) in individualistic cultures, sometimes even within the family.

The behavior of collectivists tends to be self-sacrificing toward in-group members and generally exploitative toward out-group members. Even if the in-group is not exploitative, it is formal toward outsiders, and when resources are scarce, it can become quite nasty.

When collectivists meet a potential new friend, their behavior remains "correct" for a considerable amount of time, but if they share resources, it becomes quite intimate. To repeat this important point: Collectivists behave quite differently depending on whether the other person is a member of their in-group or is out-group. If the other is an in-group member, the behavior is very associative, and in some cases it reflects self-sacrifice; if the other is an out-group member, the behavior is indifferent or dissociative. Individualists do not switch their behavior dramatically when an out-group member becomes an in-group member: collectivists do.

How you are likely to be greeted in an office in Athens, Greece, provides an interesting example of collectivist switching. Traditional Greece is collectivist, and many Athens secretaries are women from that traditional background. When you call a typical office, you often get a rather curt "What do you want?" I have relatives and friends there, and when I call their office, I am always amused by the rudeness of the first contact. But when I say "I am Harry Triandis, your boss's cousin (or friend)," the switch is dramatic. "How *lovely* to hear your voice" is the typical response!

Similarly, individualists do not show extremes of superordinate or subordinate behavior, while collectivists do. The latter show much more subordination to in-group authorities and superordination toward out-group members than do individualists (Triandis, McCusker, & Hui, 1990).

Many of the ways that distinguish collectivists and individualists are summarized in Table 6-1. You can think of all the contrasts in the table by remembering the fable of the blind men each touching a different side of an elephant. They are talking about the same thing but emphasize a different aspect of the phenomenon. However, also remember that there are a very large number of collectivist and individualistic patterns. A culture may be collectivist if its members behave according to some subset of the ways described in the left column, but different subsets will be sampled in different cultures. We need to do much more research before we know how to match each culture with each subset. The same argument applies to individualism.

TABLE 6–1 THE CONTRASTING ATTRIBUTES OF PEOPLE IN
COLLECTIVIST AND INDIVIDUALISTIC CULTURES

Horizontal collectivists	Individualists
Facet 1: Interdependent Self	*Independent Self*
CUT THE PIE OF EXPERIENCE BY FOCUSING ON	
Groups as the basic units of social perception.	*Individuals* as the basic units of social perception.
(E.g., Do people see "Mr. Smith" or "an Englishman"?)	
Relationships are the figure; the individual is in the background.	The individual is the figure; relationships are in the background.
ATTRIBUTIONS	
Behavior explained as reflecting norms.	Behavior explained by reference to personality, traits, principles, attitudes.
Success is attributed to help from others.	Success is attributed to ability.
Failure is attributed to lack of effort. (See Kashima & Triandis, 1986.)	Failure is attributed to external factors (e.g., task difficulty, bad luck).
SELF	
Is defined in terms of in-groups, relationships. (See Triandis, McCusker, & Hui, 1990.)	Is defined as an independent entity.
Change the self to fit the situation rather than the situation to fit the self (Diaz-Guerrero, 1979).	Change the situation to fit the self, rather than the self to fit the situation.
Know more about others than about self.	Know more about self than about others.
With the result that:	
The self is seen as more similar to a friend than the friend is seen as similar to the self. (See Markus & Kitayama, 1991.)	The self is seen as less similar to a friend than the friend is seen as similar to the self.
Have few self-linked memories (e.g., do poor job writing their autobiography).	Have many self-linked memories (e.g., do good job writing their autobiography).
Self includes achievement for the group:	Self includes achievement for self-glory:
I represent the group, cooperation, endurance, order, self-control.	I want to be myself. I want power.

TABLE 6–1 CONTINUED

Horizontal collectivists	Individualists
Facet 1: Interdependent Self	*Independent Self*

GOALS

Role-relevant goals are greatly valued.	Clearly articulated goals are greatly valued.
Of long duration (Hui, 1988).	Of short duration.

EMOTIONS

Tend to be most frequently other-focused (empathy) and of short duration. (See Markus & Kitayama, 1991.)	Tend to be most frequently self-focused (anger) and of long duration.

COGNITIONS

Focus on the needs of my in-group (obligations).	Focus on my needs, rights, capacity (contracts).
Cognitions are context dependent. (See Markus & Kitayama, 1991.)	Cognitions are context independent.

ATTITUDES

Favor beliefs that reflect interdependence.	Favor beliefs that reflect independence, emotional detachment from in-groups.

NORMS

Favor embeddedness in in-groups.	Favor independence from in-groups.

VALUES

Security, obedience, duty, in-group harmony, personalized relationships.	Pleasure, achievement, competition, freedom, autonomy, fair exchange.
Concern for "virtuous action" (i.e., situation-appropriate action).	Concern for "the truth" versus "action consistent with important principles."
Persistence (Blinco, 1992; Triandis et al., 1990).	

(See Schwartz, submitted; Triandis, McCusker, & Hui, 1990.)

MAJOR CALAMITY

Ostracism.	Dependence on others.

TABLE 6–1 CONTINUED

Horizontal collectivists	Individualists
Facet 1: Interdependent Self	*Independent Self*

IN-GROUPS

Few, but relationship to them is close, with much concern for their integrity.	Many; relationships are casual; little emotional involvement.
Large families; rapid population growth.	Small families; static population.
Self-sacrifice for group is "natural."	Less willingness to self-sacrifice for in-group.
In-group perceived as more homogeneous than out-group (see Kashima, 1989; Triandis, Bontempo et al., 1990).	In-group perceived as more heterogeneous than out-group.
In-group harmony is required.	Debate, confrontation are acceptable.
Conflict with out-groups is expected.	Conflict with out-groups is accepted but not desired.

(See Gudykunst, Yoon, & Nishida, 1987. Moghaddam, Taylor, & Wright, 1993, point out that in individualistic cultures there is a tendency to hide the dislike of out-groups; in collectivist cultures, such as India, negative attitudes toward out-groups are expressed very frankly.)

In-group influences many behaviors, and influence is deep.	In-group influences a few narrowly defined behaviors.

SOCIAL BEHAVIOR

Very different when the other person belongs to an in-group versus an out-group. (See Triandis, 1972, for extended discussion. See Bond, 1988; Chan, 1991; Iwata, 1992, for empirical examples.)	Only somewhat different when the other person belongs to in- versus an out-group.
Most behavior occurs in small groups.	Much behavior occurs when individual is alone or in couples.

(E.g., Korean skiers more often ski in groups than American skiers, Brandt, 1974; collectivists are more likely to eat in large groups, Triandis, 1990; Levine, 1992.)

Most interaction is between an individual and groups (Wheeler, Reis, & Bond, 1989).	Most interaction is between an individual and one other individual.

TABLE 6–1 CONTINUED

Horizontal collectivists	Individualists
Facet 1: Interdependent Self	Independent Self
Difficult entry into groups; difficult to make friends, but relationships are intimate after they get established (Gudykunst, 1983; Verma, 1992).	Easy entry into and exit from groups, but relationships mostly nonintimate. People appear very sociable, but relationship is superficial and depends on social exchanges, contracts.
Cooperation with in-group members. Communal exchanges. Mutual face-saving. Regulated by in-group norms.	Personal face-saving. Regulated by attitudes and personal values as well as cost-benefit computations and generalized public norms.
Interdependent (e.g., cobathing).	Independent (e.g., privacy).
Give little feedback about how they experience social situations.	Give much feedback about how they experience social situations.

(Since socializing is mostly in groups to which one is born, skills such as learning to give compliments or feedback about undesirable behaviors are less well developed among collectivists, while individualists have skills for giving both positive and negative feedback; Cohen, 1991.)

Select mates who will maximize family integrity (virgins, good housekeepers). (See Buss, 1990; Dion, Pak, & Dion, 1990.)	Select mates who are physically attractive and have "exciting personalities."
Proper action as defined by in-group, even if inconsistent with own attitudes.	Attitudes and behavior are supposed to be consistent.
Experience little cognitive dissonance.	Experience much cognitive dissonance.

(E.g., when a person acts in ways that are inconsistent with own attitudes, the person feels dissonance and is uncomfortable. But collectivists are so concerned with "proper behavior" that they pay little attention to their own attitudes, and if their attitudes do not match their behavior, they do not feel especially uncomfortable. Individualists consider their attitudes important, and if their attitudes do not match their behavior, they feel most uncomfortable and do something, such as change their attitudes, to reduce the dissonance; see Iwao & Triandis, in press.)

"What is mine is yours."	"What is mine is not to be used without permission."
In communication, people use "we" very frequently. Consists of context most extensively. Silence is fine.	In communication, people use "I" very frequently. Consists of content almost exclusively. Silence is embarrassing.

(In Japan silence is "strength" and considered a masculine virtue by men; Iwao, 1993).

TABLE 6-1 CONTINUED

Horizontal collectivists	Individualists
Facet 1: Interdependent Self	*Independent Self*

DETERMINANTS OF SOCIAL BEHAVIOR

In-group norms more important than attitudes. (See Bontempo & Rivera, 1992; Kashima, Siegel, Tanaka, & Kashima, 1992.)	Attitudes more important than norms.
Ascribed roles (e.g., based on gender, age, family relations).	Achieved roles.
Shame organizes social life more frequently than guilt (Creighton, 1990).	Guilt is more common than shame.
Facet 2: Same Self	*Different Self*

SELF

Modest, cooperative. (See Takata, 1987.)	Distinct from others, better than others, competitive, exhibitionistic.

EMOTIONS

They like people who are modest.	They like people who are self-assured.

(E.g., collectivists start their lectures by giving clues of modesty, such as "I have little of value to tell you"; successful individualistic lecturers take over and "control" their audiences.)

COGNITIONS

What makes me the same as my group.	What makes me different, distinguished.

NORMS

Equality and need emphasized in the distribution of resources.	Equity emphasized in the distribution of resources.

IN-GROUPS

Defined by similarity in ascribed attributes, such as kinship, caste, religion, race, village, tribe.	Defined by similarity in achieved attributes, e.g., beliefs, occupation.

SOCIAL BEHAVIOR

Reciprocity is obligatory	Reciprocity is voluntary.

(Ting-Toomey, 1986, studied three individualistic and two collectivist cultures and found that the individualists saw returning a favor as a matter of free will, while the collectivists saw it as a moral obligation. Also, the collectivists saw the obligation as long term, the individualists as short term.)

For conflict reduction, use mediators (Leung, 1988).	For conflict reduction, use courts.

TABLE 6–1 CONCLUDED

Horizontal collectivists	Individualists
Facet 2: Same Self	Different Self
Vertical collectivism	Individualism

GOALS	
In-group goals have primacy or overlap with personal goals.	Personal goals have primacy over in-group goals.
Individual and group goals are often consistent.	Individual and group goals are often inconsistent.

SOCIAL BEHAVIOR	
Hierarchical. (See Gallois, Barker, Jones, & Callan, 1992.)	Egalitarian.
Vertical relations more important.	Horizontal relations more important.
Status-asymmetric relations are comfortable.	Status-symmetric relations are comfortable.

In addition, the attributes shown in Table 6-1 have distributions like the ones shown in Figure 6-6. In other words, do not think that all the people in a collectivist culture will have a particular collectivist attribute.

Most cultures include a mixture of individualistic and collectivist elements. In the most individualistic cultures people have a very strong independent self as well as a "different self" (e.g., the upper and middle classes in the Latin countries of Europe, where the aristocratic ideals are still very strong). The moderately individualistic cultures are less extreme. In Sweden, according to Daun (1991, 1992), people are extremely independent and self-reliant, but they do not want to stand out. So they have at least one attribute, modesty, that is more frequently found in collectivist than in individualistic cultures. In the most collectivist cultures (e.g., theocracies), most people, but not the leaders, have an interdependent self and a "same self." Monks probably feel interdependent, and they do not want to stand apart from other monks.

Table 6-1 is arranged so that it distinguishes horizontal from vertical collectivism as well as two facets of horizontal collectivism-individualism. Most important is facet 1, the interdependent versus independent self, but facet 2, the contrast between the emphasis on the same and the different self, is also important. There is a relationship between these two facets, because if we manipulate the same-different self, we see a change on the interdependent-independent self.

Trafimow, Triandis, and Goto (1991) showed that you can make a person temporarily collectivist or individualist. Random assignment of students to two kinds of instructions was followed by measurement of collectivism with a standard method. The individualistic instructions were: "For the next two minutes, you will not need to write anything. Please think of what makes you different from your family and friends. What do you expect yourself to do?" The collectivist instruction was slightly different. ". . . think of what you have in common with your family and friends. . . ."

A content analysis of the responses of those who completed twenty sentences that begin with "I am" (Triandis, McCusker, & Hui, 1990) showed that those who received the collectivist instructions gave more S (social) responses (see page 145 for examples of S responses). Table 6-2 shows the percentages of the S responses obtained from different samples.

FIGURE 6–6

Theoretical distributions of contrasting attributes X versus Y in individualistic and collectivist cultures. At point A the collectivist culture has several individuals who have extreme levels of trait X, while the individualistic culture has very few such individuals. At point B the collectivist culture has a very large number of individuals who have the trait X, while the individualistic culture has just a few such people. At point C both types of cultures have modest numbers of people who have neither trait X nor trait Y. At point D the individualistic cultures have a large number of people who have trait Y, while the collectivistic culture has a few such people. Finally, at point E, the individualistic culture has a substantial number of people who are extremely high on trait Y, while the collectivist culture has very few such people.

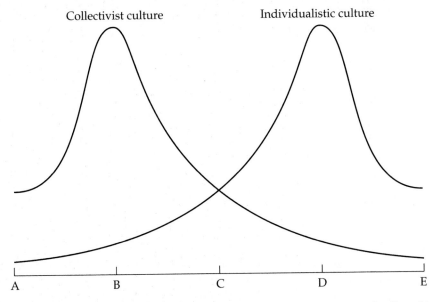

Collectivist culture   Individualistic culture

A   B   C   D   E

Attribute X   Attribute Y

TABLE 6–2 PERCENT *S* SCORES OBTAINED FROM SEVERAL SAMPLES

Sample	N	Mean	Range
Illinois students	509	19	0–60
University of Athens students	118	15	0–56
University of Hawaii students, Mainland background	28	21	10–62
University of Hawaii students, Chinese background	19	29	10–71
University of Hawaii students, Japanese background	37	28	10–65
University of Hong Kong students	118	20	10–68
People's Republic of China	34	52	28–100
Illinois students in Trafimow, Triandis, and Goto experiments			
"Think of what you have in common with your family and friends"			
With English names	24	23	
With Chinese names	18	52	
"Think of what makes you different from your family and friends"			
With English names	24	07	
With Chinese names	18	30	
Collective prime English names	24	20	
Individualistic prime English names	24	09	

SOURCE: Trafimow, Triandis, & Goto (1991). Triandis, McCusker, & Hui (1990). Copyright 1990, 1991 by the American Psychological Association. Reprinted by permission of the publisher.

In the Trafimow et al. experiment, Illinois students with English names gave 7 percent collective self-responses after receiving the "think of what makes you different" instructions, while students with Chinese names gave 30 percent collective self-responses in that condition. When the "think of what you have in common" instructions were used, the Illinois students with English names gave 23 percent collective self-responses and those with Chinese names gave 52 percent collective self-responses.

Thus, both the cultural background of the respondents and the instructions had significant effects in the expected direction. A second experiment tested forty-eight American subjects, twenty-four in each of two "priming conditions." Subjects read a story about a "king of Sumeria" who "sent a talented general" (individualistic priming condition) versus "a member of his family" (collectivist priming condition) to help another king. Again, the respondents were asked to write twenty statements that began with "I am." The results showed that 9 percent and 22 percent of the answers were "collective self-cognitions" in the individualistic and collectivist conditions, respectively. This result suggests that people have a *cognitive schema* (a set of interrelated ideas) that includes individualistic ideas and a separate one that includes collectivist ideas, and one can stimulate the schemas by priming them.

Table 6-2 also give you the means of the percent *S* responses obtained in other samples—e.g., 509 University of Illinois students average 19 percent, with a range of zero to 60. In that sample the modal (most frequent) score is *zero*! The students from the University of Athens, in Greece, are quite individualistic on this measure. The students at the University of Hawaii scored 21 percent when they had European names and 29 percent and 28 percent, respectively, when they had cultural backgrounds from China or Japan. Most of the students in the latter two samples were second or third generation from East Asia living in Hawaii. The high scores of Asian Americans on collectivism were also obtained in a study of attitudes (Triandis, Bontempo, et al., 1986).

In homogeneous-simple cultures people are expected to agree with the majority. Decisions are taken either by the authorities or by consensus. Persons who disagree and make trouble are *ostracized*. This Greek-origin word tells something about the way such societies work. In ancient Greece, if a citizen made too much trouble, there was a vote in which citizens would use an *ostrakon*, an oyster shell, to indicate that they wanted that person to be expelled from the community.

In more complex societies we cannot expel those we disagree with. But we use the vote to put those with whom we agree in positions of authority. We hope they will take care of the people with whom we disagree. This kind of democracy is linked to individualism. The French intellectual Alexis de Tocqueville, who wrote *Democracy in America* after visiting the New World in the 1840s, explicitly discussed how individualism is linked with that form of government.

The prototypic collectivist social relationship is the family, which links people with strong long-term emotional ties and common goals. Cooperation is natural, and status is determined by position within the group.

The prototypic individualistic social relationship is the market. You pay your money and you get something in return. In voluntary associations, such as the Rotary or Kiwanis Club, the relationship is also individualistic. In this cultural pattern, when people join a group they are polite and treat others with respect, but they also make sure that they remain distinct individuals. They compete with others in the group for status, which depends on their accomplishments much more than on their group memberships.

The collectivism syndrome was also identified in value studies (Schwartz, 1992, submitted). Schwartz and his associates collected data in twenty-eight countries. They asked 200 teachers and 200 "others" (students, workers, adults) to indicate the importance of fifty-six values as "guiding principles in my life." A "smallest space analysis" of the data (a statistical method that provides "maps" of the location of the values or the samples in a multidimensional space) showed that values clustered the same way in analyses of the data from each country as well as in analyses across countries.

Specifically, values like "family security," "social order," and "honoring parents and elders" clustered on one corner of the map, and values like "creative," "pleasure," and "exciting life" clustered on the opposite corner. Thus collectivist values appear to contrast with individualist values. The samples that were most collectivist were from Estonia (rural teachers, urban teachers, rural adults), Bulgaria (Turkish teachers), Turkish teachers, Taiwan teachers, and Malaysian teachers and students. The samples that were most individualist were all students from New Zealand, England, Holland, Italy, and West Germany. The U.S. teachers were in the middle of the collectivism-individualism value continuum. However, I collected these data in Danville, Illinois, and I suspect that the Midwest is more collectivist than the coasts. The Illinois students were individualists, but on these particular value measures not more so than the Japanese students.

Consequences

Children are raised to do their duty, self-sacrifice for the group, and obey authorities in collectivist cultures much more than in individualistic cultures. Conversely, children are raised to be exploratory, creative, and self-sufficient in individualistic cultures more than in collectivist cultures.

There is considerable empirical evidence that social behavior is different in collectivist and individualistic cultures (e.g., Earley, 1989). Even advertising is different and corresponds to the cultural pattern (Han, 1990), with collectivist themes (e.g., "This product is good for your family") and individualistic themes (e.g., "Use this product and you will have fun; try it, you'll like it!").

Evaluation of the Syndromes

Lest you think that extreme collectivism or extreme individualism is desirable, let me make very clear that both extremes are undesirable. The ethnic cleansing (including mass rapes, which forced large numbers of people in 1992–1993 to leave their homes) practiced by the Bosnian Serbs on the Muslims of Bosnia required extreme collectivism ("My group is all good; the other group is all bad"). High rates of delinquency, crime, homelessness, and heart attacks appear to be linked to extreme individualism. The weakening of the family reflected in high divorce rates (Brodbar & Jay, 1986), many examples of selfish child neglect (Pilisuk & Parks, 1985) and abuse (e.g., parent having fun being on drugs neglecting the child), the unwillingness to deal with national debt, and the neglect of the infrastructure in the 1990s, in most individualistic countries, probably have some relationship to the extreme forms of individualism that have emerged in the last quarter-century. We need to understand these constructs much better and move toward cultural forms that select the best elements of each cultural pattern and discard the others.

Dynamic Changes in Syndromes
Many modern, complex cultures that used to be quite collectivist are shifting toward individualism in some of their cultural patterns. A most interesting case is that of Japan, where the women born in the 1960s are spearheading the change toward individualism (Iwao, 1993). Iwao writes: "Women are less interested in following male norms of groupism in the corporate context" (p. 207). One of the symptoms of this change is that women keep their own names after marriage (p. 272). "Money has allowed them [women] to pursue goals of their own choosing—everything from a doctoral degree to a carefree sex life" (p. 28).

Of course, we should not expect a dramatic, rapid change. Most Japanese women, both old and young, are in many ways traditional, as the case of one of Iwao's students shows. She took a job arranged by her parents rather than a job that offered better chances of promotion and a good career, so as to honor the "interpersonal relations network maintained by her parents" (p. 181).

Relationships among the Cultural Syndromes

Figure 6-7 suggests that the three syndromes of tightness, complexity, and individualism may be related. The x axis reflects emphasis on tightness—severe sanctions when a person does not behave as expected from cultural norms. For a society to be tight it is necessary for people to be similar to each other so that they can agree on the norms of correct behavior in each situation. It is also more likely that there will be many clear norms when the population density is high and people feel the need to have their behavior regulated, so they will not clash unnecessarily with others. Also, when jobs are interdependent (e.g., as they would be in constructing a large irrigation ditch), they require many norms, and the breaking of norms is a great sin (e.g., diverting water from a neighbor's canal was one of the greatest sins of ancient Egypt). When activities are not interrelated (e.g., gathering berries), there are few norms, and breaking them is tolerated. Tightness is related to collectivism.

In addition, the more complex, large, and stratified a society, the more different occupations, groups, and roles there are. Complexity is related to affluence; modern industrial societies are complex and affluent. The more groups there are with different norms, the more people have to decide for *themselves* how to behave. If they make decisions that do not take the goals of others into account, they are usually not punished. In

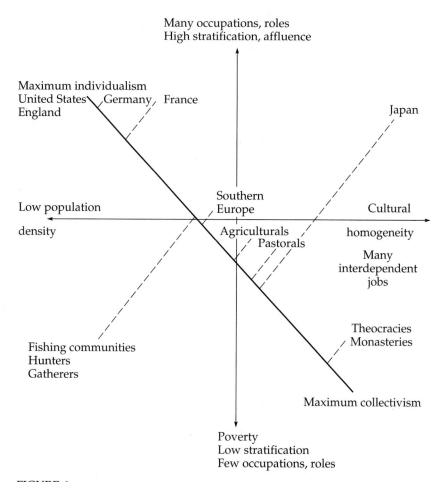

FIGURE 6–7

Probable correlates of tightness (cultural homogeneity, high population density, many independent activities needed for survival) and cultural complexity (many occupations, roles, high stratification, affluence). Individualism is maximum when a society is both complex and loose; collectivism is maximum when a society is both tight and simple.

simple societies, with only a few groups to which people belong, and with little affluence, there is a lot of common fate, and people feel interdependent. Thus, an interdependent self develops.

In this conceptualization we would expect maximum collectivism in simple, poor, low-stratification societies that are homogeneous, with interdependent activities and relatively high density, such as in theocratic regimes, monasteries, and cults (e.g., the Jim Jones cult that committed mass suicide). We would expect maximum individualism in societies that are complex and loose.

Preliterate societies are placed on this figure on the basis of information about child-rearing patterns (e.g., Berry, 1967, 1976, 1979; Hendrix, 1985) and children's personalities (e.g., Bolton et al., 1976). In short, the hunters and gatherers are more individualistic than the pastoral and agricultural societies. Edgerton (1971) reports that among the four African tribes that he studied, the pastorals were more independent than the agriculturalists but also higher in respect for authority. This suggests that they are higher on individualism but also higher in power distance. Clearly, we need more research to know precisely where each group belongs on this graph.

Some studies suggest that Japan is collectivist relative to Europe and North America, but more individualistic than the preliterate cultures. It is also fast becoming more individualistic (Iwao, 1990).

S UMMARY

In this chapter we examined four elementary forms of social behavior (communal sharing, authority ranking, equality matching, and market pricing) and linked them to three cultural syndromes (complexity, tightness, and individualism). In collectivist cultures people are more likely than in individualistic cultures to define themselves as members of groups; make attributions that focus on in-group norms; know more about others than themselves; remember more about other people; emphasize the achievement of groups; experience little dissonance when they act correctly though inconsistently with their attitudes; subordinate their personal goals to the goals of in-groups; use more other-focused emotions; favor attitudes and values that emphasize interdependence, security, duty, in-group harmony, and hierarchy; be very worried about ostracism from groups; behave very differently when the other person is an in-group versus an out-group member; accept hierarchical relationships; be reserved about joining new groups; be more intimate after they do join groups; try to save both own face and other person's face; be regulated by in-group norms; pay more attention to context during communications; be modest; and reciprocate social behavior.

QUESTIONS AND EXERCISES

1. Consider three of the behavior settings mentioned in Chapter 1. What social behaviors do you believe are most likely to occur in each setting? How many of these behaviors might be classified as related to communal sharing, authority ranking, equality matching, or market pricing?

2.   In your analysis of the previous question, how many of these behaviors were associative (e.g., helping) or dissociative (e.g., aggressive)?

3.   In your analysis of question 1, how many of these behaviors were superordinate (e.g., dominance) or subordinate (e.g., conformity)?

4.   In your analysis of question 1, how many of these behaviors were intimate (self-disclosing) or formal (doing what the etiquette of the society specifies)?

5.   Did you detect any relationships between the four relational orientations of Fiske and the behavior settings? If so, you have seen that specific behavior settings are more likely to elicit one than the others of these orientations. Did you detect some social behaviors that are more likely in one or another of these settings?

7

Culture and Communication

—————— ❖ ——————

Collectivism (Context-Dependence) and Communication ◆ *Status* ◆ Politeness Theory ◆ Content ◆ Attitude Change through Communication ◆ *Best Sources of Messages* ◆ *Medium* ◆ *Structure of Messages* ◆ *Goals* ◆ *Communication and Social Behavior* ◆ Ideologism versus Pragmatism ◆ Associative versus Abstractive Communication ◆ Paralinguistic Communication ◆ *Emotions* ◆ *Eye Contact, Distances, Body Orientations, Gestures* ◆ Summary

On a hot August afternoon, in the nineteenth century in China, two Englishmen sweated and puffed while playing tennis. When they finished, a sympathetic Chinese friend asked: "Could you not get two servants to do this for you?"

This is an amusing example of the kinds of communication difficulties that occur between cultures. If you are to be effective in your communication, you must be familiar with the subjective culture of the people you communicate with. Nothing less than knowing how they categorize experience, what associations they have among these categories, and what norms, roles, and values they have will be sufficient to protect you from miscommunications. Accuracy implies that both the source and recipient of a message assign the same meaning to it.

Gudykunst (1991) pointed out that we communicate out of *habit,* and we give ourselves instructions about how to communicate. We follow *norms,* and our communication depends on our *skills* and on how we categorize the recipients of our communication—are they in-group or out-group (Gudykunst, Gao, Schmidt, et al., 1992)? Our stereotypes also play an important role in how we communicate.

If we want to improve our communication, we need to be aware of our competence. Howell (1982) identified four stages of competence: (1) *unconscious incompetence*, where we misinterpret the other's behavior but are not aware of it (e.g., the Chinese friend of the two tennis players above); (2) *conscious incompetence*, where we are aware that we misinterpret others' behavior but do not know what to do about it; (3) *conscious competence*, where we modify our behavior to take into account the fact that we are communicating with a person from another culture; and (4) *unconscious competence*, where the correct communication pattern has become such a part of our habit structure that we no longer have to think about using a different pattern with persons from another culture.

A lot of communication is paralinguistic; that is, it does not involve the use of language, but rather emotional expression, gestures, the location of the body in relation to the other's body, eye contact, level of voice. We can insult people in other cultures quite innocently, as former President Nixon did in Brazil when he used the American signal for "OK" or "it's in the bag" (thumb and index finger in a circle), which some subgroups in Brazil use for "Let's have sex"!

Gestures are very tricky methods of communication. A gesture that means "yes" in one culture can mean "no" in another. For example, in Bulgaria and south India a nod means "no," a shake of the head, "yes." I found it very difficult to look at my south Indian assistant, whose gesture was saying "no" while her voice was saying "yes."

When people communicate, they make predictions about the effects of their communication on others. They choose their communication strategies so as to maximize their own benefits from the communication. Effective communication means that we give the same meaning to the behavior of others that they give to their own behavior.

When we give the same meaning to the behavior of others that they give, we are making *isomorphic attributions* (Triandis, 1975, 1977). Recall that an attribution is a perceived cause of a behavior. For example, there is an ancient Samurai expression of trust: "I would like to sleep with you." Now, if a Samurai said that to me and I understood it as a compliment, essentially meaning "I trust you so much that I can sleep with you in the same room, because I know you will not kill me when I am asleep," I would be making an isomorphic attribution. The attribution the Samurai made may not be exactly the attribution that I would make (that is why it is called *isomorphic* and not *identical*). Maybe the Samurai thought: "I need to tell Triandis that I feel very secure next to him." That is close enough. We are still talking about the same thing. However, if I thought the Samurai were making a sexual advance, I would be using a nonisomorphic attribution—sex—rather than an isomorphic one—trust. In Chapter 10 we will discuss how we can train people to make isomorphic attributions.

Another example of how attributions can be nonisomorphic was related to me by my friend, the Greek psychiatrist George Vassiliou (Triandis, 1975, pp. 42–43). The incident involves the interaction between an American (A) supervisor and a Greek (G) subordinate. The supervisor wants the subordinate to participate in decisions, a good management practice in the United States, but the subordinate does not know about this management style and simply expects a boss to be bossy.

Behavior	Thoughts not communicated and attributions
A: How long will it take you to finish this report?	A: Invite participation
	G: Confusion. Why does he not tell me how long it should take?
G: I do not know. How long should it take?	A: He refuses to take responsibility.
	G: I asked him for an order.
A: You are in the best position to estimate time requirements.	A: I support his judgment.
	G: What nonsense! I better give him an answer.
G: 10 days.	A: He is not good at estimating time. Let him find out from experience!
A: Take 15 days. Is it agreed you will do it in 15 days?	A: I offer a contract.
	G: He is giving me an order.

In fact, the report required much more time. The subordinate worked night and day, but still at the end of 15 days it required one more day's work.

A: Where is the report?	A: I am training him to meet deadlines.
	G: He is asking for the report.
G: It will be ready tomorrow.	A: It's not ready.
A: But we had agreed that it would be ready today.	A: I must teach him the importance of contracts.

The Greek subordinate explodes at this point. "The stupid, ungrateful boss! I worked night and day for 15 days, and he has the nerve to criticize me." He hands in his resignation. The American is totally surprised. The Greek says to himself that he simply cannot work for such a "stupid" boss.

As you can see from this example, the attributions they are making all along are mostly nonisomorphic. They are *both* in the unconscious incompetence level of communication!

It is clear from these examples that we usually do not know the thoughts and feelings of others, and we depend on them to tell us what they are thinking and feeling. We use our own framework to interpret what they are doing, and often it is completely out of line with theirs. It is also sad to say that we often do not have a clue as to the accuracy of our understanding of their communications.

Cultures differ in the way communication takes place. In the following sections we will review some major cultural differences in communication patterns.

COLLECTIVISM (CONTEXT-DEPENDENCE) AND COMMUNICATION

Greetings in collectivist cultures tend to be more extended, sometimes taking as much as twenty minutes, than in individualistic cultures. Remember, in collectivist cultures people establish a relationship between two or more groups as well as determine their positions in two hierarchies.

People in collectivist cultures pay more attention to context (emotional expressions, touching, distance between bodies, body orientation, level of voice, eye contact) when they communicate than do people from individualistic cultures (Gudykunst, 1983). The collectivist must keep relationships with in-group members at their best and looks at all the evidence to understand what is communicated. Thus, collectivists are not as explicit, direct, or clear as the individualists. The example of Saddam Hussein's brother's misunderstanding the message of Secretary James Baker (Chapter 2) is most dramatic. By paying attention to the paralinguistics but ignoring the verbal message, people from some cultures can easily misunderstand what a person from an individualistic culture is saying.

In low-context (individualistic) cultures people distrust what is not said clearly. The communicator is the focus of the communication, and the important attributes are credibility, intelligence, and expert knowledge of the subject matter. Ideally the communicator speaks clearly and well. The word "I" is used a lot. The speaker is separated from his opinions, and it is possible to discuss different viewpoints objectively. Explicit logic, proofs, linear organization of the argument (most people think X is right, but here is evidence that X is wrong; therefore we conclude that most people are wrong), emphasis on *what* is said, emphasis on specificity, and precision in word usage are valued. The best arguments are presented first (anticlimactic organization) to attract attention and generate a desire to hear the whole argument. Silence indicates disagreement, hostility, rejection, weakness, unwillingness to communicate, incompatibility, anxiety, shyness, lack of verbal skills, or a troubled person.

By contrast, in high-context cultures people value the unspoken, the implicit, and believe that saying too much may confuse. Iwao (1993) puts it this way: "There is an unspoken belief among Japanese in general that putting deep feelings into words somehow lowers or spoils their value and that understanding attained without words is more precious than that attained through precise articulation"* (p. 98). Iwao considers this a problem for the smooth functioning of Japanese marriages, because husbands rarely tell their wives that they love them. "If a Japanese woman were to get up the courage to ask her spouse if he loved her, he would become profoundly embarrassed . . . annoyed and demand 'Do I have to go *that* far in explaining'?" (pp. 98–99). Men even believe that it is "unmanly" to communicate, and it is notable that the Chinese and Japanese character for "noisy" and "talkative" consists of three small characters meaning "woman" (p. 99)!

In high-context cultures communicators focus on the perceiver of the communication (Does the other person understand me?) and train each other to understand the implicit. *How* something is said is more important than *what* is said. The word "we" is used much, and the word "I" is rare. Synthesis with intuition, ambiguity, subjectivity, generality, vagueness, and bland expressions (e.g., "probably," "maybe," "perhaps," "slightly") are common.

In collectivist cultures harmony is of the utmost importance. One says what the other wants to hear, and one does not contradict the other. Hofstede (1991, p. 58) gives the example of a collectivist (Indonesian) missionary's parable: A man had two sons. He went to the first and said: "Son, go and work in the vineyard today." The son replied, "I will go, sir," but he did not go. The man went to his second son and said the same thing, and the son replied "I will not go," but later he changed his mind and did go. Which of the two sons did the bidding of the father? The collectivist missionary argued that it was the first, because he did not contradict his father.

In high-context cultures, the argument is presented climactically. One starts with peripheral arguments and gets to the point only after the other person has reacted. Thus, one is less likely to offend the other person by presenting an argument that confronts the issue head-on.

The important attributes of the communicator are age, sex, family background, and status in the social system. There is a lot of give-and-take, thinking together, and exploration of ideas (as in the Japanese *ringi* system of consensus decision making). Personal values cannot be separated from the message (Okabe, 1983), and agreeing with the other depends very much on liking the other. Context is very important, and words are not taken at face value. Silence can mean being strong or

* *The Japanese Woman* by Sumiko Iwao. Copyright © 1993 by Sumiko Iwao. Reprinted with permission of The Free Press, a Division of Macmillan, Inc.

powerful (Condon, 1978), feeling comfortable, or simply thinking there is nothing important to say. As noted earlier, Japanese men consider silence more "manly" than talk (Iwao, 1993, p. 101).

The following example shows how the use of context can help communication and avoid loss of face. In Indonesia, a boy liked a girl and wanted to marry her. But the boy was of low social class and the girl of high social class. The boy sent his mother to visit the girl's mother. The girl's mother served the boy's mother tea and bananas. Since tea is not served with bananas, this communicated that the two (the boy and the girl) could not mix. The boy's mother understood but did not lose face, because she did not ask for the girl's hand and so did not receive a "no."

One researcher (Ueda, 1974) has identified sixteen ways the Japanese use to avoid saying "no." My guess is that there are many more than sixteen if the presentation of any incompatible or unusual stimuli can be counted as accomplishing the same end!

And if collectivists pay too much attention to context and make mistakes, it is just as likely that individualists do not pay enough attention to context. How many people from individualistic cultures would have understood the meaning of tea and bananas?

Status

Collectivists also pay more attention to status differences than do individualists. In many languages the words that one can use depend on the relative status of the speakers. As mentioned in earlier chapters, Japanese literally makes you tongue-tied until you know the relative status of the two speakers.

In regard to status in Japan, Lipset (personal communication) tells an amusing story. An American who was visiting Japan invited two Japanese colleagues to dinner at his house. They devoted considerable time trying to place each other hierarchically. This was essential, so they would know how to talk to each other and so they would know who was to go first through the dining room door. While dinner was getting cold, the exploration continued. Finally, the hungry, uncouth American shoved them into the dining room!

There are at least three levels of polite status giving in Japan when talking to the other person, and there are three levels of polite self-reference; thus, potentially, there are nine ways of talking. For example, an ordinary person talking to the emperor would use the verb endings that reflect the highest level of status difference and refer to himself or herself by using the lowest level of status. Polite practice requires that a person always give the benefit of the doubt to the other by using one or two linguistic steps that elevate the status of the other person and one or two steps that reduce his or her own status.

*P*OLITENESS THEORY

In most languages there are polite and respectful forms (*vous* in French) and less polite, familiarity-based forms (*tu* in French). The more solidarity (equality, similarity, closeness, kinship) there is between two people, the more likely they are to use *tu*. The more of a status difference, dissimilarity, social distance, and required politeness there is between them, the more likely they are to use *vous*. In French the *vous* form is also considered more "elegant" and is likely to be used by the upper class, even between spouses or parents and children, as a way to differentiate themselves from the lower classes.

There are many situations when there is nonreciprocal use of the polite and familiar forms. The larger the status difference, the more likely it is that the low-status person will use the polite form and the high-status person will use the familiar form when they talk to each other.

But this pattern can get complicated, because sometimes the closeness is so important that the status difference is eliminated; at other times that does not happen. For example, I used the familiar form of address to talk to both my paternal grandmother and my father, but my father used the formal form to talk to his mother! My grandmother adored me because I had her husband's name, and thus we were very close. But my father was one of twelve children, all raised at the turn of the century, who were taught to be most respectful to their parents.

The use of the familiar or the formal form of address is accounted for by a theory of politeness that apparently has universal features (Brown & Levinson, 1987). However, some deviations from this theory, traceable to cultural differences, have been reported in the literature (Holtgraves & Yang, 1992).

The least polite way to talk to another is direct, e.g., "Open the door" or "Give me the book." The "weightiness" of the request increases with the status (power) of the hearer, the relationship distance (e.g., stranger rather than friend), and the degree of imposition of the request (asking a lot versus a little). Brown and Levinson argue that as the request becomes weightier, speech becomes more polite. In other words, if you talk to a justice of the Supreme Court, whom you do not know, and beg for your life, you would be as polite as possible. On the other hand, if you talk to a close friend and ask to borrow some class notes, you might say: "Lend me your notes."

Brown and Levinson distinguish five levels of politeness:

Bald speech. This is the most direct—e.g., "Open the door."

Positive politeness. The emphasis is on the closeness of the hearer—
   e.g., "You will open the door, won't you?"

Negative politeness. The emphasis is on lessening the imposition—
   e.g., "Since you are close to the door, why don't you open it?" or
   "Could you open the door?"

Off-the-record. The speaker's intent is denied—e.g., "Wouldn't it be nice if the door were open?"

No performance. The speaker does not make a request.

Holtgraves and Yang (1992) found support for this theory with data from Korea and the United States. They used twenty-seven ($3 \times 3 \times 3 = 27$) scenarios describing three levels of each of the three variables (power, distance, imposition) and asked the subjects what wording they would use in each situation. They found that the theory was supported in both countries.

The theory works well in many cultures. For example, Kroger and Wood (1992) compared German use of politeness terms with Chinese, Korean, and Greek and found support for the Brown-Levinson theory.

C ONTENT

The content of communication that is most valued in one culture may not be valued in another. For example, mainstream Americans tend to use "small talk" ("How are you? Nice weather today"), but the Navajo (Salzman, 1991) do not like or engage in such talk. In fact, traditional Navajos do not want to draw attention to themselves. They fear that if they were to answer "I am well," they would be noticed by evil spirits and this would bring them misfortune.

In some cultures exaggeration is appropriate: "terrific, largest in the world." In others moderation is the rule: "not bad; will do." In some you must be definite: "This is what we will do," while in others, you are tentative: "perhaps," "probably," "maybe."

In many traditional cultures people never talk about death or death-related subjects, because they believe this may result in bringing about the event. This can produce problems with mainstream Americans who view Halloween as an opportunity for "ghosts" to walk the street and the dead to scare the living.

In a study by Triandis, Bontempo, Villareal, Lucca, and Asai (1988), Japanese and Illinois students indicated whether they would conform to or evade a confrontation with various others with whom they had a disagreement. The Japanese generally showed *less* willingness to conform to the other and *more* willingness to avoid the confrontation than did the Illinois students, especially in relationships with a close friend or a virtual stranger.

Collectivists tend to beat around the bush. They will communicate all but the most crucial piece of information, which the listener is supposed to supply in order to make the whole message comprehensible. This strategy has the advantage that it permits people to keep track of the other's feelings and avoid an argument if it is likely to disturb the harmony.

Conversely, those from individualistic cultures get to the point so quickly that the collectivist finds it shocking. Of course, for many individualists, time is money; many collectivists have more time. Nevertheless, the differences in timing can result in missed opportunities, as this example suggests:

The individualist comes into a store owned by a collectivist and is ready to buy a $2000 carpet: "What is the price?" Shocking! You simply do not do business this way. You sit down, drink some coffee, talk about the heat of the day, discuss how you spent the previous several hours. Then you look at some carpets, you discuss how the carpet market is going, you talk about the difficulties of getting supplies of carpets from different parts of the world, and so on, and half an hour later you ask the price.

By the time you ask for the price you know a lot about each other, and the price can be modified accordingly. "Bargaining can be fun," say the merchants in the bazaar. The merchant may go high if he detects that you are rich and may give you an extra good price if he knows that you are poor and deserving. The whole bargaining process is a social transaction, and the price depends on your needs, your virtue, your charm, and your bargaining skills!

This cultural difference may result in a collectivist merchant's giving a better price to an in-group member. *Advice*: If you are shopping in a collectivist culture, take one of your local friends with you to do the bargaining. When I was in Nigeria, I wanted to buy an African mask. I went to the market with a former student of mine who was with the Peace Corps and spoke Yoruba, the local language. After appropriate bargaining, he got the mask for *one-tenth* of the asking price.

ATTITUDE CHANGE THROUGH COMMUNICATION

Communication is often directed at changing attitudes. Attitude change depends on the source of the message, the content of the message, the medium used to present the message, and the audience of the message (Triandis, 1971). Let us see how these elements are affected by culture.

Best Sources of Messages

Collectivists respect older males and famous families. Individualists are most influenced by sources that are credible, expert, and intelligent and have many past achievements (e.g., winning records).

In the West, identity is dependent on previous accomplishments, experiences, and possessions. In Africa, what you express and who you are, in terms of family and tribe and unique style and movement, constitute a person's identity (Boykin, 1983). In the East, virtuous action is most important (Hofstede, 1991).

Medium

Collectivists need face-to-face contact because they depend on paralinguistics more than do individualists who are quite satisfied with written communications.

Structure of Messages

Collectivists emphasize process (what is said, done, displayed), while individualists emphasize goals (what we are supposed to get done). Individualists use linear logic, argument, and proof. Collectivists often go around in circles.

Language structures are not the same. For example, Harder (1989) points out that the appropriate response to a negative question such as "Wouldn't you go by train?" is "no" in Japanese if the respondent means he or she would go by train. In English the appropriate response is the reverse (we say: "Yes, we would go by train").

Robert Kaplan's (1966) analysis of the logical structure of English essays written by foreign students is shown in Figure 7–1.

Good English argument development reflects the influence of the great rhetoric teachers of the ancient world (Plato, Aristotle) and medieval Europe. The argument is developed linearly, either by stating several facts and drawing a conclusion (inductively) or by making a general statement and providing the supportive evidence (deductively). Kaplan analyzed more than 600 essays written in English by foreign students and found that argument development was different from English and was linked to the student's culture.

The Semitic (including Arabic, also seen in the Old Testament) development is a series of parallel arguments, linked with one or two words, such as "and," "or," or "therefore." Each parallel argument is of equal importance and either supports or contrasts with the other arguments. For example, ". . . the way of the righteous . . . / . . . the way of the wicked. . . ."

FIGURE 7–1

Five logical structures identified in English essays written by foreign students. (Kaplan, 1966. Reprinted with permission.)

English   Semitic   Oriental   Romance   Slavic

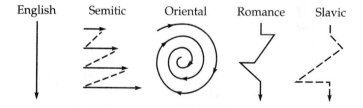

The Oriental argument development often has a "beating around the bush" structure (e.g., "It is an unusually difficult task for us to agree with this view, but we will certainly try to do so. . . .").

The Romance argument includes several digressions (e.g., "This is a very important point that philosophers have not examined, and if we examine the history of Western philosophy, . . .").

The Russian has a clear beginning and end, but in the middle there is much material that is not relevant to the development of the argument (e.g., "Most of Stalin's policies were paranoid, . . . we must consider his appreciation of Georgian music . . . and remains a dark chapter of Soviet history).

Goals

The important goal of the collectivists is harmony and saving both one's own and the other's face (Ting-Toomey, 1988). The collectivist is more concerned with virtuous action (e.g., harmony, saving the other's face) than with the truth (Iwao & Triandis, in press); the individualist is more concerned with the truth than with virtuous action.

Individualists place great value on facts and little value on the views of in-group authorities. Thus, they are likely to develop an argument by stating several facts and then coming to a generalization or conclusion.

The collectivists, on the other hand, have to link their presentation to the views of in-group authorities. No better (or more surprising) example of this can be found than in a talk I went to hear in 1960 given by a Russian psychologist at the International Congress of Psychology, in Bonn, Germany. The title of the talk was "The Study of Discrimination." The speaker started by referring to Marx, Engels, and Lenin, stating that they were all against discrimination. Then he pointed out that in order to discriminate one needs to tell the difference between stimuli. Then he revealed that his talk was about auditory discrimination! It consisted of a careful description of some very expensive equipment that enabled him to study how well people discriminate sounds.

Induction is used a great deal in argumentation in the West, while deduction is used more frequently in collectivist cultures (Glenn, 1981). This difference is also seen in emphasis on ideology rather than pragmatism. In other words, in the West the message is likely to have the structure "fact-fact-fact-conclusion." In deductive cultures the message is "conclusion, and here is the evidence."

In many Third World cultures the world is spiritual, while in the West it is often seen as material. However, there are differences in the level of spirituality. Maximum spirituality is found in Africa and India, and minimum in East Asia. The West, and even more East Asia, also places great value on balance, stability, order, predictability, and routine, while in

Africa imbalance, dynamics, surprise, energy, and movement are important goals in communication.

Communication and Social Behavior

In Chapter 6 we discussed differences in social behavior found in collectivist and individualistic cultures. These differences have implications for communication. Collectivists make friends with their relatives and with friends of the family to a much greater extent than do individualists, so they do not need highly developed skills for getting in and out of groups. That also reduces the probability that they will have highly developed verbal skills. Conversely, individualists need cocktail party skills. They develop verbal skills in order to shine in the group. Collectivists enjoy being more intimate in their relationships, and that goes well with their greater emphasis on paralinguistics, since many of the very intimate feelings cannot be discussed but are expressed.

The use of compliments lubricates social relationships. It follows, from the points we just made, that individualists will use compliments more, since they need to get in and out of groups, based on their social skills. Collectivists will not need such skills to the same extent, so they will not bother with compliments. This is exactly what was found by Barnlund and Araki (1985) when comparing the United States and Japanese rates of compliments. Barnlund and Araki interpreted their findings differently: "A society founded on the group rather than the individual, that stresses harmonious relations, is not likely to encourage comparisons that inherently weaken group membership. (Every compliment is alienating in some respect, for it introduces a comparative standard that by elevating the status of one person implies lowering of the status of others). On the other hand, a society founded on the individual, favoring confrontation with differences, is likely to promote such evaluations for they confirm the individuality of each person and encourage competition" (p. 25). It seems to me that both my explanation and Barnlund and Araki's interpretation may be valid.

Finally, collectivism and communication *in context* have important implications for the way people negotiate (Cohen, 1991). Low-context (individualistic) cultures see no need for "contrived formulas and verbal embellishments" (p. 27), which can easily be missed by the high-context cultures, resulting in misunderstandings.

In high-context cultures, the personal relationship is part of the context. Thus, it is important to establish a good relationship before serious negotiations. This takes time and must be seen as a good way to spend time since it will eventually facilitate the negotiations. Creating good relationships with verbal embellishments may mean the difference between good and bad communications and successful and unsuccessful negotiations.

High-context cultures are also more dependent on shame for social control than are low-context cultures. That means that "honor" and "loss of face" are more serious matters in the high-context cultures. People in these cultures want to find out a lot about their opponent's needs so as to satisfy as many of them as possible and will go to great lengths to avoid situations that may result in loss of face by their opponent.

*I*DEOLOGISM VERSUS PRAGMATISM

In ideological cultures the current ideology, whether it is political, like Marxism, or religious, or philosophical, dominates many judgments, and communication is likely to assume that the other person shares the same viewpoint. By contrast, pragmatic cultures concentrate on what works.

Of course, more than one ideology can exist, and many of the relious wars can be traced to such clashes of beliefs: Muslims versus Christians, Catholics versus Protestants. A modern example is the current debate over abortion (a fetus is a human being versus a woman has the right to control what happens to her). We can also analyze the abortion issue pragmatically: The evidence is very clear (Rohner, 1986) that people who do not want a child are likely to reject it, and people who reject a child are likely to contribute to a personality that is cynical, low in self-esteem, and pessimistic. Such children have a better than average chance of ending up in prison (at the cost of close to $40,000 per year to the taxpayer). This is a terrible expense for society; therefore *pragmatically* one should be pro-choice. Note that the pragmatic solution is less likely to include philosophic assumptions or emotions and more likely to consider the "bottom line."

In contrast to pragmatists, universalists try to use *one* coherent point of view and apply it to everything (Glenn, 1981). Glenn gives an example: At a United Nations conference on housing, the Russian delegate advocated the widespread use of reinforced concrete structures. The American delegates took the position that it all depends on what works well. Delegates from the Third World interpreted this exchange in favor of the Russian. They thought that the Russian was advocating that "what has worked for them should be used for us too; the Americans did not think that we are good enough to use what has worked for them."

When the universalistic person communicates with a particularistic, pragmatic opponent, the universalistic is likely to see the pragmatist as dealing with trivialities and as not having great thoughts, while the pragmatist is likely to see the universalists as theoretical, fuzzy thinking, and dealing with generalities.

In order to communicate effectively it is necessary to use the framework of the audience. But how can a person from a particularistic culture reach a universalistic audience?

Glenn (1981) provides an interesting example of how to deal with universalism when you are particularistic. Indian students are usually universalistic, and American professors who went to India under the Fulbright program were generally particularlistic. One of the major problems Americans faced in India was that their students expected them to know a general scheme that could integrate all the relevant information of their discipline. The Fulbright advisers suggested to the professors that they start their lectures by asserting *dogmatically*, "You must approach this field of study with an open mind, free of dogmatic preconceptions, so as to make it possible to judge the data impartially and thus arrive at a theoretical synthesis." In short, they started with a universalistic framework and then presented particularistic information. Reports from the professors who used this opening statement indicated that they had no problems with their Indian students. Once a broad framework was available, particularism could be used. Conversely, a lecturer with a universal framework who is going to address an audience used to particularism may do well to start with several facts and mention the framework later.

ASSOCIATIVE VERSUS ABSTRACTIVE COMMUNICATION

Some cultures are so homogeneous that people can depend on the associations of their listeners to communicate. These are associative cultures, and their communications have much in common with communications in context-dependent cultures. For instance, when a manager at NASA says "Fire!" a complex set of behaviors takes place that sends a rocket to outer space. However, in heterogeneous cultures communicators cannot assume that they can use the associations of their listeners; they use more abstract terms and define them as they communicate.

Messages are often associated with stimuli that themselves communicate some message. For example, a picture that contains many angular patterns conveys threat, while one that contains mostly rounded patterns conveys warmth (Aronoff, Woike, & Hyman, 1992). There are data suggesting that in all cultures people match the nonsense word "takete" with angular patterns and the word "maluma" with rounded patterns. Much other research provides support for Charles Darwin's speculation that humans express and recognize primary emotions such as fear and love in similar ways. In sum, the associations of a message are often important factors in communication.

Consider this example. In 1932 the finance minister of Japan was assassinated after agreeing to a 17 percent revaluation of the yen. In 1971, American Treasury Secretary Connally, oblivious to Japanese history, demanded a 17 percent revaluation of the yen. His Japanese counterpart totally rejected the demand. When Connally offered a 16.9 percent upward revaluation, the Japanese minister accepted it (Cohen, 1991, p. 133).

Communication can be frustrating when one person expects the other to use an abstractive style but the other uses an associative style. In the next example, it is unclear whether the associative speaker simply forgot he was dealing with a Westernized (abstractive) speaker or was really trying to avoid communication.

The conversation (*Los Angeles Times*, February 12, 1977) was translated verbatim by a Westernized, former Egyptian ambassador (A) to Paris, who was attempting to learn from his foreign minister (FM), a non-Westernized Arab, the results of talks between French officials and Marshal Abdel Hakim Amer, who was then the Egyptian vice president.

A: What is the news?
FM: The machine is working as usual, working.
A: I mean the news of the marshal and his Paris visit.
FM: The important thing is not the preface but the book.
A: Do you mean the preface to the visit?
FM: I mean that the essence should be as clear as the appearance, or else everything is lost.
A: Do you mean the essence of the visit and its appearance?
FM: I mean that we must not lose ourselves in formalities, and let go of the basic things.
A: I hope that the marshal has achieved something through the visit?
FM: Success may come in either way: through the strength of your own arm, or the weakness of others.
[The interview continues this way for a long time and concludes as follows:]
FM: Paris butter is like Paris.
A: Tasty?
FM: Transparent.
A: Light?
FM: Rich.
A: Wholesome?
FM: Necessary.
With that the foreign minister ushered his ambassador to the door but, before parting, admonished him: "Please treat what you have heard as a secret between the two of us." (Part I, p. 18)

By contrast, in cultures where people interact mostly with outsiders, they must define each term that they use and be very clear and explicit.

An example of associative thinking is provided by the following historic fact. In 1967, the Arabs were convinced that the Israelis had received direct, active military assistance from the Americans. In a debate in the UN Security Council the American ambassador asked for proof. The Arab delegate answered that no proof was needed, because it is "obvious that the Americans had intervened. How else could one explain that three-quarters of the Egyptian air force was destroyed in a few hours? Only a large, powerful country could do this."

Associative thinking has much in common with magical thinking. As we mentioned in Chapter 1, the two key principles of magic are propinquity and similarity. For example, anthropologists have noted numerous incidents in which one or more witnesses to an accident, such as the overturning of a canoe, were accused of killing those who drowned. The major factor was that the survivors were at the scene of the accident (propinquity).

In certain cultures people believe they can kill an enemy by taking a needle and piercing a doll that represents him or her. The *similarity* between the doll and the person represented is seen as resulting in the desired death.

Note that even in the West people burn effigies, flags, and the like, but usually they are aware that the action is symbolic. The difference with associative thinking is that the person is not fully aware of the difference between symbols and the entity they represent.

Another problem with associative thinking is that the person does not make key distinctions, such as between "my work" and "myself as a person." When such concepts overlap almost completely, it is very difficult to criticize a person's work without the person's taking the criticism personally. For example, this is the case with non-Westernized Arabs. The statement "I love you, but I think your essay is bad" makes no sense, because there is an implicit assumption in that subculture: "If you love me, you must love everything about me." To criticize in such a case requires that the non-Westernized Arab be made to think about this issue abstractly first and concretely later. A Socratic approach might work: "Is it possible for a person to love another, and yet not like one of that person's actions?" Put in this abstract way, the non-Westernized Arab is likely to agree. Then the criticism may be possible.

Similarly, who the person is and what the person does are so strongly linked in associative cultures that it is not possible to criticize a high-status individual. At the same time a low-status individual is not seen as having the right to a fair trial.

As people become more educated, they shift from associative to abstractive thinking. There is considerable evidence, reviewed by Rogoff (1990), that schooling has the effect of making communications explicit and abstract, while low levels of education result in tacit, concrete, subtle forms of communication. After all, in the classroom, events, places, and people are discussed out of context, abstractly. By contrast people without education have trouble with abstractions. For example, suppose you present the following syllogism to illiterate adults: "Wolves and bears always drink together; a bear is drinking; is the wolf drinking?" They are likely to answer: "I do not know. I have to look and see if the wolf is drinking." This is an example of concrete thinking and contrasts with abstractions that schoolchildren use every day.

Differences can also be traced to cultural values concerning the use of language, subtlety, and silence. For example, among the Navajo, talk is regarded as a sacred gift not to be used unnecessarily (Rogoff, 1990, p. 120).

Even in cultures that are highly associative, many of the educated elite think abstractly, and there are individual differences. We need to examine each case separately and not assume that simply because the individual is, say, an Arab, he will necessarily be associative and context-dependent. Westernized or highly educated Arabs are abstractive. There is also the complication that in many cultures it is "good style" to be concrete, and it "looks foreign" to be abstractive. Thus, a person may be perfectly capable of being abstractive but choose to be concrete.

*P*ARALINGUISTIC COMMUNICATION

A great deal of communication can take place without language. For example, look at Figure 7–2.

In associative communications people also depend very much on paralinguistic cues, such as looking or not looking someone in the eye, touching or not touching, keeping a certain distance from the other person, standing in a certain way (face to face, or at an angle—and how

FIGURE 7–2
Communication without words. In Japan many restaurants use plastic replicas of their offerings, including price. The replicas are constructed so well that they look fairly close to the real dish on the menu. Thus, people who do not know Japanese can order by pointing. (Triandis.)

large is the angle), using a particular level of voice, using perfume or other olfactory cues, keeping the body tense or relaxed, and so on.

There are major cultural differences in the meaning of these behaviors. What is a mild emotional expression in one culture is perceived as an emotional outburst in another.

It is not possible in this book to describe all the complexities of this field. If you wish to learn more, consult some of the references that were cited. And above all, if you travel, observe and ask for advice from local sources.

Emotions

The evidence that emotions are experienced more or less the same way around the world is fairly strong (Ekman, 1992). Enjoyment, anger, fear, sadness, disgust, and surprise appear to be basic emotions that are understandable the same way around the world. However, there are culture-specific *display rules* (Ekman & Friesen, 1971). As noted earlier in the book, Americans and Japanese subjects viewing unpleasant scenes express emotions in the same way. However, when others are present, the Japanese, more than the Americans, masked the expression of their emotion with the semblance of a smile. In short, the Japanese display rule is that one must control oneself, and not express unpleasant emotions (Ekman & Friesen, 1971).

Cultural differences are also found when the categories of emotion are studied. Some cultures have richer vocabularies than others in specific domains. For example, some distinguish different kinds of "disgust" (e.g., boredom, feelings toward a mutilated person, feelings toward dirt). It appears that people in collectivist cultures differentiate more than individualists among categories of emotions that occur in interpersonal relationships (Kitayama, 1992).

Matsumoto (1992) found support for the hypothesis that collectivists will experience more positive emotions than individualists in in-group situations and more negative emotions than individualists in out-group situations.

Eye Contact, Distances, Body Orientations, Gestures

Hall (1959, 1966) has described many cultural differences in paralinguistic behaviors, and since then, a large literature has developed that specifies them further. For example, among persons of unequal status, looking another person directly in the eye is more common in Anglo-Saxon cultures than in Latino or Native American cultures, where it is considered insolent for a low-status person to look a high-status person in the eye. Pointing with your finger toward a person is disrespectful among traditional Navajo (Salzman, 1991); if you must point, use your lips to show the direction.

Watson (1970) studied 110 male foreign students at the University of Colorado. They were asked to come to a laboratory with a person of the same language or culture. They first completed a questionnaire and then were observed through a one-way mirror, of which they were aware. They talked to each other about anything they wanted to, in their own language, while they were being observed. They were rated on a scale of 1 to 4, where 1 indicated most eye contact (focus of the eyes) and 4 indicated no eye contact. The Arabs, Latin Americans, and Southern Europeans had means of 1.25, 1.41, and 1.49, respectively, while the Asians, Indians-Pakistanis, and Northern Europeans had means of 2.06, 2.05, and 2.17. The high-contact cultures did not differ statistically from each other, but they were statistically very different from the low-contact cultures.

Table 7-1 presents the details. Touching is more common in the cultures around the Mediterranean, e.g., among Hispanics, than in Northern European cultures or among many of the Native American tribes. Most East and South Asians and Native Americans (e.g., the

TABLE 7-1 CULTURAL DIFFERENCES IN PARALINGUISTIC BEHAVIOR

		Axis	*Closeness*	*Touch*	*Visual*	*Voice*
Contact group N = 50	Arabs N = 20	2.57	3.53	6.59	1.25	3.96
	Latins N = 20	2.47	4.96	6.74	1.41	4.14
	So. Eur. N = 10	2.19	4.42	6.88	1.49	4.57
Americans	N = 16	3.00	7.66	7.00	2.86	4.43
Noncontact group N = 72	Asians N = 12	3.25	5.20	6.97	2.06	4.79
	Ind.-Pak. N = 12	3.59	3.94	6.99	2.05	4.39
	No. Eur. N = 48	3.51	5.92	7.00	2.17	4.32

CODE: *Axis* refers to whether people are face to face when they speak to each other (coded 1), or parallel (both looking forward, coded 5), or in between these two positions (coded 2, 3, and 4).

Closeness refers to whether people can potentially hold, grasp, or touch each other during a conversation. "Body contact" was coded 1, "within touching distance with forearm extended" was coded 3, while "just outside this distance" was coded 8.

Touch was coded with a 1 for "holding and caressing" and a 7 for "no contact."

Visual was coded 1 for direct eye contact and 4 for no visual contact.

Voice was coded 1 for very loud and 6 for very soft. The researcher's "normal voice level" was coded 4.

SOURCE: Watson, 1970.

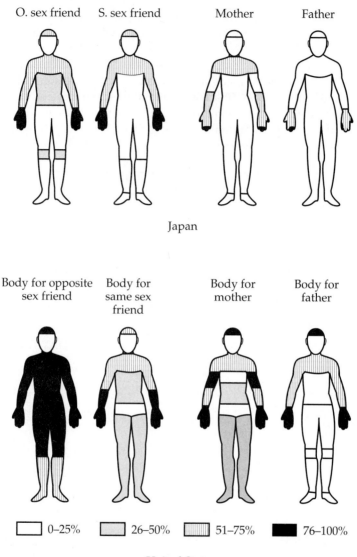

O. sex friend   S. sex friend   Mother   Father

Japan

Body for opposite   Body for   Body for   Body for
   sex friend   same sex   mother   father
                      friend

☐ 0–25%   ☐ 26–50%   ▥ 51–75%   ■ 76–100%

United States

FIGURE 7–3

One can touch certain parts of the body in one culture that are taboo in other cultures. Barnlund (1975) obtained the frequencies of touching different parts of the body. In the United States one can touch all parts of the body on an opposite-sex friend, but the region around the genitals is taboo in the case of all others. In Japan larger areas of the body, even the areas below the waist of opposite-sex friends, are taboo. You can count the number of body parts that are taboo to obtain an index of the "tightness" of the culture. (Barnlund, 1975. Reprinted by permission.)

Navajo, Salzman, 1991) do not touch even within the family, let alone among strangers. Handshakes in Latin America are expected to be soft, not hard as among mainstream Americans. Two males holding hands has a clear homosexual connotation in the United States but is a sign of friendship in the Middle East and Latin America.

The Arabs and Southern Europeans were significantly different from the Asians, Indians, and Northern Europeans; the Latin Americans, however, were not. We must remember that many Latin Americans are culturally both Mediterranean and Native American, and the latter belong to no-contact cultures. The result is that some Latin Americans behave like Southern Europeans and others like Asians, and thus there is greater variability in their scores, making it difficult to get statistically significant results.

What parts of the body a person may touch are also culturally determined. Barnlund (1975, in Argyle, 1988, p. 218) provides a chart of permissible areas for different relationships in Japan and the United States (see Figure 7–3).

Latins interact using small physical distances, while Japanese use large distances. Americans are intermediate. Sussman and Rosenfeld (1982) asked thirty-two Japanese and thirty-one Venezuelan foreign students (assigned to speak either in their native language or in English) and thirty-nine Americans to hold a five-minute conversation on a common topic with a same-sex, same-nationality confederate. It was found that when speaking their native language, the Japanese sat farther apart than the Venezuelans, with the Americans at an intermediate distance (see Figure 7–4). When speaking in English, the foreign students approximated the American conversational distances (see Figure 7–5).

In the Watson study, mentioned above, ratings of closest distance (low numbers) to farthest distance resulted in the Arabs' receiving a score of 3.53 and the Northern Europeans a 5.92.

In sum, while we can be sure that some cultural differences in the use of space are present (e.g., Arabs, Latin Americans, and U.S. Hispanics use smaller personal spaces than do North Europeans and Far Easterners), we should not expect consistently strong effects (Hayduk, 1983), because the correlations between culture and the use of space are sometimes low.

Body orientation is a very important variable and can be examined by checking the angle of conversation. Face-to-face means an angle of zero degrees. In the Watson study mentioned earlier, there was a clear statistical separation of the Arabs, Latinos, and Southern Europeans from the Asians, Indians, and Northern Europeans. Where a rating of 2 means a 45-degree angle, 3 means a 90-degree angle, and 4 means a 135-degree angle, the high-contact cultures averaged about 2.5 and the low-contact cultures about 3.5.

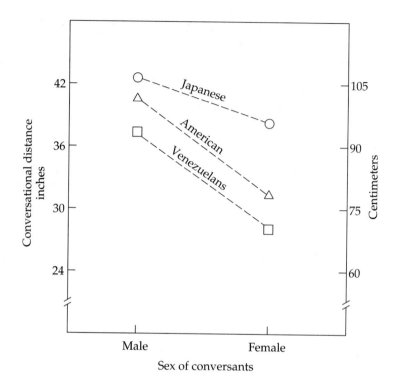

FIGURE 7-4

Conversation distance depends on both culture and gender. Here the
Japanese use more distance than the Venezuelans, especially among
females. In all three cultures males use more distance than females.
(Sussman & Rosenfeld, 1982. Copyright 1982 by the American Psychological
Association. Reprinted by permission.)

The effects of touch, distance, and body orientation can be seen in
diplomatic cocktail parties. An observer will sometimes see the high-
contact-culture diplomats "chasing" the low-contact-culture diplomats
across the floor, with the low-contact-culture diplomats retreating to a
comfortable distance. You can get some idea of these differences in the
use of space by looking at Figures 7–6 and 7–7.

The level of voice that is appropriate for conversation is also culturally
determined. The cultures around the Mediterranean, especially the Arabs,
use high levels. In fact, the Arabs believe that loud and clear is "sincere"
and soft is "devious." North of the Alps, people consider it very impolite
to disturb others with loud talk. The Navajo and many Native American
tribes also value soft voices in ordinary conversation. Americans vary on
this dimension according to social class. The upper classes use softer
levels than the lower classes. In fact, "loud" and "coarse" are often synonyms in negatively describing people in the United States.

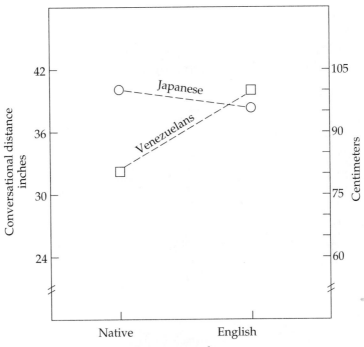

FIGURE 7–5

When respondents in the Sussman and Rosenfeld (1982) study were asked to converse in English, the cultural differences in the conversation distances were eliminated. Quite often people who are multilingual behave differently depending on the language they use. Language acts as a cue that tells them which norms to use to determine behavior. (Sussman & Rosenfeld, 1982. Copyright 1982 by the American Psychological Association. Reprinted by permission.)

Related to the Arab loud-and-clear style is the customary tendency toward exaggeration. Here is the text of a letter written by a Jordanian university administrator, thanking me for inviting him to an informal dinner—hamburgers and cold cuts. "Thank you for the extreme hospitality, dignity, and magnanimity. . . . all the ladies and gentlemen were overflowing with generosity and sociality especially at the grand supper meeting at your home. . . . the program of our visit was too perfect and beneficial. . . . "

The importance of this point is that an ordinary "thank you" sent to Jordan would most likely appear extraordinarily weak, if not insulting. Compare the previous text with something like: "I am writing to thank you for your hospitality during our visit. We enjoyed very much meeting you and appreciate the careful arrangements you have made and the

FIGURE 7–6
Same-sex conversations in
Nepal. (Roy Malpass.)

FIGURE 7–7
Same-sex conversations in Nepal. (Roy Malpass.)

dinner at your home. Thank you very much." How ordinary that is! Westerns should learn to polish and embellish their speech; otherwise they might be misunderstood in some cultures.

Gestures constitute another very important channel of communication. Many gestures are universal, but most of them are culture-specific. Argyle (1988) has assembled extensive materials on such gestures, and those interested in seeing cultural differences in gestures should consult his book. Until a traveler has learned the local gestures, it is best to avoid them. What appears totally appropriate in one culture is totally inappropriate in another. For example, the "it's A-okay" American sign, which involves two fingers forming a circle, can mean "It is not good; zero" (southern France), "Give me some money" (Japan), and "Let's have sex" (Brazil). Shaking your head means "no" in America but "yes" in Bulgaria and southern India. A firm handshake is admired in America but is seen as aggressive in many other cultures.

The timing of communications also is subject to cultural differences. Hall (1959, 1966, 1973) has discussed the difference between monochronic and polychronic use of time. In monochronic use of time a person does one job at a time or meets one person or group of persons at a time. An "appointment" means that a person devotes all the time to one activity. In polychronic use of time, several activities can occur in parallel. A person might, for instance, have appointments with two or three people and also answer the phone, go out for coffee with a friend, and in general use the time in multiple, parallel forms, rather than do one thing at a time. In many cultures, e.g., Saudi Arabia, polychronic use is more common than monochronic use of time. In sum, when monochronic time is used, a person communicates with one audience at a time; when polychronic time is used, a person communicates with several audiences simultaneously.

The non-Western willingness to use polychronic time clashes with the Western style of one dialogue at a time. That cultural difference can be understood if we take into account that polychronic communications tend to be primarily "affective exchanges" (say good or scolding things to the other), while the Western communications are primarily "cognitive exchanges" (i.e., make considerable cognitive demands on the communicator, who has to pay much attention to every word).

Furthermore, since collectivists see themselves as parts of groups, which often have long histories (ancestors over many generations; future generations), they tend to see the present as an instance within a very broad time frame. There is little concern with short-term goals and much more concern with the long-term picture. An interesting example of this view of time is the Chinese approach to the Taiwan issue. Both sides of the Formosa Strait consider Taiwan as part of China. The Taiwan government expects eventually to return to power in the Chinese Mainland, and that will "solve the problem." The government of the People's Republic of China expects that when its economic policies make it as wealthy as Taiwan, there will be a voluntary absorption of that small country into the motherland. Both sides are thinking in terms of a hundred years!

In addition to gestures and the like, communication can be accomplished by other means. In many cultures communication is accomplished with gifts. You can say "I love you" with flowers, but the color and the number of flowers is culture specific. It is best to tell the local florist exactly what you want to communicate and let a professional decide the best color, type, and number.

Toasts are an occasion for saying things that are not normally said in everyday life. In many cultures the frequency of toasts is much higher than in the United States (e.g., China, Sweden). The traveler should be prepared to give meaningful toasts as the occasion requires, being guided by hosts who will suggest it.

Limitations of space did not allow discussion of sex differences (Beck, 1988) in communication patterns, but such differences do exist and seem to have both universal and culture-specific attributes.

S UMMARY

This chapter examined patterns of communication, both linguistic and paralinguistic, across cultures. Cultures differ in the extent to which they pay attention to context and the extent to which they use associative patterns of communication. Both these attributes are more likely in collectivist cultures, where there is also much emphasis on the in-group's ideology and on harmony and hierarchy.

QUESTIONS AND EXERCISES

1. Find several persons who are likely to come from collectivist cultures and check with them about some of the generalizations made in this chapter.

2. Check with people from different cultures about the gestures that you use and how they interpret them.

3. Ask people from different cultures what nonlinguistic methods they use to say "yes" and "no" and to insult others in their culture.

4. Ask people from different cultures to role-play criticizing (a) a close friend, (b) a stranger, and (c) a disliked neighbor.

5. Ask people from different cultures to role-play how they would communicate an intensive admiration for (a) a close friend, (b) a stranger, and (c) a liked neighbor.

8

Cultural Influences on Aggression, Helping, Dominance, and Conformity

❖

In Chapter 4 I briefly mentioned a model that links subjective culture and social behavior and examines the psychological processes that intervene between these two constructs. This model is presented in Figure 8–1. It is a modification of an earlier model (Triandis, 1972, 1977, 1980) that takes into account the most recent work on the attitude-behavior relationship (Eagly & Chaiken, 1993; Fishbein et al., 1992). This chapter begins by analyzing subjective culture and

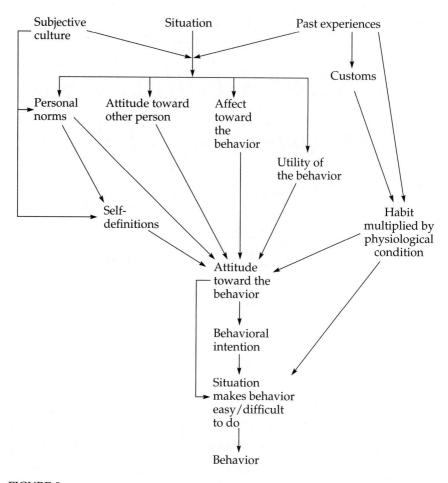

FIGURE 8–1
Subjective culture and social behavior relationships.

behavior using the concepts of the model in Figure 8–1. Next it examines aggressive behavior in terms of the concepts in Figure 8–1. Then the other social behaviors—conflict resolution, social distance, helping, sexual behavior, dominance, conformity, obedience, and self-disclosure—are discussed more briefly.

These behaviors are important in all cultures, because in all cultures people can distinguish between *associative* (helping, admiring, sexual) and *dissociative* (avoiding, aggressive) behaviors, *superordinate* (domination) and *subordinate* (conformity, obedience) behaviors, and intimate (self-disclosure) and formal (behaving as required by etiquette) behaviors (Triandis, 1978).

*S*UBJECTIVE CULTURE AND SOCIAL BEHAVIOR

Let us start with the example of the Baker-Aziz (U.S.-Iraq) cross-cultural misunderstanding described in Chapter 2. Remember, we suggested at that time that if Baker were to communicate effectively, he should have thrown the Geneva telephone book at the Iraqis. Instead, he said only, as clearly as he could have said it, that the United States will attack if Iraq does not pull out of Kuwait.

Consider then the behavior "to throw the Geneva telephone book." The variable in this model that determines that behavior is whether the situation makes it easy or difficult to do the behavior. Clearly, if the Geneva telephone book were not available, Baker would not have been able to throw it, even if he were in the habit of throwing telephone books, if he had the behavioral intention (self-instruction) of doing that, and if he had a positive attitude toward throwing telephone books. But in this case we can guess that Baker did not have the habit of throwing telephone books. If he were very angry (physiological condition), he would especially *not* be likely to do that, because habits multiply with arousal, and so people who are aroused are especially likely to do what is habitual for them. Of course, the custom in the United States does not include throwing telephone books on diplomatic occasions, and past experiences with this activity, if they had occurred, would have resulted in punishments, thus extinguishing the tendency to do it.

If Baker had gotten a briefing from cross-cultural experts, he might have realized the utility of the behavior. He might even have enjoyed the behavior (affect toward the behavior), and since he probably did not like Aziz, the attitude toward the other person would have favored the behavior. But his personal norms and self-definitions ("I am not the kind of person who throws telephone books") probably would have been quite inconsistent with the behavior, so that most likely his attitude toward the behavior would have been negative. Remember, statesmen keep an eye on how their behavior will be recorded by history, and almost certainly Baker would not have wanted history to remember him as a thrower of telephone books. When the Russian general secretary of the Communist party, Khrushchev, took off his shoe and banged it on the table in the United Nations, he produced one of the memorable events of world history, because the behavior was inappropriate in that setting. Inappropriate behavior is unlikely to come from a gentleman like Baker. Thus, his personal norms and self-definitions, which reflect the influences of upper-class U.S. subjective culture, would be very powerfully against doing what is fun to do (affect toward the behavior) or what is high in utility. The situation, also, was a diplomatic one and did not call for such behavior. In short, even if Baker had been briefed about the utility of the behavior and had liked to do it, there were too many constraints on doing it. Especially his habits would be counter to doing it. So he did what most diplomats do well: talk. But as we have seen, the talk, in this case, was misunderstood. It was too calm, not angry enough; too moderate, not extreme enough. Again, the tone resulted in a misunderstanding. A diplomat could be trained to change tone, but by examining the model we see that there are many changes (self-definitions, perception of the situation, habits, etc.) that need to be made to change a behavior. A diplomat would have to practice using a different tone for quite a while, and get many reinforcements, before the behavior changes from his or her usual habits.

This example, then, tells us that cross-cultural behavior is often ineffective, because our habits, self-definitions, and perception of the situation may be wrong for the purpose of effective behavior.

Many other examples can be given. In intercultural situations we often offend people because of our habits. In America, for example, we often cross our legs when we sit down. Some people place their feet on tables or other objects to feel comfortable. However, in many cultures (for example, Lebanon), showing the bottom of your shoes is an extreme insult. People learn to behave in ways that avoid insulting others. An American who is told not to show the bottom of his shoes will often cross his legs, remember he is not supposed to do it, and quickly uncross them, thus avoiding offending the other person. Avoiding offending his host will result in self-reinforcement. Such reinforcement will shape new habits, and the American will avoid crossing his legs. With repetition the cues of the situation (e.g., "I am in Lebanon") link with the behavior. Gradually the habit of crossing legs becomes extinguished and other behaviors replace it. To take another example, if you know that the other person is a Jain and considers all life sacred, you may well instruct yourself to abstain from killing an ant that is crawling on your arm.

While habits determine our behaviors much of the time, when we are in new situations or are surprised by events and have the time to think, we stop using habits; instead, we process whatever information we can get to make a sound decision about how to behave.

Our self-definitions require us to act in the way we think is "right" for us *in the particular situation*. There are many behaviors that we will not engage in because of our sense of what is right for us, i.e., our sense of morality. Another important element of our self-definition is self-efficacy. Do we think that we *can* do something?

Self-efficacy (Bandura, 1989) reflects the extent to which a person thinks that he or she *can* do something, in spite of barriers and difficulties that might prevent doing it. If a person does not think that he or she has the capacity or ability to reach a specific goal, that person may not even try. For example, if you think that learning a foreign language is a great idea but you do not think that you can do it, you will probably not try.

The situation is a very important determinant of behavior. Most of us act as expected in a particular situation *as we see it*. That does not mean that there are no people who desecrate churches, insult judges, hit teachers, and so on. In many of these events the person is highly aroused and acts without thinking. Self-control requires some thinking. There are also many people whose self-concept includes acting in a counternormative way (from the point of view of a particular normative system), like the herders of Sardinia we encountered in Chapter 4. In that case there are two normative systems, and the person acts according to a system that makes it "right" for him or her to steal.

Social behavior depends also on agreements made with others. This is a special kind of personal norm. For example, if you and your friend have decided to go to the movies on Wednesday at 7 p.m., that is an interpersonal agreement. In most cultures, people act as they have agreed to do. Again, that does not mean that people will never break agreements. The model includes many other factors; if some of them are inconsistent with these agreements, people will not do what they have agreed to do.

The attitude toward the other person depends on the previous experiences we had with that person and our liking of that person, as well as the actions of the other person.

The affect toward the behavior reflects the emotions that have been classically conditioned to the thought of doing something. If I hate *touching* a person (for example, a person with a mutilated face), even though my personal norms ("I should be kind and touch") and attitude toward the person (he is very nice) are positive, I may not be able to touch that person.

The utility of the behavior is a variable that reflects the perceived consequences of actions and the value of these consequences. We have beliefs about the consequences of our actions, and we also have positive or negative evaluations of these consequences. Suppose I ask you: What would happen if you studied two hours for this exam? What would happen if you went to the movies instead of studying for this exam? You would have definite ideas. You might see, for instance, that studying has the consequence of getting an A rather than a B. If an A means a lot to you, you will see much greater utility in the studying behavior than if you are satisfied with a B.

All the variables just described feed into the attitude toward the behavior. For instance, if you are the supervisor of an important student activity and your best friend is working with you and is doing a bad job, you may have to fire your friend. You hate (strong negative affect toward the behavior) to do that, but you know it is necessary. Other coworkers may have told you that you must do it, and you know that this behavior has great utility. Thus, your total evaluation of the behavior in that situation is that you have to do what you hate do to.

Your attitude toward the behavior is a kind of summary of all the influences that determine how you will instruct yourself to behave. It reflects your personal norms, self-definitions, attitudes toward the other person, affect toward the behavior, and utility of the behavior.

The attitude toward the behavior determines your behavioral intentions, that is, your self-instructions to do something. But these instructions are filtered through the realities of the situation. The fact that you have the intention to do something does not mean you will do it. It is only when the situation permits you to carry out the intentions that you will do it. (Empirical evidence supporting the relationships mentioned above has been reviewed in Davidson & Morrison, 1983, and Triandis, 1980.)

This discussion should be remembered as pointing to the *complexity* of the relationships between the elements of subjective culture and behavior. You should not assume that just because an *individual* has a particular self-concept, or endorses particular values, that individual's behavior can be predicted. The prediction of behavior requires consideration of all the factors mentioned above.

Similarly, suppose you measured a group's values and you want to predict the behavior of a member of this group from these values. Only if all the other factors mentioned above do not contradict the values can you predict that the average person in that group will act consistently with these values.

Now we turn our attention to the relationship between the elements of subjective culture and one particular behavior: aggression.

AGGRESSIVE BEHAVIOR

Aggression is a "sequence of behavior, the goal response of which is the injury to the person toward whom it is directed" (Dollard, Doob, Miller, Mowrer, & Sears, 1939, p. 9).

Incidence

Aggression varies very considerably around the globe. Goldstein and Segall (1983) review evidence that there are societies where aggression is virtually absent and societies where it occurs daily. Also, they identify significant differences in patterns of aggression. In some cultures, within-culture aggression occurs almost only when alcohol is involved (Finland) or honor is at stake (Turkey). Rates of within-culture aggression vary dramatically from very low (Iceland, Japan) to very high (Peru, Nigeria).

Interpol, the international police agency, publishes statistics that indicate large differences in murder rates among countries. For example, in Norway there is only 0.9 murder per 100,000; in Finland and the People's Republic of China the rates are 1.1 murders per 100,000 of population, while the U.S. rate is 8.6. There are even higher rates, such as

46 per 100,000 in the Philippines. The latter country has more cases of "running amok" (mass murder) than other countries. Murder is so rare in Norway that when an American committed a murder there, there was some talk about expelling all Americans! Japan has a low murder rate; Tokyo's rate is about one-twentieth of New York's.

The American Bureau of Justice reported statistics indicating that a black man in America has a 1 in 21 chance of being murdered in his lifetime. This can be compared with ratios of 1 to 131 and 1 to 369 for white males and females, respectively. Some black activists see a white "conspiracy" to eliminate black men in America. But the data do not support this view: "Currently, about 95% of murdered black males between 15 and 34 are killed by other young black males" (Sargent, 1986).

Subjective Culture

Two studies show very different rates of aggression related to culture. Brown (1986) examined aggression among the Simbu of New Guinea, a tribe administered by Australia. They engage in frequent warfare in spite of prohibitions by the Australians.

Brown found that they had very positive attitudes about aggression and admired those who were most aggressive. There was sex segregation and male domination of females; high status was associated with being male, violent, competitive, and loyal to the men's group. When a fight started, all those able to join did so. All-male groups with homogeneous attitudes were led by "big men" whose status depended on having many followers. These big men instigated fights and pressed others to join their group and fight with them. Frustration was present because there was a shortage of land, and there was no confidence in the judicial system and no possibility of equitable distribution of the available resources. It is clear, then, that this group's subjective culture is consistent with aggression.

The Simbu can be contrasted with the Semai, described by Robarchek (1986). Here attitudes toward aggression are very negative. In fact, the Semai believe that "only bad people are violent." They live in the Malaysian rain forest, where there are abundant resources and little frustration, and they associate great dangers with being alone. For the Semai the supreme value is nurturance.

Nisbett (1990) points to the large differences in homicide rates in large U.S. cities compared with cities in other countries. Specifically, the U.S. rates are hundreds of times greater than in Iceland or Israel. Even within the United States, there are large differences: The rates in the Texas panhandle are four times higher than the rates in Nebraska (p. 262). Nisbett (1990) explains the difference with reference to the cultures from which the settlers originally came: Texans in the panhandle came from the upper South; the Nebraskans originated mainly in Europe.

Members of collectivist cultures can tolerate an act of aggression when it comes from an in-group authority more than when it comes from a low-level in-group member or an outsider (Bond, Wan, Leung, & Giacolone, 1985). Bond (1992) has shown that in collectivist cultures a high-status in-group member can insult a low-status in-group member with impunity; however, a person cannot get away with insulting a collectivist's in-group! In short, aggression is interpreted differently, depending on the subjective culture of a group of people.

Situation

Nisbett (1990) provides good examples of differences in aggression, using the perspectives of evolutionary psychology. The inhabitants of Truk and Tahiti in the Pacific live in similar ecologies, but the Truk fish in the open sea, which is very dangerous; the Tahitians fish in lagoons, where there are no risks and fish are plentiful.

Both islands are tropical, but the presence of the lagoon with plenty of fish makes all the difference. The Trukese need to be aggressive and fearless in order to fish in the open sea. Thus the male Trukese are violent fighters, compete with one another in physical contests and other acts of bravado, have many love affairs, and sire children early. Women are required to be submissive, and men are extremely protective of them. By contrast the Tahitians are peaceful and cooperative and do not overprotect their women. Men are expected to be passive and submissive and to ignore slights. There is no requirement to defend one's honor.

When resources are limited and basic motives are aroused, aggression is common. Living among the nomadic Siriono of eastern Bolivia, Holmberg (1969) observed seventy-five disputes. Most concerned divisions of resources. However, the subjective culture of this tribe did not favor aggression, and while disputes existed, they seldom led to physical attacks. Warfare is rare among these tribes.

Some collectivist cultures display various forms of aggression toward out-groups and also toward in-group members who break important in-group norms. A good example can be found among the Sarakatsani (Campbell, 1964), a Greek mountain community. These shepherds steal sheep from each other and rationalize this action by saying that they do not have enough meat to feed their families. In the course of raids on the other in-group's sheep, some people get killed. Then one extended family fights with another, and ultimately there is a local war. These "family feuds" are common in collectivist cultures.

There are societies that are endogamous—people must marry within the in-group. For example, many Muslim cultures pressure the men to marry the daughter of their father's brother. In such cultures the in-group can truly remain distant from all out-groups. The honor of the family is of the utmost importance in such societies. It is greatly reduced if one of its members is killed by outsiders, in which case revenge is absolutely necessary to restore the family honor.

Large cities are more violent than rural areas, in part because of deindividuation (Zimbardo, 1969). Feeling anonymous and lacking concern for social evaluation can result in people's being more aggressive. A loss of identity can also be experienced when a person feels part of a crowd, or is disguised, masked, dressed in uniform, or hidden in darkness. Watson (1973) consulted the Human Relations Area Files to study in what cultures soldiers are especially aggressive (killing, torturing, mutilating). Deindividuation was coded when the soldiers changed their appearance before going into battle. This study found that those societies where soldiers changed their appearance were more aggressive than those societies in which soldiers did not change their appearance.

There is evidence that democracies rarely fight each other (Ember, Ember, & Russett, 1992), which suggests that when people learn how to agree to disagree and have some control over the political process, they may also learn that conflicts with other people who share similar ideas about the political process can be resolved without war. There is also evidence that ecologies that are afflicted by shortages of resources and a high frequency of unpredictable events (e.g., natural disasters) are more likely to generate aggressive cultures (Ember & Ember, 1992). Unpredictable natural disasters are linked to general distrust, and both these factors are linked to the frequency of wars. A similar phenomenon occurs among hard-core unemployed blacks: They tend to distrust all aspects of their environment (Triandis, 1976b) and also to be aggressive. Thus, frequent exposure to unpredictable negative events predisposes aggression.

In some ecologies there are more chances of conflict over resources (e.g., when groups live next to each other, and there are no rules about who has access to resources). Some ecologies are more frustrating than others (there are few resources, and other groups prevent access to them). The more frustrating the ecology, the more aggressive behavior is likely.

Several studies suggest that observing aggression can increase the probability of aggression (Geen, 1972). Parents who use physical punishment act as models of aggressive behavior and are more likely to have children who are themselves aggressive. Thus cultures and subcultures where aggression is common increase the probability of aggression.

Past Experiences

One human universal is that males commit more acts of aggression than females. Specialists are divided on whether that reflects a genetic predisposition or simply the way boys and girls are socialized around the world. Certainly, some role differentiation occurred early in the history of human evolution, with women more tied down because of childbearing and men freer to hunt and explore, resulting in different socialization patterns' being functional for the two sexes.

Males are more competitive than females (Strube, 1981), and that may be one of the many factors that increase male aggression.

Girls may learn more about alternatives to aggression (e.g., getting what they want by submitting to authorities, complimenting, providing services). Boys have more opportunities to see men as aggressive models (e.g., soldiers), may learn to aggress by imitating, and may also see aggression as defining "being a man." Parents may punish aggression in girls more than in boys.

We know that parents raise girls and boys differently. For example, Barry, Bacon, and Child (1957) examined sex differences in socialization as they appeared in the Human Relations Area Files (see Chapter 3 for a description of the files). They found that obedience was demanded of the girls twelve times more frequently than it was demanded of the boys, taking responsibility for household chores was demanded six times more frequently for girls than for boys, and training to be nurturing was found in 82 percent of the societies for girls and in none of the societies for boys. On the other hand, achievement was emphasized when rearing boys twenty-nine times more frequently than when rearing girls, and self-reliance training was provided for boys in 85 percent of the societies, but no such training was provided for girls in any of the societies. In short, there is no doubt that boys and girls are not reared the same way.

Minturn and Lambert (1964) found that children are discouraged from being aggressive in extended families, since in those cases a fight between the children can result in enmities among the adults. This was confirmed in a study by Olsen (1967) carried out in Taiwan. There was most aggression control when grandparents resided with the family.

Levinson (1989) studied family violence in the data of the Human Relations Area Files. He found wife beating in 84 percent of the societies, physical punishment of children in 74 percent, and fighting between siblings in 44 percent; these were the three most common forms of aggression within families. Adult women are most likely to be the victims of violence, and adult men are most likely to be the perpetrators. Wife beating occurs most frequently in those societies where the husband has more economic and decision power.

There is more physical punishment of children in agricultural than in hunting and food-gathering cultures. Finally, there are sixteen societies where there is no evidence of family violence of any kind.

Customs and Habits

In some cultures intertribal aggression is a custom, and people are in the habit of fighting. Conversely, people might have the habit of not fighting and have skills to avoid aggression.

Physiological Conditions

Many murders are spontaneous acts of passion rather than products of a single-minded determination to kill (Mulvihill & Tumin, 1969). There is some evidence that any kind of strong arousal, such as arousal due to extremely hot and humid temperatures (Anderson, 1987), noise, pain, insult, removal of accustomed reward, frustration (inability to reach desirable goals), hunger, and even exposure to sexual stimuli (Zillman, 1971), may facilitate aggression.

In hot climates there is more aggression than in cold ones. Anderson (1987) examined the relationship between temperature and murder, rape, and assault rates in several American cities. The relationship was strong and replicated both across time (summer-winter) and across space (U.S. South versus North) in several studies. There is more homicide, also, in hot regions of the world than in cold ones (Robbins, de Walt, & Pelto, 1972). In fact, as noted in a previous chapter, the Eskimos feel contempt for white people because they "hunt each other like animals."

Viewing violent television can increase arousal, provide information on how to carry out a crime, and suggest criminal courses of action. It can make murder seem like an ordinary event. It is estimated that the average American eighteen-year-old has seen 18,000 murders on TV! Those predisposed to aggression are most likely to view such programs. The Surgeon General's Study on Television and Social Behavior discounted the importance of this factor. But the commission excluded from its membership the seven distinguished social scientists who had done most of the research on this topic (Cisin et al., 1972).

The greater the inequality of opportunity, the greater the probability that some people will be frustrated, and this will result in aggression. For example, the frequency of crimes is related to the level of economic inequality. One interesting index of inequality is the ratio of the gross national product (GNP) controlled by the top and bottom 10 percent of the income distribution in a given country. In the United States this ratio is about 10. In Brazil it is about 50; in Iceland about 2. Crime statistics are closely related to this ratio, though many other factors are also important. For example, when I was in Iceland, I was told that there was essentially no crime, and the only people in jail were three drunks. But we must take into account the fact that the country is small (population about 260,000), that it is ethnically highly homogeneous, and that on islands crime is low because criminals cannot run away.

Social stress in general, indexed by Landau (1984) by using country statistics such as divorce rates and rates of births to unmarried mothers, is linked to crime in a sample of industrial countries.

A highly competitive environment is arousing and can lead to more crime. For example, Feldman (1968) dropped $1 and $5 bills in the streets of Boston, and equivalent amounts in the streets of Paris, France, and Athens, Greece (Table 8–1). He was interested in seeing whether people

TABLE 8-1 PROPORTION OF PEOPLE FALSELY CLAIMING MONEY IN THREE COUNTRIES

E	Lower amount[a]	Higher amount[b]
Paris (6% kept money)		
American foreigner	5	0
	(40)	(40)
French compatriot	8	10
	(40)	(40)
Athens (13% kept money)		
American foreigner	15	12
	(40)	(40)
Greek compatriot	12	10
	(40)	(39)
Boston (17% kept money)		
French foreigner	27	11
	(41)	(36)
American compatriot	10	18
	(40)	(40)

NOTE: The observed frequencies of people keeping the money in the three cities differed from the expected frequencies: $x^2 = 7.15$, $p < .05$ (n's in parentheses). Figures in percentages.
[a] Paris: 5 francs; Athens: 20 drachmas; Boston: 1 dollar.
[b] Paris: 10 francs; Athens: 50 drachmas; Boston: 5 dollars.
SOURCE: Feldman, 1968. Copyright 1968 by the American Psychological Association. Reprinted by permission.

would falsely claim that the bill belonged to them. The rates of false claim were high in Boston and low in the other two sites. When asked by another experimenter who had a tape recorder in his pocket, "What is going on here? Does this guy give money away?" the Bostonians pointed to their highly competitive environment as a justification for pocketing the money.

Physiological factors such as hypoglycemia (an abnormal glucose metabolism) also have been linked to aggression (Bolton, 1984). And there is fairly good evidence that levels of the male hormone testosterone are linked to levels of aggression as well. Dabbs and Morris (1990) analyzed the archives of U.S. military veterans and obtained information on the testosterone levels of 4462 men. They found that those who had high levels of the hormone were statistically significantly more likely to be delinquent and to have an antisocial personality (marital aggression, neglect of children, job trouble, unpaid debts, traffic offenses, nontraffic arrests, lying, violence, vagrancy).

The researchers also classified the men in their study according to their socioeconomic status. They found that those with testosterone levels in the top 10 percent of the range were likely to be members of the lower class. Aggressive behavior was a function of *both* testosterone level and lower social-class status. They found no relationship between testosterone level and aggression in the higher-social-class segment of the sample. We can reasonably infer from this that when people are frustrated *and* have high levels of the hormone, they are more likely to be aggressive.

Economic status is clearly related to the probability of frustration, since the definition of frustration is "being interrupted when attempting to reach, hence being unable to reach, desirable goals." A person who is wealthy is more likely, on the average, to be able to reach desirable goals than a person who is poor.

Attitude toward Others

Hostility toward others and their groups also depends on the stereotypes, feelings, and social distance experienced by a person toward these groups.

Utility of Behavior

Lambert (1971) showed that punishment for aggression during the socialization of children was maximal in those societies where people lived with their extended family. You cannot afford to let your son hit his third cousin, because that will split the family, which in such a case means the household. In other words, social structure is also a factor in aggression.

Self-Definition

In countries where the father-son link is weak, e.g., because of father absence, there is more crime. There is some evidence that aggressive crimes are part of a defensive reaction against feminine identification in males (see Segall, Dasen, Berry, & Poortinga, 1990, pp. 280–283, for a review).

In forty-eight societies drawn from the Human Relations Area Files, when child-father contact was minimal, there was more crime. Segall has long been a student of culture and aggression, and he takes the position that weak father-son contact may be a very important variable. Fathers tend to be absent from the family in those societies where males have more prestige than females; hence young males raised by their mothers will be especially keen to avoid being feminine. In their effort to be as masculine as possible, they overshoot and become even more masculine than the average of their society. In the six-cultures project of Whiting and Whiting (1975), the highest degree of aggression was found in the two societies with the most separation between men and women and with little contact between fathers and sons.

Situation Makes Behavior Easy

Differences in the availability and legality of firearms, as in the United States in contrast to most European countries, have an obvious impact: greater accessibility makes aggression more likely—and more likely to result in death.

In Summary

To sum it up, a large number of factors determine aggression. Factors implicated in the process include biological factors (e.g., testosterone), social-structural factors (low family cohesion, few intimate families, low father involvement, isolation from kin, deindividuation), arousal (due to frustration, viewing aggressive TV, high competition), climatic factors (hot weather), modeling (example of others, increased status), gender marking (being aggressive separates men and women), retaliation, economic factors (inequality, few resources), social stress (e.g., inflation), ease of doing (availability of weapons), and low costs (unlikely to be punished). Many of these factors are directly or indirectly related to culture.

CONFLICT RESOLUTION

Collectivist cultures are much more concerned with the maintenance of harmony in interpersonal relationships within the in-group than are individualistic cultures. This difference is reflected in the collectivists' preference for bargaining and negotiation, rather than going to court (Leung, 1988). Ting-Toomey (1988) suggested that individualists are concerned only with saving their own face and with autonomy, domination, control, and direct solutions to a conflict. As a result they prefer direct negotiation. By contrast, collectivists are concerned with saving the face of the other person as well as their own and tend to avoid direct conflict resolution. Thus, they prefer indirect negotiation strategies. In sum, arbitration and mediation are by far the preferred strategies of collectivists.

SOCIAL DISTANCE

Social distance depends on which attributes are considered to be unfavorable in a particular culture. In general, the more competition for scarce resources there is with people that have a particular attribute, the more social distance there is toward people with that attribute.

Historical factors related to conflicts over territory or resources, or dissimilarities in race, religion, language, economic position, political ideology, and other such attributes, result in unique patterns of social distance in each culture. For example, in India the caste system specifies social distance. In 1991 newspaper reports, two lovers were killed by villagers because they had eloped and married across caste lines. Even the man's male friend was killed for helping them elope.

Brewer (1968) examined the social distance among thirty tribes located in Kenya, Uganda, and Tanzania. She found that tribes that perceived other tribes as similar felt little social distance toward them. Tribes that were physically distant tended to be perceived as more different, and the tribes showed more social distance toward them than toward tribes that were located closer to their own tribe. Small social distance was also experienced toward tribes that were liked and that were familiar to the raters. Finally, the economic advancement of the out-group was an important determinant: The more economically advanced the tribe, the smaller the social distance toward it.

HELPING BEHAVIOR

An individual is likely to help depending on (1) the norms of the culture about helping, (2) moral obligations about helping, (3) self-definitions that the individual is the kind of person who helps, (4) the affect attached to helping, (5) the utility of helping, (6) the perceived difficulties of helping, (7) the costs of helping, and (8) the self-efficacy about helping (believes he or she knows how to help, has the ability to help). Once the person has helped, depending on the experienced rewards or punishments, there is an increase or decrease in the strength of the habit of helping. A broad perspective on helping can be found in Hinde and Groebel (1991).

Subjective Culture

In all cultures people are more likely to help an in-group member than an out-group member. However, the difference in the probability of helping in-group versus out-group members is larger in the case of collectivist than in the case of individualistic cultures.

Recall that exactly how a person is to be classified, i.e., as in-group or out-group, depends on the culture. There are cultures where all outsiders are out-group. There are also cultures that are extremely hospitable to outsiders, where outsiders are tentatively classified as in-group until their in-group–out-group position is determined. For example, in traditional Greek villages the *xenos* (the stranger, same root as "xenophilic" and "xenophobic") is welcome, and there are usually tentative helpful gestures that "check" if that person can be trusted and included in the in-group. Thus, traditional Greeks are more likely to help a foreigner (i.e., a potential in-group member) than a fellow Greek (Feldman, 1968; Triandis, 1972) who is clearly not a member of their in-group.

Agricultural cultures (most of them collectivist) usually have the concept of "limited good" (Foster, 1965). People in such cultures see "good" as limited, so that if something good happens to an out-group member, it follows that the in-group has less of this "good." For example, if your neighbor wins a lottery, that is bad for you. Of course, you are now at a disadvantage, since you are no longer able to compare yourself favorably to your neighbor on the wealth dimension, but in individualistic cultures that is not nearly as threatening as it is in collectivist cultures. Foster (1965) has argued that peasants are especially likely to have this point of view: Since land is the most important good for them, if an out-group member gets more land, they have less land.

Triandis and Vassiliou (1972) analyzed subjective culture judgments obtained in collectivist traditional Greek society and found support for Foster's argument that such societies have the limited-good point of view when they deal with out-groups. However, a stranger, as we have seen, is likely to be seen as a potential in-group member in that culture and so is likely to be helped.

In many collectivist cultures, however, outsiders are seen as out-group members, and thus people are less likely to help strangers, even when the costs of helping are minimal. In an experiment by L'Armand and Pepitone (1975) we see this point confirmed. They studied whether a male would help another male in Philadelphia, the United States, and in Madras, India. The procedure involved a game in which the subject waged coins representing money provided by the experimenter. In the two conditions of the experiment the subjects could help themselves or another person. The cost of helping was minimal. Americans worked as hard to help themselves as to help the other; the Indians worked harder for themselves than for the other.

The Situation

The phenomenon known as *reciprocity* (mutual exchange) can both increase and decrease the chances that a person will be helped. Reciprocity is very powerful in most human relationships, and one way to bring a stranger into the in-group, and thereby strengthen it, is to help the stranger. The stranger in turn may be helpful and in order to reciprocate will join the in-group and subsequently fight the out-group.

But reciprocity can also result in not giving help. The Japanese emphasize obligation and loyalty so much that sometimes they avoid giving help when they do not have an obligation to do so. Thus, they will not assist strangers unless they are asked very strongly, because the person assisted will have a "possibly unwanted obligation." Opinion polls asked young people (eighteen- to twenty-four-year olds), during 1977 to 1988, "Suppose you meet a man lost and trying to find his way. What would you do?" About 55 percent of the Americans answered, "Ask him if he needs help," but only 28 percent of the Japanese did (Hastings & Hastings, 1990).

Feldman (1968) recorded the helping behavior of large samples of people toward "compatriots" or "foreigners" in two individualistic settings (Boston, Massachusetts, and Paris, France) and one collectivist setting (in the early 1960s, Athens, Greece). He set up several different situations in which a person could be helpful. In one situation, the compatriots or foreigners approached people in a subway station asking them to mail a letter for them. Half the letters had a stamp and the other half did not. Since the letters were addressed to the experimenter, it was possible to check if the subjects who agreed to help did indeed help.

Table 8–2 shows the results. The unstamped letters were refused more often in Paris and Boston than in Athens. Little difference was found between behaviors toward compatriots and foreigners in Boston and Paris, but large differences were found in Athens, which at the time (Triandis, 1972) was highly collectivist. (Recent measurements, Georgas, 1989, indicate that in urban centers Greeks are now individualists, thus no longer different from U.S. samples.) Roughly about a third of the Boston and Paris samples helped a compatriot or a foreigner. The Greeks

TABLE 8-2 PERCENTAGE OF PEOPLE IN VARIOUS SAMPLES, IN THREE COUNTRIES, REFUSING TO MAIL A LETTER FOR A COMPATRIOT OR A FOREIGNER

City	*Refusals to compatriot*		*Refusals to foreigner*	
	With stamped letter	*With unstamped letter*	*With stamped letter*	*With unstamped letter*
Paris	32[a]	38[b]	12[a]	44[b]
	(73)	(81)	(57)	(89)
Athens	88[c]	97[d]	52[c]	51[d]
	(33)	(36)	(35)	(33)
Boston	15[e]	44[f]	25[e]	60[f]
	(59)	(90)	(55)	(125)

NOTE: Total $N = 765$ (*ns* in parentheses).
[a] $x^2 = 5.82$. $p < .05$. These cells differ from the findings in the other experiments.
[b] $x^2 = .33$, *ns*.
[c] $x^2 = 7.21$. $p < .01$.
[d] $x^2 = 14.30$, $p < .001$.
[e] $x^2 = .84$, *ns*.
[f] $x^2 = 4.84$, $p < .05$.
SOURCE: Feldman, 1968. Copyright 1968 by the American Psychological Association. Reprinted by permission.

helped an American about half the time, but over 90 percent refused to help a fellow Greek (who, being unknown to them, would be reliably classified as out-group).

Feldman also used fifty taxi rides with a compatriot and fifty with a foreigner to determine if the taxi drivers took the direct route (most helpful) or the long one (least helpful). He found that the Paris taxis were least helpful.

Finally, he examined the data for overpayments to random samples of pastry shops in the three cities. There were no differences in the behavior toward fellow countrymen and foreigners; in short, a customer is a customer. However, in Paris the cashiers said nothing (were unhelpful) in 54 percent of the cases; in Athens, in 50 percent of the cases; and in Boston, in 32 percent of the cases.

In other words, consistent with the point about the importance of the situation, made in several earlier chapters, the situation was *the* major determinant of the kind of cultural difference obtained.

People in large cities are especially unhelpful. Hedge and Yousif (1992) suggest that this may be a cultural universal. They found, in a comparison of the United Kingdom and the Sudan, that when the situation was not urgent and when helping entailed high personal cost, people in both countries were less helpful in the city. There were no cultural differences.

In cities people are reluctant to get involved with strangers. This is why the experts say that if you want help, you should shout "Fire!" The argument is that people are more likely to think of a fire as relevant to themselves than just hearing the word "help." We need an experiment to check on these assertions of the experts.

Wealthy nations are more likely than poor nations to help poor nations. However, there are country differences. The Scandinavian countries use a larger percentage of their gross national product (close to 0.7 percent in Sweden) in foreign aid than do other wealthy countries.

Help is more likely when the actor perceives the other person as really needing help, becomes aware of a moral obligation to help, and believes that there is a personal responsibility to help.

When other people who are possible helpers are around, a person is less likely to help. But a threshold is crossed when several people begin trying to help the person, suggesting that helping is the norm. A person who is in a good mood is more likely to help, and so people are more likely to help in cultures where they have adequate resources, a pleasant climate, or other environmental factors that make them feel good.

Self-Definition

People are more likely to help if they have a self-concept that includes the idea: "People who are like me when asked to help, do help."

In collectivist cultures people may experience a moral responsibility for helping a person in need that is not found in individualistic countries. Miller, Bersoff, and Harwood (1990) presented scenarios to Indian and United States samples in which the person requesting help was a close relative, friend, or stranger, and the need was extreme, moderate, or minor. In the case of extreme need there were no cultural differences. All said they would help. But in the case of minor need, the differences were substantial. For example, the low-need scenario involved asking a friend for directions to a store; the friend refused to interrupt reading an exciting book and thus did not help. Ninety-three percent of the Indians thought the friend had an obligation to help, but only 33 percent of the Americans thought so. In the case of strangers requesting help, the difference was 73 versus 23 percent for Indians and Americans, respectively.

Utility of Helping

The perceived consequences of offering help are important determinants of the probability that a person will help. If helping seems risky or dangerous, a person is less likely to help. Thus, in cultures where crime is very common, e.g., large American cities, people are less likely to help than in cultures where crime is rare (e.g., villages in most states).

SEXUAL BEHAVIOR

A behavior of great interest, since it perpetuates the cultural group, is sexual behavior. Patterns of this behavior around the world have been reviewed by Ford and Beach (1951). In their book they report an unbelievably wide range of sexual behaviors. For example, the preferred and accepted positions for sexual intercourse vary greatly. There are seven positions that are widely used, but none is used by more than a quarter of the cultures that have been studied. In short, what appears normal to us, the so-called missionary position, is used by only a fraction of humanity.

Kissing is a ubiquitous item of sex play that accompanies heterosexual intercourse in many cultures, but there are seven cultures where it is never used. When the Thonga of Africa first saw Europeans kissing, they laughed, expressing the sentiment: "Look at them—they eat each other's saliva and dirt" (Ford & Beach, 1951, p. 49).

There are very few cultures where homosexuality is not reported in ethnographies. In fact, in 64 percent of the societies reviewed by Ford and Beach (1951), it is considered a normal and socially accepted behavior for some member of the society. There are two cultures (the Siwans of Africa and Kerakis of New Guinea) where it is considered abnormal not to be bisexual (Kluckhohn, 1954).

Masturbation is sufficiently widespread to justify classification as a normal and natural form of sexual expression for mammals, including humans (Ford & Beach, 1951, p. 166). Nevertheless, it is disapproved of in most human societies.

DOMINANCE

Societies differ in their levels of differentiation and stratification. Differentiation is based on many attributes, in addition to money, education, and family background with which you are familiar. For example, caste or the possession of particular objects may be most important.

Some societies are relatively egalitarian, and others are very hierarchical. Dominance, of course, is much more accepted and prevalent in the hierarchical than in the egalitarian societies.

A description of extreme hierarchy was provided by Buck (1931). In the Chinese family, during the early part of this century, rations were cut during periods of starvation so that the family starved in a set order: first the girls of the family, later the boys, then the women, and then the men. The least affected were the old men. They were the most respected, and they were fed even when there was nothing left for the others.

Even in contemporary, preliterate societies food is a major motivator and the basis of stratification. Take the example of the Siriono of eastern Bolivia (Holmberg, 1969). They are nomadic hunters and gatherers living in an ecology where the supply of food is sufficient for survival but seldom abundant. People suffer food deprivation. When setting out in search of game, the chances of a successful hunt are less than three out of four. Agriculture is undeveloped, and while the forest has wild fruit, it is of low nutritive value for long-term survival.

In that society status is directly linked to being a good hunter. People who cannot get food, because they are sick or old, are abandoned. Since there are no techniques for keeping the food for a long time, it must be consumed soon after it is obtained; otherwise it will spoil. Thus, there are periods of food binges and periods of starvation. A man's status is directly linked to the minimizing of the periods of starvation. In industrial societies there is also a hierarchy linked to food. In spite of our efforts to avoid the subject, we must face the fact that there are people who go hungry every night even in the wealthiest societies.

CONFORMITY

In the classic work of Asch (1956), students were presented with several unequal lines and a standard line and they were asked to tell which line matched the standard line. On some of the trials confederates of the experimenter made false but consistent judgments, and then the naïve students had to make a judgment confronted on the one hand with the data of their own senses and on the other hand the unanimous social data that contradicted their senses.

Asch found that about one-third of the students yielded to the social group and gave a wrong answer, i.e., assumed that their senses were inaccurate. This study has been replicated in many countries (for a review see Mann, 1980, pp. 164–166). In general, rates of conformity were similar to the rates obtained in the United States. However, in the case of some of the African tribes that use severe socialization practices, the rates of conformity were very high (e.g., Bantus, 51 percent), and some countries had lower rates of conformity (e.g., Germany and Japan, low 20 percent) than did the United States.

The low rates from Japan were surprising to Frager (1970), who did the study, but we must remember that in a collectivist culture people conform to the in-group and behave uncooperatively toward out-groups. Strangers making "wrong" judgments are hardly an in-group, and a "foreigner" as the experimenter makes things even more "unnatural." So it is not too surprising that 34 percent of the Japanese showed anti-conformity—they gave the wrong answer on the neutral trials when the majority of the confederates gave the correct answer. In Matsuda's (1985) study, also done in Japan, the more cohesive the group, the more conformity there was, even though the Asch-type judgments were made in private, eliminating the possibility that the subjects agreed with the majority to avoid embarrassment.

We must note also that in many collectivist cultures decisions are taken by consensus (e.g., the Japanese *ringi* method), and this means that individuals often have an opportunity to influence the decision. In individualistic cultures, for decisions that don't involve people's egos, there may not be much discussion. Then the individual acts by imitating others. This can result in substantial levels of conformity (Doi, 1986). In short, we must not assume that collectivism will result necessarily in higher levels of conformity than individualism. It does depend on the importance of the decision.

As we have seen in previous chapters, in hunting and gathering societies, as well as in industrial societies, there is less pressure for conformity. In agricultural societies there tends to be more pressure for conformity. In densely settled, stratified societies, a good deal of socialization is directed at making children conform. Similarly, in lower social-class segments of industrial societies (Kohn, 1969) there is pressure toward conformity, which is functional, since most of these children will become workers, and it is functional for them to obey the boss and the group.

On the other hand, hunters, food gatherers, and the upper social classes in industrial societies socialize their children for self-reliance, creativity, and exploration. Again, that is functional since a hunter and food gatherer is more likely to find food if he is exploratory, and a professional is more likely to do her job well if she is creative.

Berry (1967, 1979) showed that conformity is high in agricultural societies, especially in Africa, and low in hunting and gathering societies, such as the Eskimo. The antecedents can be traced to the ecology, which made conformity functional, and to child-training patterns, which socialized children to develop behaviors that are functional in the particular ecologies.

FIGURE 8–2

Berry (1979) asked people in different cultures to indicate which of the eight lines matched the line at the top of the figure. The X was placed near the seventh line, and the respondents were "informed" that most people in their culture used that answer. The correct answer is the second from the top. Those who answered by pointing to the fourth, fifth, sixth, or seventh line showed increasing levels of conformity. (Berry, 1979. Reprinted with permission.)

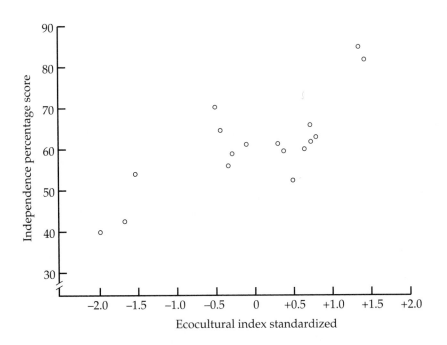

FIGURE 8–3

Berry (1979) correlated the degree of independence (nonconformity) shown by members of a sample when responding to the task shown in Figure 8–2 with that sample's position on an ecocultural dimension, where the higher position corresponds to members of the culture's being more likely to survive by being self-reliant and independent rather than obedient, because their ecology favored hunting and other independence-requiring activities. The correlation of .70, based on seventeen samples, indicates that those who were raised in environments where self-reliance is required conformed less. (Berry, 1979. Reprinted with permission.)

Berry used an adaptation of the Asch technique shown in Figure 8–2. Subjects were asked to identify the line that matches a comparison line. Note the comparison line on the top. An X was placed next to another line, which the experimenter mentioned casually was the one "most often chosen as the correct match of the top line." Conformity occurred when the subjects selected the line with the X rather than the correct line, which in this example is the second from the top.

In Figure 8–3 the x axis is the ecocultural index, which reflects the extent the ecology calls for exploration of the environment. The y axis shows how much independence subjects who performed the task shown in Figure 8–2 demonstrated. It is clear that the ecology that favored exploration was related to nonconformity; the correlation was about .70.

Classifying preliterate societies into cooperative, competitive, and individualistic, Mead (1961) suggested that there was more conformity among the cooperative than the other two types, and the cooperative had more collectivist attributes while the other two types had more individualistic attributes (see Triandis, 1988a, for a detailed review of this study).

O BEDIENCE

The famous study by Milgram (1974) has been replicated in many individualistic countries with similar results. Comparisons of the obedience rates may not be legitimate, because the time periods when the studies were done were different, and the methods of subject recruitment and the experimental procedures were not identical. In any case, while the American results showed that about two-thirds of the subjects obeyed, the German results showed an 85 percent rate of obedience and the Australian results a 40 percent rate.

It is likely that in countries where power distance (PD) is high, the rates would approach 100 percent, but there are no data on this point using the Milgram procedure. When other methods, e.g., "pick up this mess," were used, high-PD countries had higher obedience rates than low-PD countries. For a review see Mann (1980, pp. 170–172).

Food gatherers and hunters tend to be more egalitarian than agriculturists. In some modern industrial societies we find substantial differentiation, but also the ideology of equality (e.g., in the United States). Stratification is especially high when segments of a society are illiterate (e.g., in Peru), while it tends to be low when most members of a society are well educated—e.g., in Scandinavia, Israel, and Austria, where Hofstede (1980) found the least power distance. Across cultures we can find numerous status distinctions (e.g., royalty, aristocracy, gentry, wealthy people, professionals, ordinary citizens, slaves) or no such distinctions.

We must stress the importance of the in-group–out-group distinction in the area of conformity. When members of a collectivist culture are said to be more conforming, that refers explicitly to their conforming to in-groups. Such people in fact are likely to conform *less* to out-groups than are members of individualistic cultures.

I NTIMACY (DISCLOSURE) VERSUS FORMALITY

In general, cultures that are collectivist disclose more within the in-group and less toward the out-group than do individualistic cultures. Collectivists are especially opposed to "washing the family's dirty laundry in public" and go to extremes to hide unfavorable information about in-group members from outsiders.

Formality is a complex function of social distance. For low levels of social distance, such as with family members, both collectivist and individualistic cultures behave with little formality, except that in many collectivist cultures norms are observed more rigidly, especially in relation to the male and older members of the family.

At intermediate levels of social distance, such as in interactions with coworkers, neighbors, acquaintances, and the like, members of individualistic cultures show the maximum formality.

Intimacy is not widely found in individualistic cultures. It is not common, for instance, for a friend to call at two in the morning and say, "I can't sleep. Could you come to see me, so I can tell you what is bothering me?" and have the other friend comply! One way of explaining this is that people are related to a wide range of other people; they simply do not have the energy to relate to so many others intimately. Thus, relationships tend to be casual. Individualists are much more likely, when interacting with others, to talk about the weather, the latest athletic event, or politics than about themselves, their hopes and fears, their finances, their sexual life, and their problems—what kept them up worrying at night. Collectivists, on the other hand, feel strong obligations to be a "good friend" and believe self-sacrifice is a virtue and might even be enjoyable! For example, Bontempo, Lobel, and Triandis (1990) found that Brazilians had internalized obligations toward their in-group to such an extent that they did not present themselves differently to the researchers when responding anonymously or by name; Americans presented themselves considerably more positively to the researchers when responding by name than anonymously—e.g., said they would go out of their way to help a friend!

However, in individualistic societies people meet strangers easily and have excellent "cocktail party skills." Many move from person to person and group to group with great ease and start conversations with strangers without much difficulty.

In collectivist cultures people generally do not talk to strangers, and even when they find themselves in a situation where opening a conversation is appropriate, they may wait until they are properly introduced. They are so absorbed in social relationships with their kin that they have very little time for social explorations. They can be uncomfortable at a cocktail party, but they feel completely comfortable interacting with many of their kin. In extremely collectivist cultures people do not have friends who are not kin (Campbell, 1964), so they do not develop skills for social relationships with nonkin.

Gudykunst (1983) noted that collectivists are more cautious in initial social interactions and base their social perceptions on the other person's group membership, while individualists are more direct in their communication. The latter were more likely to smile, shake hands, and look directly into the eyes of the other. Gudykunst and Nishida (1986) found that Japanese saw more intimacy with acquaintances, coworkers, colleagues, and classmates than did Americans, while Americans saw more intimacy with lovers, roommates, and members of the nuclear family. A parallel cultural difference was also found by Triandis, McCusker, and Hui (1990) in the case of Chinese and Americans.

Lewin (1936) noted that in the first third of this century, Americans were easy to meet, but one could not get to know them well; Germans were difficult to meet, but if one got to know them, one was likely to know them well.

Collectivists are more formal, and in the early stages of interaction they stay on the surface (e.g., "Are you married?" "What does your father do?"). But after some time, the floodgates open (e.g., "How much money do you make?" "Do you like pornography?"). Norms about touching, kissing, and interpersonal distance, discussed in Chapter 7, are also relevant here. Clearly, such actions have much to do with intimacy.

Self-disclosure is likely to increase when this behavior is rewarded. In some cultures mutual disclosure is the norm, after people have reached a particular role relationship—e.g., in Germany the "brotherhood" relationship is marked in a special ceremony, and after that the person can disclose more.

However, there is a complication that results in the so-called passant phenomenon: Many revelations about the self can prove embarrassing at a later time, and thus one is more likely to reveal transgressions to a stranger (who is a "passant," just passing by). Of course, such revelations require certainty that one is never going to have additional interactions with that person. Similarly, behavior that is classified as a "transgression" is more likely in situations where one is unknown, and will not interact again with the same person, than in situations where one might have a continuous social relationship.

A special difficulty for disclosing to kin is that they are likely to have specific expectations about members of the family which may not have been met. People thus often present themselves as if they had lived up to the expectations of their kin. Then they are rewarded by their kin, but this behavior requires a good deal of impression management. We see more of this behavior in collectivist than in individualistic cultures, where a person is supposed to be truthful. After all, if you are autonomous, you can present yourself the way you are. If you are dependent on others, you have to present yourself the way these others expect you to be.

When individuals from different cultures interact, there is evidence that the development of intimacy and self-disclosure is inhibited. For example, Ridley (1984) reported that blacks are reluctant to self-disclose to white counselors.

Sudweeks, Gudykunst, Ting-Toomey, and Nishida (1990) give us some indications of the factors that are likely to lead to intimacy. It is probable that many of these factors operate about the same way in most cultures. The Sudweeks et al. (1990) study was concerned with relationships between Japanese and North American female students. The Japanese students were approached, asked if they wanted to be interviewed, and asked if they could give the names of North American friends. Then the North American friends were approached and asked if they wished to be interviewed. Those who agreed were paid $5.

The Japanese were interviewed in Japanese and the North Americans in English. During the interview they were asked to describe the relationship with the member of the other culture in some detail. A classification of the pairs as relatively intimate, moderately intimate, and nonintimate suggested some generalizations.

The Sudweek et al. study suggested that intimacy was most likely when the Japanese partner had the ability to speak in fluent English, when both partners showed some empathy, and when at least one of the partners accommodated by using the communication style of the other culture. For example, a Japanese would use a direct communication style, though self-consciously and apologetically, as in this case: "I asked her if she would go with me. I asked her directly. There's no other way, don't you think?" (p. 217).

The next factor was similarity. For intimacy and self-disclosure to take place, there was a need for the two partners to look at cultural differences nonjudgmentally or as a positive factor, to observe similarities in background and lifestyle (e.g., we are both students), and to note similarities in attitudes and values.

The third factor was involvement, which was reflected in the efforts of the partners to make time to interact, to increase intimacy, and to develop overlapping networks of friends. Finally, the intimate dyads did not "test the relationship" (e.g., by not calling the other for some time to see if the other would call her), but rather were responsive to each other and tried hard to understand the other's point of view.

SUMMARY

This chapter examined the most important types of social behavior across culture. We can contrast helpful and sexual behaviors, which are associative, with aggressive behaviors, which are dissociative; superordination behaviors, which are indicative of dominance, with subordination behaviors, such as conformity; intimate behaviors, such as self-disclosure, with formal behaviors. Each of these shows considerable variations across cultures. We have examined numerous factors that account for these differences.

The next chapter will examine what happens when people from different cultures find themselves in the same social situation, for example, at work together.

QUESTIONS AND EXERCISES

1.   Identify aspects of the ecology that lead to high or low levels of each of the behaviors discussed in this chapter.

2.   Identify sex differences relevant to high or low levels of the behaviors discussed in this chapter.

3.   Review and make a list of the relationships between collectivism, individualism, and the behavior patterns discussed in this chapter.

9

Dealing with Diversity and Intercultural Relations

❖

Advantages and Disadvantages of Diversity ◆ Some Factors to Consider when Dealing with Diversity ◆ *Cultural Distance* ◆ *Perceived Similarity* ◆ *Opportunities for Interaction* ◆ *Acculturation* ◆ Perceived Similarity and Culture Shock ◆ Some Complications ◆ *The Culture of Relationships* ◆ *Additive and Subtractive Multiculturalism and Cultural Identity* ◆ Attributes of Major U.S. Minorities ◆ *Attributes of African Americans* ◆ *Attributes of Hispanics* ◆ *Attributes of Asian Americans* ◆ *Other Groups* ◆ Barriers to Good Intercultural Relations ◆ *Enthnocentrism* ◆ *Intergroup versus Interpersonal* ◆ *Stereotypes in Intergroup Relations* ◆ *Intergroup Liking and Social Distance* ◆ *Some Attributes of Intergroup Relations* ◆ Summary

Modern societies are extraordinarily different on diversity. Figure 9–1 shows a group of children in a classroom in Urbana, Illinois; you can identify a good deal of diversity. Figure 9–2 shows a Japanese school group on an excursion; you can see much homogeneity.

Diversity can include differences in language, race, religion, sexual orientation, occupation, lifestyle, and many other factors. This chapter examines some of the advantages and disadvantages of this diversity and outlines some of the ways in which particular kinds of diversity operate in the United States. Then it turns to interpersonal relationships when individuals from different cultures interact. The final chapter, Chapter 10, examines some of the ways we can improve interpersonal relationships across cultures.

FIGURE 9–1
A picture of diversity (school in Urbana, Illinois, United States). (Pola Triandis.)

FIGURE 9–2
A picture of homogeneity (Japanese schoolchildren at the railroad station in Nara, Japan). (Pola Triandis.)

ADVANTAGES AND DISADVANTAGES OF DIVERSITY

Diversity results in both advantages and disadvantages (Jackson, 1991b). Advantages are suggested by evidence that heterogeneous groups, when compared with homogeneous groups, are more creative and likely to reach higher-quality decisions (McGrath, 1984; Triandis, Hall, & Ewen, 1965; Willems & Clark, 1971). For example, banks that are more innovative than the average tend to be managed by diverse teams with expertise in different functional areas (Bantel & Jackson, 1989). Homogeneity is often associated with "groupthink" (Janis, 1972, 1982), which leads to poor decisions.

Disadvantages are suggested by evidence of reduced cohesion, caused by intercultural conflict and diverse subjective cultures (Jackson et al., 1991). The long record of national, religious, racial, communal, and tribal strife in the history of the world leaves little doubt that poorly managed diversity can be disastrous.

SOME FACTORS TO CONSIDER WHEN DEALING WITH DIVERSITY

Cultural Distance

Cultures are very similar or different (distant) to the extent that they include many similar or different elements. You may want to review the discussion of this concept in Chapter 2.

Empirical findings suggest that objective cultural distance is an important variable determining how comfortable people will be in an interpersonal relationship. For example, the literature on the adjustment of foreign students to the United States indicates that those from Europe have less difficulty adjusting to the United States than those from Africa or Asia. Suicide rates among different kinds of immigrants going to different countries seem to reflect cultural distance (Furnham & Bochner, 1986). Dunbar (1992) found that U.S. personnel in managerial positions abroad had less trouble adjusting to European than to non-Western or Third World settings.

Perceived Similarity

Research indicates that those who see others as similar are attracted to them (Byrne, 1971). It is obvious that cultural distance is related to the probability that others will be perceived as dissimilar.

People differ in their experience with others who are different from themselves. In a homogeneous, isolated tribe, people have seen few others who are different. Consequently, their *level of adaptation* (Helson, 1964), or neutral point, on the "similar" versus "different" dimension is in the "very similar" region of the dimension; they will only view people who are very much like them as similar. In a cosmopolitan environment, people have levels of adaptation that are in the "somewhat different" region of the similar-different dimension and thus are likely to view people who are slightly different from them in language, clothing, or religion as "one of us."

Opportunities for Interaction

In different settings there are variations in the opportunities for people to interact. For example, neighbors are more likely to interact than are people who live far apart.

Contact by itself does not improve interpersonal relations (Amir, 1969; Stephan, 1985), but when people perceive each other as similar, contact is rewarding. When contact is rewarding, the number of positive interactions is greater than the number of negative interactions. Rewarding contact leads to more interaction. More interaction tends to make people more similar, and that increases their perceived similarity.

Acculturation

Berry (1980a) has described four ways for two cultures to relate to each other (see Figure 9–3). People may try to maintain or not maintain their

FIGURE 9–3
Berry's (1980a) acculturation framework.

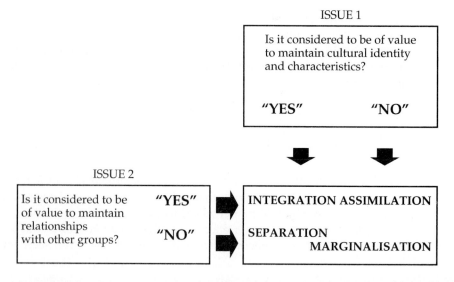

culture and may try to have or not have contact with the other culture. *Integration* is defined as the type of acculturation where each group maintains its culture and also maintains contact with the other culture. *Assimilation* occurs when a group does not maintain its culture but does maintain contact with the other culture. *Separation* occurs when the group maintains its culture but does not maintain contact with the other culture. Finally, *marginalization* occurs when neither maintenance of the group's own culture nor contact with the other culture is attempted. Berry has presented evidence that integration is most desirable, followed by assimilation, from the point of view of mental health. Marginalization is the most unfavorable condition (see Berry, Poortinga, Segall, & Dasen, 1992, p. 287).

PERCEIVED SIMILARITY AND CULTURE SHOCK

Figure 9–4 shows the variables, in intercultural situations, that determine perceived similarity and culture shock. Culture shock occurs when people interact with members of a very different culture and experience a loss of control. This happens when they cannot understand the behavior of the people from the other culture. Then they feel confused and develop both physical (e.g., asthma, headaches) and psychological (e.g., depression) symptoms (Oberg, 1954, 1960). This is discussed in more detail in Chapter 10.

As Figure 9–4 shows, perceived similarity is very high when there is no history of conflict. The greater the history of conflict (both length and intensity of conflict, wars, memories of one group killing members of the other group, etc.), the lower the perceived similarity. The same holds true for cultural distance: The greater the cultural distance, the lower the perceived similarity. On the other hand, the greater the knowledge of the other culture, as, for example, when there has been effective cross-cultural training (Landis & Brislin, 1983), the higher the perceived similarity. Intergroup relations improve with knowledge of the other culture (Stephan & Stephan, 1984). One of the methods of culture training is the culture assimilator (Albert, 1983; Fiedler, Mitchell, & Triandis, 1971); it has been shown to increase isomorphic attributions, which increase the chances of seeing the other person as similar.

Looking at the other variables in Figure 9–4, we can see that:

- The greater the actor's language competence in the other person's language, the greater the perceived similarity. Obviously, those who speak our language appear to us to be more similar than those who do not speak our language.
- The greater the network overlap with the other person, the greater the perceived similarity, because the more things two people have

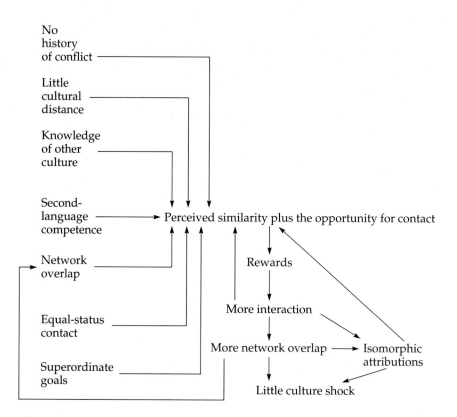

FIGURE 9–4
A theory of culture shock. (Triandis, 1992.)

in common, including friends and acquaintances, the more they will see each other as similar.

- The more equal-status contact between the two, the greater the perceived similarity.
- The more superordinate goals there are, the more perceived similarity. Of course, any element (age, gender) that people have in common will increase their perceived similarity, but goals are especially important.
- Perceived similarity plus opportunities for contact results in interpersonal situations that are rewarding. The more rewards, the more people seek interactions with those who rewarded them, and the more interactions, the greater the perceived similarity. The more interactions, the greater the network overlap (common friends). Network overlap and frequent interactions result in more isomorphic attributions. More network overlap and isomorphic attributions result in less culture shock.

The more rewarding the interaction is, more authorities approve of the contact between the two cultures. Thus, the sequence just described will be more powerful in multicultural societies or situations where the authorities promote good relationships than in societies or situations where they do not.

SOME COMPLICATIONS

The Culture of Relationships

It is important to consider each specific diversity relationship—such as men versus women, old versus young, Hispanics versus non-Hispanics, blacks versus whites, management versus union, tenured versus untenured employees, educated versus uneducated, upper class versus lower class, one religion versus another religion, and one nationality versus another nationality—and look for the kind of intergroup culture that has developed over the centuries, and especially in recent years, concerning *this* particular relationship. To understand why members of cultures act toward one another the way they do, or why they categorize experience the way they do, we need to understand the history of this relationship. The kind of acculturation pattern that is used by one group in relation to the other is also of great importance. For example, in integration a person picks elements from both cultures.

Additive and Subtractive Multiculturalism and Cultural Identity

The broad ideology of the country, corporation, or situation is a most important determinant of the cultural identity that people will develop. The so-called melting pot ideology urges each cultural group to lose some of its attributes in order to become just like the mainstream. This is what Berry called assimilation. I called it *subtractive* multiculturalism (Triandis, 1976a), because people need to subtract something, lose some of their original cultural elements, to reach their new cultural identity. By contrast, people can add skills and perspectives. That is *additive* multiculturalism, which is what Berry calls integration. Since there is evidence that ethnic groups are more mentally healthy when they add rather than lose skills (Berry, Kim, Power, Young, & Bujaki, 1989), it appears desirable for countries and corporations to adopt the policy of additive multiculturalism.

Triandis (1976a) argued that mainstream Americans can add skills relatively painlessly, and thus the policy of U.S. schools should be the increased *appreciation* of the perspectives of U.S. minorities and the teaching of skills that will permit rewarding interactions with these minorities; on the other hand, many members of minorities feel pain when they lose

ements of their ethnic identity, and thus they should not be required to
do so.

The melting pot ideology was very popular in the first third of the
twentieth century; it is now unpopular (Lambert & Taylor, 1990), except
among lower-class whites. However, it remains a subject of considerable
debate and controversy.

Cultural distance is directly related to the differences in the subjective
cultures of two cultural groups. In the next section we review some of the
cultural differences between different American ethnic groups.

ATTRIBUTES OF MAJOR U.S. MINORITIES

In discussing the attributes of U.S. minorities it is important to keep in
mind that they are very heterogeneous. First, social class makes an enormous difference. For example, the subjective culture of middle-class African Americans (AAs) is essentially the same as the subjective culture of
middle-class European Americans (EAs), but the subjective culture of AAs
who have never had a job is extremely different from the subjective
culture of AAs who have had a steady job (Triandis, 1976b). Second, the
historical influences are extremely important. For example, Hispanics
reflect influences from Africa, Europe, and the original cultures of the
Americas. A Hispanic who is culturally mostly Native American (e.g.,
some Mexicans) is very different from a Hispanic who is mostly European
(e.g., some Cubans in the United States) or one who has been strongly
influenced by African cultures (e.g., some Puerto Ricans). Third, religion
can make a difference. For example, Asian Americans (AsAs) with Hindu,
Buddhist, Christian, or Confucian backgrounds are very different from
one another; the Thais are prototypical of loose cultures, and the Japanese
are prototypical of tight cultures. Native Americans have extremely diverse cultures; for example, they vary from the aggressive (e.g., Iroquois)
to the most peaceful (e.g., Hopi).

Thus, the attributes that are presented below are "common elements"
around which there is great variability.

Attributes of African Americans

African Americans value expression in movement, sound, and the visual
modalities. European Americans value moderation in expression (though
from a worldwide viewpoint, they are average in this dimension). EAs are
more concerned with what they own as a determinant of identity (e.g., "I
am a home owner"), while AAs often emphasize what they express in
personal style and movement and "how I appear to others" (Triandis,
1976b).

Jones (1988), a distinguished black psychologist, contrasts AA and EA personalities and styles. He sees contemporary AAs as trying to find a balance between two tendencies: One tendency derives from African culture; the other from EA culture. Table 9–1 summarizes the argument. Similar points are made by Boykin (1983) and are also summarized in Table 9–1.

A large empirical study (Triandis, 1976b) concluded that:

1. The similarities in the subjective cultures of AAs and EAs are overwhelming; the differences are small.

2. The major differences occur when African Americans who have never had a job are compared with other AAs and EAs.

3. Both blacks and whites see conflict in black-white relationships.

TABLE 9-1 CONTEMPORARY AFRICAN-AMERICAN AND EUROPEAN-AMERICAN CULTURE ATTRIBUTES

African American	European American
Spiritual	Materialistic, mechanistic
Spiritual forces	Physical forces
Harmony with nature	Control nature
Present oriented	Future oriented
Time is defined by the rhythm of social relationships	Time is money; time is to be used
Oral emphasis on context	Written emphasis on content
Expressive	Controlled expression
Movement	Balance
Surprise	Predictability
Improvisation	Planning
Rejection of routine	Routine
Social responsibility	Individualism
Collectivism	Self-focus
Identity defined by: Expression Style Spontaneous activity	Identity defined by: Property Experience Record of accomplishments
Gregarious	Task oriented
Flexible	Narrowly driven
Easygoing	High achieving
Affectively driven	Calculating
Affect	Rationality

SOURCE: Jones, 1988; Boykin, 1983.

4. The major difference between blacks who have never had a job and other blacks is the ecosystem distrust. This difference can be traced to the predictability of the environments of these groups. Specifically, the non-predictability of the link between behavior and consequences for unemployed blacks (e.g., "If I apply for a job will I get one? I am uncertain") results in ecosystem distrust (Triandis, 1976b). This is a syndrome of feelings, beliefs, and behavior that includes "not trusting people, not trusting themselves, not trusting the way the establishment institutions function, and not trusting the dependability of relationships between events occurring in their environment" (Triandis, 1976b, p. 172). This syndrome is perfectly understandable as a functional reaction to an uncertain environment. How can a person who has to hustle to make a living plan? How can people trust an environment that is not predictable, where they do not know if today is the last day of their life? Figure 9–5 shows the levels of trust found in this study of unemployed black and white respondents. In that study (Triandis, 1976b) the black middle class was very similar to the white samples.

5. The second most important difference distinguishing the black unemployed from other samples is ambivalence about their self-concept. The unemployed, when compared with other samples, do not think of themselves as "important," and they value "being a powerful person" more than they value "being a nice person." This again is functional in an environment where a person has little power.

6. Another difference between the black unemployed and other samples is in their conception of social relations. The former see social relationships as involving a "pose" in which people try to appear as better than they are and more powerful. People are less open, honest, or nice than is considered ideal by other blacks.

7. The black unemployed accept conditions that exist in ghettos (crime, unemployment) as normal. This again is functional, since it helps them adjust to the environments they are forced to live in.

8. A number of behaviors, such as "fight with," "hit," "treat as brother," and "love," are seen as more appropriate by the black unemployed than by other black samples. All blacks favor formal forms of address, such as Mr./Mrs., more than whites. This behavior does not imply formality; it implies acceptance and respect.

9. The black unemployed have strong antiestablishment attitudes. The antiestablishment impulses include rejection of people who do well under the status quo, such as blacks who are successful.

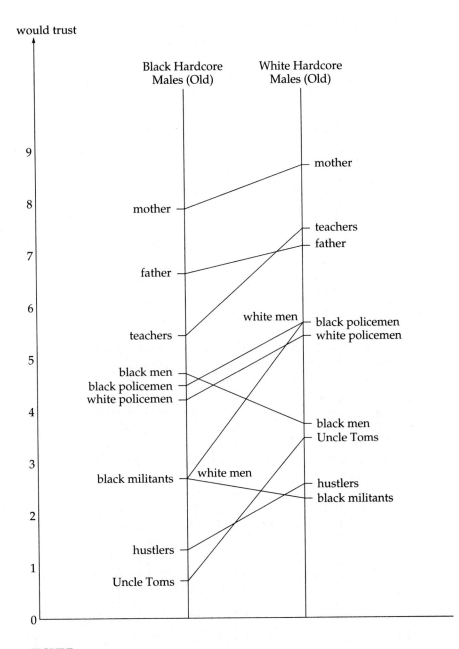

FIGURE 9–5
Rated trust toward several targets by African Americans and European Americans who have never had a job. (Triandis, 1976.)

Blacks who work with whites are especially rejected: "Here blacks reject the establishment more clearly than do whites. The establishment is seen as the police, the foremen, and others who do well under the status quo" (Triandis, 1976b, p. 154). The black unemployed see black professionals as "self-serving, intelligent egoists" (Triandis, 1976b, p. 173).

10.   Both blacks and whites think that their own group is less prejudiced than the other group.

11.   Both blacks and whites think of people in roles according to the role rather than the race. For example, "black policemen" are seen as the same as "white policemen."

We emphasize that all these statements must be viewed within the context of two major points:

1.   There are more similarities than differences in the responses of blacks and whites.

2.   There is tremendous heterogeneity in the responses of both blacks and whites.

Specifically, there are several black and white points of view. For example, some blacks are much more like the white middle class than they are like other blacks. The unemployed blacks are the only black sample that is consistently most different from the white middle class (Triandis, 1976b, p. 174).

Among some blacks, the high frequency of mothers raising sons without the help of fathers and the difficulty in gaining respectable employment due to discrimination often result in a macho identity as the boy attempts to reject the feminine identity generated by exclusive contact with females.

Black psychologist Richard Majors (Majors & Mancini-Billson, 1992) argues that black males have internalized the white male values of self-reliance and economic success, but structural barriers prevent them from being successful providers and protectors of their family. As a result, they assume what he calls a "cool pose" of toughness, willingness to use violence, and sexual promiscuity as defense mechanisms. But this cool pose also means more aggression, female abuse, and accidents, which result in homicide as the leading cause of death for young black males.

Majors and Mancini-Billson (1992) argue that "the black male is socialized to view every white man as a potential enemy, every symbol of the dominant system as a potential threat" (p. 27). They emphasize that the symbols used by some black males, such as distinctive handshakes, hairstyles, stance, walks, battle scars, turf wars, hand signals, language, and nicknames, as well as clothing and colors, are ways to increase solidarity with other black males; to be distinguished, powerful, masculine; and to provide an image of anger and struggle. The cool pose provides masks, facades, shields, fronts, and gaming that help to ensure survival.

Because whites are the majority and control most of the channels of power, minorities see the lawmaking process as disadvantageous to them, adding to their antiestablishment feelings. Blacks are particularly likely to feel exploited (Buchholz, 1978).

Attributes of Hispanics

Research (e.g., Marin & Triandis, 1985) suggests that Hispanics are more collectivist than non-Hispanics, and an aspect of this collectivism is greater expectation of harmony in in-group relationships. If the work group is to be seen as an in-group, it has to be harmonious. Hispanics use what we have called the *simpatia* cultural script (Triandis, Marin, Lisansky, & Betancourt, 1984). That is, they value people who are *simpatico* even more than do non-Hispanics. This means that they expect the other person to show more loyalty, dignity, friendliness, politeness, affection, and respect and to behave in more socially desirable ways than is usually the case for non-Hispanics. In addition, they expect, more than non-Hispanics, that the other person will not criticize them, put them down, or fight with them. It is easy to see how this cultural difference can lead to misunderstandings when Hispanics and non-Hispanics meet. Non-Hispanics may criticize, and while this behavior is very common in the Anglo culture, the Hispanics will translate this into "they are prejudiced and hostile."

Table 9–2 shows differences between Hispanics and non-Hispanics in familism. Further confidence in these results was obtained when it was found that the more acculturated Hispanics show less familism than the less acculturated (Triandis, Marin, Betancourt, & Chang, 1982). Other data indicate that Hispanics are more comfortable within their family than in work situations, while non-Hispanics often show the opposite pattern, appreciating the freedom of being independent from their family (Triandis, Marin, Hui, Lisansky, & Ottati, 1984). Hispanics also prefer cooperative to competitive situations (Triandis, Ottati, & Marin, 1982) and value being "sensitive," "loyal," "respected," "dutiful," "gracious," and "conforming" more than do non-Hispanics, while non-Hispanics value being "honest" and "moderate" more than do Hispanics (Triandis, Kashima, Lisansky, & Marin, 1982). Hispanics can tolerate, more than non-Hispanics, supervisors who are poorly organized as long as they provide them with much social support (Triandis, Hui, Lisansky, Marin, & Betancourt, 1982). Most of these attributes are consistent with collectivism, but we do not have the data concerning whether the same patterns occur in other collectivist ethnic groups. It is likely that unacculturated Americans of Asian descent also will show such attributes.

TABLE 9-2 EXPRESSED WILLINGNESS TO MAKE A SACRIFICE
TO BE WITH FAMILY (HISPANIC AND NON-HISPANIC RECRUITS)
(in percentages, decimals omitted)

Event	Mainstream (N = 81)	His-panics (N = 73)
Your father has died	50	46
Your mother has died	55	48
Your father became seriously ill	47	40
Your wife died	45	42
Your brother died	46	46
Your sister is getting married	26	33
Your daughter is getting married	43	38
Your niece is getting married	14	25
Your nephew is being baptized	07	21
Your son is being baptized	27	36
Your brother is being baptized	16	22
Your family is having a Christmas party	21	26
Your family is having a summer reunion	22	28
Your aunt from abroad is visiting	08	17
Your family is having 4th of July party	10	14
It's your parents' wedding anniversary	23	31
It's your mother's birthday	23	32
Your mother is seriously ill	50	45
It's your father's birthday	18	26

SOURCE: Triandis, Marin, Betancourt, & Chang, 1982.

Attributes of Asian Americans

There is evidence that these ethnic groups are also more collectivist than
mainstream Americans (Triandis, Bontempo, Betancourt, et al., 1986).
Of course, they are heterogeneous, and collectivism may be the only attribute they share. An excellent comparison of Americans and Chinese was
provided by Hsu (1981).

Other Groups

There are about 125 ethnic groups in the United States that have enough
members to be included in the *Harvard Encyclopedia of Ethnic Diversity and
American Ethnic Groups* (Thernstrom, 1980). Clearly, limitations of space
preclude mentioning all these other groups. We will focus instead on a
general way of analyzing intergroup relationships.

BARRIERS TO GOOD INTERCULTURAL RELATIONS

With instant communications and jet travel, intercultural relations among nationals of different countries are becoming increasingly important in a rapidly shrinking world. Sadly, many of these relationships are hostile. When you open a newspaper, you are more likely to see headlines about wars, strikes, sabotage, terrorists, economic boycotts, religious confrontations, and language conflicts than news about agreements, cooperation, and mutual benefit. Why?

Ethnocentrism and cultural distance work together to create perceived dissimilarity. Dissimilarity results in conflict, and conflict results in negative stereotypes. As a result, people make nonisomorphic attributions and experience the relationship as one in which they have no control. They feel culture shock, and they feel hostility toward the other group. In the next sections we will examine some of these phenomena.

Ethnocentrism

We are all ethnocentric, some of us more than others, especially if we have not tasted another culture. How could it be otherwise? Most of us know only our own culture, and it is natural that we will consider it as *the standard* against which to judge others. The more another culture is like our own, the "better" it is. That is the essence of ethnocentrism.

Most cultures consider themselves as the "center of the world." The Chinese called themselves the "central kingdom." The Greeks called lands to their east "the East" and lands to their West "the West." The Romans took that way of talking from the Greeks, and today this terminology is used by speakers of English.

One example will help us see how deeply we depend on our cultures in judging what is going on around us. In Chapter 4 we already reviewed the study by Shweder, Mahapatra, and Miller (1990) of children and adults in the orthodox Hindu temple town of Bhubaneshwar in Orissa, India, and similar samples in the Hyde Park area of Chicago, Illinois. Remember? They used thirty-nine scenarios describing a behavior that samples from Orissa and Illinois considered a breach of proper behavior. They asked eight standard questions about each breach, to examine how serious the misbehavior was perceived to be in the two cultures.

Let us look at scenario 4, which was "A widow in your community eats fish two or three times a week."

Here is the Indian interview, with the letters R for "respondent" and Q for "questioner":*

---

* Shweder, Mahapatra, & Miller (1990), in Kagan and Lamb, *The Emergence of Morality in Young Children*. Reprinted by permission of the University of Chicago Press.

Q: Is the widow's behavior wrong?

R: Yes. Widows should not eat fish, meat, onions or garlic, or any "hot" foods. They must restrict their diet to "cool" foods, rice, dhal, ghee, vegetables.

Q: How serious is the violation?

R: A very serious violation. She will suffer greatly if she eats fish.

Q: Is it a sin?

R: Yes. It's a "great" sin.

Q: What if no one knew this had been done? It was done in private or secretly. Would it be wrong then?

R: What difference does it make if it is done while alone? It is wrong. A widow should spend her time seeking salvation—seeking to be reunited with the soul of her husband. Hot foods will distract her. They will stimulate her sexual appetite. She will lose her sanctity. She will want sex and behave like a whore.

Q: Would it be best if everyone is the world followed the rule that widows should not eat fish?

R: That would be best. A widow's devotion is to her deceased husband—who should be treated like a god. She will offend his spirit if she eats fish.

Q: In the United States, a widow eats fish all the time. Would the United States be a better place if widows stopped eating fish?

R: Definitely, it would be a better place. Perhaps American widows would stop having sex and marrying other men.

Q: What if most people in India wanted to change the rule so that it would be considered all right for widows to eat fish. Would it be okay to change the rule?

R: No. It is wrong for a widow to eat fish. Hindu dharma—truth—forbids it.

Q: Do you think a widow who eats fish should be stopped from doing that or punished in some way?

R: She should be stopped. But the sin will live with her and she will suffer for it.

Now consider the American interview.

Q: Is the widow's behavior wrong?

R: No. She can eat fish if she wants to.

Q: How serious is the violation?

R: It is not a violation.

Q: Is it a sin?

R: No.

Q: What if no one knew this had been done. It was done in private or secretly. Would it be wrong then?

R: It is not wrong, in private or public.

Q: Would it be best if everyone in the world followed the rule that it is all right for a widow to eat fish if she wants to?

R: Yes. People should be free to eat fish if they want to. Everyone has that right.

Q: In India, it is considered wrong for a widow to eat fish. Would India be a better place if it was considered all right for a widow to eat fish if she wants to?

R: Yes. That may be their custom but she should be free to decide if she wants to follow it. Why shouldn't she eat fish if she wants to?

Q: What if most people in the United States wanted to change the rule so that it would be considered wrong for a widow to eat fish? Would it be okay to change it?

R: No. You can't order people not to eat fish. They have the right to eat it if they want.

Q: Do you think a widow who eats fish should be stopped from doing that or punished in some way?

R: No. (Shweder, Mahapatra, & Miller, 1990, pp. 168–169)

Now think about how you felt when you read this section from the Shweder et al. paper. When you were reading about the Indian responses, were you slightly amused? When you were reading about the American responses, were you slightly bored?

I suspect that this is the way you felt. Why? Because you felt rather "superior" to the Indians, and the American answers were so obvious, so totally predictable, that there was nothing really interesting there. That is exactly what ethnocentrism does. It makes us feel superior to those who are different from us, and it provides such obvious answers that we do not examine our own behavior critically.

Let us look at our own behavior for a moment. Do you see how ethnocentric it is? We assume that people have the right to eat fish because our culture is individualistic and we see social life as a series of interactions among autonomous individuals. The Indians, being collectivists, see an interdependent individual such as the widow linked to her husband for eternity. As Shweder et al. (1990) correctly put it:

> Although they disagree about the morally right thing to do, both the Indian Brahman and the American viewed the issue as a moral issue. (p. 169)

Both viewed the obligations involved as *universally binding and unalterable.*

> For the Brahman the relevant obligation was a status obligation associated with widowhood and the continued mutual reliance of husband and wife. For the American the relevant obligation was the obligation to protect the personal liberties and zones of discretionary choice of autonomous individuals. (p. 169)

Individualism-collectivism disagreements occur within the United States as well. For example, the debate over abortion reflects the issue of the freedom of women to decide (which is the very American tradition of individualism) versus the right of a collective (the church or the state) to impose its values on the individual.

Since we are all ethnocentric, the only way to improve intergroup relations is to learn to suppress our ethnocentrism (Devine, 1989).

Studies of ethnocentrism by Campbell and his associates (Brewer & Campbell, 1976; Campbell & LeVine, 1968) have suggested the following generalizations:

1. What goes on in our culture is seen as "natural" and "correct," and what goes on in other cultures is perceived as "unnatural" and "incorrect."

TABLE 9-3 CORRELATIONS BETWEEN SELF-RATINGS AND RATINGS GIVEN OUT-GROUPS

	High-contact groups	*Low-contact groups*
Evaluative Ratings	$r = .33$	$r = -.03$
Achievement Ratings	$r = .79$	$r = .53$
Potency Ratings	$r = .70$	$r = .56$

SOURCE: Brewer & Campbell, 1976.

2. We perceive in-group customs as universally valid.

3. We unquestionably think that in-group norms, roles, and values are correct.

4. We believe that it is natural to help and cooperate with members of our in-group, to favor our in-group, to feel proud of our in-group, and to be distrustful of and even hostile toward out-groups.

In a study (Brewer & Campbell, 1976) of the way thirty African tribes perceived one another, there was a tendency for similar tribes to be perceived as good and likable and dissimilar tribes to be perceived as bad. We trust people whose behavior we can predict. When we see people with strange customs, we become anxious and hostile, because we cannot predict what they are going to do.

Let us take a closer look at this study. Table 9–3 shows how self-ratings were related to received evaluative, achievement, and potency (powerful, big) ratings. In other words, "If I think I am smart, do other people also think I am smart?" Table 9–3 shows that self-ratings are positively related to received ratings, but the correlation is much higher when the tribes are in contact than when they are not in contact.

That study also found that the attraction ratings are a function of proximity. The closer the groups, the more they like each other. Because of cultural diffusion, tribes that are located next to each other are likely to be objectively similar; this similarity is reflected in the attraction ratings. In short, the more others are like us, the better they look! That is the essence of ethnocentrism. We use ourselves as the standard, and others are evaluated according to how well they meet that standard.

Intergroup versus Interpersonal

When we relate to another ethnic group, we can have an *intergroup* or an *interpersonal* relationship (Tajfel, 1974, 1982). In intergroup relationships we pay attention only to the group membership of the person. In interpersonal relationships we pay attention to the attributes of individuals. For example, suppose that a white salesperson is serving a black customer. If the salesperson pays attention mostly to the race of the customer, that is an intergroup relationship; if the salesperson pays attention mostly to the unique attributes of the customer, such as name, address, and personality, that is an interpersonal relationship.

Research shows that we are more likely to have an intergroup relationship (e.g., "I am attacking the enemy") than an interpersonal relationship when (1) there is a history of conflict between the groups; (2) there is a pattern of incompatible goals (i.e., if one group reaches its goals, the other group loses something important); (3) members experience a strong attachment to their in-group; (4) there is anonymity of group membership (e.g., the groups are too far from each other to see the faces of the members of the out-group, or people wear masks, as in a Ku Klux Klan rally); and (5) moving from one group to another is difficult, if not impossible.

Stereotypes in Intergroup Relations

Mere categorization into in-group and out-group is sufficient to produce in-group favoritism, even when the categorization is obviously and blatantly arbitrary or random. In some experiments a class of schoolchildren was divided arbitrarily into those with yellow and those with red ribbons, or those who "like or dislike Picasso's paintings" (Tajfel & Turner, 1986). When the children were asked to distribute candy to other children, they showed in-group favoritism.

In most intergroup situations individuals are categorized on the basis of attributes such as language, sex, race, religion, nationality, social class, and the like. After categorization, attributes are perceived to exist that make all members of a given category similar and at the same time different from all other members of other categories. In short, people are stereotyped.

Stereotypes result in overestimates of the link between the category and the attributes of that category. Once the stereotype is in place, it influences how we process information. We select information that fits the stereotype and reject information that is inconsistent with it. As a result, we process very easily information that is positive about the in-group and negative about the out-group. We also remember information that is consistent with our stereotypes better than other information.

When we come in contact with a group for which we have a clear stereotype, the stereotype is activated automatically (Devine, 1989). This study indicated that it requires effort to suppress the stereotypes. If we have a good enough reason to suppress them—for example, because we think of ourselves as enlightened and unprejudiced—then we can ignore them. But that can be done only if we have the time and the energy to suppress them. When we must give a response quickly, we fail to suppress our prejudices, although we would do so if we had more time to respond.

The result of this sequence is that we perceive in other groups behavior that we expect. This is known as a "self-fulfilling prophecy." Humans enjoy being good prophets! So we have a psychic investment in our stereotypes. We love them dearly.

When there is a real difference between an in-group and an out-group, there is a high probability that this difference will be exaggerated and become part of the stereotype. The greater the contrast between in-group and out-group on any dimension, the more likely is that dimension to be part of a stereotype (Campbell, 1967).

In addition there is a tendency to look at the same behavior and give a different interpretation to it depending on whether it was performed by the in-group or the out-group. Campbell (1967, p. 823) provided the examples of Table 9–4.

Once an element becomes part of a stereotype, other elements that are associated with it in the culture's "implicit personality theory" also become part of the stereotype.

Most theories of personality consider undesirable traits as related to each other and desirable traits as also related to each other. This is due to

TABLE 9-4 SELF-DESCRIPTIONS AND STEREOTYPES OF OUT-GROUPS REFLECT DIFFERENT PERCEPTIONS OF THE SAME BEHAVIOR

Self-description	Stereotype of out-group
We have pride, self-respect and revere the traditions of our ancestors.	They are egotistical and self-centered. They love themselves more than they love us.
We are loyal.	They are clannish, exclude others.
We are honest and trustworthy among ourselves, but we're not suckers when foreigners try their tricks.	They will cheat us if they can. They have no honesty or moral restraint when dealing with us.
We are brave and progressive. We stand up for our own rights, defend what is ours, and can't be pushed around or bullied.	They are aggressive and expansionistic. They want to get ahead at our expense.
We are peaceful, loving people, hating only our vile enemies.	They are a hostile people who hate us.
We are moral and clean.	They are immoral and unclean.

source: Campbell, 1967. Copyright 1967 by the American Psychological Association. Reprinted by permission.

the principle of *cognitive balance* (Heider, 1958). This principle operates universally, though more strongly in the West than in the East. In other words, inferences from one undesirable trait to another are independent of evidence. This is why stereotypes are so often invalid.

People tend to see more differences between in-group and out-group than there really are (Granberg, 1984). Conversely, people tend to see their in-group members as agreeing with them more than is the case. Stereotypes tend to decrease our information search. This makes our thinking less accurate and our judgments and decisions poor.

On the other hand, stereotypes often have a kernel of truth. There is a large overlap between autostereotypes and heterostereotypes (e.g., how Americans see Americans and how Germans see Americans, or how Germans see Germans and how Americans see Germans) that has been found in many studies (Campbell, 1967; Fischer & Trier, 1962; Triandis, Lisansky, et al., 1982; Triandis & Vassiliou, 1967). There is also evidence that those aspects of stereotypes that are easily visible are valid. For example, stereotypes that a group is tall or short may well reflect reality.

Schuman (1966) studied regional stereotypes in Bangladesh. College students were asked to choose the four adjectives that best described the people of each of the twelve districts of that country from a list of fifty characteristics. Then, a stratified random sample of urban industrial workers of rural origin was obtained so that each of the twelve districts was correctly represented. People from the twelve districts were asked specific questions about their behavior. Validity was determined by the correlation of the stereotype of members of a tribe with the answers that members of that tribe gave about their own behavior.

The findings indicated that when the trait was transparent, or easy to observe, validity was high. When it was not transparent, validity was zero. For example, an attribute such as "pious" is transparent in a Muslim country, because people can be observed very easily when praying (they turn toward Mecca, kneel, etc.). On that attribute validity was high. On the nontransparent attributes (e.g., intelligence) validity was zero.

McArthur and Friedman (1980) found that people are more likely to link undesirable behaviors to out-groups and desirable behaviors to in-groups than the other way around.

There is a relationship between the intensity of conflict among in-groups and out-groups and the ultimate fundamental attribution error. This error (Pettigrew, 1979) consists of in-group members' seeing nasty behaviors of the in-group as due to external factors ("We were forced to do it") and socially desirable behaviors of the in-group as due to internal factors (e.g., their personality); conversely, nasty behaviors of the out-group are attributed to internal factors and socially desirable behaviors of the out-group to external factors. When relationships among groups are good, the ultimate fundamental attribution error is attenuated (Hewstone & Ward, 1985).

The content of stereotypes tends to reflect the occurrence of events. Campbell (1967) gives several examples: African tribes living where there are two rainy seasons are stereotyped as "active," while tribes who live in places with one rainy season are stereotyped as "lazy." Of course, that reflects the ability of the first group to grow two crops and the inability of the second group to do that. Tribes that do much physical labor are stereotyped as "strong" and "stupid," while those that do much trading are stereotyped as "grasping" and "deceitful."

Stereotypes are inferior judgmental processes, because as Campbell (1967) has pointed out:

1. They make people think that all members of a given category have a trait (e.g., *all* men are aggressive).

2. People do not realize the extent to which they select information when they stereotype or how much their needs shape their stereotypes.

3. People see in-groups and out-groups as more different than they really are.

4. People confuse causes. For instance, they attribute behaviors to the ethnic attribute because it is salient and fail to use attributes that are correlated with ethnicity, because they are less salient. Thus they may say that "race" is the explanation when the correct factor is social class, poor jobs, age, sex, religion, or travel experiences.

5. There is a strong relationship between conflict and negative stereotyping. Yet people perceive the negative attributes of the out-group and justify their hostility by pointing to them, rather than understand that they see these attributes because they are competing with the out-group.

Contact

The more contact there is between two groups, the more accurate the stereotypes are likely to be, if other things are equal. However, in most real-life settings other things are *not* equal. Specifically, contact is associated with either positive or very negative experiences. The positive occur when two groups are similar and have nothing to divide; the negative occur when they are different and do have something to divide.

Contact is associated with similarity because it leads to diffusion of cultural traits and such diffusion increases similarity (e.g., the United States and Canada). But among cultures that have something to divide (e.g., Serbs and Croats) similarity is not helpful. They will pick on some difference, such as religion (Orthodox versus Roman Catholic) or the alphabet that they use (e.g., the Serbs use the Cyrillic, the Croats the Latin, for the same language) and will exaggerate that difference so that they perceive the "enemy"as totally different. Most wars occur among neighboring tribes or countries.

For contact to be beneficial and result in positive stereotypes, intergroup liking, and cooperative behaviors, several conditions must be met. Basically, the factors shown in Figure 9–4 must work together and make people see each other as similar. A reversal in any one of these factors is likely to result in conflict.

Clearly, cooperation occurs only under stringent conditions. Nevertheless, when *superordinate goals* were present in a number of experiments (Avigdor, 1953; Sherif, 1965), stereotypes became more positive.

The most important dimensions of stereotype content are (1) trust, (2) attraction, and (3) admiration versus distrust, repulsion and disrespect (Brewer & Campbell, 1976, p. 144). Attraction is related to cultural-linguistic similarity and geographic proximity, both of which improve the chances of contact. Admiration is related to the success of the other group, such as its level of economic development. Trust reflects the history of previous interactions. This means that there is considerable complexity in stereotypes, because some groups that are trusted are not admired, and some that are admired are not trusted.

Intergroup Liking and Social Distance

Positive stereotype content becomes one factor that leads to intergroup liking. When the content is negative, it results in intergroup disliking. When groups dislike each other, they experience social distance from each other. Social distance is often influenced by norms, i.e., ideas about what is correct behavior toward people of a certain type.

Studies have found that mere exposure to stimuli results in increases in attraction toward the stimuli (Saegert, Swap, & Zajonc, 1973; Zajonc, 1968). In other words, if you have never seen a Nepalese, the chances are that you will feel neutral or a bit anxious about this strange person. But as you become exposed to more and more Nepalese, if other factors are not present, your attraction for them will increase. Note that the fact that mere exposure leads to attraction favors the in-group (you are more likely to be exposed to in-group members) and is likely to lead to dislike of out-groups (you see few out-group members).

Interpersonal attraction also depends on physical attraction (e.g., Walster, Aronson, Abrahams, & Rottmann, 1966). Again this favors the in-group and leads to dislike of out-groups, since our standards of attractiveness often favor our own physical attributes. To many Africans, whites are so "pale" that they look "sick"! After spending several months in Africa, the explorer Stanley also felt that way when he saw white people again. But in countries where "white" is linked to "rich," the opposite pattern occurs.

In general, the more the out-group looks like the in-group, the more attractive it is, and the smaller the social distance. In a study by Jaspars, van de Geer, Tajfel, and Johnson (1965), Dutch children sorted pictures in two ways: First they sorted them according to what the people looked like, into "Dutch" versus "not-Dutch" persons. In counterbalanced order they sorted them also into "I like this" versus "I dislike this" person. The correlation between "Dutch" and "like" was very high.

Similarity is a major factor in interpersonal attraction (Byrne, 1971). There are many types of similarity: physical, age, sex, attitudes, abilities, social class, race, religion, political, and so on. Each of these types of similarity can potentially lead to attraction and small levels of social distance. Social behavior is also affected by similarity on such factors. Similarity in race is a more important determinant of attraction and low social distance for intimate behaviors than for superficial behaviors (Goldstein & Davis, 1972; Triandis & Davis, 1965).

Predictability of the other group's behavior leads to trust and attraction. Unpredictability means that we do not know how to "control" other people. Since we feel the need to control our environment (Langer, 1983), we dislike groups that are unpredictable. The self-esteem of people who are unable to control their environment is often low, and out-groups that reduce our self-esteem are unattractive.

When there are differences in power between groups, as when one group is exploiting another, social distance becomes a mechanism for keeping the other group "in its place." In this case, social distance is dictated by in-group norms. Triandis and Triandis (1960) have outlined a theory of social distance that expands this point. Note that economic, sexual, and prestige gains can be obtained by one group (e.g., whites over blacks, especially in South Africa) that would be lost if the two groups were to merge. Then social distance is a mechanism that maintains the privileges of one group.

In other situations the culture of a group may be threatened, as was the case during the persecutions of Jews by Christians in Europe. In such cases, social distance develops to protect the threatened culture on the one side and to justify the inhuman actions of the majority on the other. Thus, norms develop that prohibit contact or friendliness with the "enemy."

People differ in the extent to which they follow the norms of their culture. Those who are socially insecure are more likely to follow such norms, so that they will not be labeled as "undesirables" by their in-group. In a classic study, Bettelheim and Janowitz (1950) showed that those who had changed social class (and hence would be unsure of their social position) were more prejudiced toward minorities than those who remained in the same social class. Social mobility brings the person into an unfamiliar environment, where standards of behavior are different, and increases insecurity. In a similar vein, Kaufman (1957) found that people who were high in *status concern*, measured by agreement with statements such as "Ambition is the most important factor determining success in life" and "Raising one's social position is the most important goal of life," were more anti-Semitic ($r = .66$) than those who did not endorse such statements.

Misunderstandings between in-group and out-group are especially likely when people make nonisomorphic attributions. In Chapter 10 we will discuss how we can train people to make isomorphic attributions so as to increase intercultural understanding.

Some Attributes of Intergroup Relations

Since we have a lot of information about our in-groups, we are likely to know members of these groups who have undesirable as well as desirable traits. Thus, in-groups are often seen as heterogeneous. In the case of out-groups we have little information, and we may know only about the undesirable traits of those groups. This difference results in our thinking of our in-groups in mainly positive terms and of our out-groups in neutral or negative terms.

In the study we reviewed earlier, Brewer and Campbell (1976, p. 79) examined the view of thirty African groups about themselves and others and found only two tribes that evaluated another tribe more positively than their own. Linville (1982) showed that people have more complex schemas about their in-group than their out-group and hence make judgments about their in-group that are less extreme. For instance, whites know more about whites and less about blacks, and as a result of cognitive complexity (knowing both good and bad information) the judgments whites make about other whites tend to be less extreme. But the out-group is often seen as being monolithic. For example, "the enemy" is a single, powerful stimulus that can even lose its human qualities, as it did when the Nazis liquidated 6 million Jews, whom they regarded as one category of *Untermenschen* (subhumans).

Since people know a lot about their in-group, a behavior of an in-group member can have only a small effect on the cognitive schema that is used to think about the in-group. For example, if a person has 100 cognitions about in-group members, one more cognition is not likely to change the schema. But since people know less about the out-group, the behavior of an out-group member, especially if it is negative, can have a large impact on people's views. For example, if a person has only ten cognitions about the out-group, one cognition can make a large difference.

In-groups provide the individual with a sense of importance and, in a relatively anomic, modern society, with a sense of identity, belonging, support, shared goals, and purpose. This is an explanation for the extreme nationalistic movements that are plaguing many countries, such as the former Yugoslavia and U.S.S.R.

Brewer (1991) has proposed an *optimal distinctiveness* theory. Every person has a need to "assimilate" to some group and also to "differentiate" from other groups. For every person in each culture there is a different optimal point at which there is just the right amount of differentiation and assimilation, but not too much of either. The optimal point depends on culture. Collectivists feel most satisfied when the point is closer to assimilation and individualists when it is closer to differentiation.

The position of the optimal point depends on socialization (e.g., parents and teachers who frequently mention that "you are an X" move the point toward assimilation, while those who never emphasize this social identity move the point toward differentiation). Recent experiences can also shift the optimal point. For example, a war that threatens your group increases assimilation, but when you feel that others deal with you stereotypically, you are likely to move toward differentiation.

SUMMARY

When we read the paper, we realize that there is much intercultural conflict in the world. Conflict can be traced to ethnocentrism, seeing the other in intergroup rather than interpersonal terms, stereotyping, and differences in the ecology. In addition, exaggerations of the differences in the attributes of each culture group, insufficient opportunities to meet members of the other group, different standards of physical attraction, and low levels of similarity in attitudes, values, religion, or political orientation increase conflict. Furthermore, dissimilarities in subjective culture, lack of perceived control, norms of social distance that maintain privileges, insecurity that increases adherence to such norms, and misunderstandings of the behavior of the other cultural group also result in conflict. In the next chapter we will examine how we can train people to look at members of other cultures more accurately—and with less social distance.

QUESTIONS AND EXERCISES

1.   Think of the one group in the world you like least. What kinds of attributes do they have? Make a list of these attributes.

2.   Now think of your own group. List the attributes of your own group. Check the list of attributes you used in your answer to question 1. How much overlap is there?

3.   Now make a set of scales that consist of both sets of attributes. For example, if the attribute "intelligent" was used in answering question 2, make an item like this one: My least preferred group tends to be intelligent.

False   1   2   3   4   5   6   7   8   9   True
My own group tends to be intelligent.
False   1   2   3   4   5   6   7   8   9   True

After you finish making these scales for the attributes you listed in answer to questions 1 and 2, rate the groups on all the scales.

4.   Critically examine your ratings for question 3 against objective evidence, e.g., information you get from experts or from the library. Is there objective evidence that supports your ratings?

10

Intercultural Training

———— ❖ ————

Culture Shock ◆ Phases of Adjustment ◆ Factors Determining Success in
Intercultural Relations ◆ *The Traveler's Preparation* ◆ *The Traveler's Per-
sonality* ◆ *The Difficulty of the Assignment* ◆ Varieties of Culture
Learning ◆ Culture-General versus Culture-Specific Training ◆ Self-
Insight ◆ Experiential Training ◆ Exposure to Many Local Cultures ◆ Field
Trips ◆ The Cultural Assimilator or Intercultural Sensitizer ◆ Behavior Mod-
ification Training ◆ Other Details about Training ◆ Strategies for the
Improvement of Intercultural Relations ◆ Evaluation of Cross-Cultural
Training ◆ Summary

T he previous chapter showed that intercultural relations are often difficult. In
this chapter we examine culture shock and more fully outline various kinds
of training that can reduce culture shock and generally improve intercultural relationships. The information in this chapter is especially relevant for
those who will work with members of other cultures, either in the United States or
abroad. Diplomats, missionaries, advisers, business and educational representa-
tives, and students who spend more than a few weeks abroad will find much
material that is informative. Tourists are generally insulated from people from
other cultures, but occasionally they too come in contact with them, and so some of
the material may be of interest to tourists too.

CULTURE SHOCK

As noted in Chapter 9, when people go from one culture to another, they may
experience *culture shock* (Oberg, 1954), a phenomenon characterized by physical
and psychological symptoms (Furnham & Bochner, 1986).

The symptoms can include a combination of the following: excessive hand washing and concern for sanitation (quality of drinking water, food, cleanliness of dishes, bedding); fear of physical contact with others; absentmindedness; development of mild psychosomatic disorders; insomnia, fatigue; feelings of helplessness; fits of anger; excessive fear of being cheated, robbed, or injured; overreaction to minor physical symptoms, such as minor aches or skin irritations; abuse of alcohol or drugs; strong feelings of homesickness.

Culture shock can have severe effects. For instance, Furnham and Bochner (1986) reported that American, German, and Polish women living in Britain were twice as likely to commit suicide as British women, though there were no such differences in suicide rates for men. It would appear that it is more difficult for women than for men to adjust to a different culture.

The greater the cultural distance between the home society and the host society, the more intense the shock will be. The more experience the individual has had with exotic sites, smells, foods, and people, the less intense the shock.

One explanation of culture shock is that most of our behavior is under the control of habits. We react to specific cues and expect others to behave in ways we already know. When we are in unfamiliar environments, when people behave in ways that we do not understand, we feel that we have lost *control*. People who feel that they have little control become depressed and helpless, and they are even more likely to die than people who feel in control of their lives (Langer, 1983).

Specifically, self-efficacy (e.g., Bandura, 1989) depends on our feeling that we can control the environment. When we are able to predict what others will do, when we can act so as to get others to do what we want done, when we know how to get rewards from our environment and avoid punishments, we feel in control. In new cultures we are often not able to predict the behavior of others or get them to do what we want. People in other cultures sometimes appear to be inscrutable, and the fact that we cannot communicate with them is a great impediment.

Self-efficacy depends on the extent to which we have had experiences in mastering our environment. Our self-efficacy grows as we are able to overcome increasingly challenging barriers. The more we know about another culture, the more control we are likely to have. When we have good skills in dealing with members of the other culture, we feel more in control, and practice develops these skills. It also helps to have resources (status, money, information, goods) and to receive social support assuring us that we can control the environment. But when we are abroad, we are often faced with new situations in which we have had no previous mastering experiences. Events that we expect to occur do not; at the same time, the least expected events take place. Thus, discrepancies in *expectations* amplify our sense of lack of efficacy and loss of control.

We are used to getting rewarded with our favorite foods, sports, or cultural events, and yet in the host culture these may not be available.

In addition, in our own culture we are likely to have relatives and friends who can lend us a hand when we have a problem. *Social support* is likely to be much more available in our culture than in a strange place.

Furnham and Bochner (1986) reviewed eight theories that appear relevant in explaining culture shock and concluded that loss of control, discrepant expectations, lack of social support, and insufficient social skills are the most important factors explaining the phenomenon.

Gao and Gudykunst (1990) tested and found support for this theory: Cultural dissimilarity (distance between the two cultures), insufficient cultural knowledge, and unsatisfactory social contacts cause culture shock, which is mediated by a high level of anxiety and lack of confidence in the kinds of attributions we make. Attributions, as we have seen in previous chapters, often help us explain the behavior of people in the host culture.

As noted in Chapter 9, perceived dissimilarity between us and people of the host culture results in a lack of a sense of control. Several additional factors were mentioned that cause lack of control and poor relationships: a history of conflict, cultural distance, ignorance of the other culture, low competence in the local language, lack of friends and acquaintances, unequal status and power of the visitor and the hosts, and few superordinate goals. When a combination of these factors is present, a person is likely to experience culture shock.

Perceived dissimilarity plus the opportunity for frequent contact lead to feelings of lack of control, incompetence, and depression. These feelings are amplified when authorities, and significant others, disapprove of the contact. These feelings may result in hostility toward members of the other culture, mistakes in the attributions of the other person's behavior, and the inability to anticipate the other's acts.

These feelings have the effect of creating more negative intergroup attitudes, avoidance, and much formal social behavior. Avoidance and formality increase the perceived dissimilarity. As interaction takes place, stereotypes dominate perceptions, and people make increasingly more nonisomorphic attributions which further decreases their sense of control, causing considerable culture shock. Culture shock often sends people to the "American Club" (or equivalent), where they meet others who are also experiencing culture shock and where they drink and commiserate. They do not take advantage of being in the host culture, and they fail to learn the language and customs which would help them overcome culture shock.

The following example of culture shock will give you some sense of what can happen. This young American married a French woman, and a few months after their marriage they went to Paris to meet his in-laws. He had not traveled previously; he knew only Brooklyn and Manhattan.

Here he was in a big, strange city, surrounded by people speaking a language he did not know. They all seemed different and strange. His in-laws were nice enough, but he could not speak to them, and his wife was feeling exhausted from having to translate every word. So he spent most of his time in France at the American Information Service Library, reading American history!

Upon returning to New York, I asked him what he found most impressive in France. He replied: "The toilets at the Louvre Museum." I inquired why, and he said: "They were the only ones that worked as well as American toilets!"

When the environment is extremely different, culture shock can occur even to the experienced traveler. I experienced it the first time I went to Calcutta, India. I arrived at four in the morning. It was still dark, and as we drove from the airport to the city, the headlights of the bus illuminated thousands upon thousands of "corpses" lining the road. They were actually people sleeping along the side of the road. I later learned that most of them do so voluntarily, to save money to send back to their families in the villages. Even with that knowledge it was difficult to escape the shock.

PHASES OF ADJUSTMENT

Tourists, and others who can avoid real contact with the local culture, generally do not go through the phases of adjustment that are about to be described. However, frequently people who have to live abroad go through these phases.

Diplomats, missionaries, businesspeople, and students begin their stay in another culture with a sense of optimism and very positive feelings. They live in a hotel that looks much like hotels back home and eat foods that are much like foods back home. Often they are welcomed by associates who try to make them feel at home by arranging special events and providing privileges.

The second phase is a period when difficulties of language, inadequate schools for the children, poor housing, crowded transportation, chaotic shopping, and the like begin taking their toll. Research shows that during this period people often seek co-nationals with whom they compare notes about "how awful the natives are" and try to escape in drinking and socializing with them. As they feel less and less in control, the symptoms of culture shock become more numerous and more intense, and depression develops.

In the third phase things have reached rock bottom. They may go home a failure in the eyes of their organization as well as in their own eyes, or they may pull themselves together to learn about the local culture and thus begin coping.

In the fourth phase, new skills have been acquired so that people can cope quite well, depression becomes less severe, and optimism returns.

In the fifth phase, people know how to deal with the host culture and are about as well adjusted as at home.

Thus, the phases of adjustment form a U-shaped curve: Over time one feels good, bad, very bad, better, good, very good.

Of course, some people do not go through these phases. Tourists usually go home after phase 1. Others go home as soon as they begin feeling culture shock. About one-third to one-half of American expatriate executives, who have gone to work abroad without proper cross-cultural training, do in fact quit. This can cost their companies $250,000 per executive, create ill feelings in the host culture, and reduce the self-esteem of the executive and his or her chances for future promotions. It is a real tragedy that can be avoided if people get sufficient training.

The reactions to being abroad are quite variable. Some people join "little America," or whatever their culture, in the host country; some become bicultural with a foot in both worlds, and some "go native," adjusting so well to the local culture that they never go back to their own.

If we add the phases of coming back, which often turn out to be no less traumatic than those of going abroad, we might describe the total process as a W-curve. The first part of the W is the U we have just described; the second is the U of reentry shock.

Coming home, people go more or less through another U-shaped experience. They are greeted by family and old friends; they then have to learn to cope with differences in lifestyle, such as less money (no bonus for overseas work; often life is more expensive at home), less interesting travel, no servants, more crime, and sometimes more pollution. To make things worse, friends are often not interested in the wonderful new knowledge the person has acquired abroad.

The third phase includes learning to adjust again to the home environment, and the final one includes coping successfully with it. While the data in support of the W-curve are not very strong (Church, 1982), they obviously depend on how good an adjustment has been made to the host culture. If the person has gone native, returning home can be extremely traumatic.

The situation of those who emigrate to another culture with the intention of staying there permanently is rather different from the one just described but also consists of four phases:

1. Cultural adjustment—managing to cope with the new culture
2. Identification—changing social identity
3. Cultural competence—developing more and more skills
4. Role acculturation—adopting new culturally defined roles

In this last phase the person essentially becomes a member of the other culture, has the skills for locally approved behavior, and uses the local language well.

Though culture shock and depression occur with some frequency, they are not universal (Klineberg & Hull, 1979). They are related to (1) the traveler's preparation, (2) the traveler's personality, and (3) the difficulty of the assignment.

FACTORS DETERMINING SUCCESS IN INTERCULTURAL RELATIONS

The Traveler's Preparation

Culture shock, while common, can be avoided through proper preparation. Certainly, learning the local language is a big help. Americans are very frequently monolingual; only 4 percent of American high school students take more than two years of a foreign language (Simon, 1980). But in most parts of the world, learning several languages is common and often occurs painlessly in childhood.

When representative samples of people from the European Economic Community were asked to indicate in how many languages they could converse, nationals of small countries indicated that they learned more languages than those from bigger countries. Forty-two percent of the citizens of Luxembourg indicated that they could chat in *four* languages! By contrast, only 1 percent of the Germans, French, British, or Italians were able to do so. My guess is that the corresponding American statistics would be less than 1 percent.

If you live in a small country, you have to learn another language. When I was a child growing up in Greece, I was first exposed to French, then to German. I went to a French high school for two years. Then, during World War II, the Italians occupied Corfu, the island where I was living. They expelled all the Greek teachers from the schools, replacing them with Italian teachers, and so I learned Italian. As the war was coming to an end, English was clearly going to be the "in" language, and so at seventeen I started learning English. All of these languages came in very handy later in my professional work and when dealing with members of international psychological organizations, many of whom preferred to talk in their own languages.

Learning other languages is really very easy if you start early. When I tried to learn Chinese at age sixty, I found it impossibly hard. I got only to the point where I could do some rudimentary shopping. So here is my advice: Take advantage of your age!

Learning the host language provides a sense of being in control and a feeling of being at home in the host culture. In addition, the hosts treat you much better if you know their language. For example, in France people treat me extremely well, often asking me if I am from one of the French colonies. That experience is very different from the reports I hear from my American friends who claim that the French are inhospitable and rude.

A major advantage of learning languages is that you learn how to learn languages. A most important factor is a sense of self-efficacy ("I can do it") and confidence in being able to learn additional languages.

For that reason, all who wish to live in the modern, increasingly interdependent world should learn at least one other language. There is considerable evidence that, keeping IQ statistically under control, knowing more than one language is associated with cognitive flexibility and creativity (Segalowitz, 1980). In fact, Lambert (1992) has argued that learning languages is one way to improve intelligence.

In addition to learning the host language you should learn as much as possible about the host culture. This includes the local history and geography. Just as you are likely to look down on a visitor who does not know who George Washington was, so the locals will look down on you when you do not know their heroes. You should know about heroes and symbols (including favorite colors, foods, dress, objects) so that you will not appear foolish. Here is a story that tells it all:

An American monocultural businessman went to Lima, Peru, to sign a very important deal that his colleagues had negotiated. A party was given, where pisco sours (a rather strong local drink) were in abundance. At one point the music started, and our friend turned to the person next to him and requested: "Madam! May I have the pleasure of this dance?" The other person answered: "Certainly not! First, this is not a dance but our national anthem, and second, I am the bishop of Lima!"

You must also learn to (1) make the same attributions in explaining the behavior of the hosts that the hosts make in explaining their own behavior, (2) understand how the hosts feel about events in the environment, so as to be "tuned in" and act correctly, specifically avoiding acts that offend, and, finally (3) do what is expected and what will gratify the hosts.

To see ourselves as others see us when we travel abroad, it is useful to examine how non-Americans looked at American culture in the nineteenth century. I selected the reactions of the Japanese, because that is one of the great cultures of the world, no less sophisticated than Western culture. Here are the impressions of some Japanese visitors to the United States in the nineteenth and early twentieth centuries (Vuylsteke, 1978) taken from Japanese diaries of the period. Americans abroad can look just as ridiculous to their hosts as these visiting Japanese look to you!

On toilets:

Toilets are placed over holes in the ground; it is customary to read books in them.

On manners:

It is customary among Americans that even in front of high officials they stretch their legs on the table, rest their chins on their hands, never bow, and seem to have no etiquette. But whenever they see anyone in trouble they are extremely kind. Therefore, it is wrong to generalize that Americans are impolite.

> While the mistress of the house always stayed in the drawing room to entertain the guests, her husband—supposedly the master of the house—worked like a servant and busily moved around in and out of the room. This was the reverse of the custom in our country. How strange!

Note the overgeneralizations, the rejection of what is different, the casting of the new experiences into the framework of one's own culture, the maximizing of the in-group's positive features. These phenomena occur in most intercultural encounters, and one of the purposes of cross-cultural training is to help the trainees avoid falling into these traps.

When we study what people see abroad, we find that they use their own culture as the framework for selectively and often inaccurately perceiving the host culture. This phenomenon is well known in psychology. We tend to see events that are only slightly different from our own experiences as identical to our own experiences, a phenomenon called *assimilation*, and events that are different from our own experiences as more different than they really are, a phenomenon called *contrast* (Sherif, Kelly, Rodgers, Sarup, & Tittler, 1973).

For example, when a Swazi chief (from Africa) visited England, he was asked what he liked best, and he said he liked the policemen. Upon further inquiry it was determined that what he liked was the way the policemen directed traffic, because their gestures were identical to the gestures that the Swazi use in greeting each other. That is assimilation. The Japanese visitors noticed that male hosts move more than they do in Japan and exaggerated the difference, a contrast phenomenon. On the other hand, the presence of the hostess in the drawing room was a real difference, since this is still relatively rare in Japan, and so was an accurate perception of a real difference.

The Traveler's Personality

Selecting the right people to go abroad is very important for the organizations they will represent. Failure rates as high as 70 percent (in Africa,

Copeland & Griggs, 1985) can be avoided. As we have seen earlier, it is not just the lost salary of an executive, the cost of transporting the family, and the cost and effort of setting up an office abroad, but also the damage to the business, the lost sales, the on-the-job mistakes, and the loss of goodwill that are part of the costs.

Unfortunately, ready-made personality measures have proved to be very modest predictors of adjustment abroad, but these three have some value:

1. Conceptual complexity (Gardiner, 1972)
2. The tendency to use broad categories (Detweiler, 1980; Pettigrew, 1959)
3. Inversely, the F-scale (a measure of fascist tendencies)

People who are conceptually complex show less social distance toward people who are very different from them. People who are broad categorizers adjust to new environments better than do narrow categorizers. People who are authoritarian, rigid, and low in tolerance for ambiguity (Budner, 1962), qualities associated with fascist tendencies, do *not* do well in new environments.

Figure 10–1 shows my own example of an item from a test of narrow versus broad categorization.

Answer the question for yourself. If you saw almost all the items as belonging to one or two categories, you are a broad categorizer; if you made many categories, you are a narrow categorizer.

Detweiler's research shows that broad categorizers adjust abroad better than narrow ones. One interpretation of this finding is that broad categorizers are likely to categorize the experiences they have in the host culture together with familiar experiences they have had in their own, and so feel comfortable abroad.

It is also helpful to have high self-esteem, so that people who are different are not a threat. High self-esteem is also correlated with positive feelings toward out-groups (Ehrlich, 1973, pp. 128–136). Other desirable qualities are:

- Empathy (Taft, 1977)
- Sociability
- Critical acceptance of stereotypes
- Openness to different points of view
- Interest in the host culture
- Task orientation, provided this orientation is not excessive (Hawes & Kealey, 1979; Ruben & Kealey, 1979)

Suppose this figure is a zup.

Put a checkmark on all the zups below.

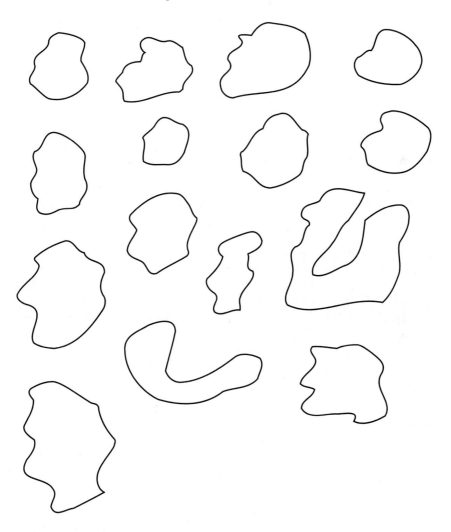

FIGURE 10–1
Example of a categorization test.

Unfortunately, there are no standard tests for most of these attributes, so they must be developed especially for the specific sample of travelers.

Predictors of success abroad (Martin, 1989) have included:

- Cultural flexibility (the ability to substitute activities in the host culture for own culture valued activities)
- Social orientation (the ability to establish new intercultural relationships)
- Willingness to communicate (e.g., use the host language without fear of making mistakes)
- Skills in conflict resolution (collaborative style)
- Patience (the ability to suspend judgment)
- Intercultural sensitivity (a willingness to search for possible cultural differences that may explain behavior that is not understood)
- Tolerance for differences among people (finding differences interesting)
- A sense of humor (the ability to laugh when things go wrong)

According to Kealey's (1989) extensive study, the individual who succeeds abroad is one who is highly motivated and who is committed to and interested in being involved in the local culture. "It seems plausible that high contact leads to increased feelings of satisfaction, for it makes these people feel successful in meeting their expectations and desires; and, as well, contact no doubt enriches in a personal way the lives of both parties so involved" (p. 409).

Other attributes identified by Kealey include low security needs (willing to take risks), low upward-mobility needs (the person does not care so much about promotions), and concern for other people.

Kealey's is an unusually good study because the instruments were administered to some of the individuals going abroad *before* they went and to some *after* they went, thus controlling for possible interactions between the experience of being abroad and the responses to the instruments.

Consultants who screen employees for corporations that plan to send them to work abroad claim to have developed inventories that provide good predictors of success abroad (Tucker, 1987). Since the validity of these measures has not been independently confirmed, it is unclear at this time that these claims can be believed.

The Difficulty of the Assignment

The cultural distance between home and host cultures makes the assignment more difficult. But there is a deceptive complication: We know from work on transfer of training, as well as from informal observations, that the most difficult place to be is one that "looks the same" and is in fact different. A place that looks the same, e.g., England for Americans, but requires different behaviors can be a trap.

Figure 10–2 shows the Skaggs-Robinson surface. This was derived from experimental psychology studies of transfer of training. Positive transfer is on the upper part of the vertical axis, and negative transfer is on the lower half of the vertical axis. Positive transfer occurs when what you learn in one setting helps you do things right in another setting. Negative transfer occurs when what you have learned in one setting leads to difficulties in the other. For example, polite Europeans, especially the French, shake hands with everybody when they arrive or leave a social situation. When they arrive at work in the morning, they go around shaking everybody's hand; before leaving work in the evening they do the same. When they come to the United States, they may try to do the same here. Most Americans would find it odd to shake hands every morning and evening. This behavior appeared even odder at an informal

FIGURE 10–2
The Skaggs-Robinson surface.

Positive   (What one learned in one's own
transfer   culture works well in new culture)

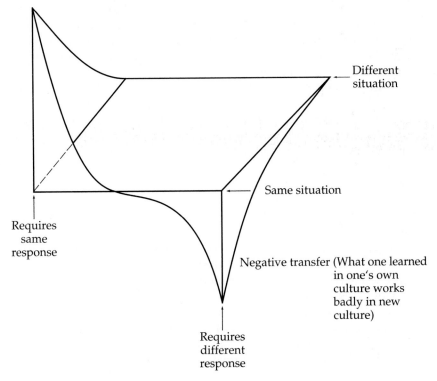

Different
situation

Same situation

Requires
same
response

Negative transfer (What one learned
in one's own
culture works
badly in new
culture)

Requires
different
response

picnic, where I saw such polite people making sure that they had not missed shaking the hand of every person there!

Figure 10-2 shows that one gets maximum positive transfer when one has the same situation, which requires the same response. The "same-different situation" is the third dimension of this graph, and it goes "into" the paper. The "requires same-different response" dimension is the horizontal axis in this figure. So you see maximum positive transfer when the same situation requires the same response, and maximum negative transfer when the same situation requires a different response. When a different situation requires a different response, there is neither positive nor negative transfer.

In sum, the easiest condition is the one where the environment looks the same as at home and what you have learned to do at home is the right thing to do abroad. The most difficult condition is the one where the environment looks the same, but a very different behavior is correct. When the environment looks very different, we know we should behave differently. The difficulty with the situation that looks familiar but requires a very different behavior is that it is deceptive and can cause the unwary to fall into a trap.

VARIETIES OF CULTURE LEARNING

There are numerous ways you learn about another culture. You can spend time with members of the other culture, you can read about them, you can ask people who have been there. Each of these methods can be effective, but each has limitations.

It is important to train the whole accompanying family as well as the person who is going abroad. Experience has shown that the most common reason for American executives to return from abroad early is that the spouse could not adjust to the host environment. Predeparture training that includes the spouse and children, if any, can be extremely valuable.

When the training is realistic, many trainees inform their employer that going abroad is not for them. This is an excellent outcome, because it is far better for the person to drop out before much damage has been done.

One of the major problems in culture learning is convincing a person that culture training is worthwhile. Most people are ethnocentric and feel that others must learn about their culture rather than that they should learn about other cultures. Many also feel that they already know enough. Thus very little training is done relative to what is needed.

Specifically, only about a third of U.S. multinational companies offer *any* formal cross-cultural training (Tung, 1981). By contrast, two-thirds of the European and Japanese multinationals offer it (Tung, 1988). Some

American managers seem to be more arrogant than their counterparts in other industrial countries because they feel they have little to learn from their competitors, while the Europeans and Japanese think they have a lot to learn from theirs (Kupfer, 1988). Resistance to training can be traced also to the belief that the training is ineffective. But the empirical evidence indicates that some training is helpful (Black & Mendenhall, 1990). Some forms of training have been tested with random assignment of trainees to experimental (training) and control (no training) groups, and the differences were significant, involving improvements on the order of 20 percent. Finally, while everybody is ethnocentric, some individuals are more ethnocentric than others, and some organizational cultures encourage ethnocentrism more than others. Corporations that are ethnocentric and do not believe that training is effective will not invest in this activity.

CULTURE-GENERAL VERSUS CULTURE-SPECIFIC TRAINING

There are many topics relevant to getting along in other cultures that are not specific to any culture. These include:

1. Know that we are all ethnocentric. Try to catch yourself when you are ethnocentric.

2. Know that the attributions that hosts will make about their own behavior are likely to be different from the attributions that you will make about their behavior. Look for discrepancies in the attributions people are making.

3. Learn to sort what is personal from what is national. When people abroad react to you, they are often seeing you as a "representative" of your own country. They may be hostile, not because they do not like *you*, but because they do not like the policies of *your country*. Also, people may be reacting to a cultural trait (e.g., do not like people who eat meat) rather than to a personal trait.

4. Learn that it is most difficult to act correctly in an environment where the situation looks just as it does in your own culture but where the required behavior is very different.

5. Learn how to initiate conversations in the host culture so as to learn more about it.

6. Learn to avoid co-nationals so that you can practice the local language and learn the new skills required to do well in the host culture as quickly as possible.

7. Learn to find enjoyable activities in the host culture.

8. Learn to see a positive aspect in every situation.

9. Learn to suspend judgment, to live with ambiguity, to categorize broadly (e.g., while a host's response is different from what we do at home, it is not *that* different).

10. Learn how people react when they are confronted by differences in attitudes and values: They are likely to:
    a. Ignore the difference.
    b. Bolster their position ("I am obviously correct, and your are stupid") by finding additional arguments to strengthen their own position or by getting social support from co-nationals who agree.
    c. *Differentiate*—it is okay for them to do it that way and for us to do it our way.
    d. *Transcend*—both are correct under some conditions; our way is best under conditions X and their way is best under conditions Y.

Once you know these four ways of reacting to what is different, try to suppress the first two and use the last one more frequently.

SELF-INSIGHT

The emphasis in this kind of training is on the development of an understanding of how culture affects a person's behavior. This technique uses an actor to behave in the opposite way from the way that is prescribed by the culture of the trainee. For example, in training Americans, the actor behaves like a "contrast-American" (Stewart, 1966).

Topics include the following: Americans emphasize material goals versus other cultures stress spiritual goals (e.g., India); Americans emphasize achievement versus some cultures emphasize ascribed status based on family prestige; Americans see competition as desirable versus many cultures see it as undesirable; Westerners in general emphasize planning, while traditional cultures emphasize fate; Westerners also place reliance on self, while in high-power-distance cultures reliance on superiors is more likely; similarly in low-power-distance cultures the emphasis is on equality, while status differences are most important in high-power-distance cultures. Other contrasts: The belief that knowledge through observation is superior to knowledge received from authorities; the belief that thoughts cannot influence events versus the belief that they can do so.

The actor interacts with the trainee, and the session is videotaped. The trainer then spends time with the trainee going over the tape and explaining how the trainee's behavior is determined by culture.

This method is good because the trainee learns about his or her own culture. However, the trainee does not learn anything specific about the host culture.

EXPERIENTIAL TRAINING

This technique involves bringing the trainees into contact with members of the host culture in situations where the trainees can make mistakes that will not hurt long-term relationships. It also can help prospective travelers understand the problems they will face abroad.

For example, in the early 1960s, the Peace Corps used an exact replica of a South Pacific village (no electricity, no movies, no running water, etc.) in a valley on the island of Hawaii (Brislin, 1993). Trainees spent several weeks learning the languages and customs of such villages while interacting with trainers from South Pacific cultures. Many trainees exposed to the rigors of that environment decided to drop out, saving the Peace Corps the expense of early repatriation and the volunteer the embarrassment of failure on the job.

This method, however, is expensive and depends on trial-and-error learning, which is slow. Nevertheless, it produces results if the training organization can spend the money and the trainees have the time.

EXPOSURE TO MANY LOCAL CULTURES

It is assumed that the more experience trainees have had in entering, learning about, and leaving cultures, the better equipped they will be to deal with their new environment abroad. This type of training was developed by the late psychiatrist Bryant Wedge. It encourages the trainees to join different urban subcultures, such as the police, the fire department, unions, top management of corporations, school boards, religious groups, political groups, pickpockets, prostitutes, and so on. Each of these groups has a unique culture, and the skills required to join it should be valuable. One has to learn how to scout, enter, explore, terminate, evaluate the new skills, and transfer them to the next culture. The trainer helps the trainee get in and out of each subculture and discusses the experiences of the trainees once a week in review sessions where each trainee's problems in getting in and out of each culture are examined.

This method has a number of practical difficulties. It is difficult for a trainee to get into some of these groups (e.g., in one case, when a trainee wanted to join some stevedores, they attacked him with a knife). And while there is much to be said for the process skills that are acquired, trainees do not learn much content about the host culture they will visit.

FIELD TRIPS

Many companies send their executives abroad to visit the potential host country for two weeks to become familiar with the environment. At that point the trainee can decline the opportunity to work abroad. This method can be used as a self-selection device, but it teaches very little in depth about the local culture.

THE CULTURE ASSIMILATOR
OR INTERCULTURAL SENSITIZER

We already examined the importance of learning to make isomorphic attributions (Triandis, 1975). In order to train people to make isomorphic attributions, this technique was developed and validated (e.g., Fiedler, Mitchell, & Triandis, 1971) and found to work. It is the only cross-cultural training method that has been evaluated so far, with random assignment of trainees to experimental and control groups, and it has been shown to be effective (Albert, 1983). That does not mean that the other methods do not work; it only means that rigorous studies have not yet been reported.

The culture assimilator is a programmed learning approach to cultural training. It consists of a set of 100 to 200 episodes, i.e., scenarios where people from two cultures interact. Each episode is followed by four or five explanations of why the member of the other culture has acted in a specific way. The trainee selects one of the explanations and is asked to turn to another page (or computer screen) where feedback is provided concerning the chosen explanation.

Let us look at the simplest example. Suppose you are teaching a white middle-class foreman to understand the behavior of a Hispanic lower-class worker. If the foreman understands the worker's viewpoint, that is considered successful training.

EPISODE: Hispanic worker looks down when spoken to.

QUESTION: Why did the worker look down?

ATTRIBUTIONS:

1. He was distracted. Turn to page 50.
2. He was fearful. Turn to page 51.
3. He was respectful. Turn to page 52.
4. He was hostile. Turn to page 53.

When the trainees turn to pages 50, 51, or 53, they find negative feedback, along lines such as this: "No, this is incorrect; try another explanation."

When the trainees turn to page 52, they get feedback such as: "Excellent! That is correct. When we presented this question to a sample of 80 Hispanic workers and 95 non-Hispanic foremen, 85 percent of the workers considered this answer to be the correct one, and only 36 percent of the non-Hispanic foremen thought that this was correct."

Note that the construction of assimilator training is culture specific. It requires the use of samples of people from the two cultures, who study the episode and the attributions and select the attribution they consider to be correct. Thus, the training is validated as it is being constructed.

In addition, the feedback gives the percentages of samples who agree or disagree with each answer. This avoids teaching stereotypes. Instead, you learn that your judgments about why people acted in a given way are probabilistic, and the probabilities differ across cultures.

Of course, in constructing assimilators it is necessary to have many more episodes than will be used in the final training, because some will not discriminate the two samples of subjects and thus must be discarded.

The construction of the episodes is based on interviews with people who have wide experience in the two relevant cultures; sometimes it is based on research that has identified differences in the subjective culture of the two relevant samples. Any item of cultural difference can be included. For example, to teach the meaning of words, we would include the information that in continental Europe the "first floor" of a building is called "earth level," or has some other culture-specific name, and the "first floor" corresponds to the American "second floor."

In training persons from an individualistic culture such as the United States to go to a collectivist culture such as the Far East, we might include a variety of items such as:

1. Differences in norms; e.g., do not bring a present of a certain color.

2. Differences in roles; e.g., in some collectivist cultures, the parent-child role is almost sacred (so that if one's spouse disagrees with one's parents, it is obligatory to take the side of one's parents).

3. Differences in the way behaviors can express intentions; e.g., frequently "no" must be expressed *most* indirectly—perhaps by serving two substances that are usually not served together (see Chapter 7).

4. Differences in self-concepts; e.g., collectivist selves are more likely to be appendages of groups than to be autonomous.

5. Differences in what behaviors are valued; e.g., in collectivist cultures people use a modest introduction in beginning their lecture, such as "What I have to tell you is not very important."

6. Differences in the kinds of associations that people make; for instance, in collectivist cultures people are more likely to associate the word "progress" with national than with personal progress.

7. Differences in the kinds of differentiations that people make;

e.g., in collectivist cultures there will be more differentiations on the vertical axes than on the horizontal axes of social relationships.

8. Differences in the important determinants of behavior—in collectivist cultures behavior is more likely to reflect norms than attitudes.

9. Differences in the kinds of reinforcements that people expect for particular behaviors in particular situations—in collectivist cultures one is supposed to give a gift in many situations in which in individualist cultures one would pay.

Triandis, Brislin, and Hui (1988) advised individualists going to a collectivist culture to pay attention to group attributes more than they do in their own culture, to learn about the in-groups and out-groups, to expect sharp differences in behavior when the collectivist interacts with members of such groups, and to expect more harmony within the in-group, e.g., no criticism of high-status people. The individualists were also told to cultivate long-term relationships, be modest when presenting a lecture, stress equality and need when distributing resources, and give more gifts than is customary in their own culture.

Construction of a typical assimilator begins with 200 or so episodes extracted either from discussions with people who know both cultures or from relevant ethnographies, both of which have been analyzed to identify a set of four or five attributions for each episode. Then the episodes and the attributions are presented to samples from the trainee's and host's culture, and differences in the response patterns are examined statistically. Episodes that do not discriminate the relevant samples are discarded. Then the assimilator is printed in a book or placed in a computer.

Each trainee can work through the book or computer program alone, or the trainer may select some of the more interesting episodes and present them for discussion. Trainees may also role-play the content of some of the episodes.

In principle, this method can be expanded for use with an interactive disk technology; this way the trainee sees videotaped actors performing the episode and participates by pushing buttons that indicate what responses the trainee thinks are appropriate. Feedback from the computer in the form of praise or criticism can make this task most interesting.

Evaluations of the training, where randomly assigned trainees received or did not receive the training (e.g., Weldon, Carlston, Rissman, Slobobin, & Triandis, 1975), have shown that people learn to make isomorphic attributions, they expand the range of explanations they give for specific behaviors, they become less ethnocentric, and they develop more accurate expectations concerning appropriate behavior.

Assimilator training increases cognitive complexity. Cognitive complexity makes it possible to consider the subjective culture of the other cultural group as "valid" and thus lessens prejudice (Gardiner, 1972).

However, culture assimilator training does not strongly increase liking for the other group or reduce social distance toward it. Liking depends on the number of pleasant experiences one has shared with the other group. Just knowing how the other group thinks does not change emotions.

Stephan and Stephan (1984) used a culture assimilator to increase "knowledge of Chicano culture" among Anglo students in New Mexico. The so-called path model of Figure 10–3 shows that in this case there was a small improvement in liking (attitudes toward Chicanos) among those who were trained. The numbers suggest the strengths of the relationships among the variables of this study.

The study indicates that Anglo students' attitudes toward Chicanos in the American Southwest are related to three factors: (1) how much they know about Chicano culture, (2) how much contact they have with Chicanos, and (3) their parents' attitudes toward Chicanos. Contact with Chicanos was determined by the attitudes of their friends toward Chicanos. Finally, contact increased knowledge of Chicano culture, and the assimilator training boosted that knowledge a bit more, and so that those who were trained had more positive attitudes than those who were not trained.

Stephan and Stephan concluded their 1984 study as follows: "Simple intergroup contact, such as the contact that typically occurs in desegregated schools, is not likely to improve intergroup relations. However, specially designed educational programs, designed to reduce ignorance of the outgroup, do appear to improve intergroup relations" (p. 249).

Social distance often depends on the norms of our own group. If our own group urges us to get along with the other group, we are more likely

FIGURE 10–3

In a sample studied by Stephan and Stephan (1984) in New Mexico, attitudes toward Chicanos were more positive among those who had greater knowledge of Chicano culture, obtained in part through direct contact with Chicanos and in part through culture assimilator training. Contact depended on the attitudes of friends. Positive attitudes toward Chicanos by the parents of the respondents were also related to positive attitudes toward Chicanos.

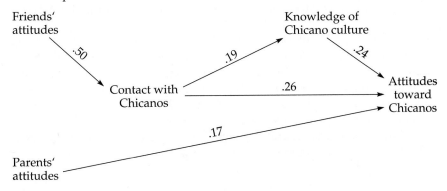

to do so than if it opposes such friendliness. As in the Stephan and Stephan study, when the friends favor contact, there is likely to be an improvement in relationships.

For these reasons culture assimilator training is only *one* component of cross-cultural training. It is not sufficient by itself. It needs to be supplemented with other methods, such as the self-insight method, which is likely to increase the motivation of the trainees to learn about the other culture, and experiential training, which can change emotions. Also, the norms of social interaction between the two cultures need to be changed to modify social distance.

Another limitation of assimilator training is that it does not change behavior. It is one thing to know how one is supposed to behave and quite another to behave correctly. To achieve the latter goal one needs to do behavior modification training.

In addition to assimilators that focus on a specific culture, there is a general assimilator (Brislin, Cushner, Cherrie, & Yong, 1986). It deals with the fact that it is natural and to be expected that trainees will feel anxious abroad, experience disconfirmed expectancies, be unable to feel that they belong to the local culture, experience ambiguity about what they should do, and be exposed to local prejudices. It teaches trainees that they must learn to control their own prejudices.

The general assimilator also teaches trainees to expect differences in the way people view work, the relationship of work and social interactions, time, space, language, roles, groups, rituals, hierarchies, and values.

It also helps the trainees to understand differences in categorization, differentiation (e.g., some people know more about some subjects than you do), the importance of the in-group–out-group distinction (e.g., between collectivists and individualists), learning styles (not everyone learns best the same way), and attributions (how to make isomorphic attributions).

The general assimilator has been successfully evaluated (Cushner, 1989). Twenty-eight trained adolescents from the Pacific Rim visiting New Zealand were better adjusted than twenty-two control adolescents hosted by New Zealanders. The trained adolescents completed a number of tasks measuring cross-cultural sensitivity better than the control subjects did.

A final point about assimilators: When you are warned that there will be problems when interacting abroad, you are more likely to be able to deal with these problems than if you are naïve about them. This phenomenon is parallel to findings with hospital preoperative patients: Those who were told that they will feel quite uncomfortable after the operation dealt better with the postoperative pain than those who had been told nothing. In general, the more the training creates realistic expectations about events in the host culture, the better.

BEHAVIOR MODIFICATION TRAINING

Behavior modification techniques work. They require that people be rewarded for desirable behaviors and be made to do an incompatible behavior whenever they have the urge or tendency to do an undesirable behavior. For example, in Latin America it is customary among friends to give an *abrazo*, a kind of embrace with the arms. Also, holding hands, touching, and other behaviors between good friends of the same sex are common. North Americans have to be trained to carry out such behaviors. If they behave as is expected by the Latinos, they will be liked better than if they behave as they do at home. If they don't behave as expected, the locals will think of them as cold and undemonstrative "gringos." But without proper training North Americans who force themselves to behave in the Latino way will feel that they are behaving inappropriately.

Conversely, some behaviors have to be eliminated. For example, in some cultures (e.g., Greece), to show the palm of your hand, especially if the hand is open, is an insult. It is called a *moutza* and reflects utmost contempt. However, many people are in the habit of greeting others by waving an open hand. For these people to stop doing this requires training. Most people wave without thinking. A trainer must catch them in the act and tell them not to do it. Self-correction after such acts can change the habit, so that the person waves with the palm turned toward the self.

Some habits are especially difficult to change. For example, for Westerners going to Bulgaria or southern India it is necessary—and a challenge, to put it mildly—to learn to nod to say "no" and shake the head to say "yes" as is the custom there. Here trainees need a lot of practice to get over well-established habits.

Some people feel that behavior modification is unethical, because it forces people to act differently. But is it better for people to act incompetently and insult their hosts?

OTHER DETAILS ABOUT TRAINING

Kohls (1985) has suggested that the optimal time to provide cross-cultural training is two months to two weeks before departure. However, others have argued that training after arrival in the host culture is more effective, because the trainee is more motivated. On the other hand, the trainee may not be able to afford to make mistakes during the first weeks after arrival. Probably some basic training before and some training after arrival in the host culture would be optimal.

Most corporations try to provide their own training; however, they often lack a sufficient number of trainees to develop a high-quality program. Consultants offer training, but they usually do not present data about training effectiveness. It is likely that trainers are quite variable, some being much better than others, but there are essentially no data on this.

STRATEGIES FOR THE IMPROVEMENT OF INTERCULTURAL RELATIONS

As a way to summarize many of the points made in the last two chapters, here are some major strategies for improving intergroup relations:

Use decategorization. This approach (Brewer & Miller, 1988; Gaertner, Mann, Murrell, & Dovidio, 1989) works on undermining the distinction between in-group and out-group. For example, we might argue that it is useless to use the out-group category, because we cannot predict, with odds better than chance, anything about the people in that category.

Increasing the complexity of intergroup perceptions. Prejudiced individuals view the out-group as extremely homogeneous. The "enemy" is a single entity. Brewer and Miller (1988) suggest that we can reduce prejudice by presenting information indicating that the out-group is in fact very heterogeneous. The more people think of the out-group as heterogeneous, the more fuzzy is their heterostereotype. Fuzzy stereotypes seem undependable, which reduces prejudice.

Use classical conditioning of the category. This strategy involves having positive experiences in the presence of the members of the out-group. Effective behaviors (e.g., after behavior modification training) in the presence of the other cultural group are likely to result in such positive experiences and will avoid embarrassing experiences. The use of superordinate goals is a form of classical conditioning. People see the other group as being helpful, as enabling them to reach important goals. The association of the other group with the positive emotions about reaching these goals results in feeling good about the other group.

Increase awareness of similarities. This strategy emphasizes similarities: Members of the out-group, just like members of the in-group, want physical and mental health, recreation, travel, leisure time, a happy old age, a good standard of living for their family, security, independence, success in their activities, a good job, a happy family life. When relating to others, follow the advice of the German philosopher Kant: Act in such a way that if everyone else in the world acted that way, you would like the world better than you do now.

Decrease the dissimilarities. Train people to overcome the importance they give to dissimilarities. Many of the "lessons of history" point to previous conflicts that make people look different. Do not believe all you read about how wonderful the in-group is and how awful the out-group is. People in authority often profit from such conflicts. Be critical when they tell you to hate others. Ask: Are they profiting from this hatred? Quite often one of the best ways for a politician to get reelected is to create a foreign policy crisis. Take a good look at the evidence. Furthermore, learn to make isomorphic attributions by placing yourself in the shoes of the out-group.

Look for superordinate goals. Reduce competition, and look for win-win situations and for superordinate goals. Find common elements, and talk more about "we" and less about "us" and "them."

Value diversity. Multiple viewpoints are more likely to result in good decisions when people from different cultures look at a decision. *Groupthink* (Janis, 1972, 1982) occurs when people uncritically accept the prevailing viewpoint, and it leads to poor decisions and to major mistakes. For example, General Motors marketed the Nova in Latin America without asking a few Latinos to examine that name. Had GM asked, it would have saved millions of dollars, because No Va (does not go) is hardly a good name for a car! It failed in that part of the world.

Train yourself and your children for complexity. Things are never all good or all bad. Every cloud has a silver lining, and there is usually a cloud even on the best day. A broad information search for both the positive and the negative evidence leads to better decisions. Once a person learns to do this, it is likely that complex stereotypes and attributions will be linked only weakly to specific events, and the person will be less likely to jump to conclusions.

Learn to deal with conflict constructively. Learn to recognize the legitimate needs of your opponent. Tell the opponent that you are concerned about such needs. Strive for equal power in a negotiation and for win-win solutions. Do not threaten the self-esteem of your opponent. Link positive consequences to cooperation. Help your opponents with their internal problems. Make the issues under dispute specific and limited. Argue about the specifics, not the principles, after affirming the principles on which there is agreement. Avoid conflict over the rules of how to settle conflict.

EVALUATION OF CROSS-CULTURAL TRAINING

Cross-cultural training can be effective. Black and Mendenhall (1990) reviewed twenty-nine studies that measured effectiveness. They found that all the studies that measured how people felt about the training had positive results, all the studies that measured effective interpersonal relationships found improvements, all the studies that measured changes in perception found them, and all that tried to reduce culture shock succeeded in doing so. Two-thirds of the studies that measured performance obtained improved performance.

In general the effects were found in field studies, but not in laboratory studies. This may be due to the limited time we can use in the laboratory. A few hours of training are not enough to produce major changes. Furthermore, field studies involve volunteers who are motivated to succeed abroad. If we tried to train the general public, perhaps we would not have positive results. No matter how good the training or the trainer, if the trainees do not wish to change, they won't. Nevertheless, the studies with control groups and longitudinal designs reviewed by Black and Mendenhall (1990) show some impressive results which should encourage more cross-cultural training. A meta-analysis that statistically combines the results from many studies has also found that cross-cultural training is effective (Deshpande & Viswesvaran, 1992).

Training is provided more frequently by Japanese and Korean corporations than by U.S. corporations. However, recently, faced with high failure rates among employees who work abroad, American corporations have started doing some training. For example, General Motors is spending about half a million dollars a year training 150 Americans and their families headed abroad (Lublin, 1992). Most of the training provided by consulting firms has not been evaluated. They take the position that it can do no harm, so why bother to evaluate it. However, if cross-cultural training is to become "scientific," it should be studied and modified as indicated by the evaluations.

Summary

This chapter has described the symptoms of culture shock usually experienced by people who change cultures and examined the ups and downs over time of feeling comfortable in other cultures. Several factors have been identified that minimize culture shock and maximize success in other cultures: the traveler's preparation, the traveler's personality, and the ease of the assignment. A wide variety of methods of culture training were reviewed, and suggestions were made on how to obtain strong effects from such training. Evaluations of this training have indicated that the training is beneficial.

A scientific understanding of how culture affects social behavior—and the use of this understanding to improve relationships across cultures—has just begun. I hope this book makes a small contribution toward these developments.

QUESTIONS AND EXERCISES

1. Construct a general assimilator item by talking to friends who have traveled abroad. Show this item to several people who differ in sophistication about behavior abroad, and check to see what kinds of people make many mistakes and what kinds of people get the right answer at once.

2. Construct a specific culture assimilator item about a familiar culture. Do what was done for exercise 1.

3. Imagine that you are the training director of a multinational corporation. Specify a situation that seems plausible to you, i.e., state the attributes of the corporation, the trainees, and the host culture, that can be used in exercise 4.

4. For the particular case of the multinational corporation mentioned in exercise 3, what is the best training? (That is, what mixture of training experiences is likely to be optimal?) Think of who is to be trained, when and where, and by what means.

References

❖

ABELSON, R. P., ARONSON, E., McGUIRE, W. J., NEWCOMB, T. M., ROSENBERG, M. J., TANNENBAUM, P. H. (Eds.). (1968). *Theories of cognitive consistency: A sourcebook*. Chicago: Rand McNally.

ACHEBE, C. (1967). *Arrow of God*. New York: John Day.

ADAMOPOULOS, J. (1984). The differentiation of social behavior. *Journal of Cross-Cultural Psychology, 15*, 487–508.

ADAMOPOULOS, J., & BONTEMPO, R. (1984). A note on the relationship between socialization practices and artistic preference. *Cross-Cultural Psychology Bulletin, 18*, 4–7.

ADAMOPOULOS, J., & BONTEMPO, R. (1987). Diachronic universals of interpersonal structures. *Journal of Cross-Cultural Psychology, 17*, 169–189.

ADAMOPOULOS, J., SMITH, C. M., SHILLING, C. J., & STOGANNIDOU, A. (submitted). Cross-cultural invariance in the perception of social environments: A rule-theoretical approach to situational classification.

ADER, R. (Ed.). (1981). *Psychoneuroimmunology*. New York: Academic Press.

ADORNO, T. W., FREKEL-BRUSWIK, E., LEVINSON, D. J., & SANFORD, R. N. (1950). *The authoritarian personality*. New York: Harper.

ALBERT, R. D. (1983). The intercultural sensitizer or culture assimilator: A cognitive approach. In D. Landis & R. W. Brislin (Eds.), *Handbook of intercultural training* (Vol. 2). New York: Pergamon Press, pp. 186–217.

ALTMEYER, B. (1981). *Right wing authoritarianism*. Minneapolis: University of Minnesota Press.

AMERICAN PSYCHOLOGICAL ASSOCIATION. (1972). *Ethical standards for research with human subjects*. Washington, D.C.: APA.

AMIR, Y. (1969). Contact hypothesis in intergroup relations. *Psychological Bulletin, 71*, 319–342.

AMIR, Y., & SHARON, I. (1987). Are social psychology's laws cross-culturally valid? *Journal of Cross-Cultural Psychology, 18*, 383–470.

ANDERSON, C. A. (1987). Temperature and aggression: Effects on quarterly, yearly, and city rates of violent and nonviolent crime. *Journal of Personality and Social Psychology, 52*, 1161–1173.

ARGYLE, M. (1988). *Bodily communication*. London: Methuen.

ARGYLE, M., HENDERSON, M., BOND, M., IIZUKA, Y., & CONTARELLO, A. (1986). *International Journal of Psychology, 21*, 287–315.

ARONOFF, J., WOIKE, B. A., & HYMAN, L. M. (1992). Which are the stimuli in facial displays of anger and happiness? Configurational bases of emotion recognition. *Journal of Personality and Social Psychology, 62,* 1050–1066.

ASCH, S. (1956). Studies of independence and conformity: A minority of one against a unanimous majority. *Psychological Monographs, 70,* No. 9 (Whole No. 416).

AVIGDOR, R. (1953). Etudes experimentales de la genese des stereotypes. *Cahiers Internationales de Sociologie, 5,* 154–168.

BANDURA, A. (1989), Perceived self-efficacy in the exercise of personal agency. *The Psychologist: Bulletin of the British Psychological Society, 10,* 411–424.

BANTEL, K. A., & JACKSON, S. E. (1989). Top management and innovations in banking: Does the composition of the top team make a difference? *Strategic Management Journal, 10,* 107–124.

BARKER, R. (1968). *Ecological psychology: Concepts and methods for studying the environment of human behavior.* Stanford, CA: Stanford University Press.

BARNLUND, D. C. (1975). *Public and private self in Japan and the United States.* Tokyo: Simul Press.

BARNLUND, D. C., & ARAKI, S. (1985). Intercultural encounters: The management of compliments by Japanese and Americans. *Journal of Cross-Cultural Psychology, 16,* 9–26.

BARRY, H. (1980). Description and uses of the Human Relations Area Files. In H. C. Triandis & J. W. Berry (Eds.), *Handbook of Cross-Cultural Psychology* (Vol. 2). Boston: Allyn and Bacon, pp. 445–478.

BARRY, H., BACON, M., & CHILD, I. (1957). A cross-cultural survey of some sex-differences in socialization. *Journal of Abnormal and Social Psychology, 55,* 327–332.

BECK, A. (1988). *Love is never enough.* New York: Harper & Row.

BELLAH, R. N., MADSEN, R., SULLIVAN, W. M., SWIDLER, A., & TIPTON, S. M. (1985). *Habits of the heart: Individualism and commitment in American life.* Berkeley, CA: University of California Press.

BENJAMIN, L. S. (1974). Structural analysis of social behavior. *Psychological Review, 81,* 392–425.

BERKOWITZ, L., & WALSTER, E. (1976). Equity theory: Toward a general theory of social interaction. In L. Berkowitz (Ed.), *Advances in Experimental Social Psychology.* New York: Academic Press, pp. 1–263.

BERLIN, B., & KAY, P. (1969). *Basic color terms.* Berkeley, CA: University of California Press.

BERLYNE, D. (1980). Psychological aesthetics. In H. C. Triandis & W. J. Lonner (Eds.), *Handbook of Cross-Cultural Psychology* (Vol. 3). Boston: Allyn and Bacon, pp. 323–362.

BERRY, J. W. (1967). Independence and conformity in subsistence level societies. *Journal of Personality and Social Psychology, 7,* 415–418.

BERRY, J. W. (1976). *Human ecology and cognitive style.* Beverly Hills, CA: Sage.

BERRY, J. W. (1979). A cultural ecology of social behavior. In L. Berkowitz (Ed.), *Advances in experimental social psychology* (Vol. 12). New York: Academic Press, pp. 177–207.

BERRY, J. W. (1980a). Acculturation as varieties of adaptation. In A. Padilla (Ed.), *Acculturation: Theory, models, and some new findings.* Boulder, CO: Westview, pp. 9–25.

BERRY, J. W. (1980b). Social and cultural change. In H. C. Triandis & R. Brislin (Eds.), *Handbook of Cross-Cultural Psychology*. Boston: Allyn and Bacon, pp. 211–280.

BERRY, J. W. (1990). The psychology of acculturation. In *Nebraska Symposium on Motivation, 1989*. Lincoln: University of Nebraska Press, pp. 201–234.

BERRY, J. W., & BENNETT, J. A. (1992). Cree conceptions of cognitive competence. *International Journal of Psychology, 27*, 73–88.

BERRY, J. W., KIM, U., POWER, S., YOUNG, M., & BUJAKI, M. (1989). Acculturation attitudes in plural societies. *Applied Psychology, 38*, 185–206.

BERRY, J. W., POORTINGA, Y., SEGALL, M., & DASEN, P. (1992). *Cross-cultural psychology*. New York: Cambridge Press.

BETTELHEIM, B., & JANOWITZ, J. (1950). *Dynamics of prejudice*. New York: Harper.

BILLINGS, D. K. (1989). Individualism and group orientation. In D. M. Keats, D. Munroe, & L. Mann (Eds.), *Heterogeneity in cross-cultural psychology*. Lisse, The Netherlands: Swets & Zeitlinger, pp. 92–103.

BLACK, J. S., & MENDENHALL, M. (1990). Cross-cultural training effectiveness: A review and theoretical framework for future research. *Academy of Management Review, 15*, 113–136.

BLINCO, P. M. A. (1992). Task persistence of young children in Japan and the United States: A cross-cultural study. In S. Iwawaki, Y. Kashima, & K. Leung (Eds.), *Innovations in cross-cultural psychology*. Amsterdam/Lisse: Swets & Zeitlinger, pp. 311–318.

BLUMBERG, L., & WINCH, R. F. (1972). Societal complexity and family complexity: Evidence for the curvilinear hypothesis. *American Journal of Sociology, 77*, 896–920.

BOCHNER, S. (1980). Unobtrusive methods in cross cultural experimentation. In H. C. Triandis & J. W. Berry (Eds.), *Handbook of Cross-Cultural Psychology* (Vol. 2). Boston: Allyn and Bacon, pp. 319–388.

BOGARDUS, E. S. (1925). Measuring social distance. *Journal of Applied Sociology, 9*, 299–308.

BOLTON, C., BOLTON, R., GROSS, L., KOEL, A., MICHELSON, C., MUNROE, R. L., & MUNROE, R. H. (1976). Pastoralism and personality: An Andean replication. *Ethos, 4*, 463–481.

BOLTON, R. (1984). The hypoglycemia-aggression hypothesis: Debated versus research. *Current Anthropology, 25*, 1–53.

BOND, M. H. (1988). *The cross-cultural challenge to social psychology*. Newbury Park, CA: Sage.

BOND, M. H. (1992). Continuing encounters with Hong Kong. In W. J. Lonner & R. S. Malpass (Eds.), *Readings in Psychology & Culture*. (Mimeo.).

BOND, M. H., & CHEUNG, M. (1984). Experimenter language choice and ethnic affirmation by Chinese trilinguals in Hong Kong. *International Journal of Intercultural Relations, 8*, 347–356.

BOND, M. H., & PANG, M. K. (1989, May). Trusting the Tao: Chinese values and the re-centering of psychology. Paper presented at the Conference on Moral Reasoning in Chinese Societies, Taipei, Taiwan.

BOND, M. H., WAN, K-C., LEUNG, K., & GIACALONE, R. A. (1985). How are responses to a verbal insult related to cultural collectivism and power distance? *Journal of Cross-Cultural Psychology, 16*, 111–127.

BOND, M. H., & YANG, K. (1982). Ethnic affirmation vs cross-cultural accommodation: The variable impact of questionnaire language on Chinese bilinguals in Hong Kong. *Journal of Cross-Cultural Psychology, 13,* 169–185.

BONTEMPO, R., LOBEL, S., & TRIANDIS, H. C. (1990). Compliance and value internalization in Brazil and the U.S.: Effects of allocentrism and anonymity. *Journal of Cross-Cultural Psychology, 21,* 200–213.

BONTEMPO, R., & RIVERA, J. C. (1992). Cultural variation in cognition: The role of self-concept in the attitude-behavior link. Paper presented at the August meetings of the Academy of Management, Las Vegas, Nevada.

BOWEN, E. S. (1954). *Return to laughter.* New York: Harper. Also in paperback (1964): Garden City, N.Y.: Doubleday.

BOYD, R., & RICHERSON, P. J. (1985). *Culture and the evolutionary process.* Chicago: University of Chicago Press.

BOYKIN, A. W. (1983). The academic performance of Afro-American children. In J. Spence (Ed.), *Achievement and achievement motives.* New York: Freeman, pp. 328–371.

BRABECK, M. (1989). *Who cares? Theory, research and educational implications of the ethic of care.* New York: Praeger.

BRANDT, V. S. (1974). Skiing cross-culturally. *Current Anthropology, 15,* 64–66.

BREWER, M., & CAMPBELL, D. T. (1976). *Ethnocentrism and intergroup attitudes: East African evidence.* New York: Halsted/Wiley.

BREWER, M., & MILLER, N. (1988). Contact and cooperation: When do they work? In P. Katz & D. Taylor (Eds.), *Eliminating racism.* New York: Plenum, pp. 315–328.

BREWER, M. B. (1968). Determinants of social distance among East African tribal groups. *Journal of Personality and Social Psychology, 10,* 279–289.

BREWER, M. B. (1985). The role of ethnocentrism in intergroup conflict. In S. Worchel & W. G. Austin (Eds.), *The social psychology of intergroup relations.* Chicago: Nelson Hall, pp. 88–102.

BREWER, M. B. (1991). The social self: On being the same and different at the same time. *Personality and Social Psychology Bulletin, 17,* 475–485.

BRISLIN, R. W. (1980). Translation and content analysis of oral and written materials. In H. C. Triandis & J. W. Berry (Eds.), *Handbook of cross-cultural psychology* (Vol. 2). Boston: Allyn and Bacon, pp. 389–444.

BRISLIN, R. (1993). *Understanding culture's influence on behavior.* Fort Worth, TX: Harcourt Brace Jovanovich.

BRISLIN, R., CUSHNER, K., CHERRIE, C., & YONG, M. (1986). *Intercultural interactions: A practice guide.* Beverly Hills, CA: Sage.

BRODBAR, N., & JAY, Y. (1986). Divorce and group commitment. The case of the Jews. *Journal of Marriage and the Family, 48,* 329–340.

BROWN, D. E. (1991). *Human universals.* Philadelphia: Temple University Press.

BROWN E. D., & SECREST, L. (1980). Experiments in cross-cultural research. In H. C. Triandis & J. W. Berry (Eds.), *Handbook of Cross-Cultural Psychology* (Vol. 2). Boston: Allyn and Bacon, pp. 297–318.

BROWN, H. P. (1990). The counter revolution of our time. *Industrial Relations, 29,* 1–15.

BROWN, P. (1986). Simbu aggression and the drive to win. *Anthropological Quarterly, 59,* 165–170.

BROWN, P., & LEVINSON, S. (1987). *Politeness: Some universals in language use.* Cambridge, England: Cambridge University Press.

BROWN, R. W., & LENNEBERG, E. H. (1954). A study of language and cognition. *Journal of Abnormal and Social Psychology 49,* 454–462.

BUCHHOLZ, R. A. (1978). An empirical study of contemporary beliefs about work in American society. *Journal of Applied Psychology, 63,* 219–227.

BUCK, P. (1931). *The good earth.* New York: Grosset & Dunlop.

BUDNER, S. (1962). Intolerance of ambiguity as a personality variable. *Journal of Personality, 30,* 29–50.

BURTON, M. L., MOORE, C. C., WHITING, J. W., & ROMNEY, A. K. (1992, February). World cultural regions. Paper presented to the Santa Fe, NM, meetings of the Society for Cross-Cultural Research.

BUSS, D. M. (1990). International preferences in selecting mates. *Journal of Cross-Cultural Psychology, 21,* 5–47.

BYRNE, D. (1971). *The attraction paradigm.* New York: Academic Press.

CAMPBELL, D. T. (1967). Stereotypes and the perception of group differences. *American Psychologist, 22,* 817–829.

CAMPBELL, D. T. (1975). On the conflicts between biological and social evolution and between psychology and moral tradition. *American Psychologist, 30,* 1103–1126.

CAMPBELL, D. T. (1986). Science's social system of validity enhancing collective belief change and the problems of the social sciences. In D. W. Fiske & R. A. Shweder (Eds.), *Metatheory in social science.* Chicago: University of Illinois Press, pp. 108–135.

CAMPBELL, D. T. (1988). *Methodology and epistemology for social science.* Chicago: University of Chicago Press.

CAMPBELL, D. T., & LEVINE, R. (1968). Ethnocentrism and intergroup relations. In R. P. Abelson et al. (Eds.), *Theories of cognitive consistency: A sourcebook.* Chicago: Rand McNally, pp. 551–564.

CAMPBELL, J. K. (1964). *Honor, family and patronage.* Oxford: Clarendon Press.

CARNEIRO, R. L. (1970). Scale analysis, evolutionary sequences, and the ratings of cultures. In R. Naroll & R. Cohen (Eds.), *A handbook of method in cultural anthropology.* New York: Columbia University Press.

CHAGNON, N. (1968). *Yanamano: The fierce people.* New York: Holt, Rinehart, & Winston.

CHAN, K-S. D. (1991). Effects of concession pattern, relationship between negotiators, and culture on negotiation. Unpublished master's thesis, University of Illinois, Department of Psychology.

CHINESE CULTURAL CONNECTION (1987). Chinese values and the search for culture-free dimensions of culture. *Journal of Cross-Cultural Psychology, 18,* 143–164.

CHIU, C. Y. (1990). Normative expectations of social behavior and concern for members of the collective in Chinese society. *Journal of Psychology, 124,* 103–111.

CHURCH, A. T. (1982). Sojourn adjustment. *Psychological Bulletin, 91,* 540–572.

CIBOROWSKI, T. (1980). The role of context, skill and transfer in cross-cultural experimentation. In H. C. Triandis & J. W. Berry (Eds.), *Handbook of Cross-Cultural Psychology* (Vol. 2). Boston: Allyn and Bacon, pp. 279–296.

CISIN, I. H., COFFIN, T. E., JANIS, I. L., KLAPPER, J. T., MENDELSOHN, H., OMWAKE, E., PINDERHUGHES, C. A., POOL, I., SIEGEL, A. E., WALLACE, A. F. C.,

WATSON, A. S., & WIEBE, G. D. (1972). *Television and growing up: The impact of television violence.* Washington, DC: U.S. Government Printing Office.

COHEN, L. A. (1987). Diet and cancer. *Scientific American, 257,* 42–48.

COHEN, R. (1991). *Negotiating across cultures.* Washington, D.C.: United States Institute of Peace Press.

COLE, M. (1975). An ethnographic psychology of cognition. In R. W. Brislin, S. Bochner, & W. Lonner (Eds.), *Cross-cultural perspectives on learning.* New York: Wiley.

CONDON, J. C., JR. (1978). Intercultural communication from a speech communication perspective. In F. L. Casmir (Ed.), *Intercultural and international communication.* Washington, DC: University of America Press, pp. 383–406.

COOLEY, C. H. (1902). *Human nature and the social order.* New York: Scribner.

COPELAND, L., & GRIGGS, L. (1985). *Going international.* New York: Random House.

CREIGHTON, M. R. (1990). Revisiting shame and guilt cultures: A forty-year pilgrimage. *Ethos. 18,* 279–307.

CUSHNER, K. (1989). Assessing the impact of a culture-general assimilator. *International Journal of Intercultural Relations, 13,* 125–146.

DAAB, W. Z. (1991, July). Changing perspectives on individualism. Paper presented at the Helsinki meeting of the International Society of Political Psychology.

DABBS, J. M., JR., & MORRIS, R. (1990). Testosterone, social class, and antisocial behavior in a sample of 4, 462 men. *Psychological Science,1,* 209–211.

DALBY, L. C. (1983). *Geisha.* Berkeley: University of California Press.

DAUN, A. (1991). Individualism and collectivity among Swedes. *Ethnos, 56,* 165–172.

DAUN, A. (1992). Modern and modest: Mentality and self-stereotypes among Swedes. In A. Sjoegren & L. Janson (Eds.), *Culture and management.* Stockholm: Institute of International Business, Invandrarminnesarkivet Series A-7.

DAVIDSON, A. R., JACCARD, J., TRIANDIS, H. C., MORALES, M. L., & DIAZ-GUERRERO, R. (1976). Cross-cultural model testing: Toward a solution of the emic-etic dilemma. *International Journal of Psychology, 11,* 1–13.

DAVIDSON, A. R., and MORRISON, D. M. (1983). Predicting contraceptive behavior from attitudes: A comparison of within- versus across-subjects procedures. *Journal of Personality and Social Psychology, 45,* 997–1009.

DESHPANDE, S. P., & VISWESVARAN, C. (1992). Is cross-cultural training of expatriate managers effective: A meta analysis. *International Journal of Intercultural Relations, 16,* 295–310.

DETWEILER, R. (1980). The categorization of the actions of people from another culture: A conceptual analysis and behavioral outcome. *International Journal of Intercultural Relations, 4,* 275–293.

DEUTSCH, M. (1975). Equity, equality and need: What determines which value will be used as the basis of distributive justice? *Journal of Social Issues, 31,* 137–149.

DEUTSCH, M. (1990). Forms of social organization: Psychological consequences. In H. T. Himmelweit and G. Gaskell (Eds.), *Societal psychology.* London: Sage.

DEVINE, P. G. (1989). Stereotypes and prejudice: Their automatic and controlled components. *Journal of Personality and Social Psychology, 56,* 5–18.

DeVore, I., & Konner, M. J. (1974). Infancy in hunter-gatherer life: An ethnographic perspective. In N. F. White (Ed.), *Ethology and psychiatry.* Toronto: University of Toronto Press, pp. 113–141.

Diaz-Guerrero, R. (1977). Culture and personality revisited. *Annals of the New York Academy of Sciences, 285,* 119–130.

Diaz-Guerrero, R. (1979). The development of coping style. *Human Development, 22,* 320–331.

Diener, E., Emmons, R. A., Larsen, R. J., & Griffin, S. (1985). The satisfaction with life scale: A measure of life satisfaction. *Journal of Personality Assessment, 49,* 71–76.

Dion, K. K. (1985). Social distance norms in Canada: Effects of stimulus characteristics and dogmatism. *International Journal of Psychology, 20,* 743–749.

Dion, K. K., Pak, A. W., & Dion, K. L. (1990). Stereotyping physical attractiveness: A socio-cultural perspective. *Journal of Cross-Cultural Psychology, 21,* 378–398.

Doi, T. (1986). *The anatomy of conformity: The individual versus society.* Tokyo: Kadansha.

Dollard, J., Doob, L., Miller, N., Mowrer, O. H., & Sears, R. (1939). *Frustration and aggression.* New Haven, CT: Yale University Press.

Doob, L. W. (1971). *Patterning of time.* New Haven, CT: Yale Press.

Draguns, J. (1990). Normal and abnormal behavior in cross-cultural perspective: Specifying the nature of their relationship. In J. Berman (Ed.), *Nebraska Symposium on Motivation, 1989.* Lincoln: University of Nebraska Press, pp. 235–278.

Draper, P. (1973). Crowding among hunter-gatherers: The !Kung bushmen. *Science, 182,* 301–303.

Draper, P. (1976). Social and economic constraints on child life among the !Kung. In R. B. Lee & I. DeVore (Eds.), *Kalahari hunter-gatherers: Studies of !Kung San and their neighbors.* Cambridge, MA: Harvard Press.

Duley, M. I., & Edwards, M. (Eds.). (1986). *The cross-cultural study of women: A comprehensive guide.* New York: Feminist Press.

Dunbar, E. (1992). Adjustment and satisfaction of expatriate U.S. personnel. *International Journal of Intercultural Relations, 16,* 1–16.

Eagly, A. H., & Chaiken, S. (1993). *The psychology of attitudes.* Fort Worth, TX: Harcourt Brace Jovanovich.

Eagly, A. H., & Kite, M. E. (1987). Are stereotypes of nationalities applied to both women and men? *Journal of Personality and Social Psychology, 53,* 451–462.

Earley, P. C. (1989). Social loafing and collectivism: A comparison of the United States and the People's Republic of China. *Administrative Science Quarterly, 34,* 565–581.

Edgerton, R. (1971). *The individual in cultural adaptation: A study of four East African peoples.* Los Angeles: University of California Press.

Edwards, A. L. (1957). *Techniques of attitude scale construction.* New York: Appleton-Century-Crofts.

Ehrlich, H. J. (1973). *The social psychology of prejudice.* New York: Wiley.

Eibl-Eibesfeldt, I. (1974). The myth of the aggression free hunter and gatherer society. In R. L. Holloway (Ed.), *Primate aggression, territoriality and xenophobia: A comparative perspective.* New York: Academic Press.

EISENSTEIN, H. (1983). *Contemporary feminist thought.* New York: Hall.

EKMAN, P. (1992). Facial expression of emotion: New findings, new questions. *Psychological Science, 3,* 34–38.

EKMAN, P., & FRIESEN, W. (1971). Constants across cultures in the face and emotion. *Journal of Personality and Social Psychology, 17,* 124–129.

EMBER, C. R., & EMBER, M. (1992). Resource unpredictability, mistrust, and war. *Journal of Conflict Resolution, 36,* 242–262.

EMBER, C. R., EMBER, M., & RUSSET, B. (1992). Peace between participatory polities: A cross-cultural test of the "Democracies rarely fight each other" hypothesis. *World Politics, 44,* 573–599.

EMBER, C. R., & LEVINSON, D. (1991). The substantive contributions of worldwide cross-cultural studies using secondary data. *Behavioral Science Research, 25,* 79–140.

ERKMAN, F. (1992). Support for Rohner's parental acceptance-rejection theory as a psychological abuse theory in Turkey. In S. Iwawaki, Y. Kashima, & K. Leung (Eds.), *Innovations in cross-cultural psychology.* Amsterdam/Lisse: Swets & Zeitlinger, pp. 384–395.

ETIENNE, M., & LEACOCK, E. (1980). *Women & colonization: Anthropological perspectives.* New York: Praeger.

FELDMAN, R. E. (1968). Response to compatriot and foreigner who seek assistance. *Journal of Personality and Social Psychology, 10,* 202–214.

FIEDLER, F. E., MITCHELL, T., & TRIANDIS, H. C. (1971). The culture assimilator: An approach to cross-cultural training. *Journal of Applied Psychology, 55,* 95–102.

FISCHER, H., & TRIER, U. P. (1962). *Das Verhaeltnis zwischen Deutschschweizer und Westschweizer: Eine sozialpsychologische Untersuchung.* Bern: Hans Huber.

FISHBEIN, M., & AJZEN, I. (1975). *Belief, attitude, intention and behavior: An introduction to theory and research.* Reading, MA: Addison-Wesley.

FISHBEIN, M., BANDURA, A., TRIANDIS, H. C., KANFER, F. H., BECKER, M. H., & MIDDLESTADT, S. E. (1992). Factors influencing behavior and behavior change. Final Report on Theorists Workshop. Champaign, IL: University of Illinois Department of Psychology.

FISKE, A. P. (1990). *Structures of social life: The four elementary forms of human relations.* New York: Free Press.

FISKE, A. P. (1992). The four elementary forms of sociality: Framework for a unified theory of social relations. *Psychological Review, 99,* 689–723.

FISKE, A. P., HASLAM, N., & FISKE, S. T. (1991). Confusing one person with another: What errors reveal about the elementary forms of social relations. *Journal of Personality and Social Psychology, 60,* 656–674.

FISKE, D. W. (1986). Specificity of method and knowledge in social science. In D. W. Fiske & R. A. Shweder (Eds.), *Metatheory in social science.* Chicago: University of Chicago Press, pp. 61–82.

FISKE, D. W., & SHWEDER, R. A. (1986). *Metatheory in social science.* Chicago: University of Chicago Press.

FOA, U. (1961). Convergence in the analysis of the structure of interpersonal behavior. *Psychological Review, 68,* 341–353.

FOA, U., & FOA, E. (1974). *Societal structures of the mind.* Springfield, IL: Thomas.

FOA, U., TRIANDIS, H. C., and KATZ, E. W. (1966). Cross-cultural invariance in the differentiation and organization of family roles. *Journal of Personality and Social Psychology, 4,* 316–327.

FORD, C. S., & BEACH, F. A. (1951). *Patterns of sexual behavior*. New York: Harper.

FOSTER, G. (1965). Peasant society and the image of limited good. *American Anthropologist, 67*, 293–315.

FRAGER, R. (1970). Conformity and anti-conformity in Japan. *Journal of Personality and Social Psychology, 15*, 203–210.

FRANKENHAEUSER, M., LUNDBERG, U., & CHESNEY, M. (Eds.). (1991). *Women, work, and health: Stress and opportunities*. New York: Plenum.

FRAZER, J. G. (Originally published in 1890; 1959). *The new golden bough: A study of magic and religion (abridged)*. New York: Macmillan.

FREDERICHS, R. R., CHAPMAN, J. M., NOURJAH, P., & MAES, E. F. (1984). *Cardiovascular diseases in Los Angeles, 1979–1981*. Los Angeles: American Heart Association.

FREGER, R. (1970). Conformity and anti-conformity in Japan. *Journal of Personality and Social Psychology, 15*, 203–210.

FREUD S. (1909/1976). Notes upon a case of obsessional neurosis. In J. Strachey (Ed. and Trans.), *The complete works* (Vol. 10). New York: Norton.

FURNHAM, A., & ALIBBAI, N. (1983). Cross-cultural differences in the perception of female body shapes. *Psychological Medicine, 13*, 829–837.

FURNHAM, A., & BOCHNER, S. (1986). *Culture shock: Psychological reactions to unfamiliar environments*. London: Methuen.

GAERTNER, S. L., MANN, J., MURRELL, A., AND DOVIDIO, J. F. (1989). Reducing intergroup bias: The benefits of recategorization. *Journal of Personality and Social Psychology, 57*, 239–249.

GAILEY, C. W. (1987). Evolutionary perspectives on gender hierarchy. In B. B. Hess & M. M. Ferree, *Analyzing gender: A handbook of social science research*. Newbury Park, CA: Sage, pp. 32–67.

GALLOIS, C., BARKER, M., JONES, E., & CALLAN, V. (1992). Intercultural communication: Evaluations of lecturers by Australian and Chinese students. In S. Iwawaki, Y. Kashima, & K. Leung (Eds.), *Innovations in cross-cultural psychology*. Amsterdam/Lisse: Swets & Zeitlinger, pp. 86–102.

GAO, G., & GUDYKUNST, W. B. (1990). Uncertainty, anxiety, and adaptation. *International Journal of Intercultural Relations, 14*, 301–317.

GARDINER, G. S. (1972). Complexity training and prejudice reduction. *Journal of Applied Social Psychology, 2*, 326–342.

GEEN, R. G. (1972). *Aggression*. Morristown, N.J.: General Learning Corporation.

GEERTZ, C. (1973). *The interpretation of cultures*. New York: Basic Books.

GEORGAS, J. (1986). *Social Psychology*. Athens: University of Athens Press (in Greek).

GEORGAS, J. (1989). Family values in Greece: From collectivist to individualist. *Journal of Cross-Cultural Psychology, 20*, 80–91.

GIELE, J. Z., & SMOCK, A. C. (1977). *Women: Roles and status in eight countries*. New York: Wiley.

GILLIGAN, C. (1982). *In a different voice: Psychological theory and women's development*. Cambridge, MA: Harvard University Press.

GLENN, E. (1981). *Man and mankind: Conflicts and communication between cultures*. Norwood, N.J.: Ablex Co.

GLICK, J. (1968). Cognitive style among the Kpelle. Paper presented at the meetings of the American Educational Research Association, Chicago.

GOLDSTEIN, A. P., & SEGALL, M. H. (1983). *Aggression in global perspective.* New York: Pergamon.

GOLDSTEIN, M., & DAVIS, E. E. (1972). Race and belief: A further analysis of the social determinants of behavioral intentions. *Journal of Personality and Social Psychology, 22,* 346–355.

GOLDSTEIN, M. C. (1987). When brothers share a wife. *Natural History, 96* (2), 38–49.

GOODENOUGH, W. H. (1980). Ethnographic field techniques. In H. C. Triandis & J. W. Berry (Eds.), *Handbook of Cross-Cultural Psychology* (Vol. 2). Boston: Allyn and Bacon, pp. 29–56.

GOTTFREDSON, M. R., & HIRSCHI, T. (1990). *A general theory of crime.* Stanford, CA: Stanford University Press.

GRANBERG, D. (1984). Attributing attitudes to members of groups. In J. R. Eisler (Ed.), *Attitudinal judgment.* New York: Springer.

GUDYKUNST, W. (1991). *Bridging differences.* Newbury Park, CA: Sage.

GUDYKUNST, W. B. (Ed.). (1983). *Intercultural communication theory.* Beverly Hills, CA: Sage.

GUDYKUNST, W. B., GAO, G., NISHIDA, T., NADAMITSU, Y., & SAKAI, J. (1992). Self-monitoring in Japan and the United States. In S. Iwawaki, Y. Kashima, & K. Leung (Eds.). *Innovations in cross-cultural psychology.* Amsterdam/Lisse: Swets & Zeitlinger, pp. 185–198.

GUDYKUNST, W. B., GAO, G., SCHMIDT, K. L., NISHIDA, T., BOND, M. H., LEUNG, K., WANG, G., & BARRACLOUGH, R. A. (1992). The influence of individualism-collectivism, self-monitoring, and predicted-outcome value on communication in ingroup and outgroup relationships. *Journal of Cross-Cultural Psychology, 23,* 196–213.

GUDYKUNST, W. B., & NISHIDA, T. (1986). The influence of cultural variability on perceptions of communication behavior associated with relationship terms. *Human Communication Research, 13,* 147–166.

GUDYKUNST, W. B., & TING-TOOMEY, S. (1988). Culture and affective communication. *American Behavioral Scientist, 31,* 384–400.

GUDYKUNST, W. B., YOON, Y., & NISHIDA, T. (1987). The influence of individualism-collectivism on perceptions of communication in ingroup and outgroup relationships. *Communication Monographs, 54,* 295–306.

GUIORA, A. Z. (1985). The psychodynamic aspects of bilingualism. Paper given at the meetings of the American Psychological Association, Los Angeles.

GUPTA, B. (1976). *The Andamans: Land of the primitives.* Calcutta: Jijnasa Publications.

GUPTA, U., & SINGH, P. (1982). Exploratory studies in love and liking and types of marriages. *Indian Journal of Applied Psychology, 19,* 92–97.

HALL, E. T. (1959). *The silent language.* Greenwich, CT: Fawcett. (1973) New York: Anchor Books.

HALL, E. T. (1966). *The hidden dimension.* Garden City, NY: Doubleday.

HAN, S. P. (1990). Individualism and collectivism: Its implications for cross-cultural advertising. Doctoral dissertation. Urbana: University of Illinois Department of Communications.

HARAWAY, D. J. (1991). *Simians, cyborgs, and women.* New York: Routledge.

HARDER, B. (1989). Weaving cultural values on the loom of language. *Media Development, 3,* 25–28.

HARDING, S. (Ed.). (1987). *Feminism and methodology.* Bloomington, IN: Indiana University Press.

HARE-MUSTIN, R., & MARECEK, J. (1990). *Making a difference: Psychology and the construction of gender.* New Haven, CT: Yale University Press.

HARLOW, H. F., & HARLOW, M. (1962). Social deprivation in monkeys. *Scientific American, 207,* 136–146.

HARRE, R. (1985). Review of R. M. Farr and S. Moscovici (Eds.), Social representations. *British Journal of Psychology, 76,* 138–140.

HARRISON, J. K. (1992). Individual and combined effects of behavior modeling and culture assimilator in cross-cultural management training. *Journal of Applied Psychology, 77,* 952–962.

HARUKI, Y., SHIGEHISA, T., NEDATE, K., WAJIMA, M., & OGAWA, R. (1984). Effects of alien-reinforcement and its combined type on learning behavior and efficacy in relation to personality. *International Journal of Psychology, 19,* 527–545.

HARVEY, O. J., HUNT, D. E., & SCHROEDER, H. M. (1961). *Conceptual systems and personality organization.* New York: Wiley.

HASTINGS, E. H., & HASTINGS, P. K. (1990). *Index of international public opinion, 1988–89.* New York: Greenwood Press.

HATFIELD, E., & RAPSON, R. L. (1993). Historical and cross-cultural perspectives on passionate love. In K. T. Strongman (Ed.), *International review of emotion.* New York: Wiley.

HAWES, F., & KEALEY, D. J. (1979). *Canadians in development: An empirical study of adaptation and effectiveness on overseas assignment.* Ottawa: Canadian International Development Agency.

HAYDUK, L. A. (1983). Personal space: Where we now stand. *Psychological Bulletin, 94,* 293–335.

HEDGE, A., & YOUSIF, Y. H. (1992). Effects of urban size, urgency, and cost of helpfulness: A cross-cultural comparison between the United Kingdom and the Sudan. *Journal of Cross-Cultural Psychology, 23,* 107–115.

HEIDER, F. (1958). *The psychology of interpersonal relations.* New York: Wiley.

HEISE, D. R. (1979). *Understanding events: Affect and the construction of social action.* New York: Cambridge University Press.

HELSON, H. (1964). *Adaptation level theory.* New York: Harper & Row.

HENDRIX, L. (1985). Economy and child training reexamined. *Ethos, 13,* 246–261.

HENRY, J. P., & STEPHENS, P. M. (1977). *Stress, health and social environment.* New York: Springer.

HERSKOVITS, M. J. (1955). *Cultural anthropology.* New York, Knopf.

HEWSTONE, M., & WARD, C. (1985). Ethnocentrism and causal attribution. *Journal of Personality and Social Psychology, 48,* 614–623.

HILL, R. (1979). *Hanta Ho.* Garden City, N.Y.: Doubleday.

HINDE, R. A., & GROEBEL, J. (1991). *Cooperation and prosocial behavior.* Cambridge: Cambridge University Press.

HOFSTEDE, G. (1980). *Culture's consequences.* Beverly Hills, CA: Sage.

HOFSTEDE, G. (1991). *Cultures and organizations.* London: McGraw-Hill.

HOLLOWAY, S. D., KASHIWAGI, K., HESS, R. D., & AZUMA, H. (1986). Causal attributions by Japanese and American mothers and children about performance in mathematics. *International Journal of Psychology, 21,* 269–286.

HOLMBERG, A. R. (1969). *Nomads of the long bow: The Siriono of eastern Bolivia.* Garden City, N.Y.: Natural History Press.

HOLTGRAVES, T., & YANG, J. (1992). The interpersonal underpinnings of request strategies: General principles and differences due to culture and gender. *Journal of Personality and Social Psychology, 62,* 246–256.

HOLTZMAN, W. H. (1980). Projective techniques. In H. C. Triandis & J. W. Berry (Eds.), *Handbook of Cross-Cultural Psychology* (Vol. 2). Boston: Allyn and Bacon, pp. 245–278.

HOWELL, W. S. (1982). *The empathic communicator.* Belmont, CA: Wadsworth.

HSU, F. L. K. (1971). *Kinship and culture.* Chicago: Aldine.

HSU, F. L. K. (1981). *Americans and Chinese: Passage to differences.* Honolulu: University of Hawaii Press.

HSU, F. L. K. (1983). *Rugged individualism reconsidered.* Knoxville, TN: University of Tennessee Press.

HUI, C. H. (1988). Measurement of individualism-collectivism. *Journal of Research on Personality, 22,* 17–36.

HUI, C. H., & TRIANDIS, H. C. (1985). Measurement in cross-cultural psychology: A review and comparison of strategies. *Journal of Cross-Cultural Psychology, 16,* 131–152.

HUI, C. H., & TRIANDIS, H. C. (1986). Individualism and collectivism: A study of cross-cultural researchers. *Journal of Cross-Cultural Psychology, 17,* 225–248.

HUI, C. H., & TRIANDIS, H. C. (1989). Effects of culture and response format on extreme response style. *Journal of Cross-Cultural Psychology, 20,* 296–309.

HULIN, C. L., DRASGOW, F., & PARSONS, C. K. (1983). *Item response theory: Applications to psychological measurement.* Homewood, IL: Irwin.

IGLITZIN, L. B., & ROSS, R. (Eds.). (1976). *Women in the world: A comparative study.* Santa Barbara, CA: Clio Books.

INKELES, A. (1983). The American character. *The Center Magazine,* November–December 1983, pp. 25–39.

INKELES, A., & LEVINSON, D. J. (1969). National character: The study of modal personality and sociocultural systems. In G. Lindzey & E. Aronson (Eds.), *The handbook of social psychology.* Reading, MA: Addison-Wesley.

INKELES, A., & SMITH, D. H. (1974). *Becoming modern.* Cambridge, MA: Harvard University Press.

IRVINE, S., & CARROLL, W. K. (1980). Testing and assessment across cultures: Issues in methodology and theory. In H. C. Triandis & J. W. Berry (Eds.), *Handbook of Cross-Cultural Psychology* (Vol. 2). Boston: Allyn and Bacon, pp. 181–244.

IWAO, S. (1988, August). Social psychology's models of man: Isn't it time for East to meet West? Invited address to the International Congress of Scientific Psychology, Sydney, Australia.

IWAO, S. (1990). Recent changes in Japanese attitudes. In A. D. Romberg & T. Yamamoto (Eds.), *Same bed, different dreams: American and Japanese— Societies in transition.* New York: Council for Foreign Relations.

IWAO, S. (1993). *The Japanese woman: Traditional image and changing reality.* New York: Free Press.

IWAO, S., & TRIANDIS, H. C. (in press). Validity of auto- and hetero-stereotypes among Japanese and American students. *Journal of Cross-Cultural Psychology.*

IWATA, O. (1992). Comparative study of person perception and friendly/altruistic behavior intentions between Canadian and Japanese undergraduates. In

S. Iwawaki, Y. Kashima, & K. Leung (Eds.), *Innovations in cross-cultural psychology*. Amsterdam/Lisse: Swets & Zeitlinger, pp. 173–183.

JACKSON, S. E. (1991a, Sept. 29). Implications of work force diversity for assessment practices. Lecture given at the "Assessment: A Changing View" conference, Minneapolis.

JACKSON, S. E. (1991b). Team composition in organizational settings: Issues in managing an increasingly diverse work force. In S. Worchel, W. Wood, & J. Simpson (Eds.), *Group process and productivity*. Newbury Park, CA: Sage, pp. 138–171.

JACKSON, S. E., & ALVAREZ, E. B. (1992). Working through diversity as a strategic imperative. In S. E. Jackson & Associates (Eds.), *Diversity in the workplace: Human resources initiatives*. New York: Guilford Press, pp. 13–36.

JACKSON, S. E., & ASSOCIATES (1992). *Diversity in the workplace: Human resources initiatives*. New York: Guilford Press.

JACKSON, S. E., BRETT, J. F., SESSA, V. I., COOPER, D. M., JULIN, J. A., & PEYRONNIN, K. (1991). Some differences make a difference: Individual dissimilarity and group heterogeneity as correlates of recruitment, promotions, and turnover. *Journal of Applied Psychology, 76*, 675–689.

JANIS, I. L. (1972). *Victims of group think*. Boston: Houghton-Mifflin.

JANIS, I. L. (1982). *Groupthink* (2d ed.). Boston: Houghton-Mifflin.

JANSZ, J. (1991). *Person, self, and moral demands: Individualism contested by collectivism*. Leiden, The Netherlands: DSWO Press.

JASPARS, J. M. F., VAN DE GEER, J. P., TAJFEL, H., & JOHNSON, N. (1965). *On the development of international attitudes*. Leiden, The Netherlands: Psychological Institute.

JONES, J. M. (1986). Racism: A cultural analysis. In J. F. Dovidio & S. L. Gaertner (Eds.), *Prejudice, discrimination and racism*. Orlando, FL: Academic Press.

JONES, J. M. (1988). Racism in black and white. In P. A. Katz & D. A. Taylor (Eds.), *Eliminating racism*. New York: Plenum, pp. 117–135.

JOSEPHS, R. A., MARKUS, H. R., & TAFARODI, R. W. (1992). Gender and self-esteem. *Journal of Personality and Social Psychology, 63*, 391–402.

KAPLAN, R. B. (1966). Cultural thought and patterns in inter-cultural education. *Language Learning, 16*, 1–20.

KASHIMA, E. S. (1989). Determinants of perceived group heterogeneity. Unpublished doctoral dissertation. Champaign, IL: University of Illinois, Department of Psychology.

KASHIMA, Y., SIEGEL, M., TANAKA, K., & KASHIMA, E. S. (1992). Do people believe behaviors are consistent with attitudes? Towards a cultural psychology of attribution processes. *British Journal of Social Psychology, 31*, 111–124.

KASHIMA, Y., & TRIANDIS, H. C. (1986). The self-serving bias in attributions as a coping strategy: A cross-cultural study. *Journal of Cross-Cultural Psychology, 17*, 83–98.

KAUFMAN, W. C. (1957). Status, authoritarianism, and anti-Semitism. *American Journal of Sociology, 62*, 379–382.

KAY, P., & KEMPTON, W. (1984). What is the Sapir-Whorf hypothesis? *American Anthropologist, 86*, 65–79.

KEALEY, D. J. (1989). A study of cross-cultural effectiveness: Theoretical issues, practical applications. *International Journal of Intercultural Relations, 13*, 378–428.

KIDDER, L. H. (1992). Requirements for being "Japanese": Stories of returnees. *International Journal of Intercultural Relations, 16*, 383–394.

KIDDER, L. H., & KOSUGE, N. (in press). Family-work in modern Japan: The reproduction of sons and mothers. In M. Lerner & G. Mikula (Eds.), *Entitlements and the affectional bond*. New York: Plenum.

KITAYAMA, S. (1992, February). Culture and emotions. Paper presented at the Santa Fe, NM, meetings of the Society for Cross-Cultural Research.

KITAYAMA, S., MARKUS, H. R., KUROKAWA, M., TUMMALA, P., & KATO, K. (1991). Self-other similarity judgments depend on culture. Technical Report No. 91-17, Department of Psychology, University of Oregon, Eugene, OR.

KLINEBERG, O. (1954). *Social psychology*. New York: Holt.

KLINEBERG, O., & HULL, W. F. (1979). *At a foreign university: An international study of adaptation and coping*. New York: Praeger.

KLUCKHOHN, C. (1954). Culture and behavior. In G. Lindzey (Ed.), *Handbook of social psychology*. Cambridge, Mass.: Addison-Wesley (Vol. 2), pp. 921–976.

KLUCKHOHN, F., & STRODTBECK, F. (1961). *Variations in value orientations*. Evanston, IL: Row, Peterson.

KOHLBERG, L. (1969). Stage and sequence: The cognitive developmental approach to socialization. In D. A. Goslin (Ed.), *Handbook of socialization theory and research*. New York: Rand McNally.

KOHLBERG, L. (1981). *The philosophy of moral development: Moral states and the idea of justice*. San Francisco: Harper & Row.

KOHLS, R. (1985). Intercultural training. In W. R. Tracey (Ed.), *Human resource management and development handbook*. New York: American Management Association, pp. 1125–1134.

KOHN, M. L. (1969). *Class and conformity*. Homewood, IL: Dorsey.

KOHN, M. L. (1987, August). Cross-national research as an analytic strategy. Presidential Address to American Sociological Association.

KROEBER, A. L. (1917). *Zuni kin & clan*. New York: Trustees.

KROEBER, A. L., & KLUCKHOHN, C. (1952). *Culture: A critical review of concepts and definitions* (Vol. 147, No. 1). Cambridge, MA: Peabody Museum.

KROGER, R. O., & WOOD, L. A. (1992). Are the rules of address universal? Comparison of Chinese, Korean, and German usage. *Journal of Cross-Cultural Psychology, 23*, 148–162.

KUHN, M. H., & McPARTLAND, R. (1954). An empirical investigation of self attitudes. *American Sociological Review, 19*, 68–76.

KUPFER, A. (1988, May 14). How to be a global manager. *Fortune*.

LAMBERT, W. E. (1992). Challenging established views on social issues: The power and limitations of research. *American Psychologist, 47*, 533–542.

LAMBERT, W. E., & TAYLOR, D. (1990). *Coping with cultural and racial diversity in urban America*. New York: Praeger.

LAMBERT, W. W. (1971). Cross-cultural backgrounds to personality development and socialization of aggression: Findings from the Six Cultures study. In W. W. Lambert & R. Weisbrod (Eds.), *Comparative perspectives on social psychology*. Boston: Little, Brown, pp. 49–61.

LAMBERT, W. W., TRIANDIS, L. M., & WOLF, M. (1959). Some correlates of beliefs in the malevolence and benevolence of supernatural beings: A cross-cultural study. *Journal of Abnormal and Social Psychology, 58*, 162–169.

LANDAR, H. J., ERVIN, S. M., & HOROWITZ, A. E. (1960). Navaho color categories. *Language, 36,* 368–382.

LANDAU, S. F. (1984). Trends in violence and aggression. A cross-cultural analysis. *International Journal of Comparative Sociology, 24,* 133–158.

LANDIS, D., & BRISLIN, R. (1983). *Handbook of intercultural training* (3 vols.). New York: Pergamon.

LANGER, E. J. (1983). *The psychology of control.* Beverly Hills, CA: Sage.

L'ARMAND, K., & PEPITONE, A. (1975). Helping to reward another person: A cross-cultural analysis. *Journal of Personality and Social Psychology, 31,* 189–198.

LAZARUS, R. S., & AVERILL, J. R. (1972). Emotion and cognition with reference to anxiety. In C. D. Spielberger (Ed.), *Anxiety: Contemporary theory and research.* New York: Academic Press.

LEBRA, T. (1984). *Japanese women: Constraint and fulfillment.* Honolulu: University of Hawaii Press.

LEDERER, R. (1987). *Anguished English.* Charleston, SC: Wyrick.

LEE, R. B., & DEVORE, I. (Eds.). (1976). *Kalahari hunter-gatherers: Studies of !Kung San and their neighbors.* Cambridge, MA: Harvard Press.

LEE, Y., & OTTATI, V. (1990). Determinants of ingroup and outgroup perceptions of heterogeneity: An investigation of Sino-American stereotypes. (Mimeo.)

LEUNG, K. (1987). Some determinants of reactions to procedural models of conflict resolution: A cross-national study. *Journal of Personality and Social Psychology, 53,* 898–908.

LEUNG, K. (1988). Some determinants of conflict avoidance. *Journal of Cross Cultural Psychology, 19,* 125–136.

LEUNG, K. (1989). Cross-cultural differences: Individual vs culture-level analysis. *International Journal of Psychology, 24,* 703–719.

LEVINE, E. M. (1981). Middle class family decline. *Society, 18,* 72–78.

LEVINE, R. V. (1992, February). Personal communication, Santa Fe, NM, meetings of Society for Cross-Cultural Research.

LEVINE, R. V., & BARTLETT, K. (1984). Pace of life, punctuality, and coronary heart disease in six countries. *Journal of Cross-Cultural Psychology, 15,* 233–255.

LEVINSON, D. (1989). *Family violence in cross-cultural perspective.* Newbury Park, CA: Sage.

LEWIN, K. (1936). *Principles of topological psychology.* New York: McGraw-Hill.

LINVILLE, P. W. (1982). The complexity-extremity effect and age-based stereotyping. *Journal of Personality and Social Psychology, 42,* 193–211.

LIPSET, S. M. (1990). *Continental divide.* New York: Routledge.

LIPSET, S. M. (submitted). *American exceptionalism in Japanese perspective.*

LOMAX, A., & BERKOWITZ, N. (1972). The evolutionary taxonomy of culture. *Science, 177,* 228–239.

LONGABAUGH, R. (1980). The systematic observation of behavior in naturalistic settings. In H. C. Triandis & J. W. Berry (Eds.), *Handbook of Cross-Cultural Psychology* (Vol. 2). Boston: Allyn and Bacon, pp. 57–126.

LONNER, W. (1980). The search for psychological universals. In H. C. Triandis & W. W. Lambert (Eds.), *Handbook of Cross-Cultural Psychology* (Vol. 1). Boston: Allyn and Bacon, pp. 143–204.

LONNER, W. (Ed.). (1985). Television in the developing world. *Journal of Cross-Cultural Psychology, 16,* 259–397.

LONNER, W., & BERRY, J. (1986). *Field methods in cross-cultural research*. Beverly Hills, CA: Sage.

LOTT, B. (1990). Dual natures or learned behavior: The challenge to feminist psychology. In R. T. Hare-Mustin & J. Marecek (Eds.), *Making a difference: Psychology and the construction of gender*. New Haven, CT: Yale University Press, pp. 65–101.

LOW, B. S. (1989). Cross-cultural patterns in the training of children: An evolutionary perspective. *Journal of Comparative Psychology, 103*, 311–319.

LUBLIN, J. S. (1992, Aug. 4). Companies use cross-cultural training to help their employees adjust abroad. *Wall Street Journal*, p. B-1.

LUMMIS, M., & STEVENSON, H. W. (1990). Gender differences in beliefs and achievement: A cross-cultural study. *Developmental Psychology, 26*, 254–263.

LYKES, M. B. (1985). Gender and individualistic vs collectivist notions of the self. In A. Stewart & B. Lykes (Eds.), *Gender and personality*. Durham, NC: Duke University Press.

MA, H. K. (1988). The Chinese perspectives on moral development. *International Journal of Psychology, 23*, 201–227.

MAJORS, R., & MANCINI-BILLSON, J. (1992). *Cool pose*. New York: Lexington Books.

MALINOWSKI, B. (1922). *Argonauts of the Western Pacific* (2 vols.). London: Routledge.

MALPASS, R. S. (1977). Theory and method in cross-cultural psychology. *American Psychologist, 32*, 1069–1079.

MALPASS, R. S., & POORTINGA, Y. H. (1986). Strategies for design and analysis. In W. J. Lonner & J. W. Berry (Eds.), *Field methods in cross-cultural research*. Beverly Hills, CA: Sage, pp. 47–84.

MANDELBAUM, D. G. (1988). *Women's seclusion and men's honor*. Tucson, AZ: University of Arizona Press.

MANN, L. (1980). Cross-cultural studies of small groups. In H. C. Triandis & R. W. Brislin (Eds.), *Handbook of Cross-Cultural Psychology* (Vol. 5). Boston: Allyn and Bacon, pp. 155–210.

MANN, L., RADFORD, M., & KANAGAWA, C. (1985). Cross-cultural differences in children's use of decision rules: A comparison between Japan and Australia. *Journal of Personality and Social Psychology, 49*, 1557–1564.

MARIN, G., GAMBA, R. J., & MARIN, G. V. (1992). Extreme response style and acquiescence among Hispanics. *Journal of Cross-Cultural Psychology, 23*, 498–509.

MARIN, G., & MARIN, B. V. (1991). *Research with Hispanic populations*. Newbury Park, CA: Sage.

MARIN, G., & TRIANDIS, H. C. (1985). Allocentrism as an important characteristic of the behavior of Latin Americans and Hispanics. In R. Diaz-Guerrero (Ed.), *Cross-cultural and national studies in social psychology*. Amsterdam: North Holland, pp. 85–104.

MARIN, G., TRIANDIS, H. C., BETANCOURT, H., & KASHIMA, Y., (1983). Ethnic affirmation versus social desirability: Explaining discrepancies in bilinguals' responses to a questionnaire. *Journal of Cross-Cultural Psychology, 14*, 173–186.

MARKUS, H., & KITAYAMA, S. (1991). Culture and self: Implications for cognition, emotion and motivation. *Psychological Review, 98*, 224–253.

MARMOT, M. G., & SYME, S. L. (1976). Acculturation and coronary heart disease in Japanese Americans. *American Journal of Epidemiology, 104,* 225–247.

MARTIN, J. N. (1989). Intercultural communication competence. *International Journal of Intercultural Relations, 13,* 227–428.

MATSUDA, N. (1985). Strong, quasi- and weak conformity among Japanese in a modified Asch procedure. *Journal of Cross-Cultural Psychology, 16,* 83–97.

MATSUMOTO, D. (1992, February). Culture and emotion. Paper presented at the Santa Fe, NM, meeting of the Society for Cross-Cultural Research.

McARTHUR, L., & FRIEDMAN, S. A. (1980). Illusory correlation in impression formation: Variations in the shared distinctiveness effect as a function of distinctive person's age, race, and sex. *Journal of Personality and Social Psychology, 39,* 615–624.

McCLELLAND, D. C. (1980). Motive dispositions: The merits of operant and respondent measures. In L. Wheeler (Ed.), *Review of Personality and Social Psychology,* Beverly Hills, CA: Sage, pp. 10–41.

McGRATH, J. (1984). *Groups: Interaction and performance.* Englewood Cliffs, NJ: Prentice-Hall.

MEAD, M. (1961). *Cooperation and competition among primitive peoples.* Boston: Beacon Press.

MILGRAM, S. (1974). *Obedience to authority.* New York: Harper.

MILLER, J. G. (1984). Culture and the development of everyday social explanation. *Journal of Personality and Social Psychology, 46,* 961–978.

MILLER, J. G., BERSOFF, D. M., & HARWOOD, R. L. (1990). Perceptions of social responsibilities in India and the United States: Moral imperatives or personal decisions? *Journal of Personality and Social Psychology, 58,* 33–47.

MILLER, N., & BREWER, M. B. (1984). *Groups in contact.* San Diego, CA: Academic Press.

MINER, H. (1958). Body ritual among the Nacirema. *American Anthropologist, 58,* 503–507.

MINTURN, L., & LAMBERT, W. W. (1964). *Mothers of six cultures.* New York: Wiley.

MOGHADDAM, F. M., TAYLOR, D. M., & WRIGHT, S. C. (1993). *Social psychology in cross-cultural perspective.* New York: Freeman.

MOORE, H. L. (1988). *Feminism and anthropology.* Minneapolis: University of Minnesota Press.

MOSCOVICI, S. (1961/1976). *La psychanalyse: Son image et son public.* Paris: Presses Universitaires de France.

MULVIHILL, D. J., & TUMIN, M. M. (Eds.). (1969). *Crimes of violence. Volume II Staff Report of National Commission on the Causes and Prevention of Violence.* Washington, DC: U.S. Government Printing Office.

MURDOCK, P., & PROVOST, C. (1973). Measurement of cultural complexity. *Ethnography, 12,* 379–392.

NADER, L. (1975). Anthropological perspectives. In M. J. Lerner (Ed.), The justice motive in social behavior. *Journal of Social Issues, 31,* 151–170.

NAIDOO, J. C., & DAVIS, J. C. (1988). Canadian South Asian women in transition: A dualistic view of life. *Journal of Comparative Family Studies, 19,* 311–327.

NAROLL, R. (1983). *The moral order.* Beverly Hills: CA: Sage.

NAROLL, R., MICHIK, G. L., & NAROLL, F. (1980). Holocultural research methods. In H. C. Triandis & J. W. Berry (Eds.), *Handbook of cross-cultural psychology* (Vol. 2). Boston: Allyn and Bacon, pp. 479–522.

NETO, F., & TRIANDIS, H. C. (submitted). Allocentrism vs idiocentrism among Portuguese students.

NIELSEN, J. (1990). *Feminist research methods*. Boulder, CO: Westview Press.

NISBETT, R. E. (1990). Evolutionary psychology, biology, and cultural evolution. *Motivation and Emotion, 14*, 255–263.

OBERG, K. (1954). *Culture shock*. The Bobbs-Merrill Reprint Series, No. A-329.

OBERG, K. (1960). Culture shock: Adjustment to new cultural environments. *Practical Anthropology, 7*, 177–182.

OGILVIE, D. M. (1987). The undesired self: A neglected variable in personality research. *Psychological Review, 52*, 379–385.

OKABE, R. (1983). Cultural assumptions of East and West: Japan and the United States. In W. B. Gudykunst (Ed.), *Intercultural communication theory: Current perspectives*. Beverly Hills, CA: Sage, pp. 21–44.

O'KELLY, C. G., & CARNEY, L. S. (1986). *Women and men in society* (2d ed.). Belmont, CA: Wadsworth.

OLSEN, N. J. (1967). The effect of household composition on the child rearing practices of Taiwanese families. Cornell University dissertation in *University Microfilms, 71–22, 933*.

ORTNER, S. B., & WHITEHEAD, H. (1981). *Sexual meanings: The cultural construction of gender and sexuality*. New York: Cambridge University Press.

OSGOOD, C. E., MAY, W., & MIRON, M. (1975). *Cross-cultural universals of affective meaning*. Urbana: University of Illinois Press.

OUSMANE, S. (1976). *Xala*. Westport, CT: Lawrence Hill.

PAREEK, U., & RAO, T. V. (1980). Cross-cultural surveys and interviewing. In H. C. Triandis & J. W. Berry (Eds.), *Handbook of cross-cultural psychology* (Vol. 2). Boston: Allyn and Bacon, pp. 127–180.

PELTO, P. J. (1968, April). The difference between "tight" and "loose" societies. *Transaction*, 37–40.

PEPITONE, A., & TRIANDIS, H. C. (1987). On the universality of social psychological theories. *Journal of Cross-Cultural Psychology, 18*, 471–498.

PETTIGREW, T. (1959). The measurement of correlates of category width as a cognitive variable. *Journal of Personality, 26*, 532–544.

PETTIGREW, T. (1979). The ultimate attribution error: Extending Allport's cognitive analysis of prejudice. *Personality and Social Psychology Bulletin, 5*, 461–476.

PHILLIPS, H. P. (1965). *Thai peasant personality: The patterning of interpersonal behavior in the village of Bang Chan*. Berkeley: University of California Press.

PIAGET, J. (1966). Necessité et signification de recherches comparatives en psychologie genetique. *International Journal of Psychology, 1*, 3–13.

PIKE, K. L. (1967). *Language in relation to a unified theory of the structure of human behavior*. The Hague: Mouton.

PILISUK, M., & PARKS, S. (1985). *The healing web*. Hanover, NH: University Press of New England.

PLOMIN, R. (1990). *Nature and nurture: An introduction to behavioral genetics*. Pacific Grove, CA: Brooks/Cole.

RAHE, R. H. (1969). Multicultural correlations of life change scaling: America, Japan, and Denmark. *Journal of Psychosomatic Research, 13*, 191–195.

RAHE, R. H. (1972). Subjects' recent life changes and their near future illness reports. *Annals of Clinical Research, 4*, 250–265.

RAZRAN, G. (1940). Conditioned response changes in rating and appraising socio-political slogans. *Psychological Bulletin, 37,* 481.

REINHARZ, S. (1992). *Feminist methods in social research.* New York: Oxford Press.

RIDDLE, J. M., & ESTES, J. W. (1992). Oral contraceptives in ancient and medieval times. *American Scientist, 80,* 226–233.

RIDLEY, C. R. (1984). Clinical treatment of the nondisclosing Black client: A therapeutic paradox. *American Psychologist, 39,* 1234–1244.

ROBARCHEK, C. A. (1986). Helpfulness, fearfulness, and peacefulness: The emotional and motivational context of Semai social relations. *Anthropological Quarterly, 59,* 165–170.

ROBBINS, M. C., DE WALT, B. R., & PELTO, P. J. (1972). Climate and behavior: A biocultural study. *Journal of Cross-Cultural Psychology, 3,* 331–344.

ROBERTS, J. M. (1951). Three Navaho households: A comparative study of small group culture. *Papers of Peabody Musuem, 40* (3).

ROGOFF, B. (1981). Schooling and development of cognitive skills. In H. C. Triandis & A. Heron (Eds.), *Handbook of cross-cultural psychology* (Vol. 4). Boston: Allyn and Bacon, pp. 233–287.

ROGOFF, B. (1990). *Apprenticeship in thinking.* New York: Oxford University Press.

ROHNER, R. P. (1984). Toward a conception of culture for cross-cultural psychology. *Journal of Cross-Cultural Psychology, 15,* 111–138.

ROHNER, R. P. (1986). *The warmth dimension: Foundations of parental acceptance-rejection theory.* Newbury Park, CA: Sage.

ROKEACH, M. (1960). *The open and closed mind.* New York: Basic Books.

ROKEACH, M. (1973). *The nature of human values.* New York: Free Press.

ROKEACH, M., & MEZEI, L. (1966). Race and shared belief as factors in social choice. *Science, 151,* 167–172.

ROSALDO, M. Z., & LAMPHERE, L. (1974). *Woman, culture and society.* Stanford, CA: Stanford University Press.

ROSS, L., & NISBETT, R. E. (1991). *The person and the situation.* New York: McGraw-Hill.

ROZIN, P., MILLMAN, L., & NEMEROFF, C. (1986). Operation of the laws of sympathetic magic in disgust and other domains. *Journal of Personality and Social Psychology, 50,* 703–712.

RUBEN, B., & KEALEY, D. (1979). Behavioral assessment of communication competency and the prediction of cross-cultural adaptation. *International Journal of Intercultural Relations, 3,* 15–47.

SAEGERT, H. A., SWAP, W., & ZAJONC, R. B. (1973). Exposure context and interpersonal attraction. *Journal of Personality and Social Psychology, 25,* 234–242.

SAFIR, M., MEDNICK, M. T., ISRAEL, D., & BERNARD, J. (Eds.). (1985). *Women's worlds: From the new scholarship.* New York: Praeger.

SALZMAN, M. B. (1991). *A Navajo intercultural sensitizer.* Fairbanks, AK: Center for Cross Cultural Studies of The University of Alaska.

SAPIR, E. (1951, originally 1929). The status of linguistics as a science. In D. Mendelbaum (Ed.), *Selected writings.* Berkeley: University of California Press, *5,* 207–214.

SARGENT, E. D. (1986, Mar. 2). The black "fratricide" epidemic. *Washington Post.*

SCHEPER-HUGHES, N. (1985). Culture, scarcity, and maternal thinking: Maternal detachment and infant survival in a Brazilian shantytown. *Ethos, 13,* 291–317.

SCHLEGEL, A. (1989). Gender issues and cross-cultural research. *Behavior Science Research, 23,* 265–280.

SCHMITZ, C. (1992). Collectivism and patriotism. B.A. honors thesis. Champaign, IL: University of Illinois Department of Psychology.

SCHUMAN, H. (1966). Social change and the validity of regional stereotypes in East Pakistan. *Sociometry, 29,* 426–440.

SCHWARTZ, S. H. (1992). Universals in the content and structure of values: Theoretical advances and empirical tests in 20 countries. In M. Zanna (Ed.), *Advances in Experimental Social Psychology* (Vol. 25). New York: Academic Press.

SCHWARTZ, S. H. (submitted). Cultural dimensions of values: Toward an understanding of national differences. In U. Kim, H. C. Triandis, & G. Yoon (Eds.), *Individualism and collectivism: Theoretical and methodological perspectives.*

SCHWARTZ, S. H., & BILSKY, W. (1987). Toward a universal psychological structure of human values. *Journal of Personality and Social Psychology, 53,* 550–562.

SEARS, D. O. (1986). College sophomores in the laboratory: Influences of a narrow data base on social psychology's view of human nature. *Journal of Personality and Social Psychology, 51,* 515–530.

SEGALL, M. H., DASEN, P. D., BERRY, J. W., & POORTINGA, Y. H. (1990). *Human behavior in global perspective.* New York: Pergamon Press.

SEGALL, M. H., CAMPBELL, D. T., & HERSKOVITS, M. J. (1963). Cultural differences in the perception of geometric illusions. *Science, 193,* 769–771.

SEGALOWITZ, N. S. (1980). Issues in the cross-cultural study of bilingual development. In H. C. Triandis & A. Heron (Eds.), *Handbook of cross-cultural psychology* (Vol. 4: Developmental). Boston: Allyn and Bacon, pp. 55–92.

SEN, P. K. (1962). *Land and people of the Andamans.* Calcutta: Post-Graduate Book Mart.

SETIADI, B. N. (1984). Schooling, age, and culture as moderators of role perceptions. Unpublished doctoral dissertation. Champaign, IL: University of Illinois Department of Psychology.

SHERIF, C. W., KELLY, M., RODGERS, H. L., JR., SARUP, G., & TITTLER, B. I. (1973). Personal involvement, social judgment, and action. *Journal of Personality and Social Psychology, 27,* 311–328.

SHERIF, M. (1965). Superordinate goals in the reduction of intergroup conflict: An experimental evaluation. In M. Schwebel (Ed.), *Behavior, science, and human survival.* Palo Alto, CA: Science and Behavior Books.

SHWEDER, R. A., & BOURNE, E. J. (1982). Does the concept of person vary cross-culturally? In A. J. Marsella & G. M. White (Eds.), *Cultural conceptions of mental health and therapy.* London: Reidel, pp. 97–137.

SHWEDER, R. A., & LEVINE, R. (1984). *Culture theory.* Chicago: University of Chicago Press.

SHWEDER, R. A., MAHAPATRA, M., & MILLER, J. G. (1990). Culture and moral development. In J. W. Stigler, R. A. Shweder, & G. Herdt (Eds.), *Cultural psychology.* New York: Cambridge University Press, pp. 130–204.

SIMON, P. (1980, May). The U.S. crisis of foreign language. *The Annals of the American Academy,* pp. 31–40.

SKINNER, B. F. (1981). Selection by consequences. *Science, 213,* 501–504.

SNAREY, J. R. (1985). Cross-cultural universality of social-moral development: A critical review of Kohlbergian research. *Psychological Bulletin, 97,* 202–232.

STEPHAN, W. G. (1985). Intergroup relations. In G. Lindzey & E. Aronson (Eds.), *Handbook of social psychology* (2d ed.). New York: Random House, pp. 599–658.

STEPHAN, W. G., & STEPHAN, C. W. (1984). The role of ignorance in intergroup relations. In N. Miller & M. B. Brewer (Eds.), *Desegregation: Groups in contact.* New York: Academic Press, pp. 229–256.

STEVENS, S. S. (1966). Matching functions between loudness and ten other continua. *Perception and Psychophysics, 1,* 5–8.

STEWART, E. (1966). The simulation of cultural differences. *Journal of Communication, 16,* 291–304.

STRODTBECK, F. (1951). Husband-wife interaction over revealed differences. *American Sociological Review, 16,* 468–473.

STRODTBECK, F. (1964). Considerations of meta-method in cross-cultural studies. *American Anthropologist, 66,* 223–229.

STRUBE, M. J. (1981). Meta-analysis and cross-cultural comparison: Sex differences in child competitiveness. *Journal of Cross-Cultural Psychology, 12,* 3–20.

SUDWEEKS, S., GUDYKUNST, W., TING-TOOMEY, S., & NISHIDA, T. (1990). Developmental themes in Japanese-North American interpersonal relationships. *International Journal of Intercultural Relations, 14,* 207–234.

SULLIVAN, J., PETERSON, R. B., KAMEDA, N., & SHIMADA, J. (1981). The relationship between conflict resolution approaches and trust: A cross cultural study. *Academy of Management Journal, 24,* 803–815.

SUSSMAN, N. M., & ROSENFELD, H. M. (1982). Influence of culture, language, and sex on conversational distance. *Journal of Personality and Social Psychology, 42,* 66–74.

SZALAY, L. (1970). *A communication dictionary of cultural meanings.* Washington, DC: American Institutes for Research.

SZALAY, L. B. (1985). Psychocultural findings. In H. W. Sinaiko, P. M. Curran, B. T. King, & J. M. Schneider (Eds.), *Hispanic subpopulations and naval service.* Tech. Report SI/MRAS/TR-11. Washington, DC: Office of Naval Research.

TAFT, R. (1977). Coping with unfamiliar cultures. In N. Warren (Ed.), *Studies in cross-cultural psychology.* London: Academic Press, pp. 121–154.

TAJFEL, H. (1974). Social identity and intergroup behavior. *Social Science Information, 13,* 65–93.

TAJFEL, H. (1982). *Social identity and intergroup relations.* New York: Cambridge University Press.

TAJFEL, H., & TURNER, J. (1986). The social identity theory of intergroup relations. In S. Worchel & W. Austin (Eds.), *Psychology of intergroup relations* (2d ed.). Chicago: Nelson-Hall, pp. 7–24.

TAKATA, T. (1987). Self-deprecative tendencies in self-evaluation through social comparison. *Japanese Journal of Experimental Social Psychology, 27,* 27–36.

TANAKA, Y. (1972). A study of national stereotypes. In H. C. Triandis (Ed.), *The analysis of subjective culture.* New York: Wiley, pp. 117–179.

TAPP, J. L., KELMAN, H. C., TRIANDIS, H. C., WRIGHTSMAN, L., & COELHO, G. (1974). Continuing concerns in cross-cultural ethics. *International Journal of Psychology, 9,* 231–249.

THERNSTROM, S. (1980). *Harvard Encyclopedia of Ethnic Diversity and American Ethnic Groups.* Cambridge, MA: Harvard Press.

THORNE, B., KRAMARAE, C., & HENLEY, N. (1983). *Language, gender and society.* Cambridge, MA: Newbury House.

THURSTONE, L. L. (1931). The measurement of social attitudes. *Journal of Abnormal and Social Psychology, 26,* 249–269.

TING-TOOMEY, S. (1986). Interpersonal ties in intergroup communication. In W. B. Gudykunst (Ed.), *Intergroup communication.* London: Edward Arnold.

TING-TOOMEY, S. (1988). A face-negotiation theory. In Y. Kim & W. Gudykunst (Eds.), *Theories of intercultural communication.* Newbury Park, CA: Sage.

TODD, E. (1983). *La troisieme planete.* Paris: France Editions du Seuil.

TORREY, E. F. (1986). *Witchdoctors and psychiatrists: The common roots of psychotherapy and its future.* New York: Harper.

TRAFIMOW, D., TRIANDIS, H. C., & GOTO, S. (1991). Some tests of the distinction between the private and the collective self. *Journal of Personality and Social Psychology, 60,* 649–655.

TREIMAN, D. J., & ROOS, P. A. (1983). Sex earning in industrial society: A nine-nation comparison. *American Journal of Sociology, 89,* 612–650.

TRIANDIS, H. C. (1964). Cultural influences upon cognitive processes. In L. Berkowitz (Ed.), *Advances in Experimental Social Psychology* (Vol. 1). New York: Academic Press, pp. 1–48.

TRIANDIS, H. C. (1967). Toward an analysis of the components of interpersonal attitudes. In C. Sherif & M. Sherif (Eds.), *Attitudes, ego-involvement and change.* New York: Wiley, pp. 227–270.

TRIANDIS, H. C. (1971). *Attitudes and attitude change.* New York: Wiley.

TRIANDIS, H. C. (1972). *The analysis of subjective culture.* New York: Wiley.

TRIANDIS, H. C. (1975). Cultural training, cognitive complexity, and interpersonal attitudes. In R. W. Brislin, S. Bochner, and W. J. Lonner (Eds.), *Cross-cultural perspectives on learning.* Beverly Hills, CA: Sage.

TRIANDIS, H. C. (1976a). The future of pluralism. *Journal of Social Issues, 32,* 179–208.

TRIANDIS, H. C. (1976b). *Variations in black and white perceptions of the social environment.* Urbana: University of Illinois Press.

TRIANDIS, H. C. (1977). *Interpersonal behavior.* Monterey, CA: Brooks/Cole.

TRIANDIS, H. C. (1978). Some universals of social behavior. *Personality and Social Psychology Bulletin, 4,* 1–16.

TRIANDIS, H. C. (1980). Values, attitudes and interpersonal behavior. In H. E. Howe & M. M. Page (Eds.), *Nebraska Symposium on Motivation, 1979.* Lincoln: University of Nebraska Press, pp. 195–260.

TRIANDIS, H. C. (1988a). Collectivism and individualism: A reconceptualization of a basic concept in cross cultural psychology. In G. K. Verma & C. Bargley (Eds.), *Personality, attitudes, and cognitions.* London: Macmillan, pp. 60–95.

TRIANDIS, H. C. (1988b). Cross-cultural contributions to theory in social psychology. In M. Bond (Ed.), *The cross-cultural challenge to social psychology.* Newbury Park, CA: Sage, pp. 122–140.

TRIANDIS, H. C. (1989). Self and social behavior in differing cultural contexts. *Psychological Review, 96,* 269–289.

TRIANDIS, H. C. (1990). Cross-cultural studies of individualism and collectivism. In J. Berman (Ed.), *Nebraska Symposium on Motivation, 1989.* Lincoln: University of Nebraska Press, pp. 41–133.

TRIANDIS, H. C. (1992). Cross-cultural research in social psychology. In D. Granberg & G. Sarup (Eds.), *Social judgment and intergroup relations: Essays in honor of Muzafer Sherif*. New York: Springer Verlag, pp. 229–244.

TRIANDIS, H. C. (1993). Cross-cultural industrial and organizational psychology. In H. C. Triandis, M. Dunnette, & L. Hough (Eds.), *Handbook of Industrial-Organizational Psychology* (Vol. 4). Palo Alto, CA: Consulting Psychologists Press.

TRIANDIS, H. C., & J. W. BERRY (Eds.). (1980). *Handbook of Cross-Cultural Psychology* (Vol. 2). Boston: Allyn and Bacon.

TRIANDIS, H. C., BONTEMPO, R., BETANCOURT, H., BOND, M., LEUNG, K., BRENES, A., GEORGAS, J., HUI, C. H., MARIN, G., SETIADI, B., SINHA, J. B. P., VERMA, J., SPANGENBERG, J., TOUZARD, H., & DE MONTMOLLIN, G. (1986). The measurement of etic aspects of individualism and collectivism across cultures. *Australian Journal of Psychology, 38,* 257–267.

TRIANDIS, H. C., BONTEMPO, R., LEUNG, K., & HUI, C. H. (1990). A method for determining cultural, demographic, and personal constructs. *Journal of Cross-Cultural Psychology, 21,* 302–318.

TRIANDIS, H. C., BONTEMPO, R., VILLAREAL, M. J., ASAI, M., & LUCCA, N. (1988). Individualism and collectivism: Cross-cultural perspectives on self-ingroup relationships. *Journal of Personality and Social Psychology, 54,* 323–338.

TRIANDIS, H. C., BRISLIN, R., & HUI, C. H. (1988). Cross-cultural training across the individualism-collectivism divide. *International Journal of Intercultural Relations, 12,* 269–289.

TRIANDIS, H. C., & DAVIS, E. E. (1965). Race and belief as determinants of behavioral intentions. *Journal of Personality and Social Psychology, 2,* 715–725.

TRIANDIS, H. C., DAVIS, E. E., & TAKEZAWA, S. (1965). Some determinants of social distance among Americans, German, and Japanese students. *Journal of Personality and Social Psychology, 2,* 540–551.

TRIANDIS, H. C., HALL, E., & EWEN, R. (1965). Member heterogeneity and dyadic creativity. *Human Relations, 18,* 33–55.

TRIANDIS, H. C., HUI, C. H., ALBERT, R. D., LEUNG, K., LISANSKY, J., DIAZ-LOVING, R., PLASCENCIA, L., MARIN, G., BETANCOURT, H., & LOYOLA-CINTRON, L. (1984). Individual models of social behavior. *Journal of Personality and Social Psychology, 46,* 1389–1404.

TRIANDIS, H. C., HUI, C. H., LISANSKY, J., MARIN, G., & BETANCOURT, H. (1982). Perceptions of supervisor-subordinate relations among Hispanic and mainstream Navy recruits. Technical Report No. 11. Champaign IL: University of Illinois Department of Psychology.

TRIANDIS, H. C., KASHIMA, Y., LISANSKY, J., & MARIN, G. (1982). Self-concepts and values among Hispanic and mainstream Navy recruits. Technical Report No. 7. Champaign IL: University of Illinois Department of Psychology.

TRIANDIS, H. C., KASHIMA, Y., SHIMADA, E., & VILLAREAL, M. (1986). Acculturation indices as a means of confirming cultural differences. *International Journal of Psychology, 21,* 43–70.

TRIANDIS, H. C., LAMBERT, W. W., BERRY, J. W., LONNER, W. J., HERON, A., BRISLIN, R., & DRAGUNS, J. (Eds.). (1980–1981). *Handbook of Cross-Cultural Psychology* (6 vols.). Boston: Allyn and Bacon.

Triandis, H. C., Lisansky, J., Setiadi, B., Chang, B., Marin, G., & Betancourt, H. (1982). Stereotyping among Hispanics and Anglos: The uniformity, intensity, direction, and quality of auto- and heterosterotypes. *Journal of Cross-Cultural Psychology, 132,* 409–426.

Triandis, H. C., & Marin, G. (1983). Etic plus emic versus pseudoetic: A test of a basic assumption of contemporary cross-cultural psychology. *Journal of Cross-Cultural Psychology, 14,* 489–500.

Triandis, H. C., Marin, G., Betancourt, H., & Chang, B. (1982). Acculturation, biculturalism, and familism among Hispanic and mainstream Navy recruits. Technical Report No. 15. Champaign, IL: University of Illinois Department of Psychology.

Triandis, H. C., Marin, G., Hui, C. H., Lisansky, J., & Ottati, V. (1984). Role perceptions of Hispanic young adults. *Journal of Cross-Cultural Psychology, 15,* 297–320.

Triandis, H. C., Marin, G., Lisansky, J., & Betancourt, H. (1984). *Simpatia* as a cultural script of Hispanics. *Journal of Personality and Social Psychology, 47,* 1363–1375.

Triandis, H. C., McCusker, C., & Hui, C. H. (1990). Multimethod probes of individualism and collectivism. *Journal of Personality and Social Psychology, 59,* 1006–1020.

Triandis, H. C., Ottati, V., & Marin, G. (1982). Social attitudes among Hispanic and mainstream Navy recruits. Technical Report No. 10. Champaign, IL: University of Illinois Department of Psychology.

Triandis, H. C., & Triandis, L. M. (1960). Race, social class, religion, and nationality as determinants of social distance. *Journal of Abnormal and Social Psychology, 61,* 110–118.

Triandis, H. C., & Triandis, L. M. (1962). A cross-cultural study of social distance. *Psychological Monographs, 76.* No. 21 (Whole of No. 540).

Triandis, H. C., & Vassiliou, V. (1967). Frequency of contact and stereotyping. *Journal of Personality and Social Psychology, 7,* 316–328.

Triandis, H. C., & Vassiliou, V. (1972). Comparative analysis of subjective culture. In H. C. Triandis (Ed.), *The analysis of subjective culture.* New York: Wiley, pp. 299–338.

Triandis, H. C., Vassiliou, V., & Nassiakou, M. (1968). Three cross-cultural studies of subjective culture. *Journal of Personality and Social Psychology, Monograph Supplement 8* (4), 1–42.

Trier, J. (1931). *Der Deutsche Wortschatz in Sinnbezirk des Verstandes: Die Geschichte eines Sprachfeldes.* Heidelberg: Carl Winters.

Truswell, A. S., Kennelly, B. M., Hansen, J. D. L., & Lee, R. B. (1972). Blood pressure of !Kung bushmen in northern Botswana. *American Heart Journal, 84,* 5–12.

Tucker, M. F. (1987). Predicting success on foreign assignments. *Relocation/Realty Update, 3,* Sec. 24.

Tung, R. L. (1981). Selection and training of personnel for overseas assignment. *Columbia Journal of World Business, 16,* 68–78.

Tung, R. L. (1988). *The new expatriate.* Cambridge, MA: Ballinger.

Ueda, K. (1974). Sixteen ways to avoid saying "No" in Japan. *Patterns of communication in and out of Japan.* Tokyo: ICU Communication Department.

VASSILIOU, V., TRIANDIS, H. C., VASSILIOU, G., & MCGUIRE, H. Interpersonal contact and stereotyping. In H. Triandis (Ed.), *The analysis of subjective culture.* New York: Wiley, pp. 89–116.

VERMA, J. (1992). Allocentrism and relationship orientation. S. Iwawaki, Y. Kashima, & K. Leung (Eds.), *Innovations in cross-cultural psychology.* Amsterdam/Lisse: Swets & Zeitlinger, pp. 152–163.

VONTRESS, C. E. (1991). Traditional healing in Africa: Implications for cross-cultural counseling. *Counseling and Development, 70,* 242–249.

VUYLSTEKE, R. (1978). Asian views of Americans during the 1800's and 1990's. *East-West Center Magazine,* Spring–Summer issue.

WALSTER, E., ARONSON, V., ABRAHAMS, D., & ROTTMANN, L. (1966). Importance of physical attraction in dating behavior. *Journal of Personality and Social Psychology, 4,* 508–516.

WARWICK, D. P. (1980). The politics and ethics of cross-cultural research. In H. C. Triandis & J. W. Berry (Eds.), *Handbook of Cross-Cultural Psychology* (Vol. 2). Boston: Allyn and Bacon, pp. 319–372.

WATERS, M. C. (1990). *Ethnic options: Choosing identities in America.* Berkeley: University of California Press.

WATSON, O. M. (1970) *Proxemic behavior.* Paris: Mouton.

WATSON, R. I., JR. (1973). Investigation into deindividuation using a cross-cultural survey technique. *Journal of Personality and Social Psychology, 25,* 342–345.

WEINER, B., FRIEZE, I., KUKLA, A., REED, L., REST, S., & ROSENBAUM, R. M. (1972). In E. E. Jones et al. (Eds.), *Attribution: Perceiving the causes of behavior.* Morristown, NJ: General Learning Corporation.

WELDON, D. E., CARLSTON, D. E., RISSMAN, A. K., SLOBODIN, L., & TRIANDIS, H. C. (1975). A laboratory test of effects of culture assimilator training. *Journal of Personality and Social Psychology, 32,* 300–310.

WERNER, O., & CAMPBELL, D. T. (1970). Translation, working through interpreters and the problem of decentering. In R. Naroll & R. Cohen (Eds.), *A handbook of method in cultural anthropology.* New York: American Museum of Natural History, pp. 398–422.

WHEELER, L., REIS, H. T., & BOND, M. H. (1989). Collectivism-individualism in everyday social life: The Middle Kingdom and the melting pot. *Journal of Personality and Social Psychology, 57,* 79–86.

WHITING, B. B., & WHITING, J. W. M. (1975). *Children of six cultures—A psycho-cultural analysis.* Cambridge, MA: Harvard Press.

WHITING, J. W. M. (1964). Effects of climate on certain cultural practices. In W. Goodenough (Ed.), *Explorations in cultural anthropology.* New York: McGraw-Hill, pp. 496–544.

WHITING, J. W. M. (1968). Methods and problems of cross cultural research. In G. Lindzey & E. Aronson (Eds.), *The handbook of social psychology.* Reading, MA: Addison-Wesley, pp. 693–728.

WHORF, B. L. (1956). *Language, thought and reality* (J. B. Carroll, Ed.). New York: Wiley.

WILLEMS, E. P., & CLARK, R. D., III (1971). Shift toward risk and heterogeneity of groups. *Journal of Experimental Social Psychology, 7,* 304–312.

WILLIAMS, J., & BEST, D. L. (1982). *Measuring sex stereotypes: A thirty-nation study.* Beverly Hills, CA: Sage.

WILLIAMS, J., & BEST, D. L. (1990). *Self and psyche: Gender and sex viewed cross-culturally.* Newbury Park, CA: Sage.

WITKIN, H. A., & BERRY, J. W. (1975). Psychological differentiation in cross-cultural perspective. *Journal of Cross-Cultural Psychology, 6,* 4–87.

WITKOWSKI, S. R., & BROWN, C. H. (1982). Whorf and universals of color nomenclature. *American Anthropological Research, 38,* 411–420.

WOBER, M. (1972). Culture and the concept of intelligence: A case in Uganda. *Journal of Cross-Cultural Psychology, 3,* 327–328.

WRIGHT, G. N., & PHILLIPS, L. D. (1980). Cultural variation in probability thinking: Alternative ways of dealing with uncertainty. *International Journal of Psychology, 15,* 239–257.

YAMAGUCHI, S. (submitted). Collectivism among the Japanese: A perspective from the self. In U. Kim, H. C. Triandis, & G. Yoon (Eds.), *Individualism and collectivism: Theoretical and methodological perspectives.*

YANG, K-S., & BOND, M. H. (1980). Ethnic affirmation by Chinese bilinguals. *Journal of Cross-Cultural Psychology, 11,* 411–425.

ZAJONC, R. B. (1968). Attitudinal effects of mere exposure. *Journal of Personality and Social Psychology, Monograph Supplement, 9,* Part 2, pp. 2–27.

ZILLER, R. C. (1965). Toward a theory of open and closed groups. *Psychological Bulletin, 64,* 164–182.

ZILLMAN, D. (1971). Excitation transfer in communication-mediated aggressive behavior. *Journal of Experimental Social Psychology, 7,* 419–434.

ZIMBARDO, P. G. (1969). The human choice: Individuation, reason, and order versus de-individuation, impulse, and chaos. In *Nebraska Symposium on Motivation, 1969.* Lincoln: University of Nebraska, pp. 237–307.

ZIPF, G. K. (1949). *Human behavior and the principle of least effort.* Cambridge, MA: Addison-Wesley.

Name Index

Page numbers in italics indicate figures; page numbers followed by t indicate tables.

Subject Index

Page numbers in italics indicate figures; page numbers followed by t indicate tables.

AAs (*see* African Americans)
Abortion, 251
Abstractive communication, 195
  associative communication and, 194–197
Acculturation, 19
  accommodation in, 38
  in culture change, 38
  diversity and, *238*, 238–239
Acculturation framework, *238*, 238–239
Acculturation indexes, 63–65, *64*
Activity (A) factors, 98
Adaptive interactions, defining culture and, 16–17, *18*
Additive multiculturalism, 241
Admiration, stereotype content and, 257
Affect toward a behavior, 209
Affluence
  cultural complexity and, 177–178
  cultural distance and, 33
  helping behavior and, 224
  individualism and, 165
African Americans (AAs), attributes of, 242–247, 243t, 245t
Age, in-groups and, 116
Aggression, observed, 215, 217
Aggressive behavior, cultural influences on, 212–220
  attitude toward others and, 219
  customs and habits, 216
  incidence of, 212–213
  past experiences, 215–216
  physiological conditions and, 217–219, 218t
  self-definition and, 219–220
  situation and, 214–215, 220
  subjective, 213–214
  utility of behavior and, 219

Agrarian societies
  helping behavior in, 222
  male-female relationships in, 130–131
  pressure for conformity in, 227–229, *228, 229*
Agreements with others, social behavior and, 211
Alcoholism, 41
American Bureau of Justice, murder statistics of, 213
American Psychological Association, 36, 288
Androcentric bias, in cross-cultural research, 85
Animism
  in traditional beliefs, 10
  in traditional healing, 11
Antecedent-consequent method, for study of word meanings, 99–100
Antecedents of disease, 41–44, *42*
Antiestablishment attitudes, of African Americans, 244–246
AR (authority ranking), 149
Argument, climactic presentation of, 185
Arranged marriages, 135–136
Arrow of God (Achebe), 12
AsAs (Asian Americans), 242, 248
Asian Americans, collectivism of, 248
Asian Americans (AsAs), 242
  attributes of, 248
Assimilation, 239, 269
Associations
  of categories, 95
  intercultural training in, 279
Associative behaviors, 5, 208
Associative communication, 195
  abstractive communication and, 194–197